INTERNATIONAL INDUSTRIAL LAW

International Industrial Law

Editor:

Veronica Cinti

Delve Publishing
www.delvepublishing.com

International Industrial Law
Editor: **Veronica Cinti**

708 3rd Avenue, 6th Floor
New York, NY 10017
United States of America

www.delvepublishing.com

ISBN: 978-1-68095-706-8

Library of Congress Control Number: 2016953782

About the Editor

Veronica Cinti

Experienced researcher and content creator, Veronica Cinti has covered different roles in academia and the private sector. Among other things, she served as researcher and teaching associate at University, and as managing editor and journalist in the media industry.

Contents

List of Contributors

Ana Alba Betancourt
National Autonomous University of Mexico (UNAM), MX

Thomas Farkas
Institute for Innovation and Competition/Free University Berlin

jose roberto herrera diaz
Munich Institute of Intellectual Property (MIPLC)

Marnix T. Croes
WODC, Dutch Ministry of Safety and Justice, NL

Merja Pentikäinen
University of Turku, FI

Sandra van den Braak
Commercial Law at the Molengraaff Institute of Private Law

Chilenye Nwapi
Consultant and Researcher, University of Calgary, Canada and Senior Fellow, OGEES Institute, Nigeria

Emmanuel Lazega
University of Paris – Dauphine

Rutger Claassen
Associate Professor of Political Philosophy at Utrecht University's Department of Philosophy & Religious Studies (the Netherlands), NL

Anna Gerbrandy
Professor of Competition Law at the Utrecht University School of Law (the Netherlands), NL

Eva Lachnit
Utrecht University School of Law

Louise Vytopil
Utrecht University School of Law, NL

Preface

Industrial Law is the branch of Law that deals with legal aspects of three different but inter-related set of entities - Industries, Labor and Governmental agencies. Governments across the world have been promoting setting up of industries but at the same time are controlling them actively. They always have given importance to Labor-welfare and needless to say, many laws are brought to mitigate, address and solve industry-labor disputes in the most amicable manner. At the same time, erring industries are always punished.

Modern Industrial Jurisprudence changed the concept of master-servant. Under the modern sense, one who invests capital is no more than a master and one who puts in labor is no more a servant. Since the industrial revolution the labor movement has been concerned how economic globalization would weaken the bargaining power of workers, as their employers could move to hire workers abroad without the protection of the labor standards at home. International labor law is the body of rules spanning public and private international law which concern the rights and duties of employees, employers, trade unions and governments in regulating the workplace. The International Labor Organization and the World Trade Organization have been the main international bodies involved in reform labor markets. The International Monetary Fund and the World Bank have indirectly driven changes in labor policy by demanding structural adjustment conditions for receiving loans or grants. Conflict of laws issues arise, determined by national courts, when people work in more than one country, and supra-national bodies, particularly in the law of the European Union, has a growing body of rules regarding labor rights. With a wide range of application and a dynamic development, industrial law covers a pivotal role in society. High level of internationalization, normative harmonization of natural persons and legal entities, and strengthening of control authorities are a few of the pillars upon which industrial law builds itself. From patent disputes to labor law topics, passing through copyright and competition regulation, this book presents, through practical examples, the analysis of some of the prominent issues characterizing the legal aspects of industrial activities and their application.

Editor

Veronica Cinti

INTRODUCTION

Law is essential to any society in that it provides the rules by which people and businesses interact. Law affects almost every function and area of industry. This is because almost every industry decision has legal repercussions, including deciding whether to incorporate an industry, obtaining financing, protecting proprietary knowledge used to develop products/services, entering into contracts to purchase raw materials, ensuring that products meet safety standards, disposing of plant wastes, promoting and pricing products/services, entering into contracts to sell products/services, and providing product warranties and aftersales service. At all stages of industry, running afoul of the law can hurt an industry, while playing within the boundaries of the law can help the industry to succeed. For this reason, accountants, who play a key role in almost every aspect of operations, must have a solid working knowledge of the law.

Industrial Law relates to the laws governing industrial enterprises. These can include a wide range of legal topics, from employment laws to environmental concerns, contracts, industrial relations, and worker safety regulations. Industries vary widely and the policies for each is as unique as the business to which it relates. Employment and labor laws are relevant to any commercial enterprise, and industry is no exception. Indeed, industrialization led not only to the modern conveniences of our technological age, but also the rise of organized labor unions. Employment and labor issues in industrial enterprises are particularly important, given the often hazardous nature of the work. Another major area of concern to industrial laws is accidents. Industrial workplaces vary widely depending on industry and purpose, from the clean rooms of high-tech manufacturing, to the often dangerous and noisy welding floors of heavy industry. Factories, warehouses, chemical plants, refineries, and many other facilities may also be considered industrial workplaces. Common industrial accidents include forklift accidents, falling objects, slips, trips, and falls, machinery or equipment injuries, explosions or blast injuries, and chemical burns or inhalation. Industrial accident injuries can often be more severe than other workplace injuries given the nature of the work. Indeed, according to the Bureau of Labor Statistics, it is estimated that two out of every 1,000 industrial workers will lose their life from a workplace accident. As a result, personal injury laws are a major area of practice related to industrial laws.

The phrase 'international industrial laws' is used in develop country, as elsewhere, synonymously and denote those laws and legal rules which regulate the employer employee relations. Some of these laws, though not directly dealing with such relations, nevertheless impose certain obligations or confer certain rights upon the employers or the employees so that in the ultimate analysis they can be deemed to impinge upon employer-employee relations. The literature on industrial laws, however, must confine itself to those laws which directly and substantially, and not remotely and incidentally, deal with the relationship between employees and employers. "A code of civil procedure may prohibit the attachment of the wages of a servant in execution of a decree. An educational act may indirectly eliminate children's entry into industry by providing for their compulsory education. Yet, surely, these cannot be called industrial laws". By law, of course, is not meant merely the acts of legislature. Customs and agreements having the force of law or giving rise to laws should legitimately be included in the term industrial laws. So also case law or judge-made law which, at any rate in this country, has been enormous especially in matters like bonus, scales of pay, discipline in industry etc.

Purpose of Industry Law

Industry laws exist to create reliable standards for organization to follow. Most industry transactions fall under contracts law, concerning themselves with issues such as uniformity and creating standards that are easy to follow in the ordinary course of industry.

- Industry laws create consistent, predictable standards. While laws that govern industries vary by state, they all have certain requirements that reduce risk and uncertainty between parties that enter into formal agreements.
- Many industry relationships form over contracts. In order to encourage the formation of industry relationships, laws must provide enforcement that allows contractual relationships to stay intact.
- Predictable industry laws allow people in organization to enter into multiple transactions with the assurance that each transaction receives a certain level of protection. For example, a commercial leasing business may sign multiple leases in a single day. They can do this because of the predictable ways in which states govern lease transactions.
- Uniformity saves time in industry law. When industry owners rely on the same laws to conduct in organization, they need to know that state agencies and courts apply the laws in a uniform fashion. Judges frequently consider the potential for uniformity when they interpret any area of industry law.

Importance of Labor Laws in the Industries

Labor laws clarify and codify industry owners' obligations to their employees. The labor movement has a long history of lobbying for laws that protect worker's rights, improve worker safety, prevent child labor and increase workers' bargaining power relative to their employers. While labor laws might seem like a bureaucratic hassle for the industry, these laws help keep your employees safe, healthy and happy, and satisfied employees tend to be more productive.

Proper Classification

Independent contractor's people who work for themselves and who control the time and method of their work are not covered by most labor laws, and employers do not have to pay payroll taxes on independent contractors. The Fair Labor Standards Act prevents employers from improperly classifying employees as independent contractors in an attempt to save money. This prohibition ensures that employees are not overburdened with taxes, that employers pay into worker's compensation insurance where required and that employees are eligible for minimum wage. If you're not sure whether your employees are independent contractors, examine the nature of their work. If you can control how, when and where they do their work, they're probably employees. But if you hire someone to complete a specific task and that person works on their own schedule, he may be an independent contractor.

Child Protection

The federal Fair Labor Standards Act prohibits employment of children under the age of 14, unless they work in a parent's industry. The law also regulates the hours children between 14 and 16 can work and prohibits dangerous occupations for all children under 18. The documentation requirements of the FLSA can help you avoid inadvertently running afoul of child labor laws.

Fair Wages

The FLSA establishes a federal minimum wage $7.25 an hour as of 2013. Employers cannot pay their employees less than this hourly wage, but employees under 20 can be paid the youth minimum wage of $4.25 per hour during their first 90 days of employment. The federal minimum wage can provide you guidance about how to pay your employees; even employees who make more than minimum wage often use minimum wage as a guideline for fair pay.

Employee Protections

Several labor laws offer protections that guard against unfair treatment and unsafe working conditions. The industry, for example, must take reasonable safety precautions. If you work in certain hazardous industries, such as construction or coal mining, you'll be subject to additional regulations and oversight to ensure your employees remain safe. The Department of Labor's Whistleblower Protection Program prohibits employers from retaliating against employees who report workplace safety problems and other legal violations, and also bars employers from terminating employees who sue them or file complaints with government agencies.

Reasonable Hours

Prior to the FLSA, employers could force employees to work extended hours with little compensation. The FLSA, however, mandates that most employees who work in excess of 40 hours in a given work week are compensated at time-and-a-half. Employers must also keep records of employee hours and have a reliable way of tracking when and how long employees work. This statutory requirement can make it much easier to manage employee scheduling and to avoid breaking the FLSA.

Important Industrial Laws and its Objectives

Industrial Laws help to put an end to unfair labor practices and provides for the rights, privileges, obligations and responsibilities of the workforce. Industrial legislation helps both workers and management to know exactly about their rights, duties and obligations and also the liabilities.

The objectives of Industrial laws are:

- To safeguard the workers against exploitation.
- To maintain good relationship between employees and employers.
- To provide and improve the welfare, amenities of workers.
- To settle industrial disputes.

Industry and the law of Tort

A tort is a civil wrong. Unlike the obligations voluntarily accepted by the parties to a contract, a tort consists of the breach of a duty imposed by the law. The law of tort seeks to provide a legal remedy for the victims of certain forms of harmful conduct. Tort duties are owed to a wide range of persons and are not dependent on the existence of a contractual relationship. Although this area of law is often referred to as the law of tort, in reality a number of distinct areas of tortious liability have been developed to protect people from the many forms of wrongful conduct which may occur in modern society. So it is probably more accurate to refer to a law of torts. Examples of the kinds of harmful conduct which the law provides protection against include:

- Interference with a person's ownership or possession of land or personal property, e.g. the torts of trespass to land and trespass to goods;
- Injury to business or personal reputations, e.g. tort of defamation;
- Interference with a person's use and enjoyment of land, e.g. tort of nuisance;
- Damage to land, e.g. tort of negligence, the rule in Rylands v Fletcher;
- Personal injury and death, e.g. torts of negligence and trespass to the person;
- Damage to commercial interests, e.g. torts of deceit, passing-off, inducement of breach of contract, conspiracy

Basis of tortious liability

Liability in tort is essentially 'fault-based'. This means that a claimant must prove that the defendant acted intentionally or negligently and was, therefore, blameworthy. The defendant's reasons or motive for committing a wrongful act are generally not relevant to liability in tort. However, the presence of malice is relevant to some torts: malice is an essential ingredient of some torts, e.g. conspiracy requires proof of an intention to injure the claimant rather than to promote the defendant's legitimate interests; proof of malice can defeat certain defenses to defamation, e.g. qualified privilege will not protect a defendant who acted maliciously; malice may make an otherwise reasonable act unreasonable so as to establish liability, e.g. in the tort of nuisance.

There are two situations where tortious liability may be imposed despite the defendant not being at fault.

1. Torts of strict liability. These are torts where the claimant can recover compensation for loss or damage without having to prove fault or intention on the part of the defendant. Part I of the Consumer Protection Act 1987, for example, provides that a manufacturer is strictly liable for injuries caused by his defective products. The rule in Rylands v Fletcher, breach of statutory duty and conversion are further examples of torts imposing strict liability.
2. Vicarious liability. In certain situations one person may be held liable for the torts of another. This type of liability is known as vicarious liability. An employer, for example, is vicariously liable for the torts of his employees committed during the course of their employment. Vicarious liability may also arise between partners and between a principal and agent. There are various justifications for the principles of vicarious liability:

   Liability is incurred by the person best able financially to meet any award of damages (usually because the risk is covered by insurance);

   The claimant is given an additional defendant to sue, who is more likely to be able to satisfy any judgment;

   Harm may be prevented by imposing liability on the person in control of the activity;

   The claimant is provided with a defendant in cases where it is impossible to establish precisely who was responsible within a particular organization for the wrongful conduct.

Proof of damage

The law of tort is concerned with providing a remedy for certain forms of wrongful conduct. In most torts, the claimant must prove that he has suffered some damage, e.g. personal injury or damage to his property, in order to establish liability. However, the fact that the claimant has suffered damage is not sufficient on its own to establish liability. The claimant must also prove that the damage was caused by the defendant's infringement of a right vested in the claimant which is recognized by the law. For example, the construction of an out-of town shopping Centre may result in a loss of trade for town Centre shops, but since the law does not provide a right to protection from competition, affected shopkeepers will not have a remedy, no matter how severe their losses. Although proof of damage is an essential component of most torts, some rights are regarded as so important that the law will provide a remedy even though the claimant has not suffered any damage. These torts are said to be 'actionable per se' (actionable in itself) and the most important examples are libel and trespass. Nominal damages can be recovered in respect of these torts even though no loss has occurred.

1

CHAPTER

CROSS-BORDER PATENT DISPUTES: UNIFIED PATENT COURT OR INTERNATIONAL COMMERCIAL ARBITRATION?

Ana Alba Betancourt

Keywords: Unified Patent Court, Patents, Arbitration, Conflicts of Law, Intellectual Property, Jurisdiction, Enforcement

INTRODUCTION: CROSS-BORDER LITIGATION OF PATENT DISPUTES AND THEIR PROBLEMS

This paper was inspired by the conflict between Apple and Samsung, in which these international companies that have patents registered globally1 for which they are business partners, entered into conflicts related to the same patents. An assumption is made that other companies with products holding patents and having a global trade activity, being business partners, are likely to have that type of conflicts. Given the territoriality of the registration and protection of patents currently, such companies have to litigate in each of the national courts where they want to protect and enforce their patents. Apple and Samsung have been referred to as 'Frenemies'2 a conjunction of the words 'friends' and 'enemies', because of their high reliance on one another in developing products, all the while being locked in multiple conflicts with each other involving patents before different national courts. On one hand, according to the Bloomberg supply-chain analysis, 8.8% of Samsung revenue (ca. 7.5 million of US dollars) comes from Apple.3 Moreover, ahead of the launch of the iPhone in 2007, Apple asked Samsung to provide them with a microprocessor, making Samsung the manufacturer of the logic memory chips which are at the heart of the iPhone and iPad.4Hence about 20% of the iPhone is comprised of Samsung technology.5 On the

Citation: Ana Alba Betancourt, Cross-Border Patent Disputes: Unified Patent Court or International Commercial Arbitration?, 32(82) Utrecht Journal of International and European Law, pp. 44-58 (2016). DOI: http://doi.org/10.5334/ujiel.262.

other hand, despite having very strong business links, the companies sued each other in more than 10 jurisdictions.6 The extraordinary number of litigation procedures has been subject to a high level of coverage by the press, academic articles and general blogs which have referred to the dispute.7

It has been observed that due to the different approaches taken by different national courts to a single patent-right, and the vast possibilities that the current litigation system offers to the opponent parties, big enterprises have come to abuse it, without necessarily reaching an efficient solution to their dispute. Taking the example of the Apple-Samsung patent litigation, the companies did not reach a conclusive solution through the multiple national litigation actions, but ended up in negotiation outside of court.8

Given the observation that current cross-border litigation of a single patent right between the same parties may reach different conclusions, this paper aims to analyse on one side, the future Unified Patent Court (UPC) which represents an effort from several countries in the European Union (EU) to have a harmonised patent system. On the other side, the characteristics of the UPC will be compared with those of a commercial arbitration procedure, where parties can solve their cross-border patent conflict.

This paper will not address the issue of arbitrability of a patent dispute. It is considered that this has already been widely discussed; both in light of international arbitration as an *inter partes* procedure and due to the *erga omnes* effect of intellectual property rights (IPRs).9 It is understood that the biggest problem concerning the arbitrability of IPRs is related to adjudicating on the validity of the rights in a private procedure. On one hand, it is believed that even when arbitration is a private procedure, as long as the arbitrators are considered experts there is no reason why their decision would be any less appropriate than the Courts' decisions. However, for the arbitration award to be enforceable it would have to comply with the public policy of the respective country which opens up the risk that the national laws consider that the validity of patents cannot be arbitrated. In order to avoid this result, this paper agrees that the effect of the award is exclusively between the parties and that they may still enforce their rights against third parties.10

Hence, leaving aside the question of arbitrability in this kind of disputes, this article will discuss the origins and reasoning behind the UPC system. Part III submits that the UPC system's main advantages are the fact that it will consist of a single procedure that will decide cross-border conflicts all over Europe, as well as the neutrality of the decision makers. These two characteristics are considered face-to-face with characteristics of commercial arbitration that represent the same advantages.

In Part IV, procedural aspects of the UPC vis-à-vis arbitration will be analysed. These are considered of high relevance given that they answer the following issues of the cross-border conflicts of patents:

Jurisdiction (where are the parties to a cross-border patent conflict going to take their action?);

Preliminary injunctions (when a patent infringement takes place, it is extremely important for the affected parties to rely on the concession of injunctions);

Choice of law (since cross-border disputes involve several jurisdictions, which law will remain applicable to a single procedure?); and

Enforcement of the decision (how will a single decision be enforced in different jurisdictions?)

The article concludes that although UPC presents a very good alternative to tackle the issues surrounding a cross-border patent dispute, there is still uncertainty as to the procedure. Moreover there is the need for a more international solution, which can be reached by a single arbitration procedure.

The main methodological approaches used in this article are qualitative research methods in the form of case studies, comparative approaches, literature review and experts' opinions gathered from attending conferences with academics and practitioners. The secondary sources of the paper were drawn from newspapers, technology magazines and IPRs blogs, given that they provided the latest updates on UPC.

It is known that qualitative research gives a deeper understanding of experiences of the law and its application.11 With that in mind, and given that the UPC is not yet in force, the author analysed several articles and other material available on UPC's website. Moreover the author attended conferences with patent experts, where the UPC system was analysed and debated, and the most relevant findings are quoted throughout the paper. Given that the UPC system has not been ratified, the different issues in question remain a matter of opinion. Therefore the conversations, debates at conferences and one-on-one interviews, attended and carried out by the author, were critical in order to gather enough data to analyse and answer the research question. Information was gathered from a variety of experts and active contributors of the patent system in Europe, including patent lawyers,12 patent chiefs of innovative companies,13 patent judges, professors and representatives of the European Patent Office (EPO).

EUROPEAN APPROACH TO CROSS-BORDER CONFLICTS OF PATENTS: THE UNIFIED PATENT COURT

In 1949, after the Council of Europe had just been created, the French Senator Longchambon made a proposal for a regional patent system. While this proposal was rejected, the belief in the need for a patent office and supporting laws to facilitate integration found several supporters. Over the next years other proposals surged, which in combination helped to set the agenda for the creation of a European patent.14 The European Patent Convention (EPC) was signed in Munich in 1973, and became effective in 1977.15 The EPC established 'a system of law, common to the Contracting States, for the grant of patents for inventions'16 and a European Patent Organisation with administrative and financial autonomy;17 that is, a single procedure and office for what it is called the 'European patent'.

Even though it established a single procedure for the application for a patent, the system does not grant a unitary right, but rather a bundle of national patents that are subject to the laws of the contracting states in which protection is sought.18 The validity of the grant of the European patent is conditioned upon said patent being translated into the language of each Contracting Member State where the patent is to have effect.19 Hence, the European patent is a fragmented patent system, where each Contracting State's patent laws govern that State's fractional share of the European patent (*e.g.* the remedies are not addressed in the EPC).20 In addition, when it comes to post-(patent)granting issues, such as amendment, revocation and infringement, litigation must take place at the national level.21 One must note, however, that the EPC was only intended to be the first step; a provisional tool which was to be followed by further harmonisation.

In February 2013, several European countries signed the Agreement on the Unitary Patent (which is part of the EU patent package). It will enter into force as soon as 13 states, including France, Germany and the United Kingdom have ratified it.22 The EU patent package establishes the creation of:

A Unified Patent Court;

The unitary patent or 'European patent with unitary effect', meaning a patent granted by the EPO which, upon request of the patent holder, will have unitary effect for the territory of the 25 Contracting States participating in the Unitary Patent Scheme (UPS), and that will co-exist with national patents and the classical European patents.23

This unitary system intends to end the different and sometimes contradictory decisions in the national courts under the current European patent system. In the following section, the characteristics of the system will be analysed against those of commercial arbitration.

ADVANTAGES OF UPC AND ARBITRATION

The UPC system will potentially solve the issue of having to litigate in several national courts in the EU when aiming to defend a single patent—registered in different jurisdictions—against a singular opponent. It intends to have a unitary patent abolishing the bundle system and it will also unify the procedure for the Signatory States. This part of the essay will explain two advantages that the UPC system will offer in the case of a cross-border patent conflict: to be able to draw several conflicts into one single procedure, and the neutrality of the decision makers. Such advantages are considered similar to characteristics of Commercial Arbitration and hence they are explained as follows.

Single Procedure

The first characteristic to analyse is the fact that UPC will establish a single procedure for the same conflict between the same parties in several jurisdictions. First, this section describes the single procedure in the UPC, then, the arbitration procedure in the UPC and finally how commercial arbitration may work as a single procedure englobing a cross-border patent conflict.

UNITARY PATENT COURT

According to the EPO, the fact that national courts and authorities of the contracting states of the EPC are the ones to decide on the infringement and validity of European patents gives rise to a number of difficulties when a patent proprietor wishes to enforce a European patent in several countries. Such problems may include high costs, risk of diverging decisions, and lack of legal certainty.24 Overcoming these difficulties represents one of the justifications for the UPC.

The main characteristics of the UPC are the following:

A Court of First Instance with local, regional, and central divisions located in the Contracting States;

- A Common Court of Appeal;
- A referral system to the Court of Justice of the European Union (CJEU) for preliminary rulings whenever a question of EU law requires interpretation;
- The UPC will have jurisdiction for both the new unitary patents and the non-unitary European patents which are currently granted by the EPO;25
- The Court will have exclusive jurisdiction to hear *inter alia*, actions for infringement of patents and of supplementary protection certificates, counterclaims for revocation, revocation actions, actions for provisional and protective measures and injunctions, and actions against decisions of the EPO relating to unitary patents; and
- A possibility for the claimant to opt out and choose another forum during a 7-year transitional period (extendable).26 This period was set to allow patent owners, experts and lawyers to learn and adjust to the new system.
- Once the UPS starts working, it will give rise to four parallel patent systems in the EU, some of which will overlap:
- National patents based on national applications;
- National patents based on an EPO application within the UPC Agreement system;
- National patents based on an EPO application outside the UPC Agreement system (owing to non-ratification or in non-Member States); and
- European patents with unitary effect.

The UPC system also provides the possibility of having a single arbitration or mediation procedure. According to the Agreement on a Unified Patent Court (UPC Agreement or UPCA), the judge in the UPC may suggest to the parties of a conflict that instead of continuing with the litigation, they solve the conflict via the Arbitration and Mediation Centre (the Centre or Arbitration Centre).27 The latter will have the capability of ruling over the conflict with the same unified effect as the UPC, hence providing alternative dispute resolution methods as a single procedure ruling over the unitary patent.

It is still in doubt how the Centre will operate during the transitional period of the UPC, given that the EPC system will coexist during this time, as explained above. Assuming that the patent is under the bundle system of the EPC, it is understood that if both of the parties agree to solve the conflict in the UPC Centre, they are giving their tacit consent for the award to be valid in all of the Contracting States of UPC.

Therefore, given the coexistence of the EPC with the UPC for the transitional period of 7 years, and the uncertainty of the relation between the two, it is possible to conclude that the UPC system by ways of litigation or arbitration, will not immediately achieve the unity that it is looking for, at least not until the transitional period has elapsed.

INTERNATIONAL COMMERCIAL ARBITRATION

Under the current system, if parties want to submit their cross-border patent conflict to a single arbitration procedure, it is possible to do so. To start an arbitration procedure it is necessary that the parties enter into an arbitration agreement. When the parties have a contractual relationship, *e.g.* a license contract, they can include in it an arbitration clause (agreement for future disputes). In that case, that clause will constitute the arbitration agreement.28 If the parties enter into a dispute without having a previous contract relationship, it is also possible for the parties to sign a submission agreement for arbitration.29

Both agreements for future disputes (*i.e.* the contractual arbitration clause) and submission agreements require that the parties to the conflict agree to take their dispute to arbitration, and through the arbitration agreement, the parties can specify the dispute that they want to submit to arbitration. A basic principle in international arbitration is that of party autonomy, endorsed by Article 19(1) of the UNCITRAL Model Law on International Commercial Arbitration.30 The autonomy of the parties to the arbitration agreement is restricted by issues of public policy.31 The UPC system will allow a single procedure for a cross-border conflict of patents and therefore we can affirm that the agreement for arbitration for such type of conflicts will not be in prejudice of public policy. Hence, if the parties agree, it is possible that they submit to a single commercial arbitration for a patent conflict that involves several jurisdictions.

NEUTRALITY OF DECISION MAKERS

Unified Patent Court

One of the important characteristics of the new system is the neutrality of the decision makers and the assurance that they will be knowledgeable in the respective patent field. In the UPC, the judges that will sit on the case will be chosen from a 'Pool of Judges' and it is considered that this measure will ensure the neutrality of the Court. According to the UPCA: '[t]he Pool of Judges shall be composed of all legally qualified judges and technically qualified judges from the Court of First Instance [(CFI)] who are full-time or part-time judges of the Court'.32 Moreover, according to Article 8(1) of the same agreement '[a]ny panel of the Court of First Instance shall have a multinational composition'. Having international decision-makers who are not known to the parties beforehand is positive from a neutrality point of view and negative from a practice point of view, mainly because practitioners will fear the unknown quality of the judges' decisions. The UPC Agreement tries to counteract such fear, since in Article 18(3) states that the allocation of judges shall take into account their legal or technical expertise, linguistic skills and relevant experience, in order to guarantee the same high quality as on all panels of the CFI.

At the time of writing there is still no regulation of the arbitration procedure of the UPC, but it is likely to work on the same basis as the CFI, with arbitrators chosen from a pool of experts.

INTERNATIONAL COMMERCIAL ARBITRATION

One of the advantages of arbitration is that the parties have the freedom to choose the arbitrators that are going to preside over their conflict. Thus, they can secure which experts will be analysing their case. In this part of the essay it will be examined very briefly how the arbitrators are appointed. There is vast literature regarding the rules to appoint arbitrators and the proven knowledge and ethics that are desirable for arbitrators. It is not the aim of this work to analyse this issue deeply, but only to provide an overview, in order to ascertain if the freedom of the parties to select arbitrators is an advantage when dealing with cross-border conflicts of patents. Subject to the applicable law and the chosen institutional rules, if any, the principle of party autonomy generally will govern the selection and nomination of the arbitral tribunal.

Number of Arbitrators

The principal factors that affect the decision on the number of arbitrators are the size, value, and complexity of the dispute.33 In general, appointing a sole arbitrator for smaller cases is more appropriate. The greater the number of arbitrators appointed, the greater the delay and expense likely to be incurred during the proceedings.34 Appointing a three-member tribunal may permit the parties to combine different types of experience, legal and technical expertise and linguistic skills.35 In the field of patents, this would mean that it would be possible to appoint an arbitrator that has knowledge and skills in the technical field of the protection of the patent.

If the parties decide to conduct the arbitration according to institutional rules, the different dispositions regarding the number of arbitrators are the following:

The World Intellectual Property Organization (WIPO) Arbitration Rules specify in Article 14 that the Tribunal will consist of the number of arbitrators that has been agreed by the parties;36

Articles 10(1) and 10(2) of the UNCITRAL Model Law, provide that the parties are free to determine the number of arbitrators but failing such determination the number of arbitrators shall be three. Although Rule 7(1) adds that if the responding party fails to designate its choice for the second member, the appointing authority may designate a sole arbitrator;

Rule 15 of the American Arbitration Association (AAA) Rules of Arbitration states that without agreement of the parties the default is one arbitrator, unless the administrator determines that three are appropriate because of the circumstances of the case. Three arbitrators will be the default if the claim amounts to one million dollars or more;37

Article 12(2) of the International Chamber of Commerce (ICC) Rules of Arbitration, establishes a presumption in favour of a sole arbitrator participation when the parties failed to agree upon the number of arbitrators, unless it appears that the dispute warrants three arbitrators;38

In summary, a panel of three arbitrators is likely to be chosen by the parties of a cross-border conflict of patents, although the parties may decide to have more. This decision will, of course, have an impact in the cost of the procedure.

Arbitrator Selection Procedures

It has been established that the parties to an arbitration will have the freedom to choose how many arbitrators they will want on the panel. In this part of the essay, we will address the way parties will be able to select them.

Appointment by the Parties

According to Cook and Garcia, in the IPR context this method is advantageous because the parties are able to appoint individuals who possess the technical and legal expertise needed to understand the particular facts and legal aspects of the case.39 If the parties have decided to have a tribunal of three arbitrators and there are two parties in the procedure, normally each of them would appoint one arbitrator and they then would jointly appoint the third arbitrator.40 If the parties cannot agree on the appointee, it is advisable that the parties agree on the methodology by which the Tribunal will be selected. Otherwise the parties will lose control over the characteristics of the tribunal itself.41

Appointment in Institutional Arbitrations

When the arbitration is institutional and the parties do not agree on the arbitrators, the institution will usually be entitled to appoint the arbitrators:

Under WIPO Arbitration Rules, Article 19, it is specified that when the parties fail to agree on the appointment of an arbitrator, there will be a special mechanism conducted by the WIPO Centre in order to find a person that would be suitable for both parties.42 In case the system fails, the WIPO Centre will then be authorised to appoint the sole or presiding arbitrator;43

UNCITRAL Rules point out in Article 11(3) that where the parties fail to appoint arbitrator(s), the appointment shall be made by the Court or another authority specified by the State that is enacting the Model Law;

Rule 13 of the AAA Rules of Arbitration, specifies that where the parties do not appoint an arbitrator, either within a specific period to do so, or after a notice from the AAA to do so, then the AAA will make the appointment;

Article 12(8) ICC Rules specifies that in the absence of a nomination, and when the parties are unable to agree on a method for the constitution of the arbitral tribunal, the Court will appoint the arbitrators and will designate one of them to act as president.

As stated above, the parties will typically have the freedom to choose the people that will arbitrate their conflict. Barring that, they are able to set up a mechanism to choose the arbitrators. According to Bridgeman,44 the parties can also specify the qualifications they wish to be represented within the tribunal, for instance the profession and professional experience of arbitrators. It is said that among the personal characteristics of an arbitrator are courage, decisiveness and case management ability.45

Even though the process to appoint arbitrators may be criticised for being long, if the arbitration is conducted under the ICC provisions, there is the possibility of having emergency arbitrators to grant interim relief before the Tribunal is constituted. This avoids the need of parties having to go to court to attempt to obtain such relief, since appointing an arbitrator will take two days.46 In matters of intellectual property (IP) disputes it can be of key importance to obtain an urgent injunctive relief.47 If the arbitration is being conducted by an institution, such as WIPO, it might be an assurance for the parties that they will have experts in IPRs on an international scale.

In summary, both the UPC and Arbitration share the advantage that cross-border conflict of patents may be resolved by a single procedure, with the only difference being that in order to submit it to arbitration under UPC the parties have to sign an agreement. From the UPC perspective, it is considered a disadvantage to have a seven-year transition period, as explained in Part III (Section A), where four parallel patent systems remain. Regarding the neutrality of the decision-makers, the Pool of Judges system of the UPC seems to ensure that experienced and neutral experts will sit on the cases. In this regard, if the arbitration is administered by an institution, the selection of experts might be the same as in the UPC procedure, it will only make a difference if the parties wish to choose the arbitrators themselves.

Procedures of UPC and Arbitration

After talking about the advantages that UPC and arbitration procedures will offer in contrast to current cross-border litigation, this section will analyse certain aspects of the procedures in order to assess whether these procedural elements will aid the type of conflicts in question.

Jurisdiction

This section will analyse which is the appropriate forum when having a dispute that involves several jurisdictions.

UNIFIED PATENT COURT

The international jurisdiction of the UPC is established by Regulation 1215/2012.48 As a basic rule, the claimant may start the proceedings at the place where the alleged infringement has taken place. However, in a conflict (such as the one between Apple and Samsung) in which the infringement takes place in several Member States, the claimant will have to choose the jurisdiction where to start the proceeding. Article 33(2) of the UPC Agreement depicts the forum rules as follows:

If there is an action between the same parties on the same patent, the division49 first chosen will be competent for the whole case, and any division chosen later will declare the action inadmissible;

If there is an action pending before a regional division and the infringement occurred in the territories of three or more regional divisions, the concerned division, at the request of the defendant, shall refer the case to the central division;

In Article 33(5) it is specified that if an action for revocation is pending before the central division and there is an action for infringement between the same parties and related to the same patent, it may be brought before any division or before the central division.

Véron has pointed out that Article 33(2)(b) has puzzled numerous European lawyers that consider it an 'anti-regional division weapon'. The rule provides that as soon as a third division starts operating in the case, parties can transfer the case to the central division. This action will withdraw the case from the regional division which, in turn, will arguably bring some political play in action.50

Article 33(1)(b) provides the claimant the option to bring the infringement action where the defendant has its residence. In the case of multiple defendants, it could be the place where one of the defendants has its residence or principal place of business, while bearing in mind that the action against multiple defendants may be brought only where they have a commercial relationship and the action relates to the same alleged infringement. All the rules can apply to non-EU defendants, as they can be sued at the place of infringement.

Finally, according to Article 33(7), in all cases it is possible that the parties of the conflict agree to bring the action before the division of their choice, including the central division. However, as Véron points out, this is rather exceptional and needs a certain degree of maturity and good connection between the parties.51

According to Heusch (Head of Nokia's European litigation), the basic principle is that everybody should be sued at their domicile; the idea of suing *locus delicti* (the place of infringement) was first introduced in the EU by the Brussels Regulation to protect the claimant against foreign laws or courts.52 Nowadays, however, given the broader market and technological facilities, it is possible to offer a product online (protected by patent) all over the world, meaning that the claimant is free to choose the most favourable jurisdiction within which to sue. This situation is an unintended consequence of the Brussels Regulation.53

It is important to point out that given the nature of the system, the judgment of one of the divisions will be binding in all the UPC Contracting States. This is in contrast to the EPO system, where a decision is only valid in the jurisdiction where the Court has its seat. It is therefore possible to assume that forum choice is likely to be made strictly based on cost efficiency for the parties. However, practitioners have identified other factors that are likely to play a role in the selection of the forum and these are:

Injunctions: It will have to be taken into account the place of manufacture, the main distribution facilities or larger markets of the products. In practice it is important to choose the forum that will be as instrumental as possible.54 In the UPC system, every local division will be able to issue an injunction for all of Europe and assess damages on behalf of the Contracting States. Though some practitioners have expressed that having the same procedural rules does not secure that the courts will take the same approach, as they will be biased by their traditions: 'like different chefs following the same recipe, they will flavour the dish in a different way'.55

Bifurcation: Practitioners would be concerned with either starting or abstaining from an action in different courts if they think that the judges are likely to bifurcate.56 Jörg Thomaier, chief of patent litigation in Bayern, is of the opinion that having technical experts as judges is enough to improve the decisions in the system regarding infringement and validity, and he believes that the concerns of practitioners regarding bifurcation will be eradicated when there is a technical judge on the panel.57

Taking of evidence: Even though the rules for taking evidence will be the same, it is believed that the application will be influenced by the traditions of the forums. Hence, depending on the need of the patents, practitioners will be tempted to go to one local division or another. For instance it is thought that UK courts are more open to taking witness testimonies than French courts.58

Time efficiency of the decisions: According to Heusch, with the new courts the regional and local divisions will want to attract cases, in principle to justify their existence.59Because of this, litigants are afraid that there will be competition between courts to be the most patentee-friendly. Although this may involve timing issues, these are qualitative decisions as well. For this reason, Nokia and other companies proposed the addition of Rule 19B, suggesting that the court with the closest connection to the case should sit on it.60 At the time of writing, 19B has not incorporated into the UPC Agreement.61

It is submitted then, that even when the substantive law is harmonised the different approaches will still play a role during the first years of the UPC and only when a balance is achieved the selection of the forum will be less important. A final point of concern is that regardless of the different 'local flavours' of the different divisions, they will all meet in the Court of Appeal (CoA) in Véron (n 50). It will be interesting to see how this CoA will navigate the harmonisation here, and also begs the question of whether it will add its own local flavour. This issue will only be answered in the long run.

The UPC Agreement has a positive list of the actions that fall within the jurisdiction of the courts.62 It is important to note that the current rules of jurisdiction of the UPC were inspired by the rules of the Brussels Convention, which has been in existence for more than 40 years and which gives a proper balance to the interest of the stakeholder.63

ARBITRATION UNDER THE UPC

Article 35 of the UPCA indicates that a patent Arbitration and Mediation Centre shall have its seats in Ljubljana and Lisbon. According to De Werra, the decision of having two seats for the Centre was made from a political perspective, however, it raises questions regarding what would happen to the freedom of the parties to choose the arbitral seat.64Would the parties who wanted to use arbitration to solve their conflict over a European patent be obliged to use the facilities of the Centre? In terms of the seat of arbitration, would it be considered to be Lisbon or Ljubljana? Or elsewhere in Europe?

The selection of the arbitration seat impacts the costs of the proceedings, the applicable law, and potentially the enforcement of the award. In terms of disputing a European patent with unitary effect only, the question of applicable law would be solved, and the parties will not have to fear any potential application of the *lex fori.*

The answer to the above question may be found in the freedom of the parties to choose arbitration. The use of the UPC Arbitration Centre is just one option open to the parties. If the parties want to solve their patent dispute through arbitration they may choose any arbitration institution or even an *ad hoc* procedure to manage it. If they do want to go to this Centre it is clear that the sites will then be Lisbon and Ljubljana. This is not problematic as it is possible to have both the seat of the arbitration in one State and (for reasons of cost or location convenience) to have audiences in another State.

INTERNATIONAL COMMERCIAL ARBITRATION

If the arbitration is conducted by an institution and the parties do not agree on a seat, the administration will choose the location for them.65 If, however is an arbitration that is not subject to an institution (*ad hoc*) and the parties cannot agree on a seat, this complicates the procedure. The applicable procedural law of the *ad hoc* arbitration, depends upon the seat. But if a seat has not been decided by the parties, the arbitrator will have to apply procedural law in order to determine the appropriate seat. The question is then, which procedural law will the arbitrator apply in order to determine the seat?

Article 20 of the UNCITRAL Model Law states that the arbitral tribunal, taking into account the circumstances of the case and the convenience of the parties, will decide the place. Therefore, if the arbitrator follows the UNCITRAL Model law it will just need to evaluate the circumstance of the case, including convenience for the parties.66 However, the application of this disposition will depend on whether the country where the award is going to be enforced follows the Model Law or not. For the parties it is important to take into consideration the law of the place where they are likely to enforce the award.67

For cross-border conflicts of patents the ideal scenario would be for the parties to choose a place that is neutral to the countries where the award is going to be enforced. Taking into account that the aim would be to enforce the decision in several States it would be possible for the parties to choose a seat in any country they considered to be 'arbitration friendly'.68 Alternatively, the arbitrators may prefer another jurisdiction to the countries where they will attempt to enforce the award, while ensuring that it is also a signatory party of the New York Convention (NYC).69

PRELIMINARY INJUNCTIONS

Unitary Patent Court

Article 32(c) states that the UPC will have competence over actions for provisional and protective measures and injunctions. At the time of writing the Rules of Procedure are yet to be approved. Rule 10 of the latest draft of the Rules of Procedure lays down the most important aspects of it to the extent that it is possible to conclude that in a single procedure there is a decision of the merits.

Article 62 of the UPC Agreement makes it clear that there is a possibility of obtaining a preliminary injunction against an infringer and that there should be some way of compensating the person against whom the injunction is granted. The court is meant to balance the interests of the parties and decide whether to grant the injunction or not. This seems to come from the Anglo-Saxon approach of considering injunctions without trying to decide whether the party is likely to be successful in an interim hearing.70Therefore, instead of focusing on the relative harm that each party would suffer if the injunction were granted, it is assumed that there is a dispute between the parties that will be determined at trial.

Under the EPC system, the CJEU in the cases *Gat v Luk* and *Roche v Primus*, decided that a cross-border injunction would only be granted when the defendant is based in the country of the court that is deciding on the injunction, and the validity of the patents is not disputed.71

INTERNATIONAL COMMERCIAL ARBITRATION

In respect of preliminary injunctions, Article 29 of the ICC Rules accounts for a procedure for the appointment of an emergency arbitrator which a party in need of urgent or conservatory measures can apply for. The process involves submitting an application for emergency measures to the Secretariat.72 An award made by the Centre will be enforceable *mutatis mutandis* according to the enforcement rules of the decisions of the UPC. Regarding injunctions, Article 83(2) establishes that '[w]here appropriate, the enforcement of a decision may be subject to the provision of security or an equivalent assurance to ensure compensation for any damage suffered, in particular in the case of injunctions.' This provision will facilitate the enforcement of an interim award if the parties decide to submit their dispute to the Centre. There are, however, several factors regarding the enforcement of awards in the UPC system that need to be taken into consideration and they are studied below in the enforcement section.

CHOICE OF LAW

Unified Patent Court

Article 24 of the UPC Agreement determines the law in which UPC should base its decisions on:

Union law, including Regulation (EU) No 1257/2012 and Regulation (EU) No 1260/2012;73

The UPC Agreement;

The European Patent Convention;

Other international agreements applicable to patents and binding on all the Contracting Member States; or

National law.

Article 24(3) opens the possibility that the law of Non-Contracting States apply when designated by application of the rules referred to in Paragraph 2, which regulates the application of national laws in the UPC.74

INTERNATIONAL COMMERCIAL ARBITRATION

It is a principle of international arbitration that the parties in conflict are free to choose the legal system they want the tribunal to base the decision on. However, if the parties do not agree on the choice of law then they can decide that the tribunal will choose for them. This raises the question what the rule should be to determine the applicable law. In international arbitration literature this has been discussed extensively.

Similarly, when the parties decide on an institutional arbitration, the procedural rules of the institution will provide for the rules to choose the substantive law. This essay focuses on matters that would be considered in a cross-border patent conflict. One of the limitations to the freedom of the parties to choose a substantive law has to do with public policy. The parties cannot choose a legal system in which the application will affect the public policy of the place of enforcement. In matters of patent disputes, the importance of such policy materialises generally in matters of competition law. Nevertheless, even the EU competition authority has suggested arbitration as a means to solve conflicts related to European patents.75

With the increasing harmonisation of national IP laws through multilateral agreements such as the TRIPS Agreement,76 and now the UPC, it may often be fair and reasonable for the court to presume that affected State(s)' norms are the same as those of the State of arbitration.77 Nevertheless, in the field of patents it is perceived that there is reluctance by practitioners to break the territoriality of the substantive law protecting the patents.78Therefore, in order to maintain the territoriality of the substantive laws applicable to a patent conflict, it may be suggested that all of the national laws related to the conflict will apply. This approach is known as a 'mosaic of national laws'. It resembles the approach taken in *Actavis v LillyEWHC 1511.* (Pat) where a UK judge took into account the national laws of all of the jurisdictions involved in the dispute (*e.g.* France, Spain among others).79 This case shows that where there is a cross-border conflict over the same patent, it is possible to apply the laws of all of the countries that were involved in the dispute. The author is of the opinion that in terms of substance, the European laws that deal with IPRs are more or less homogenised;80 the slight differences that may exist between them, are a result of the interpretation of the law by the decision makers, rather than an objective difference.

It is recommended that the mosaic approach should be followed in regard of applicable law in the case of an arbitration of cross-border patent disputes, in order to include the different interpretations of the law. This approach will have more acceptability as long as it does not involve a decision on the validity of the patent.

ENFORCEMENT

Unitary Patent Court

Article 82 of UPC states that the decisions and orders of the court will be enforceable in any Contracting State. The order for enforcement will be appended to the decision. Therefore it is possible to conclude that the enforcement of the decisions under the UPC will come automatically with the judgment. This represents an advantage over the EPC system, where the enforcement of foreign national judgments is not mandatory. In the case of injunctions, under the UPC the enforcement of a decision may only be subject to the provision of security or an equivalent assurance to ensure compensation for any damage suffered.

The enforcement procedures shall be governed by the law of the Contracting State where the enforcement takes place.81 Moreover, any decision of the court shall be enforced under the same conditions as a decision made in the Contracting State where the enforcement takes place. This is called 'automatic enforcement' and it intends to be mandatory. Article 82(4) states that if a party does not comply with the terms of an order of the court, that party may be sanctioned with a penalty. The individual penalty shall be proportionate to the importance of the order to be enforced and shall be without prejudice to the party's right to claim damages or security.

Arbitration Award and Its Enforcement

First, to obtain recognition and enforcement of an international arbitral award, it is necessary that both the agreement to arbitrate and the award exist.82 The NYC establishes the formal proof of the existence of the foreign awards in its Article IV: 'A party seeking recognition and enforcement of an award must supply (a) the duly authenticated original of the award or a duly certified copy thereof, and (b) the original arbitration agreement or a duly certified copy thereof'.

Fulfilling the requirements described above will constitute *prima facie* evidence of the entitlement of the applicant to enforcement of the award.83 There will be no need to start an enforcement procedure if the parties comply with the award voluntarily. However, if they do not, the interested party will have to go to a national court to ask for enforcement. There is vast regulation and experience regarding the enforcement of international awards under the NYC in different national courts, which is not considered necessary to reproduce for the purposes of this article.

Enforcement of Arbitration Award under the UPC System

Article 35 of UPC provides for the formation of a patent Arbitration and Mediation

Centre, and Paragraph 2 states that '[...] Article 82 shall apply mutatis mutandis to any settlement reached through the use of the facilities of the Centre, including through mediation [...]'. The provisions of Article 82 are for the enforcement of decisions and orders. Therefore, it can be inferred that either the settlement outcome from a mediation or the arbitral award will be enforced in the same way as formal decisions rendered by the UPC.84 This means that the award will be labelled with the status of a sentence and will achieve the character of *res judicata*. This would be a clear advantage of the arbitration over the court procedure as there would be no appeal and hence a potentially faster procedure.

However, it is noticeable that Article 35 quoted above only talks about 'settlement' and not specifically about 'award'. An arbitration decision is not a settlement *per se*, it is a decision taken by a third party (arbitrator). It is questionable whether the intention of the legislator was that the Centre would be exclusively used by the parties to reach an agreement (and not to arbitrate their dispute), and perhaps this is why the word 'settlement' is continuously used. One can hope that this does not cause confusion in the future, when parties ask for the enforcement of an award rendered by the Centre.

In this respect, the ICC Rules, in Article 32, recognise that if the parties reach a settlement and they transmit85 it to the arbitral tribunal, then this settlement will be recorded in the form of an award made, if the parties so wish. Therefore, from the experience of other arbitration institutions, it is possible to convert a settlement into an arbitration award. The advantage of converting a settlement into an award is that, if in the future one of the parties refuses to comply with the settlement, the other party can make the award enforceable.

According to De Werra, the provision in Article 35 of UPC leaves the question open about whether the parties will be able to submit a dispute regarding a European patent with unitary effect to another arbitration service provider. Even though this is an issue that will have to be clarified to ensure the successful implementation of the Alternative Dispute Resolution methods used for solving European patent disputes, he is of the mind that the parties will be free to choose the arbitration institution they prefer.86 It is proposed then, that this theory finds confirmation when taking into account that the basis of the arbitration is the consent of the parties, and therefore they should be able to choose the institution that will be more efficient for them.

Given this scenario, if the parties choose another institution different to the UPC Centre, the enforcement of the arbitral award begs the question: Are the parties going to be able to enforce the award according to the UPC scheme/rules?

It is important to take into account that the award deals with a patent registered in the EU, either a European patent or a European patent with unitary effect. And it is also important to note that during the transitional period, the parties can opt out of the scheme of UPC and choose the forum where they want their action to be heard (Article 83(1) of UPC).87 Then, if the contended patent is a European patent (without unitary effect) and the owner opts out of the UPC system, the answer to the question is straightforward as the parties to the arbitration will be able to enforce their award, based on the mechanism of the NYC.

According to Article 83(1) of UPC, during the transitional period actions may be brought before the national courts. As such, it can be concluded that the parties can use the national courts to enforce the arbitration awards if they so wish, regardless of whether the patent has unitary effect or not. It remains in question whether an award not rendered at the Centre would be enforceable under UPC. In order to answer this, it is necessary to analyse Article 82 of UPC and the enforcement-related articles at the current draft for Rules of Procedure. Article 82 specifies that the decisions (and orders) shall be enforceable in any Contracting State. This means that UPC's will not have jurisdiction to enforce their decisions. Hence our question is defined a little bit more by the following: is it possible that an award that deals with a European patent with unitary effect be levelled up to a decision of the UPC court, even considering that the award was not rendered by a UPC institution, but rather another arbitration institution?

Rule 354 of the draft for Rules of Procedure reads:88 '[s]ubject to Rule 118.9 and Rule 352 decisions and orders of the Court shall be directly enforceable from their date of service in each Contracting Member State. Enforcement shall take place in accordance with the enforcement procedures and conditions governed by the law of the particular Contracting Member State where enforcement takes place'. It is submitted that this provision rules out decisions taken by other institutions that are not part of the UPC scheme. Consequently, the awards provided by arbitration institutions (*e.g.* WIPO, ICC) that relate to an EU patent with unitary effect will have to be enforced by means of the institutions' rules and the NYC.

On the other hand, if the parties have an award from the UPC Centre, can they enforce it outside of the EU? It is submitted that if the award was rendered by the UPC Arbitration Centre, but the parties wish to enforce it outside of the EU, the fact that the Centre has dealt with the arbitration would be regarded as if any other arbitration institution had administered it. The award will then be enforced as well by virtue of the NYC. Initially, the seat of those arbitrations would be either Portugal (Lisbon) or Slovenia (Ljubljana) and both of the countries are part of the mentioned convention.89

CONCLUSION

This paper elaborates on the submission that the current litigation system of cross-border conflicts of a single patent between the same parties, in different jurisdictions, results in an abuse of the litigation system by the parties and results in different and sometimes contradictory decisions. This submission was stated after following the multijurisdictional litigation between Apple and Samsung. Hence, the paper studies the possible solution of using a single procedure to resolve these types of conflicts; the decision of which can be enforced in the different jurisdictions where the parties market their products. It is submitted that the European efforts to achieve a single procedure has finally come to reality with the creation of the UPC. It represents a single procedure and it will ensure the neutrality of the decision-makers. Nevertheless this paper shows that commercial arbitration can be advantageous as it harbours the possibility of a wider effect of the award (beyond the EU).

Furthermore, this paper analysed four elements of procedure in the new UPC vis-à-vis those same elements in commercial arbitration. First, with regard to jurisdiction, the new UPC system will be defined by rules that at the time of writing are still not definitive. On the other hand, several arbitration institutions have definitive rules that would help the parties to decide a forum for their dispute and provide flexibility to the convenience of the parties.

Concerning the Preliminary Injunctions procedures in arbitration it is stated that the parties can rely on this method. This is particularly the case when the parties had a previous contract where they agree to arbitrate the disputes regarding IPRs because the arbitral tribunal can help in rendering an express award if it is considered to have found an infringement.

Regarding the applicable law, it is submitted that a mosaic approach would be suitable for cross-border patent conflict. This consists of taking into account all of the applicable laws that are relevant and decide under each of the laws the different decisions of the conflict. An example of this approach is seen in the *Actavis* case. It is submitted that if such an approach is possible in litigation, the practice is also viable for arbitration.

Finally, regarding the enforcement of international arbitration awards, it is recognised that the NYC provides for a mechanism of enforcement regardless of the award involving a EU patent with or without unitary effect and that, if the parties so wish, it can be enforced outside Contracting States of the UPC. On the other hand, if the parties opt to take their dispute to the UPC Arbitration Centre, the award will be enforced in the EU in the same way as a decision made by the UPC. Outside of the EU, this award might also be enforced under the terms of the NYC. Therefore, it is submitted that although the UPC represents an extraordinary procedure that will bring a special advantage to cross-border patent conflicts, its limitations, given that it only has effect within the EU signatory parties, and the present uncertainties in the proceedings, opens the possibility for reliable institutional commercial arbitration to fill the gaps during these types of disputes.

COMPETING INTERESTS

The research for this article was conducted during the PhD studies of the author, which were financed by CONACYT (Mexico) and the Centre of Commercial Law Studies of Queen Mary University of London (UK).

NOTES

[1]See eg Jack Purcher 'Apple & Samsung Dramatically Secured More Patents in 2012' (*Patently Apple*, 10 January 2013) <http://www.patentlyapple.com/patently-apple/2013/01/apple-samsung-dramatically-secured-more-patents-in-2012> accessed 11 March 2016; Laura Gaze and John Roderick, *Inside the iPhone Patent Portfolio* (Thomson Reuters IP Market Report 2012).

[2]See eg Nigam Arora, 'Apple May Pay Billions to Samsung for New iPad' (*Forbes Magazine*, 15 March 2012) <www.forbes.com/sites/greatspeculations/2012/03/15/apple-may-billions-to-samsung-for-new-ipad/> accessed 11 March 2016; Kartik Chillakanti, 'Apple and Samsung: Frenemies for Life' (*Huffington Post*, 24 July 2013)

<www.huffingtonpost.com/fueled/apple-and-samsung-frenemi_b_3640858.html> accessed 11 March 2016.

[3]Ian King and Adam Satariano, 'Apple Ties to Samsung in Sharp Contrast to Courtroom Clash' (*Bloomberg Magazine*, 7 August 2012) <www.bloomberg.com/news/2012-08-07/apple-ties-to-samsung-in-sharp-contrast-to-courtroom-clash> accessed 11 March 2016.

[4]ibid.

[5]ibid.

[6]ibid.

[7]A Google search, using the term 'Apple vs Samsung' gives around 416 million results; see <https://www.google.co.uk/?gfe_rd=cr&ei=QThMU_LAH43R8geY9oHICQ#q=apple+vs+samsung> accessed 14 April 2014.

[8]Apple and Samsung negotiated all patent procedures outside of the US, see Amid Chowdhry, 'Apple and Samsung Drop Patent Disputes Against Each Other Outside of the U.S.' (*Forbes Magazine*, 6 August 2014) <http://www.forbes.com/sites/amitchowdhry/2014/08/06/apple-and-samsung-drop-patent-disputes-against-each-other-outside-of-the-u-s/#2b783eeca5e1> accessed 20 March 2016.

[9]See eg Julian Lew, Loukas Mistellis and Stephan Kröll, *Comparative International Commercial Arbitration* (Kluwer Law International 2003); Trevor Cook and Alejandro Garcia, *International Intellectual Property Arbitration* (Wolters Kluwer 2010); Anne Martin and J Derek Manson, 'Arbitration: A Quick and Effective Means for Patent Dispute Resolution' (*Oblon*, December 2011) <http://www.oblon.com/publications/arbitration-a-quick-and-effective-means-for-patent-dispute-resolution/> accessed 11 March 2016; and Gari Born, *International Arbitration Law and Practice* (Kluwer Law International 2012).

[10]This opinion is shared with Cook and Garcia (n 9); see also Thierry Calame and Martin Aebi, 'Enforceability' in Thomas D Halket (ed), *Arbitration of International Intellectual Property Disputes* (Juris Publishing 2012).

[11]Qualitative research aims to understand the meaning of human action, relying on text data rather than numerical, it also asks open questions about the phenomena as it occurs in context. See Stacy Carter and Miles Little, 'Justifying Knowledge, Justifying Method, Taking Action: Epistemologies, Methodologies and Methods in Qualitative Research' (2007) 17 QHR 1316.

[12]Recognised patent lawyers in the EU, specialised in patent litigation.

[13]From companies such as Nokia, Bayern and Caterpillar.

[14]Justine Pila, 'The European Patent: An Old and Vexing Problem' (2013) 62 ICLQ 917.

[15]Vincenzo Di Cataldo, 'From the European Patent to a Community Patent' (2002) 8 Colum J Eur L 19.

[16]Convention on the Grant of European Patents [1973] 13 ILM 268 (European Patent Convention), art 1.

[17]ibid art 4.

[18]Pila (n 14).

[19]European Patent Convention art 137(2b).

[20]Di Cataldo (n 15) 20.

[21]Erika Ellyne, 'European Patent Law: A Foreseeable Future in the Wake of the European Court of Justice Opinion 1/09 on the Compatibility of the Draft Agreement Creating a Unified Litigation Patent System with the Founding European Treaties?' (2012) 2 QMJIP 345.

[22]For recent updates on ratifying parties, see <http://www.consilium.europa.eu/en/documents-publications/agreements-conventions/agreement/?aid=2013001> accessed 10 March 2016.

[23]EPO, 'Unitary Patent and Unified Patent Court' (29 January 2015) <http://www.epo.org/law-practice/unitary.html> accessed 12 March 2016.

[24]EPO, 'The Unified Patent Court' (29 January 2015) <www.epo.org/law-practice/unitary/patent-court.html> accessed 11 March 2016.

[25]ibid.

[26]ibid.

[27]Agreement on a Unified Patent Court [2013] OJ C175/1, art 52(2).

[28]Jacques De Werra, 'Can Alternative Dispute Resolution Mechanisms Become the Default Method for Solving International Intellectual Property Disputes?' (2012) 43 Cal W Intl LJ 39.

[29]See WIPO, 'Recommended Contract Clauses and Submission Agreements' <http://www.wipo.int/amc/en/clauses/#4> accessed 12 March 2016 (for an example of such a submission agreement).

[30]United Nations Commission on International Trade Law Model Law on International Commercial Arbitration (adopted 21 June 1985, amended 2006) 24 ILM 1302 (UNCITRAL Model Law) (reflecting a worldwide consensus on key aspects of the arbitration practice).

[31]Alan Redfern and others, *Law and Practice of International Commercial Arbitration* (4th edn, Sweet & Maxwell Publishing 2004) 315.

[32]UPC Agreement art 18(2).

[33]James Bridgeman, 'Choice of Arbitrator' in Thomas D Halket (ed), *Arbitration of International Intellectual Property Disputes* (Juris Publishing 2012).

[34]Redfern and others (n 31) 221.

[35]Cook and García (n 9) 143.

[36]Arbitration Rules of the World Intellectual Property Organization (2014) <http://www.wipo.int/amc/en/arbitration/rules> accessed 5 September 2015 (WIPO Arbitration Rules).

[37]Commercial Arbitration Rules and Mediation Procedures of the American Arbitration Association (2013) <https://www.adr.org/aaa/ShowProperty?nodeId=/UCM/ADRS

TG_004103&revision=latestreleased> accessed 5 September 2015 (AAA Rules of Arbitration).

[38]Rules of Arbitration of the International Chamber of Commerce (2012) <http://www.iccwbo.org/products-and-services/arbitration-and-adr/arbitration/icc-rules-of-arbitration/> accessed 11 March 2016 (ICC Rules).

[39]Cook and García (n 9) 144.

[40]See UNCITRAL Model Law art 11(3); and ICC Rules art 12(5) (both suggesting that each party will appoint one arbitrator while the third one will be appointed by the Court).

[41]Bridgeman (n 33) 235.

[42]This mechanism, consist briefly in the following steps: The WIPO Centre sends to each party an identical list of a three candidates (such names will come from a list drawn from the WIPO Centre) then each party may delete the name of any candidate that they object to, and will leave the candidates in order of preferences, the Centre then will invite a person to be arbitrator.

[43]ibid; see also WIPO Arbitration Rules (n 36).

[44]Bridgeman (n 33) 240.

[45]Karen Fong, 'Arbitration of IP Disputes: Eyes Wide Shut' (*The In-House Lawyer*, 14 December 2009) <http://www.inhouselawyer.co.uk/index.php/intellectual-property/7673-arbitration-of-ip-disputes-eyes-wide-shut> accessed 12 March 2016.

[46]See ICC Rules art 29 and Appendix V.

[47]Katie McConnell and Nathan Searle, 'Would You Take a Patent Dispute to the ICC for an Arbitration?' (*PatLit*, 21 September 2011) <http://patlit.blogspot.co.uk/2011/09/would-you-take-patent-dispute-to-icc.html> accessed 12 March 2016.

[48]Council Regulation (EU) 1257/2012 of 17 December 2012 on implementing enhanced cooperation in the area of the creation of unitary patent protection [2012] OJ L361/1.

[49]A division of the UPC will entail a first instance Court and they will be categorised in local, regional and central divisions. Every Contracting Member State may set up a local division (or more if needed). Contracting Member States that do not have much patent litigation may set up a regional division together. The central division is based in Paris, with sub-central divisions in London and Munich, which will each be assigned a specialty of the patent matter (eg technological, biological field). See EPO, 'What are the Main Features of the Unified Patent Court?' <www.epo.org/law-practice/unitary.html> accessed 12 March 2016.

[50]Pierre Véron, 'The Unified Patent Court Explained in Detail' (European Patent Reform Forum, Munich, 19 September 2013).

[51]ibid.

[52]Clemens Heusch, 'Consultation Panel: Feedback and Ideas Regarding Draft Proposals for Rules of Procedure' (European Patent Reform Forum, Munich, 19 September 2013); Council Regulation (EC) No 44/2001 of 22 December 2000 on jurisdiction and the recognition and enforcement of judgments in civil and commercial matters [2001] OJ L12/1 (Brussels I Regulation) (that was later replaced by Regulation (EU) No

1215/2012).

[53]ibid.

[54]Jörg Thomaier, 'Inter-Industry Debate: International Litigation Considerations' (European Patent Reform Forum, Munich, 19 September 2013).

[55]Véron (n 50).

[56]UPC Agreement art 33(3) (clarifies that the local division has the discretion to either proceed with both the action for infringement with the counterclaim for revocation, or refer the counterclaim for revocation of decision to the central division and suspend (stay) or proceed with the action for infringement). The latter alternative is, at the moment, called 'bifurcation' in Germany—though it is uncertain which term will be applied in the future.

[57]Jörg Thomaier, 'Consultation Panel: Feedback and Ideas Regarding Draft Proposals for Rules of Procedure' (European Patent Reform Forum, Munich, 19 September 2013).

[58]Thomaier, 'Inter-Industry Debate' (n 54).

[59]Although, he also points out the fact that they will want to attract the big cases as a matter of prestige; see Heusch (n 52).

[60]ibid. For example, if 19% of the products are distributed in one or two countries, the dispute should not be brought before a minor market where there is only the presence of a webpage since that would not constitute a close (enough) connection.

[61]See Rules of Procedure of the Unified Patent Court (17th draft, 31 October 2014) <http://www.unified-patent-court.org/images/documents/UPC_Rules_of_Procedure_17th_Draft.pdf> accessed 12 March 2016 (UPC Rules of Procedure) (containing a preliminary set of provisions for the UPC).

[62]UPC Agreement art 32.

[63]Véron (n 50).

[64]Gyooho Lee, Keon-Hyung Ahn and Jacques De Werra, 'Euro-Korean Perspectives on the Use of Arbitration and ADR Mechanisms for Solving Intellectual Property Disputes' (2014) 30 Arb Intl 91.

[65]See WIPO Arbitration Rules art 39; and ICC Rules art 18.

[66]A similar rule is followed by other non-UNCITRAL countries, eg the Swiss Rules of International Arbitration (2012) <https://www.swissarbitration.org/files/33/Swiss-Rules/SRIA_english_2012.pdf> accessed 10 February 2016 (Swiss Rules), art 16(1) (which reads '[i]f the parties have not determined the seat of the arbitration, or if the designation of the seat is unclear or incomplete, the Court shall determine the seat of the arbitration, taking into account all relevant circumstances, or shall request the arbitral tribunal to determine it').

[67]Thomas D Halket and Susan H Nycum, 'The Arbitration Agreement' in Thomas D Halket (ed), *Arbitration of International Intellectual Property Disputes* (Juris Publishing 2012).

[68]London and New York are the most preferred seats of arbitration specified in

international arbitration clauses; see Norton Rose Fulbright, *11th Annual Litigation Trends Survey* (May 2015) <http://www.nortonrosefulbright.com/files/20150514-2015-litigation-trends-survey_v24-128746.pdf> accessed 12 March 2016, 70.

[69]The Convention on the Recognition and Enforcement of Foreign Arbitral Awards (adopted 10 June 1958, entered into force 7 June 1959) 330 UNTS 38 (New York Convention) (which applies to the recognition and enforcement of foreign arbitral awards and the referral by a Court to arbitration). For a complete list of signatories see <http://www.newyorkconvention.org/contracting-states/list-of-contracting-states> accessed 12 March 2016.

[70]Alex Wilson, 'The Unified Patent Court Explained in (European Patent Reform Forum, Munich, 19 September 2013).

[71]Timothy Siaw, 'The Netherlands' in Massimo Sterpi and Thierry Calame (eds), *Patent Litigation: Jurisdictional Comparisons* (2nd edn, Sweet and Maxwell 2012) 300; Case C-4/03*Gesellschaft für Antriebstechnik mbH & Co. KG v Lamellen und Kupplungsbau Beteiligungs KG*[2006] ECR I-6509; Case C-539/03 *Roche Nederland BV and Others v Frederick Primus and Milton Goldenberg* [2006] ECR I-6535.

[72]ICC Rules Appendix V.

[73]Regulation 1257/2012 (n 48) (containing provisions concerning the effect, exhaustion, licenses on the unitary patent, and rules over the administrative tasks of the patent office); Council Regulation (EU) 1260/2012 of 17 December 2012 on implementing enhanced cooperation in the area of the creation of unitary patent protection with regard to the applicable translation arrangements [2012] OJ L361/89 (taking into account the official languages of the UPC).

[74]See UPC Agreement art 24(2)-(3). When the conflict involves UPC Agreement arts 25-26 (on the right of the patent owner to prevent the direct or indirect use of an invention), art 27 (on the limits of the effect of the patent), or art 28 (on the right based on prior use of the invention); the application of national laws is allowed. National laws will also be applicable during the procedure when there are questions concerning the burden of proof (arts 54-55); corrective measures in infringement procedures (art 64); award of damages (art 68); and the period of limitation for bringing an action (art 72).

[75]See Commission, 'Antitrust: Commission Accepts Legally Binding Commitments by Samsung Electronics on Standard Essential Patent Injunctions' (29 April 2014) <http://europa.eu/rapid/press-release_IP-14-490_en.htm> accessed 12 March 2016.

[76]Marrakesh Agreement Establishing the World Trade Organization (adopted 15 April 1994, entered into force 1 January 1995) 33 ILM 1144, Annex C, Agreement on Trade-Related Aspects of Intellectual Property Rights (TRIPS Agreement).

[77]American Law Institute, *Intellectual Property, Principles Governing Jurisdiction, Choice of Law, and Judgments in Transnational Disputes* (American Law Institute 2008).

[78]See eg David Caron, 'The World of Intellectual Property and the Decision to Arbitrate' (2003) 19 Arb Intl 451.

[79]See *Actavis UK Limited and others v Eli Lilly & Company* [2014] EWHC 1511 (Pat)

(Judgment on the merits).

[80]Ever since the TRIPS Agreement entered into force, the standards provisions have the same effect in all of the countries that took part in it.

[81]UPC Agreement art 82(3).

[82]Calame and Aebi (n 9).

[83]ibid.

[84]Lee, Ahn and De Werra (n 65) 120.

[85]ICC Rules art 16 (which requires the transmission of a settlement to pass by the Secretariat of the ICC as part of the administrative procedures of the aforementioned organisation).

[86]Lee, Ahn and De Werra (n 65).

[87]UPC Agreement art 83(1) (stating that '[d]uring a transitional period of 7 years [...] an action for infringement or revocation of a European patent [...] may still be brought before national courts [...]').

[88]See UPC Rules of Procedure (n 61).

[89]See (n 70).

2
CHAPTER

TRADEMARK PROTECTION FOR STORE DESIGNS

Thomas Farkas

INTRODUCTION

Companies spend significant sums implementing a special look for their products and brands in order to stand out from the competition. With the competition not only taking place within a country but across the globe the need to give the consumer a unique brand experience is more important than ever. The extension of intellectual property rights and their scope of protection play a vital role in this scenario. In Europe for example, not only has the legislator introduced new means of protection but also extended the scope of protection of existing intellectual property rights. In the course of the harmonization of the European trademark regime, the Trademark Directive ("tmdir") and the Trademark Regulation , the European legislator widened the protection offered by trademarks. First of all, the possibility to register a throughout the European Community with a single application extends its territorial scope. Secondly, the term for signs being capable of registration has been extended. Art. of the trade mark regulation stipulates the criteria for a sign to be eligible for trademark protection . Said provision introduced new types of trademarks such as color marks , olfactory marks6 , sound marks and haptic marks into the legal system of the EU. The industries reaction on said extension of trademark law followed in an instant. Hence in both, the U.S. and the EU regime, a more extensive and rigorous use of trademarks can be observed. Companies will equip and up value their products utilizing position marks , color marks and will at least try to obtain protection via shape marks for the products itself. Often the same products are also registered as designs according to the new EU framework for Design right. Simultaneously their features could also be protected as copyright or according to unfair competition law/passing-off

Citation: Thomas farkas, trademark protection for store designs, http://revistas.uexternado.edu.co/index.php/propin/article/view/3920/4213.

Besides the practice of cumulative protection for goods offered through the whole arsenal of intellectual property rights, a relatively new phenomenon could be on the rise, at least from an EU perspective: the protection of the get-up of business venues. This article aims to analyze the legal basis for the protection of a business venue's get-up via intellectual property rights. The analysis focuses on the current framework in the US and in the EU. While it will be shown that the US-American Law has been familiar with the phenomenon of the protection as a "trade dress", the legal evaluation of the protection of business venues in the EU as such is still in its infancy. Finally this article will assess if such protection is desirable.

IMPLICATIONS OF DESIGNING A BUSINESS VENUE

Especially in recent years the enhanced and sophisticated design of business venues such as retail stores and restaurants alike demonstrate the emphasis on the will to stand out from the competition; furthermore such an advanced design communicates the message of the brand to the consumer. It is the ultimate goal of any company to gain a recognition value amongst the target consumers for the design of the business venue. A consumer's positive experience is likely to drive him into a business venue on a more regular basis. In order to successfully gain consumer loyalty, companies make circumspect investments not only financially but also with thought through marketing strategies. In the end a lot of effort and investments are spent on the design of the business venue in order to give the consumer said special brand experience. Due to these investments companies have a well-reasoned urge to protect these investments utilizing intellectual property rights. But due to the crisp details and the comprehensive design of the venue in question it is often not easy to accomplish said protection for the whole design of the business venue. While single features can be protected by design law, copyright and trademark law it proves rather difficult to protect the get-up, the sign of a business venue as whole.

Despite the legal issues when protecting the get-up of a business venue companies are keen to design their venue with a distinct overall appearance. Companies such as Apple, the German based electronic warehouses Saturn Hansa and media markt, apparel retailers Hollister, Abercrombie & Fitch, Tommy Hilfiger and Restaurant chains McDonalds, Vapiano or Crepes and Waffles emphasize on creating a consumer experience of the same atmosphere, store concept, store design and the same menus. The educated customer recognizes these business venues on first sight and even more when entering their facilities. The following part analyzes the protection of the get-up of these business venues according to the legal institutes of trademark and unfair competition law in the U.S. and the EU.

MEANS OF PROTECTION FOR BUSINESS VENUES/STORES

US Law - Trade Dress

The protection of trade dresses is well established in the U.S.'s legal system. Section 43 (a) (1) of the Lanham Act defines the protection offered by a trade dress. It reads as follows: Any person who, on or in connection with any goods or services, or any container for goods, uses in commerce any word, term, name, symbol, or device, or any combination thereof, or any false designation of origin, false or misleading description of fact, or false or misleading representation of fact, which

a. Is likely to cause confusion, or to cause mistake, or to deceive as to the affiliation, connection, or association of such person with another person, or as to the origin, sponsorship, or approval of his or her goods, services, or commercial activities by another person, or

b. In commercial advertising or promotion, misrepresents the nature, characteristics, qualities, or geographic origin of his or her or another person's goods, services, or commercial activities, shall be liable in a civil action by any person who believes that he or she is or is likely to be damaged by such act.

In General, visual but non-verbal marks are collectively known as trade dress. The protection of a trade dress is only historically different to that of trademark protection. Today trade dress protection is coined by the notions of trade mark law20. According to the provision mentioned above, the design and shape of the materials in which a product is packaged, the product configuration, the design and shape of the product itself, can be considered as a form of trade dress. The International Trademark Association inta confirms that a trade dress can be incarnated as the "overall commercial image (look and feel) of a product or service that indicates or identifies the source of the product or service and distinguishes it from those of others. It may include the design or configuration of a product; the labeling and packaging of goods; and/or the décor or environment in which services are provided. Trade dress can consist of such elements as size, shape, color and texture, to the extent such elements are not functional. In many countries, trade dress is referred to as "get-up" or "product design".

According to the U.S. law, protection for a trade dress is available, if the feature for which trade dress protection is claimed bears the same source-identifying function as a trademark. The protection of trade dress has raised multiple issues not encountered in word marks. The issues concern amongst others the anticompetitive effects of trade dress protection and its conflicts with other intellectual property rights such as patent law and copyright. Although the current legal system in the U.S. offers protection for a trade dress also by registration as a trademark; practical reasons implicate that most trade dress and product configurations are protected without registratio. If the trade dress is unregistered, the trade dress owner has to overcome the hurdle of precisely demonstrating which features of his product or packaging constitute the trade dress. Furthermore he has to prove that the alleged trade dress is protectable; he must establish that there is a likelihood of confusion. The assessment of similarity will be evaluated by comparing the respective trade dress designs. With regards to the other factors to prove likelihood of confusion it should be mentioned that these are in principal the same as when comparing traditional trademarks or logos. In regards to trade dress protection for services it must be assessed whether or not the consumer is predisposed to view the trade dress as a source indicator. For both, the registered and the unregistered trade dress, the criteria to be assessed are distinctiveness, non-functionality and infringement by likelihood of confusion. Furthermore the indication of origin is in the center of trade dress protection: the features that indicate the trade dresses origin are to be protected; ingredients of innovation and creativity cannot be protected by trade dress or trade mark law. So in what cases does a trade dress offer protection to business venues?.

Case Law - Two Pesos v. Cabana Inc.

One of the leading cases in the U.S. covering trade dress protection for a business venue is the Supreme Court decision in Two Pesos Inc. v. Taco Cabana. The case concerns the protection of the get-up of a Mexican themed restaurant, respectively Taco Cabana. Restaurants of the Taco Cabana chain are designed in a typical Mexican way. Both, the exterior and the interior of these fast food restaurants bear typical distinct Mexican style features and motives. The restaurants of the Taco Cabana chain all incorporate the same features as a matter of their corporate identity. The claim was made against the direct competitor Two Pesos. The defendant Two Pesos utilizes the same style elements in his restaurants as the plaintiff. The US Supreme Court confirmed the decision of the previous instance. This case demonstrates the assessment of trade dress infringement according to the following criteria:

Eligibility for Trade Dress Protection

First of all, the get-up of the business venue, the restaurant Taco Cabana, must be eligible for trade dress protection. Due to the fact that Taco Cabana did not register their get-up as trade dress, the competent courts could only judge on a claim for an unregistered trade dress. As mentioned above, the protectable features are defined as any word, any name, any symbol or devise or any combination thereof that can be used by a person to mark their goods. The legal protection of a trade dress relates especially to the elements that are able to enhance the sale of goods or services. The U.S. Supreme Court did not comment if the get-up of a business venue is eligible as a unitary mark. Instead the competent Court argued in favor of a strong protection for designs. Trade dress protection shall hence be available a get-up showing the intent to protect the marketing investments made and the resulting value of the business. This includes also the protection of the consumer's ability to differentiate the business of those of competitors. It was argued that the federal protection of a mark is desirable as such trade dresses would enhance competition and the quality of the businesses output; in this regard the protection would secure the reputation and the good will of the business in question. Consequently the Supreme Court did not see an issue positioning the get-up of Taco Cabana's business venues under the umbrella of trade dress protection even if the get-up would consist of multiple single features.

Distinctiveness

In order to obtain trade dress protection the relevant feature(s) must be capable of distinguishing the goods and services of the right owner to those of a competitor. According to the US approach to distinctiveness it must be differentiated between signs that are inherently distinctive and such that acquired secondary meaning. The get-up of a product or service is only then inherently distinctive if it is suggestive, arbitrary or fanciful; a generic or merely descriptive feature can only acquire distinctiveness through secondary meaning. In this regard the defendant in Taco Cabana v. Two Pesos stated that the get-up of the plaintiff's business venues was merely descriptive: he argued that the get-up merely constituted an indication of Mexican food being served. The defendant compared the get-up in question to a factual sign stating that Taco Cabana is a "Mexican restaurant". On behalf of the defendant it was consequently argued that the plaintiffs get-up could only be regarded as distinctive if it already acquired secondary meaning. The U.S. Supreme Court did not accept this argument; he held the plaintiffs get-up to be inherently distinctive. Furthermore the property interests of the plaintiff in his unique and valuable marketing device, the get-up of the restaurants, were to be recognized irrespective of the relevant consumer associations that would prove acquired distinctiveness through secondary meaning. In its judgment the U.S. Supreme Court pointed out that the requirement of an additional secondary meaning could harm competition as it would stifle the start-up phase of small businesses. It should be noted that in other cases U.S. courts focussed on secondary meaning in order to grant protection. In a more recent judgment the U.S. Supreme Court pointed out, that in order to obtain trade dress protection acquired secondary meaning must be proven unless the case would concern a get-up constituting the product itself.

Functionality Doctrine

According to Sec. 43(a) (3) of the Lanham Act the claimant must prove that the get-up for which protection is sought is not merely functional. From the spirit and the purpose of the provision a merely functional design should be free for all to use and imitate as long as no other intellectual property rights appl. Otherwise the freedom of competition would be too harshly restricted. Therefore it must be assessed whether or not the features of the get-up in question are essential for the usage or the purpose of the goods or services and if these features influence the value or the quality of the goods or service. The functionality of single features does not necessarily lead to the conclusion that the get-up as such is also merely functional. On the other hand the possibility to have a different design or proven distinctiveness does not preclude functionality. In case the feature of the get-up is also protectable as a patent concedes it to be functional even if the patent is exhausted. In Taco Cabana v. Two Pesos the U.S. Supreme Court held the plaintiffs get-up not to be functional. This argument is correct in so far, as the design of a business venue is not essential for the service it provides. Even if single features of the get-up, such as the menu, would fulfill the criteria for the functionality doctrine, this does not convey functionality on the get-up as a whole. Even when applying the Inwood test the get-up of the plaintiff's restaurant does not directly concern the quality and the pricing of the respective goods and services. Even if the sophisticated design of the business venue will influence the costs of the offered goods and services this indirect influence was not regarded to be sufficient to reason for functionality. According to this argument the functionality doctrine will not be an effective hurdle for the get-up of a business venue to obtain trade dress protection.

(Reputation of the Get-Up)

The reputation of the get-up as such is not an obligatory requirement for protection. This becomes even clearer when considering the fact that distinctiveness must not per se be proven through secondary meaning. Nevertheless the threshold for distinctiveness cannot be judged with certainty according to the current legal status. The protected get-up of restaurants such as Dunkin'Donuts and Taco Cabana are mainly operated via franchise systems. The judgment in Taco Cabana v. Two Pesos implies that the operation of multiple franchise restaurants with identical design and corporate identity strengthens the distinctiveness because of their presence. Also this conclusion can be drawn from another case involving the get-up of a business venue, respectively a barber shop chain. Here the get-up of the single business venues were not identical and contained slight modifications. The protection of the get-up was regarded as not eligible for trade dress protection due to the above mentioned differences.

OTHER CASE LAW

The competent court in Best Cellars, Inc. v. Wine Made Simple, Inc., held that the overall décor and the design of the plaintiff's wine retail store constituted protectable trade dress. This decisions was made despite the existence of a number of elements that were utilitarian or commonplace in the industry (i.e., the placement of informational cards in front of wine bottles and arranging wine bottles horizontally in racks). As for registered trade dresses the fast food restaurant chain "Chipotle" owns a registration for its restaurant layout as shown below; the description reads "a restaurant evoking a neo-industrial feel through the use of unpainted galvanized or stainless steel" with "natural wood finishes as accents on the table and/chair edges, bench seating, wall finishes, and/ or chairs", and the "use of industrial-look light fixtures". The first illustration shows the registration, the second photograph The illustrative comparison below demonstrates how such a description translates into the interior of a Chipotle restaurant:

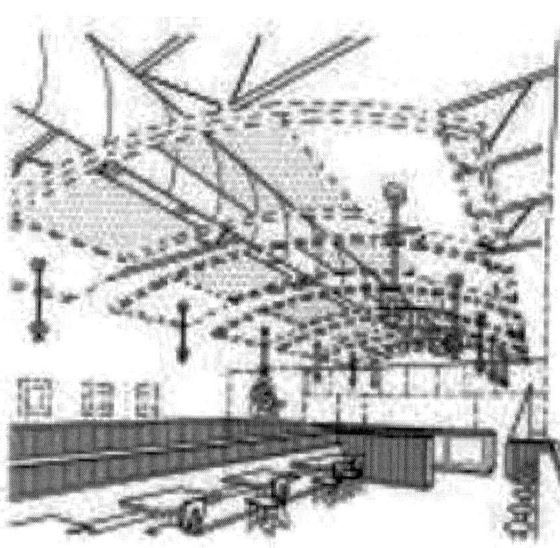

Picture taken from the article by Devin Cooke and Julia Anne Matheson, "Is Your Store Design Unique? Trademark It", last visited 20th September 2014 at [www.finnegan.com/resources/articles/articlesdetail.aspx?news=cec05725- e298-4d22-8025-521e46e99ea0].

Picture taken from the article by Devin Cooke and Julia Anne Matheson, "Is Your Store Design Unique? Trademark It", last visited 20th September 2014 at [www.finnegan.com/resources/articles/ articlesdetail.aspx?news=cec05725-e298-4d22-8025-521e46e99ea0].

The restaurant "Potbelly Sandwich" also owns trademark registrations covering aspects of its restaurant layout and décor. This includes the U.S. registration No. 3494208. It describes the trade dress mark as "appearance and design of the interior of a restaurant produced by a combination of multiple counters of different heights forming a multi-level counter structure, a built-in glass front drink cooler, cubbyhole-style shelving, banner stanchions with chains/ropes and tile behind serving area. The solid lines show the positioning of the mark in connection with the restaurant and those features claimed by the applicant as its mark". The illustration below shows said registration:

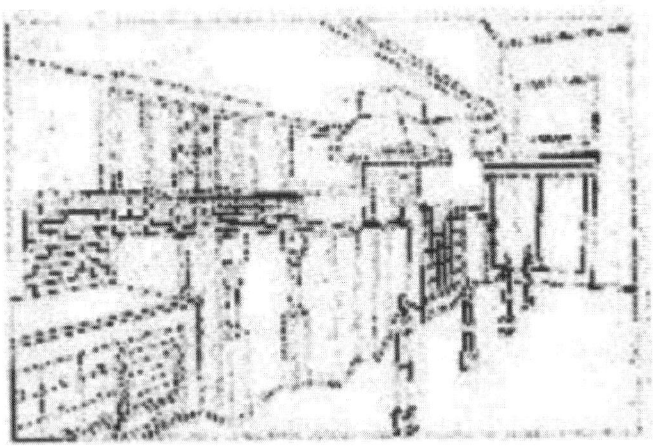

Picture taken from the article by Devin Cooke and Julia Anne Matheson, “Is Your Store Design Unique? Trademark It”, last visited 20th September 2014 at [www.finnegan.com/resources/articles/articlesdetail.aspx?news=cec05725- e298-4d22-8025-521e46e99ea0]. The illustration shown above prove demonstrate that registrations of a business venue’s get-up do exist and also that it will be difficult to judge an infringement based on these illustrations.

THE APPLE STORE CASE IN THE US

Especially when Apple found out that a store in China featured the white Apple logo, among other design details, was so authentic that even salespeople who worked there believed that they worked for Apple, they decided to attempt for further protection. In early 2013 the U.S. Patent and Trademark Office (uspto) granted Apple’s request for trademark protection for the minimalist design and layout of its retail stores comprised of “a clear glass storefront by a paneled façade” and the signature “oblong table with stools set below video screens flush mounted on the back wall”. During the two-year trademark examination process, the uspto was especially concerned with issues related to the functionality doctrine and the criterion of distinctiveness regarding Apples business venue. Apple was requested to explain as to why the claimed store design features were neither functional nor so standard in the industry as to be unprotectable. Furthermore Apple had to demonstrate that the trade dress had come to serve a source identifying function. Accordingly Apple refined the trade dress features for which it sought protection multiple times. In the course of these arguments Apple also obtained and submitted a consumer survey to support its claim of acquired secondary meaning. The uspto requested an even narrower description of the relevant features. Finally Apple submitted inquiries with hundreds more pages of documentation of secondary meaning to the uspto. These included the following evidence: substantial business activity generated by the Apple stores, promotional events that were tied to Apple stores, photographs of the stores on Apple’s website, and numerous unsolicited media articles about the store design. Ultimately, Apple was able to persuade the uspto to allow its mark to be published for third-party objection. After the deadline for opposition period passed without objection, Apple’s marks matured to registration. Apple was able to successfully demonstrate to the uspto that the get-up of their business venue is non-functional and has acquired distinctiveness sufficient to qualify for registration as a trade dress.

EU LAW

Introduction

The most recent jurisprudence in the EU regarding the protection of get-up of a business venue has its origin from German jurisprudence. The German Federal Patent Court (“Bundespatentgericht”, abbreviated BPatG) referred questions to the ecj on how to interpret the European Trade mark Law regarding the protection of Apple’s trademark application for its store design. Therefore the following part will discuss the protection of the get-up of a business venue according to German Law. Subsequently the ecj decision answering the questions of the BPatG will be analyzed.

Trade Dress Protection According to German Law

According to German Law the get-up of a store can mainly be protected by trade mark and unfair competition law. Despite the fact that the origins of German Trademark law stems from the Act against unfair competition ("uwg") unfair competition law, the former should at least in theory be less woven into unfair competition law as is the case in the U.S..

Federal Patent Court - "Apple store" case

While the former German trade mark law denied the registration for three-dimensional shapes, the current trade mark law explicitly constitutes the possibility to register three-dimensional shapes. Obviously the possibility to register threedimensional shapes as trademarks raises some concern in regards of an overlap to other intellectual property rights. Can a technical feature which is contained in a three dimensional shape be registered? If so, how is it justified to have a perpetual monopoly granted by a trademark for a technical invention expressed in a threedimensional shape if in prior a patent for the feature was obtained? The same considerations are relevant for the overlap of trademark law and design rights/Copyright law: should a three-dimensional shape be registrable as a trademark if a design right or copyright protection could be obtained as well? Shape marks that consist of a patentable innovation or an aesthetic feature protectable as a design right/copyright will make the other intellectual property rights, which offer only a limited term of protection and bear customized protection criteria, superfluous. The European legislator was aware of the issue of overlapping protection. In order to prevent such an unwanted overlap he introduced relevant sections in both, the trademark Regulation and Directive. The wording of Section 3 (1) (e) Trademark Directive reads as follows: The following shall not be registered or, if registered, shall be liable to be declared invalid:

signs which consist exclusively of:

- The shape which results from the nature of the goods themselves;
- The shape of goods which is necessary to obtain a technical result;
- The shape which gives substantial value to the goods.

Despite the extension of protection offered by intellectual property rights in recent years the protection for trade dresses is rather a phenomenon occurring in the U.S. Especially when considering that a store design, the performance of a band or the atmosphere of a restaurant are protectable as well. The principal German view on the protection of such features is rather skeptical. It was only in 2013, where the Federal Court of Patents had to decide on the registrability of above shown store design72 by Apple Inc. as a trade mark73. The details of the case can be summarized as follows: The plaintiff demanded extension of the internationally registered threedimensional shape mark to the German territory. The color of the illustration is "steel gray and light brown", illustration as shown in the online accessible database of the uspto74. The illustration shown in the mentioned database is registered for the following services of class 35 of the Nice classification: "Retail store services featuring computers, computer software, computer peripherals, mobile phones, consumer electronics and related accessories, and demonstration of products relating thereto". The registration offers the following description: "The mark consists of distinctive design and layout of a retail store". The competent department of the German Trademark Office has denied the protection of said illustration of a retail store reasoning that it would lack inherent distinctiveness. The illustration of the store was held to be exhausted in the illustration of the store and thus in the representation of the core features of the offered services. The design of retail stores and sales facilities is an effective and important marketing tool for the sale of consumer goods. The illustration of the retail store in question was found not to be distinctive from other retail stores offering electronic consumer goods. The difference of the illustration in question to the design of large warehouses specializing in electronic consumer goods would only stem from the latter bigger variety of goods and brands offered to the end consumer. Finally it was held that, the function as indication of origin for retail stores is usually achieved by the use of logos and brand names. Thus perceiving the get-up of a store, the consumer would draw conclusions to the quality and price range of the relevant goods, but not to their source. Apple submitted a complaint to the BPatG seeking to reverse said decision and reasoned as follows:

The illustration for which protection was assumed to be inherently distinctive as it is unique for the relevant market. Trademark protection for a three-dimensional mark could not be denied with the argument that it is not intellectually separable from the offered services. Instead Apple assumed that it is in the nature of things that a three dimensional mark subsides with the subject matter of the application. They argued that due to the fact that services are immaterial, an illustration cannot be denied trademark protection simply because it illustrates the service itself. A service should not be exhausted in providing said service; it goes further. It is not reasonable to demand a higher threshold for the trademark protection for the get-up of a store than for any other three-dimensional shape. The illustration for which protection is sought must be regarded as inherently distinctive if it is different from the store designs used by competitors. Factually there are a significant number of unique features contained in the store design represented by the illustration: the lack of a recognizable cashier area, the pure presentation of the goods, the use of old style table without the use of retail platforms, the lack of point of sale palettes, the overwhelming strict observance of form and clear symmetric arrangement of the facilities. These details bear a strong recognition value. Even toy manufacturers, when offering a doll house store, officially refer to the model as "Apple Store".

Furthermore the Complainant Added the Following Description to the Illustration:

Protection is sought with regards to the colors light brown and steel grey. The mark reflects the design and the arrangement of a retail store. The get-up of the store consists of a transparent glass front, surrounded by a steel grey façade construed by panels. The glass front consists of rectangular oblong panels with slimmer panels attached to the sides. Inside the retail store there is a rectangular lighting system built into the ceiling displayed over the whole length of the retail store. The walls on the side of the retail store bears light brown cantilever boards for displaying goods. The side walls bear cupboards with multiple racks. The middle section of the retail store features light brown rectangular tables, arranged in a row and parallel to the walls. They are arranged from the beginning to the end of the retail store. In the back of the retail store a rectangular table with bar stools is arranged below the back wall and in the same height of the TV Screens. Finally the illustration shows dotted lines where products are to be displayed, which are not intended to be covered by the trade mark. Nevertheless the position is regarded to be part of the mark. Taking the view that the dispute raises fundamental questions concerning harmonized European trade mark law, the BPatG decided to stay the proceedings and to refer the following questions to the Court of Justice: (1) Is Article 2 of Directive [2008/95] to be interpreted as meaning that the possibility of protection for the 'packaging of goods' also extends to the presentation of the establishment in which a service is provided? (2) Are Articles 2 and 3(1) of Directive [2008/95] to be interpreted as meaning that a sign representing the presentation of the establishment in which a service is provided is capable of being registered as a trade mark? (3) Is Article 2 of Directive [2008/95] to be interpreted as meaning that the requirement for graphic representability is satisfied by a representation by a design alone or with such additions as a description of the layout or indications of the absolute dimensions in metres or of relative dimensions with indications as to proportions? (4) Is Article 2 of Directive [2008/95] to be interpreted as meaning that the scale of the protection afforded by a trade mark for retail services also extends to the goods produced by the retailer itself?.

The senate of the Federal Patent Court made the following considerations when referring the questions mentioned above to the ecj: The subject matter of the registrability of a three dimensional get-up of a store as a trademark for retail services is not regulated by law nor decided by the German Courts. The target to have streamlined criteria for obtaining a trade mark registration mentioned in the eighth recital of the Directive stipulates the need to refer this matter to the ecj. With regards to the first question the Federal Patent Court made the following considerations: The senate tends to accept the protectability of the scope extension of the get-up as it takes the view that there are substantial differences to the get-up of competitors. Thus it is relevant for a final decision if the ecj will regard the criteria of Art. 2 of the tmdir as fulfilled. The provision does not define the term of a „sign“; however it's nonexhaustive wording names the following examples: „words, including personal names, designs, letters, numerals, the shape of goods or of their packaging“. However it does not mention the get-up of a service. This could reflect the intention of the legislator due to the fact that (1) the service mark was known before the introduction of the Directive; and (2) a service is immaterial and thus does not inherently have a get-up of its own. On the other hand objects that are used to offer the service can be regarded as their embodiment e.g. the vehicle with regards to the service of transportation or as in the case at hand a get-up of a store with regards to retail services. Additionally and as already mentioned the wording of Art. 2 is non-exhaustive. Excluding the protection of the get-up of a service would contravene the intention to harmonize the internal market. With regards to the second question the Federal Patent Court gave the following opinion: A sign reflecting the get-up embodying the service must be graphically representable and capable of distinguishing the services of those of a competitor. Furthermore it must not fall into the categòries for absolute grounds for refusal.

Should the ecj conclude that the get-up of a service falls under the nonexhaustive categories of Art. 2 tmdir, then this second question is relevant for the issue, if the absolute grounds for refusal in Art. 3 tmdir also apply to the mark in question. According to the wording of Art. 3 tmdir only those signs fall under the absolute grounds for refusal that consists of the shape of goods. From the wording alone, this provision does not apply to two dimensional signs. The Senate takes the view, that an extended applicability of these grounds for refusal beyond their wording is only justified in rare cases. Nevertheless the grounds for refusal should be applicable in the case at hand as the same criteria must be applicable for goods and services alike. Otherwise competition would be distorted and marks consisting of get-up of services would be privileged if the absolute grounds for refusal would not apply. The ratio of the provision could also speak for an extension of the grounds for refusal: the public interest of free access to goods and services should outweigh the interest of the trade mark owner for a perpetual monopoly if the goods and services in question are already protected by other intellectual property rights, e.g. patent and design law.

In the case at hand it is especially the Art. 3 i lit. e iii of the tmdir that could constitute an absolute ground for refusal. Ann application will be denied according to Art. 3 i lit. e iii tmdir if the get-up consists of a shape that adds substantial value to the service. The get-up of a retail store is the main feature in order to judge the quality of the shopping experience. Despite this fact the get-up of the shopping venue does not constitute the most relevant feature of the service "retail store". To the same extent the shopping experience is to be judged by the quality of the goods and the other relevant services offered in the venue. The senate asked but tends to deny the question, if a part of the bundle of services is sufficient to apply the absolute grounds for refusal. With regards to the third question the senate of the Federal Patent Court made the following statements: The Senate holds the get-up of a retail store as principally able to be a valid trademark. Despite this argument, the illustration in question must also be graphically representable according to Art. 2 tmdir. According to the ecj jurisprudence a sign can be a trade mark, if the illustration at hand is clear (not ambiguous), precise (e.g. a color cannot merely be described as 'purple'), self-contained (e.g. music notes), easily accessible (e.g. the Pantone international database), intelligible, durable (the graphical representation must remain consistent), and objective. The registration system alongside with its guarantee function is only efficient, if these criteria are fulfilled. Only then will there be legal certainty. The ecj has yet to decide how in particular the illustration of the get-up of a retail store must be represented in order to fulfill these criteria. In principal an illustration with a perspective of the retail store can be regarded as fulfilling the Sieckmanncriteria, if the scope of protection can be determined when perceiving the illustration. The illustration of the retail store for which registration is sought shows it's facilities. Nevertheless it does not give any certainty or guidelines to the degree of actual size of the retail store, it's furniture, facilities and there relation in size to each other. Especially the size of the entrance area in relation to the depth of the retail store cannot be judged by perceiving this illustration. Hence it is only its overall impression that can be assumed when perceiving the illustration. Subject to these considerations it must be stressed if Apple's application for registration fulfills necessary "Sieckmann" criteria of clarity and precision. Despite these reasonable doubts the senate of the Federal Patent court took the view that an additional measurement chart would suffice to overcome the lack of certainty and precision. It then held a preliminary decision by the ecj necessary in order to determine the criteria for the graphical representation in question. With his fourth and final question the senate of the Federal Patent Court asked the ecj, if the scope of protection of a service mark for retail stores does also cover goods that are produced by the retailer himself. The ecj has yet to decide this question, if a retailer can obtain protection only for goods of other traders or if his own label products are also covered by such protection. In addition the national courts are yet to decide on this question. The senate took the view that the retailer must refer goods manufactured by third parties in order to obtain trademark protection for these services. Otherwise, in case of own label goods the distribution of such goods is regarded as only a supportive service for which trademark protection is to be available. Thus the senate opined that only the distribution of goods manufactured by third parties reaches the holy land of trademark protection. The retailer that distributes his own label goods primarily competes with other manufacturers. Hence the protection by trademark law can only cover protection of a trademark for the goods themselves. In case he distributes goods manufactured by third parties he is competing with other distributors. This is the reason that he then only can obtain trade mark protection for the service of distribution.

On the other hand there a valid argument could be that the distribution of own label goods in a retail store does not necessarily cover the whole range of goods. Instead the retailer often varies his range of offered products towards a certain target group from different regional areas with different taste and purchasing power. It could be argued that this selection also offers a valuable service beyond the mere distribution which would consequently speak for trademark protection. With regards to all four questions the BPatG found that a preliminary decision of the ecj was necessary; this decision will be discussed:

Ecj Decision - "Apple Store" Case

The ecj answered the questions of the BPatG in the "Apple Store Case". The decision can be summarized as follows: In regards of the first three questions the ecj came to the conclusion that "In the light of all the foregoing considerations, the answer to the first to third questions is that Articles 2 and 3 of Directive 2008/95 must be interpreted as meaning that the representation, by a design alone, without indicating the size or the proportions, of the layout of a retail store, may be registered as a trade mark for services consisting in services relating to those goods but which do not form an integral part of the offer for sale thereof, provided that the sign is capable of distinguishing the services of the applicant for registration from those of other undertakings and that registration is not precluded by any of the grounds for refusal set out in that directive". In regards of the fourth question the ecj found that it was inadmissible.

German act Against Unfair Competition ("UWG")

In contrary to the U.S. Law the German Law also offers protection to such threedimensional designs by the Act against Unfair Competition. Outside of the scope of intellectual property rights a fundamental element of German Law is the basic principle of freedom of competition and imitation. This principle underlines the notion that only intellectual property rights offer protection to creative output. If a creative output is not protected by an Intellectual property right, the output shall be free to copy. As an exception the Act against unfair competition can offer protection against the imitation of products or creative ideas only then, if there is an act of copying and an unfair element. The mere act of copying as such should not be regarded as unfair.

The Court of First Instance Münster had to decide on the protection of the get-up of a restaurant chain according to the uwg. The restaurant chain "Vapiano" claimed infringement of the trade dress of their business venue and seek to court to grant a preliminary injunction.

According to the facts of the case the plaintiff operates a system catering chain bearing the name "Vapiano". All business venues of the plaintiffs chain offer an Italian style cuisine and all venues are identically designed in regards of both, the exterior and the interior. All furniture, decorations and menus are designed by a well-reputed designer. The designs have largely been made exclusively for the plaintiff. The defendant operates a restaurant in the neighborhood of one of the plaintiff's venues offering Chinese style fast food with a similar font as the plaintiff use for their trade name. The plaintiff proved that its customers regularly assume that both businesses are connected. Furthermore the plaintiff submitted evidence that the design of its business venue is honored by the press. Especially Vapiano's atmosphere and the design features experience appreciation. The competent court granted the plaintiff injunctive relief regarding the features of Vapiano's get-up. It held that the defendants business venue caused a „preventable confusion“ and an „unfair dilution“ according to Sections §§ 3, 4 Nr. 9a and b uwg. In an analogous application of the supplementary protection of related rights under competition law the court held that this protection would also cover immaterial features, namely the design concept of the plaintiff's business venue, which was found to be new and distinctive in comparison to those of competitors in the market. The protection offered by the uwg extends to the design concept as such, that was almost identically copied. The deviations in the offered goods and in the name were found to be only marginal. The relevant market could still assume a business connection between the plaintiff's and the defendant's business venue.

CONCLUSION

Both, the U.S. and the German Law system offer protection for the get-up of business venues. Furthermore both systems offer protection for single features of the get-up with their intellectual property system. According to the U.S. Law the protection of the get-up of a business venue is provided by the institute "trade dress"; a claim for the infringement of a business venue's the get-up based on unfair competition law will not suffice. In order to obtain trade dress protection the get-up of the business venue must be distinctive, either inherently or acquired though secondary meaning. Furthermore the get-up must not be functional. Lastly, a likelihood of confusion must be determined by the alleged infringing get-up. According to German Law protection can be afforded by both, trademark and unfair competition law. With regards to the ecj decision in the "Apple Store" it remains to be seen how the BPatG will decide after its questions have now been answered by the ecj. In its decision the ecj made clear that the high threshold for shape marks will also be applicable for the get-up of business venues. Only if the get-up is substantially distinctive from the standard design, it will be inherently distinctive. In this regard it remains to be seen how franchises such as "Vapiano" and the "Body Shop" will attempt to register their unique, but not necessarily inherently distinctive store designs. Questions also remain in regard of the enforcement of such trade mark applications. Competitors are not likely to advertise with the illustration from the trademark register, but instead will use single features of the get-up that are shown by the illustration. Complex issues concerning the degree of similarity between the marks could arise. Further it will be difficult to prove an infringing use of the trademark due to the criterion of secondary meaning. The consumer is likely to appreciate the get-up of a business venue in its aesthetic and technical design; despite this it is less likely that he will associate the design with goods and services offered in the business venue. The ecj decision does give some wiggle room for the BPatG: only such a sign is capable of being a trade mark for retail services, if goods by other manufacturers are to be sold. The protection of the illustration of a store design would then only cover retail with such goods by other manufacturers. Flagship stores as utilized by Apple, Gucci or Nike could not even argue to fulfill the criteria of compulsory use if they only sell their own. Finally, an excessive protection of get-up and store design does raise some concern. The notion of freedom to copy could be undermined. A perpetual monopoly for designs and get-up would stifle competition. This issue can be solved by raising the threshold for protection, e.g. the level of required distinctiveness. While the court was rather generously accepting inherent distinctiveness of the restaurants designs in the Taco Cabana v. Two Pesos case, more recent decisions show a more reluctant assessment. In Wal-Mart Stores, Inc. v. Samara Brothers the U.S. Supreme Court leaned towards the assumption that for the protection of a products get-up distinctiveness acquired through secondary meaning must be proven. The functionality doctrine also prevents an overlap of protection with design and copyright law. But for business venues such as restaurants it will be not likely that the get-up as a whole will be regarded merely functional. This doctrine should be sharpened in order to lead to cut clear results regarding such trade dress cases. As discussed above, In Germany, § 3 MarkenG limits the protectability of signs that consist of a shape, similar to the functionality doctrine. The protection via the unfair competition law does have a different approach. Thus it is questionable if the set of unfair competition protection is available parallel to trade mark protection. Companies could utilize cumulatively the mentioned intellectual property rights in order to protect their concepts of store design. Sometimes protecting and nurturing the classic elements of one's brand is more efficient than a financial burdensome fight for new means of protections. With the words of designers: "sometimes less is more".

REFERENCES

1. Bassewitz, Katharina von, Trade Dress und Functionality - Ein Vergleich des marken- und wettbewerbsrechtlichen Schutzes von Produktformen in den usa und Deutschland - Zugleich eine Anmerkung zum Urteil Antioch Co. v. Western Trimming Corp., grur Int 2004, 390-395.
2. Bornkamm, Joachim, Markenrecht und wettbewerbsrechtlicher Kennzeichenschutz zur Vorrangthese der Rechtsprechung, grur 2005, 97-102.
3. Cooley, Amanda Harmon, Trade dress protection of business décor: What is this tertium quid?, Southern Law Journal,vol. 18 (2008), [www.southernlawjournal.com/2008/02_.pdf], visited 20th September 2014.
4. Dinwoodie, Graeme B., Trade dress and design law, New York, Austin, 2010.
5. Dinwoodie, Graeme B., Trademarks and unfair competition, Law and policy, Third ed., 2010.
6. Dinwoodie, Graeme B. & Janis, Mark D., Trade dress and design law, New York, Austin, 2010.
7. Eck (ed.), Wettbewerbsrecht, 2010 (cited: Eck).
8. Fezer, Karl-Heinz (ed.), Markenrecht, 2009 (cited: Fezer).
9. FLJ-29-1-sum-2009_sandberg, [www.swlaw.com/assets/pdf/publications/2009/07/ 01/FLJ-29-1-sum-2009_Sandberg.pdf] (visited 18th September 2014).
10. Gausling, T., German Federal Supreme Court expands design protection: 'Birthday Train', Journal of Intellectual Property Law & Practice 9 (2014), 549-550.
11. Goldmann, Michael, Eintragung der Darstellung einer Laden-Ausstattung als Marke, grur-Prax 2014 (21.09.2014), 349, [https://beck-online.beck.de/Default.aspx?vpath=bibdata/zeits/grurprax/2014/cont/grurprax.2014.349.1.htm&po s=4 &hlwords=apple%c3%90+apple+#xhlhit] (visited 21st September 2014).
12. Henning-Bodewig, Frauke, International handbook on unfair competition, Munich, C.H. Beck.
13. Hilliard, David Craig; Welch, Joseph N. & Widmaier, Uli, Trademarks and unfair competition, 9th ed., New Providence, NJ, 2012.
14. Jacobs, Hara K.; Lee, Melissa L., Mitchell, Glenn & Wadyka, Steven J., U.S. trade dress law, A Primer for the new millenium, New York, NY, 2002.
15. Köhler, Jürgen, Das Verhältnis des Wettbewerbsrechts zum Recht des geistigen Eigentums - Zur Notwendigkeit einer Neubestimmung auf Grund der Richtlinie über unlautere Geschäftspraktiken, grur 2007, 548–554.
16. Matheson, Julia Anne & Cooke, Whitney Devin, Is Your Store Design Unique? Trademark It, 2013 (visited 13th September 2014).
17. McCarthy, J. Thomas, McCarthy on trademarks and unfair competition, vol. 1, Darfield, IL 2007.
18. McConnell, Akila Sankar, Making Wal-Mart Pretty: Trademarks and Aesthetic

Restrictions on Big-Box Retailers, Duke Law Journal 53 (2004), 1537-1567, in: [http:// scholarship.law.duke.edu/cgi/viewcontent.cgi?article=1223&context=dlj] (visited 20th September 2014).

19. Navigating Fashion Law, Leading lawyers on exploring the trends, cases, and strategies of fashion law, Boston, Mass., 2012.
20. Ohly, Ansgar & Sosnitza, Olaf (ed.), uwg, 6. Ed. 2014 (cited: Ohly & Sosnitza).
21. Pagenberg, Jochen, Trade Dress and the Three-Dimensional Mark - The Neglected Children of Trademark Law?, International Review of Intellectual Property and Competition Law, 2004, 832-843.
22. Sandberg, Scott C., Trade Dress: what does it mean?, Franchise Law Journal, 2009, [www.swlaw.com/assets/pdf/publications/2009/07/01/FLJ-29-1-sum-2009_sandberg.pdf] (visited 10th September 2014).
23. Sander, Charlotte, Der Schutz von Geschäftsraumgestaltungen durch das Immaterialgüter- und Wettbewerbsrecht im deutschen und amerikanischen Recht, grur Int. 2014, 215-228.
24. Suthersanen, Uma, Design law, European Union and United States of America, 2nd ed., London, 2010.

3
CHAPTER

OWNERSHIP OF COPYRIGHT IN WORKS CREATED IN EMPLOYMENT RELATIONSHIPS

Jose Roberto Herrera Diaz

INTRODUCTION

Great quantities of copyrighted works around the world are produced in the context of labor law Relationships. The ownership of these works has been regulated in different ways by the national laws of each country, and the only attempt of legal harmonization has been found in the European Community regarding computer programs created in the course of employment. The sovereignty and territoriality principles by with each country can enact its own laws in its territory to rule on the ownership question has been applied by countries. As an example, Germany and United States have regulated the subject in their respective national copyright laws. Nonetheless, there are similarities in the ways that these two countries regulate the ownership of economic rights. In other countries, such as Colombia, lawmakers have established a legal rule regarding the ownership of moral rights in copyrighted works, but have not ruled on the important issue of the economic rights in such works. This ambiguity has caused legal uncertainty, raising the question as to whether these types of rights belong to employees or employers.

This paper will make a comparative study of the laws of Colombia, Germany and the United States of America, taking into account the current issues that can arise in works created in employment relationships and the ensuing consequences. The structure of the comparison will be focused on the following two central points of analysis.

First, this thesis will concentrate on the differences in the laws and case law of the three countries with regard to the ownership of the copyright in employment relationships. In order to determine how each country addresses the ownership question, other aspects such as authorship and the differences between the author's right system and the Anglo American Copyright system (i.e., the treatment of moral rights) will

Citation: Herrera Diaz, Jose Roberto, Ownership of Copyright in Works Created in Employment Relationships. Revista la Propiedad Inmaterial, No. 14, pp. 91-139, 2010. Available at SSRN: http://ssrn.com/abstract=1705516.

be analyzed as well. Likewise, the diverging theories underlying the author's rights systems in these countries, with Colombia being a dualistic system and Germany being a monistic system, and the effect of the silence of the parties to a contract with respect to the point of ownership, are both issues that must be explored to render a thorough understanding of the subject.

Secondly, not only the differences, but also the similarities between each system will be explored. In this regard, the paper will analyze whether, in works created in employment relationships, there is a tendency of the monistic and dualistic author's right systems to approach to the Anglo American Copyright System. In other words, any similarities between the laws and practices of Colombia and Germany and the American "work made for hire" doctrine will be addressed. Most important, if the philosophies by which the two main copyright systems were created are currently applicable to works created in employment relationships. This issue will address whether the interest in protecting the human being's original expression and thus the interests of the employed authors prevails over the interest in protecting the utilitarian character of the works.

Furthermore, the study will focus on the topic of ownership as it relates to specific kinds of works, such as computer programs regulated in the European Community Directive 91/250. On this point for example, the same approach will be followed, analyzing whether the German implementation of this directive is creating a tendency for the author's right system to become similar to the American copyright system.

Despite the fact that the focus of the paper is on copyright provisions, some aspects of labor law, such as scope of employment and employment relationships, will be analyzed in order to have a integral understanding of the topic. Since labor law provisions and copyright provisions are different fields of law, the difficulties that may arise in knowing which area of law to apply will be examined.

Finally, issues concerning to works created by independent contractors in Colombia, Germany, and the United States will be analyzed, in particular the same copyright provisions regarding the ownership of the works that can apply to employees and independent contractors. In a similar context, the treatment of works created by public servants or private employees may reveal similarities and differences to the treatment of public employees in these three countries.

WHY WORKS CREATED IN EMPLOYMENT RELATIONSHIPS?

When the topic under study has been analyzed in the legal literature, the usual terms by which the authors refer to it are: works made for hire,[1] works created by employees,[2] or works created in employment relationships.[3] This diversity of terms creates a difficulty to analyze the subject, as the significance of each expression may bring different results on the ownership point. For instance, the first option, work made for hire, is a popular term for common law countries in which the employer is considered the author and owner of the copyright. The problem using this term is that is of no use in continental tradition countries where in almost all the situations the authorship of the copyright vest in the employee, as well as the ownership of the moral rights. Regarding the second option, works created by employees, despite being common in the continental tradition countries, in which usually the authorship and ownership vest in the employee, one may find difficulty in establishing if the work is always created by an employee. In some cases, the original expression of the copyrighted work may come from the employer and the employee's freedom to produce the work can be limited by the employer's orders. For instance, an employer that is dictating a literary work to his secretary cannot be prevented from being the original author of the work, despite the fact the secretary fixed the expression of the copyrighted work. Thus, one must carefully observe the term *creation*, because in the context of an employment relationship, it can cause misleading interpretations such as, for example, that every function of an employee constitutes creation. For these reasons, it is more impartial to use the concept *works created in employment relationships*, since it addresses not only the employers' interests, but also the employees'.

WHAT IS AN EMPLOYMENT RELATIONSHIP?

Before entering into the analysis of the Copyright law, it is necessary to understand the concept of *employment relationships.*

The International Labor Organization (ILO) has identified three common elements in labor law contracts around the world.[4] Those elements are not always defined by the law or case law of each country. However, not only the ILO, but also the labor law doctrine in all the countries of the world, have established a consensus on the existence of three elements.[5] The first element, called the personal element, means that only a natural person can be considered an employee.[6] Second is the subordination element by which the employer is entitled to give orders to the employees; this element involves a hierarchical aspect. The third and final element is the salary that employers pay to their employees as a retribution for their work.[7] Colombia is one of the countries by which said elements can be clearly found. Article 22 of the labor law code defines labor law contract as: "one in which a natural person promises to give his services to another legal or natural person, under continuous subordination (i.e., receiving orders from the employer), with remuneration in exchange for the services".[8]

When these three elements are present, there is a presumption of existence of a labor law contract. [9] In Colombia the main distinction of a labor law contract and other contracts is the so called subordination. In the course of services provided under civil law contracts, there are orders given to the person providing the services, but the autonomy that the provider of services has is broader than those in an employment contract.[10]

The term *employment* is not only linked to works created under a labor law contract. In most jurisdictions the term *employment* is a generic term by which not only labor contracts are included, but also contracts by which a person agrees to provide services to another are included.[11] Despite the fact that the focus of this study is the employment relationships in the narrow sense, meaning, labor law contracts, one cannot ignore other kinds of agreements that are included within the generic concept of employment. For instance, works created by independent contractors in the United States or works created under contracts to provide services in Colombia, are mandatory examples that show the broad understanding of the term *employment.* Likewise, these other kinds of relationships can provide answers in some cases to ownership issues in the labor law contract.[12] Thus the following analysis will not only review labor law contracts, but also non labor law relationships in each country by which employment and works are created.

LABOR OR IP LAWS?

One important question for the analysis is whether the ownership of the copyright in works created in *employment relationships* should be regulated by labor or intellectual property laws. As the present topic combines both fields of law, intellectual property provisions can be found in labor law statutes and vice versa. One may ask if it is better if only one field of law rules on the topic or if it is better that both fields can rule some part of the topic.

As we will see later, there are some issues that have been exclusively ruled by the labor or agency law. For instance, the definitions of an employee, a labor law relationship or the elements of a labor law relationship are usually found within employment statutes.

Regarding the central topic of study, some countries regulated the topic under a labor law statue. For example, Spain regulated the ownership of the copyright of the works created by employees in a labor law provision, the employees' statute.[13] However, after some years, the Spanish lawmakers followed the global trend of regulating IP topics exclusively in IP laws. Thus, the Spanish Intellectual Property Law derogated previous labor law rules and provided an answer to the ownership of the copyright in employment relationships.[14] As it will be shown in the next Chapters, Germany and the United States have regulated the ownership point on Intellectual Property laws (Copyright acts) following the mentioned global trend. In the case of Colombia, as there is not a specific answer to the economic ownership point, one cannot have certainty on whether the Author's Right law contains a provision that rules the topic.

Germany. Legal rules and Analysis

Applicable Law

Germany has many different laws regarding the Copyrights. However, for the purpose of this study, the analysis will concentrate mostly in the Copyright and Related Rights Act of 1965. Although this Act has been modified by several amendments, the most pertinent for analysis is the Amendment of June 9, 1993, by which the E.C. Directive on the Legal Protection of Computer Programs was implemented.

Regarding Labor Law provisions, Germany does not have a codified Labor

Law Act. Instead, there are different legal sources such as the Federal Legislation, collective agreements, work agreements and case law.[15] Likewise, the Civil Code is another important provision as it defines employment relationship[16] in section 622 with the trilogy of elements previously analyzed. Although the Civil Code sets forth the elements to define employment relationships, there is no definition of employee in

Germany. However, German Courts have said that employee is a natural person that receives instructions on the way to do work[17]. Also, they have said that despite the fact that a person can be greatly autonomous in doing work, a clear indicia of classifying someone as an employee is the act of fulfilling a schedule ordered by the employer.[18]

The German Continental Law Tradition

The philosophy of the classical author's right system created under the continental legal models is based on the idea that the work is always of property of the author. Consequently, the author can only transfer or license his economic rights, and not his moral rights, to third parties.[19]

However, this is the Classical notion of the author's right system that is evident in France, representing some clear differences with Germany, where neither the economic and moral rights can be transferred.[20]

German Copyright Law is classified as continental law, as opposed to common law tradition. This enhances many differences among the Copyright system existing in Germany and non-continental countries such as the usa.

The first and the most important effect is that the continental tradition is based on the protection of rights of flesh and blood authors.[21] This means that the main goal of the continental legal family is protecting the rights of natural persons that create copyrighted works. The continental Tradition does not directly protect the legal persons as they are not human minds that produce works. However, despite the differentiation of natural and legal persons, the continental System protects some economic rights of legal persons by the so-called "neighboring rights".[22]

The second effect of the continental legal system in relation to copyright law is strongly related to the first. As the focus of the protection is centered on flesh and blood authors, the law protects not only the economic basis of their lives, but also their intimate moral interests tied up in their works.[23] For this reason, as Dietz says: "The German term Urheberecht, usually translated into English by copyright or copyright law, is better translated by the French term droit d'auteur, meaning "author's right" or author's right law". [24]

Thus, the term *author* is a clue word in the continental system as it is focused merely on the protection of the personal and economic interests of the authors as natural persons.

The German Author's Rights System and Its Effect on Works Created in Employment Relationships

The author's rights system structure was brought into practice in the German Law through Copyright and Neighboring Rights (Urheberrechtsgesetz, UrhG) in Article 11. This Article established that the ownership of the copyright belongs to the creator of the work, demonstrating how important it was for the German lawmaker to protect the traditional concept of author by giving him, in all cases, the ownership of the copyright. When Article 11 states that the "Copyright shall protect the author with respect to the intellectual and personal relationship with his work",[25] the personal aspect characterized in the author's right system is clearly shown. Even when there are matters by which the so-called works made for hire are present, the German law claims for the importance of recognizing the ownership to the natural person that creates the work.[26] As will be seen later in the United States analysis, the work made for hire doctrine allows that a person other than the creator of the work can be considered as the author. Hence, in the United States, despite the fact that in some situations an employer may not participate in the creation of a copyrighted work, he can still be considered as the author and owner of a work created by an employee. An important difference between these two countries lies in the consequences of these differing systems. In Germany, if the parties do not agree otherwise, the economic rights will always be employee's property. By contrast, in the United States, if the parties do not agree otherwise, the copyright will belong to the employer. As one can see, on the same *de facto* situation, the results in these two countries may be the opposite.

For some commentators, like Goldstein, there is no significant difference in the results between common law jurisdictions and civil law jurisdictions. In the words of Goldstein: *"Copyright shall protect the author with respect to his intellectual and personal relationship with his work, and also with respect to utilization of his work"*. Translation provided by wipo. Text Available at: http://www.iuscomp.org/gla/statutes/UrhG.htm.

Civil law and most Common law jurisdictions take different roads to essentially the same result in assigning rights to works made in the course of an employment relationship. Common law countries provide that, absent an agreement to the contrary, copyright in works created in the course of employment initially vests in the employer, not the employee.[27]

Goldstein further explains: "Civil law countries generally reverse the common law presumption and provide that copyright in works created in the course of employment vests in the employed author, so that a transfer by the employee is required for the employer to obtain copyright."[28] Thus, in Goldstein's opinion, the difference lies in the way by which each system reaches the result, but not on the result as such, since usually the copyright ownership vest with the employer. We have to distinguish however, that in the author's rights system, what the employee transfers to the employer are not all rights upon the work. Only the economic rights are transferred and the employed author retains the moral or personal rights in the work.

Two German Particularities

Having addressed the generalities of the German Author's Right system, is the turn to focus on two characteristics in the German context of works created in employment relationships.

The first important aspect to point out is that German law treats works created under employment relationships as works created on commission.[29] Thus, a work created by an independent contractor in Germany will have the same copyright ownership as a work created by an employee. The copyright will still vest on the employee or independent contract, if there is no agreement otherwise. By contrast, as will be seen in chapters vi and vii, in the United States and Colombia, there are certain differences regarding the treatment of independent contractors and employees.

Second, the fact that Germany does not recognize initial ownership to employers does not mean that an employer cannot claim the rights of a copyrighted work created by an employee at his service. However, the way by which the employer can enjoy the economic rights is different in comparison to most of the countries with a continental law tradition. On this point, some commentators like Dietz said that this is due to the fact that Germany has the monistic theory of author's right, by which economic and moral rights are indivisible.[30] In words of Dietz:

German law governing copyright transfer is articulated in Subchapter 2 on

"Copyright Licenses" within Chapter V of part I of the Copyright Act. The particular thrust of this law can only be understood against the background of the so-called monistic theory of German Copyright. According to this concept, copyright as a whole, that is, author's right, safeguard both the financial and the personal or intellectual interests of an author.[31]

On article 11 of the Copyright Act this monistic approach is applied when the article states: that the "Copyright shall protect the author with respect to his intellectual and personal relationship with his work, and also with respect to utilization of his work". In Germany, this rule leads to the conception of the Copyright as a whole, by including in one body the "*personal relationships to the work*" (moral rights) and the "*utilization of his work*" (economic rights). This feature of the German system is another important distinction from the traditional author's right systems, such as France or Belgium. In these two countries, the economic rights are freely alienable and employees can transfer their economic rights to the employer in the employment agreement or otherwise[32].

As was mentioned above, the inalienability of the economic rights does not mean that the employer does not has rights to a work created by an employee. By the so called "*contractual right to use*", German law makes it possible for the employer to exercise the economic rights in the work.[33] The fact that the employer does not receive the ownership of these rights, because there is not a transfer of right, can raise some questions, such as whether the employer has standing to sue when there is a copyright infringement.[34]

The German Copyright Act only permits the transferability of the copyright by inheritance, but the law clearly states that no other means are possible. Article 29 of the Act provides:

"Copyright may be transferred in execution of a testamentary disposition or to coheirs as part of the partition of an estate. *Copyright shall not otherwise be transferable*".

Furthermore, the English translation of Article 31[35] expresses that the author may grant the exploitation right to use to another. For dietz, this is what the literal translation of the German provision must be, as the English term "license" cannot be used here. In the words of dietz: "Although used in some English translations, the English term '*license*' does not fully translate the German conception of such contractual transfer. The Copyright Act only speaks of the granting of 'simple or exclusive rights of use'".[36]

The exclusive right of use is twofold. On the one hand, Article 31 (2) refers to the non-exclusive exploitation right to use. On the other, Article 31 (3) refers to an exclusive right to use. The main difference of both provisions is that in the latter, the exclusive right gives the power to the party to exclude others from use, even to the author. Dietz compares these two provisions to the traditional notions of exclusive and simple licenses. However, he states that in comparison to the German contractual right to use, the contractual terms by which the parties negotiate their interests are in the framework of the copyright contract law[37] located in subsection 2 of the Copyright act. The framework includes different rules oriented to protect authors in the contractual grants. The first important rule of subsection 2 is the prohibition to grant uses that are not yet known at the time of a grant (Article 31 (4) German Copyright Act).[38] Second, Article 31(5) establishes the principle of "purpose-restricted transfer." This principle states that the author is not to be held to have granted more extensive rights that would be required by the purpose pursued in the grant[39]. Finally, Article 37[40] establishes that in cases of doubt concerning the extent of certain types of transfers, the authors retain specific rights. Usually, when the author grants the right to use, he reserves the rights to make it available to the public and to exploit derivative works. Likewise, when the author grants the right to reproduce, the author reserves the right to fix the work on sound or visual recording [41].

For the purpose this analysis, one has to take into account that these rules also apply to the employer who is the party that would receive the right to use the work created by the employed author. Hence, it is important to stress that, in technical terms, there is no transfer of rights to the employer in Germany and the employer receives a right to use the work. The power of exercise that the employer has will be represented by an exclusive right to use or a simple right to use.

As will be seen later, to constitute a work made for hire for independent contractors in the United States, the law requires a written agreement. Likewise, in the following chapter, we will see that in Colombian law as well, the transfer of economic rights requires a written agreement. By contrast, the German Copyright Act does not provide general formalities for the grant of the exploitation rights.[42] The only exception can be found in Article 40[43] which requires a written agreement for the granting of exploitation rights in future works. Perhaps a possible explanation for the flexibility of the German system is that, as there is not a transfer of right, there is no need for the law to establish a strict formality to protect the interest of the author. Despite some limitation to the author, such as the impossibility to use the work in the case of an exclusive grant, he will still be considered as the author and owner of the work.

Finally, regarding other formalities such as the registration of transfer,[44] the German law does not impose any obligation to record transfers of copyrighted interests.[45]

By contrast, as we will see in Colombia and the United States, in some cases the process of registration may be necessary.

Article 43 of the German Copyright Act

Article 43[46] of the German Copyright Act, together with Article 69b[47], are the most important provisions for the German law analysis as they regulate expressly the topic of works created in employment relationships.

As it was said before, the general rule in Germany is that the employee is the owner and author of the copyrighted work produced under the course of his employment. Likewise, if the employee wants to grant the right to use to the employer, he will have to do it by contract.

The copyright contract rules are established in subsection 2 (Exploitation rights) from Articles 31 through 42 of the Copyright Act. When Article 42 states that "the provisions of this subsection shall also apply if the author has created the work in execution of his duties under a contract of employment or service", it is referring to the rules of subsection 2 analyzed before. However, the provisions of subsection 2 may not be applicable to employment relationships as the second sentence of Article 43 states: "provided nothing to the contrary transpires from the terms or nature of the contract of employment or services". This second sentence has created some critics within the legal commentators. For example, Dietz states: "This somewhat vague and unsatisfactory final clause in Section 43 in practice merely serves as a means to make it easier to find and interpret implied clauses in favor of employers".[48] Furthermore, dietz remarks: "This provision may be read as containing a sort of indirect presumption to the effect that all rights necessary for the activities of the employer or the commissioning party have been granted".[49]

As we can see, it is not completely clear in Germany whether the employers have to expressly sign an agreement with the employees to receive the right to use the exploitation rights. The wording of the article may consequently produce situations wherein an implied grant is concluded.

However, as already mentioned, there is a clear consensus that the Copyright as a whole, moral rights and economic rights vest in the employed or commissioned author.[50] Likewise, the rules of contracts of subsection 2 (e.g. prohibition to grant uses that are not known, principle of purpose restricted transfers, and favorability for the author in cases where it is unclear as to what type of grant) are applicable to the employed author and can help to minimize the effect of an implied clause that may grants rights to the employer, and hence, affects his interests.

The scope of Employment requirement

In addition to the grant of the economic rights that the employer has to receive from the employee, another important requirement in making a valid grant is that the work must be created in execution of the employee's duties. To determine the employee's duties or the scope of employment, labor law regulations, rules in union agreements and the labor law contract have to be analyzed.[51] Likewise, courts have said that factors such as location and the time by which the employee creates the work (working hours) are not suitable criteria for evaluating the scope of employment.[52] Thus, the functions that the employee has are the main factor to determine if a work was created under the scope of employment.[53] The previous rule does not imply that the employee cannot grant the economic rights from works created outside the scope of employment. However, some commentators have noted that under this hypothesis, the employee will not be remunerated just with the salary, and extra remuneration will have to be given to the employee.[54]

The general tendency regarding the employee remuneration is that it is given within the current wage. No additional remuneration is provided. This is a topic under discussion, as some commentators state that paying the employee with only the wage will infringe the general principle by which the author must receive reasonable compensation for the exploitation of his work.[55]

This is an issue for debate, since another argument that can arise under an extra compensation theory will be that not all the works that employees produce are protected under copyrights. In fact, most of the works are not protected. Thus fixing a mandatory extra remuneration as a general rule can be a fair retribution to the employed author for accomplishing the intellectual property protection of his creation. Likewise, if a mandatory extra remuneration is created, employed authors will have an incentive to create. Also, the progress of arts, which is one of the main objectives of copyright law, could be easily furthered by stimulating creation for employees.

On January 18 of 2002 the last version of the Employees' Invention Act was enacted in Germany.[56] The Act gives an extra remuneration to the employees that create patents. The employed inventors in Germany are not only remunerated by their salary, in virtue of the said act, Employed inventors received an extra sum that awards their creation, and at the same time creates an incentive for other employees to invent. Despite the fact, that the said act does not contain copyright provision, this is an example of an extra remuneration that may be reasonable to put into practice in the context of works created in employment relationships. As most of the times the employer exercise the economic rights, and the employee only receives its salary in return of his creations, an extra remuneration can be a fair solution to protect the interest of the employed authors.

The rights Granted by the employee

Typically in the employment contract, the employee grants the exploitation rights to the employer. If this is the case, preference has to be given to these agreements.[57] Likewise, when the employee grants the use of economic rights to the employer, these rights are given exclusively to him.[58] However, the tendency is that the parties do not agree on the ownership of the copyright in the contract, and the courts[59] find implied clauses that grant economic rights to the employer. In fact, some commentators state that there is a general obligation in the employment contract for the employee to grant economic rights to the employer.[60] For instance, Rojahn states that there are two arguments that may justify a general obligation for the employee to grant the economic rights to the employer. The first argument is that there must be an analogy with the Employees Inventions Act of 2004. In Section 18 and 19 of the Act, there is a general obligation for the employee to offer the license of rights to the employer.[61] Thus, Rojahn states that the economic rights of the employee in the copyrighted work should be licensed to the employer, as in the patent right. Both are intellectual property rights, so there should be a general obligation to offer a license.

The second argument is based on the labor law principle by which there must be a general relationship of trust between employee and employer.[62] Consequently, as Rojhan states, a demonstration of trust lies in the fact that the employee offered a license to the employer.

The topic of implied license has not only been analyzed by commentators but also addressed by courts. The Federal Court of Justice (decision reference: bgh grur 1974, 480/483) in fact went further and said that there was a presumption of a license when the employee has handed the work to the employer.[63]

Other criteria stated used to determine implied grants of economic rights, as stated by Kirchberger, include looking objectively to the labor law contract and checking if the works created are related to the normal functions of the employer company. By contrast, the subjective elements, such as the intention of the employee to grant the economic rights, are not taken into account.[64]

Apart from looking to the labor law contract, another tool used to determine implied clauses that grant economic rights to the employer in lack of express agreements can be found in Germany in Union Agreements (tarifvertraege).[65] Some examples of Union Agreements in which economic rights are granted to the employer can be found in the following areas: press (newspaper, magazines), radio and television (public as well as private television companies), movie, theater and design.[66]

Fortunately for the employee, despite the implied grants of economic rights that a court may find or an employer may argue, some of the economic interests in the work can still be protected. As it was already mentioned there are different provisions in subsection 2 orientated to protect the interests of the author, such as the prohibition to grant uses that are not yet known at the time of a grant (Article 31(4) German Copyright Act);[67] the principle of purpose restricted transfer[68] and the principle of favorability to the author in case of doubts concerning the extent of certain types of transfers.[69]

Regarding the term by which the employee grants the use of the economic rights to the employer, Krasser states that the usual practice is that even after the end of the labor law contract, the employer keeps the economic rights.[70] Likewise, dreier calls attention that the employee cannot use the economic rights in the course of a new employment contract with a new employer, if in a previous contract the old employer was exercising the economic rights. The old employer will still have the power to exercise the economic rights of the work created by the employee.[71] However, we have to take into account that, as the grant of rights is ruled by a contract, the employee can agree with the employer that after the

The E.C. Directive 91/250 on the Legal Protection of Computer Programs and the Article 69 B) of the German Copyright Act

The E.C. Directive was issued in 1991 in response to the amount of differences existing in the legislation of the Member States regarding this kind of works. One of the differences in Member States' legislations was the authorship of this works. But the other one related to the topic under study, was works created in employment relationships.[72]

The main aim of the Directive however was to codify the special standard of protection to computer programs, as there were many differences in the level of originality required to protect this type of work.[73] Germany was in fact one of the European countries characterized by its high originality requirements for considering a work protected under copyright. The German legislation required the author's personal intellectual creation that was interpreted by courts with a narrow standard oriented to a high originality level for protection.[74]

In fact, before the Directive the German Supreme Court said in 1998 in *Computer Edge v Apple Computer*, that only "above average" creative result in the field of programming, an estimated 20 to 30 percents of all programs, would be eligible for protection.[75] Thus, the problem that German courts faced was in harmonizing the statutory standard of protection fixed in the Directive with the high originality standard. However, in implementing the Directive, the German government adopted the mandatory standards of the Directive in Article 69 of the German Copyright act.[76] Article 69a(3) of the German Copyright Act set the new originality standard by saying that the computer program has to express the "author's own intellectual creation" as is also stated in Article 1(3)[77] of the Directive.[78]

This topic is still under debate on the legal literature, because the interpretation of the terms *"author's own intellectual creation"* can vary between courts in different states.[79] However, for the purpose of this study, it is important to take into account that if an employee in Germany creates a computer program in the execution of his duties, the terms that have to be used to analyze the level of originality required for protection is the one established in Article 69(a) of the German Copyright Act; that is, the work must reflect the author's (employee's) own intellectual creation.

For the topic under analysis Article 2[80] of the Directive is the central focus of the analysis, as this Article contains the E.C. rule for Authorship and ownership in the employment relationships.

Article 69(b) of the German Copyright Act is the national implementation of article 2 of the EC directive. As already explained, there is an exception to the general rule of granting of economic rights, as the Article directly entitles the employer to economic rights. As in the case of works created by employees which are not computer programs, Article 69(b) requires that the works must be created in the execution of the employee's duties. In order to decide the scope of the obligations, the previous considerations under the subtitle, scope of employment, should be applied here, meaning that the labor law contract, the main area of business of the employer and union agreements, have to be taken into consideration.[81]

Just as in Article 42 of the German Copyright Act, Article 69(b) also applies to works created in the course of services contracts. However, one important difference with the directive should be made here, as the Directive do not regulate the topic of freelancers. However, Dreier states that the initial proposal of the directive was to include freelancers in article 2(3). In his words:

Contrary to the Commission's initial proposal, the directive does not specifically regulate the authorship of commissioned computer programs. The main reason seems to have been the intention not to impair too heavily the interests of freelance programmers, in order not to hinder programming activities in the EC. Consequently, in the absence of special regulation on the national level, authorship of commissioned works is vested in the person(s) who created the program and the exercise of the exclusive rights is left to contractual provisions.[82]

After reading the previous passage, another open question for analysis is: Why does the German lawmaker give the exercise of economic rights to the employer in service relationships if the Directive did not regulate this topic? Bearing in mind that the author's rights tradition of Germany by which the protection of the author may be considered bigger than in the Anglo-American Copyright System, the application of the same rules to the independent contractor may be considered contradictory.

Furthermore, Article 2 (3) of the Directive keeps silent on whether the fact that the employer exploits the economic rights means that he receives a license, a transfer of rights, or if it is an initial ownership of the exclusive right.[83] As will be mentioned later in Chapter vi, in the United States, the employer has the initial ownership of the copyright if there is a work made for hire. Hence, in the United States the third result would be applied. In the German case, the most similar result under these three options is that the employee grants a license[84] to use the work to the employer, but the employer would not have the ownership of the Copyright.

As previously stated, Article 69(b) establishes a clear rule that the economic rights in a computer program created by an employee can be freely exploited by an employer without the need for the employer to receive a contractual grant from the employee. The situation described in Article 69 is different from the situation of Article 43, in which the employee will have to agree with the employer the grant of the economic rights or the employer may have to find some implied argument[85] that will grant him the exploitation rights. The situation is oppositely different in computer programs, since Article 69(b) allows employers and employees to agree otherwise, meaning that the general rule wherein the exercise of economic rights vest on the employer can be changed by the consensus of the two parties. Thus, the employee will still have a way to freely exploit the economic rights in virtue of the Directive. Moreover, the basic principle by which the author of a work is protected by copyright is also applicable in the case of computer programs.[86]

Regarding the general practice of remuneration for the employee by the creation of computer programs, the tendency is the same as Article 43 (non computer programs works created by employees). There is no extra remuneration for the employee in addition to the salary that the employer pays, and the employee cannot demand licensing fees.[87] However, if the computer program is created outside of the employee's duties, and the employer is exercising his economic rights, the result is the same as in non-computer program creations and an extra remuneration must have to be given to the employee.[88]

Despite the fact that the general practice in Germany is that the employee does not get an extra remuneration when he creates a computer program, one may conclude that under this hypothesis the practice should be different. The situation of computer programs sets forth a different hypothesis from the general rule of Article 43. In computer program created works, the employer has the power to exercise all the economic rights.[89] Thus, in this case, it may be reasonable to consider an extra remuneration for the employee despite the fact that in practice it is not provided. As previously stated, the German Employee´s Inventions Act gives extra remuneration to employed inventors. In the case context of computer programs created by employees is even clearer to think about a similar mechanism, as the employer exercise directly the economic rights.

It is important to ask why the drafters of the Computer Programs Directive gave the employer the direct power to exercise economic rights. Some question to open the debate could be:

Was it because the employee has less autonomy in creating the works in a computer as opposed to other kinds of works? Or is it because the normal practice before the directive was that by implied clauses or express agreements the rights were exercised by the employer, and thus, the drafter of the Directive saw this de facto situation and put it into the law?

Furthermore, and most important, as it will be mentioned latter, the interests of the software industry companies which were usually based on an Anglo American Copyright System were taken into account in the negotiations of this directive.[90] The solution that the Directive took can be considered however, a fair solution as it allowed the exercise of the economic rights to the employer, without giving him the ownership of the copyright. It can be considered a fair balance between the two main systems of Copyrights: the Anglo American Copyright System and the Author's right System.

The silence of the parties before the E.C. Computer Programs Directive

The Directive made a clear change to German copyright law in works created by employees depending whether the work is a computer program or not, as in the first case, without agreement of the parties the economic rights will rest with the employer. Before this Directive, silence of the parties in Germany did not give the economic rights to the employer. In other European Countries, the directive did not make any changes to the National law. That is the case of Spain, where before the Directive if employer and employee were silent about the ownership of a copyrighted work, the economic rights vested were transferred to the employer.[91] Thus, Spain did not suffered a change with the computer programs works, as before the Directive employers were exercising the economic rights of all kind of works created by employees if there was not agreement to the contrary.

Moral Rights

As already mentioned, German law is based in the monistic theory of author's right by which both economic rights and moral rights are included in one body. Moreover, there are no assignments of these rights, and third parties can only acquire the exercise of economic rights by agreeing with the copyright owner on a contractual right to use.

Regarding moral rights, the primary difference from economic rights is that they are completely inalienable and third parties cannot even exercise this type of right like they can with exploitation rights. Nonetheless, as will be addressed below, in certain types of works such as computer programs, some moral rights can be limited in their exercise.

The application of economic and moral rights is sometimes difficult to differentiate as the interests involved are related. As described by Dietz: *"It is therefore not very easy to state precisely whether, as a general matter, many provisions of the Copyright Act partake more of a moral or more of an economic nature".*[92] The said difficulty to distinguish in some cases if an economic or personal right is recognized is applicable as well to employees who, as already mentioned, are authors and thus owners of the moral and economic rights.

Regarding the point of moral rights in the E.C. Directive of Computer Programs, it is important to state that the directive remained silent on this point and left the power to Member States to regulate the topic.[93] The German lawmakers do not mention in article 69 b) any provision regarding moral rights, hence, there is no difference at least by law, on the application of moral rights in computer programs.

The German Copyright Act primarily recognizes the two classical moral rights: the right of paternity or right of recognition of authorship (Article 13) and the right of integrity (Article 14). The Act also recognizes another important moral right, the right of publication or right to control disclosure (Article 12).[94] Unlike the exploitation rights, as already explained, the moral rights are not alienable in any author rights system. Articles 43 and 69(b) of the Copyright Act, regarding works and computer programs works created in employment relationships, do not affect directly the moral rights in Germany. Nonetheless, as Kirchberger states, some moral rights can be limited in the exercise:

... the author has the right of recognition of authorship. This right can, in general, neither be transferred nor waived. It can, however, be limited to the extent of the special nature of the employment.[95]

Moreover, when Kirchberger refers to the effect of the computer programs Directive on moral rights, she states:

... the regulation deals solely with the economic rights and does not affect the moral rights of the creator as such. The execution of the personal rights can however be limited. The author's right to prohibit any distortion or any other mutilation of the work is often limited as computer programs are usually further developed and a prohibition to alter software programs would reduce the employer's possibility to do so.[96]

After reading the previous conclusion of Kirchberger, one may question if the differences between an author's right system and a pure copyright system are really clear. If one of the main difference of the copyright system from the author's right system is that the latter protects moral rights, it is important to evaluate how effective is this protection. On this regard, Prof. Lehman has commented on the difficulty to protect Moral Rights in computer program works. In his words: "Thus, given the rather industrial character of computer programs, in practice moral rights only play a subordinate role, and it has been argued that legally they should also have to stand back". [97]

Another argument that has been raised to explain the reason why the integrity right is limited lies in the possibility of this right being waived.[98] On this point, dietz states: "the fact that the obligation to respect the integrity of a work subject to a license under Section 39 is made dependent on the condition that there is no agreement to the contrary shows that this moral right, to some degree at least, can be contractually waived*".[99]

Thus, despite the effect of new technologies that affect the integrity moral right, the fact that this right can be waived creates the possibility for companies to alter the works of their employees without their authorization.

Despite the weaknesses of the moral rights that can be presented in some works, in some situations there are authors that underline the importance of this right. For example, in the following phrase, dietz calls attention to the importance of the moral right of public disclosure: *"The separate statutory recognition of this right stresses the importance of this moral aspect of copyright law, which guarantees that no person other than the author himself is allowed to decide whether and in what way his work shall be disclosed, eventually to the public".*[100] Applying Dietz's statement to this study, the employed author is the only one that can decide the public disclosure of the work. However, this phrase can be clear under the hypothesis of an independent author in which the employer can exercise many of the exploitation rights and even, the employee has limitations on exercising his moral rights. Thus, another question for the debate is whether the right of public disclosure is limited in the exercise in the course of employment, and whether, for example, the employee cannot impede the employer to disclose a work in an unauthorized way.

Exercising the Right of Authorship, the author can determine whether his work is to bear his name, signature or other designation and what designation is to be used.[101] In this situation, the same question raised earlier will be applied. In the case of an individual author, he will decide to put his name. However, in the course of employment, it is important to check if an employee has the power to decide this matter and request to the employer that his name should appear on the work. As already seen in the analyzed Computer Programs Directive, the computer industry was influencing the adoption of the Directive in order to give legal persons (employers) the exercise of economic rights. Thus, the right of authorship is in practice claimed to a far lesser extent than is possible because of the interest of the software house in question.[102] One may conclude that the possibility for legal persons to exercise the economic rights in computer programs, gave a back door to the computer industry to limit the exercise of moral rights.

It is worth inquiring if in the computer software that we usually use, we can see the names of the employees who actually created those works. At least in the software created by Microsoft, an American Company, the names of the software developers are not mentioned. If one sees the product package or the dvd's or cds in which these programs are contained, there are no indications of the names of the employees who create those works. This is probably due to the fact that the copyright system in America does not recognize this moral right. Thus, the task will be to see if software created in an employment relationship under German law shows the name of the author or authors.

A paradoxical situation is found in France, where limitations on moral rights are not only present in the usual practice as in Germany, but also the law provides a limitation. Article 46 of the French Author's right law provides that "unless otherwise stipulated, the author may not oppose adaptation of the software within the limits of the rights he has assigned nor exercise his right to correct or to retract".[103] This rule can be considered as paradoxical because it contradicts France's reputation for staunchly protecting all of the author's moral interests. However, within Article 46 a 'personal rights protection' is not reflected, as parties waive their moral rights of integrity and revocation in the case of silence.

Furthermore, in spite of the previous critics of the application of moral rights in the studied topic, there are some cases in which there is a clear application of moral rights in Germany that can make a clear differentiation between the author's right system and the copyright system. For instance, German cases[104] dealing with the integrity moral right in architectural and cinematographic works are famous examples of the application of this right. However, there are not known cases dealing with the application of moral rights in works created in employment relationships that can lead to the conclusion that there are big differences between author's right system and copyright systems. Thus, the legal theory can be different as the German law recognizes different moral rights. Nonetheless, the practice can bring very similar situations as the ones found in the Anglo-American Copyright System, where the employer is in most of the cases the one that exercises the economic rights.

After analyzing the current practice on moral rights, a question for future policy making is whether the legal system's philosophy regarding author's rights will recognize, not only the economic, but also the moral rights of employers. Examples of this can already be found globally. For instance, the Japanese Copyright Act in its Section 15 provides for the transferability to the employer of, not only the exploitation rights, but also the moral rights.[105] This provision was made in order to centralize the rights of author on the employer and to facilitate exploitation.[106]

Finally, it is important to bear in mind that as Germany has the monistic theory of author's right, the duration of the moral right is the same as in the economic rights. Article 64 of the Copyright Act establishes that the duration of the rights is seventy years after the author's death. Thus, the heirs of the employee will only have 70 years of moral and economic rights. The heirs will not have a perpetual moral right as in the case of countries with dualistic theory of moral rights. As will be addressed below, Colombia adopted the French author's right system, in which moral and economic rights are divided, and thus, the heirs of an employee in Colombia will enjoy the perpetual moral right.

Works Created By Public Servants

The Works created by employees working for the German government are initially owned by employees, as is also the case with employees working in the private sector. On this point, German law keeps in line with the philosophy of the French author's right system, and does not recognize government or corporate works initially owned by legal entities.[107] It is important to specify that the list of Government works in Article 5 of the

German Copyright Act, which states those works not protected under copyright. Thus, what is protected are the works not listed in Article 5.[108] Nonetheless, as it happens to the private employment relationships[109], in the public employment relationships,[110] the ownership of these works belongs to the employees and the government can only receive the exploitation rights to use the work.[111]

The German provision highlights a difference in comparison to United States and Colombia, where the State is the owner of the copyright in the United States and of the economic rights in Colombia, despite the Colombian author's right system.[112] Consequently, another particularity of the German system lies in the fact that the copyright is given to the employed author and his interests prevail over the economic interests that the State may have on the work created by the public servant. An open question for debate will be why does article 69 (b) of the German Copyright gave the economic rights to the employer? If one may think that the interest of the state is more important that the interest of an employer that orders the production of computer programs?

UNITED STATES. LEGAL RULES AND ANALYSIS

In a different sense from Germany and Colombia, which are continental law systems characterized by statutes as the only primary source of law, the United States is a common law system in which case law is the main source of law. In fact, in the United States, common law principles first established that the ownership of the copyright presumptively belongs to the person that commissioned a work.[113] This rule was later brought under statute in the Copyright Act of 1909 that established that the employer is the author and initial holder of works made for hire.[114] However, as Garlock says, the 1909 statute did not define terms such as employer or work made for hire.[115] It was not until the 1976 Copyright Act that in the United States the term *work made for hire* appeared in a statute.

This study will focus on the analysis of section 201 of the 1976 Act which is the current applicable law. An examination of the background surrounding the enactment of the law is essential as starting point.

Despite the fact that the topic under study is 'works created under employment relationships', in Germany and in Colombia, the term 'employment' is a generic term in which not only labor law contracts but other type of private law contracts can be included. In the United States one of the examples of a private law relationship by which great amount of works are produced, is the case of works created by independent contractors. These types of contractors are not subject to the normal direction and supervision that can be seen in a labor law contract. However, since the Bratlleboro case[116] in 1966, the second circuit applied the work for hire doctrine to independent contractors.[117] Years later, in 1974, in the Siegel case[118] the second circuit developed a test to determine when an independent contractor was included into the 'work made for hire' doctrine. This was the so called 'instance and expense test' by which the employer was considered as the owner of the copyright if the employer was the motivating factor to produce the creation.[119] Under this test, the employer did not need to direct and supervise the work he ordered. Simply having the right to control the process was enough to make him the copyright owner.[120]

Furthermore, in Murray v. Gelderman,[121] the fifth circuit extended the work for hire doctrine under the 1909 act. In opinion of Garlock, after this case: "the common law interpretation of the work made for hire doctrine under the Copyright Act of 1909 developed into a virtually irrebuttable presumption that anyone who paid another to create a copyrightable work was the statutory author and thereby entitled to a copyright in the product".[122]

Thus, notwithstanding that the work made for hire was not defined in the 1909 statute, courts in the usa created this doctrine to give an answer to the ownership of the copyright question. Not only the direction and supervision factors were taken into account to determine a work made for hire, also the economic factor by which the one who paid the work can be considered the author were important elements for Courts to determine a work made for hire. The utilitarian aspect of copyright law, characterized by a copyright system, was clearly shown by giving the ownership of the copyright to the person that paid another one for the production of a work, even without having any labor law contract. This utilitarian aspect is also represented by the fact that the employer is considered the author of the work. The employee who may be sometimes the original creator of the work is not considered to be the author in the United States, as happens in continental systems such as Germany and Colombia.

However, in the United States, as Nimmer points out, there have been problems caused by naming an employer the author. In words of Nimmer, "According to some commentators, a constitutional question arises, given the notion of 'author' in the Copyright Clause, as to whether the employer is considered the 'author' of a work by operation of law or as the transferee of the Actual creator. See *Scherr vs.*

Universal Match Corp".[123]

Despite criticism of naming an employer as the author of a work created by an employee, the fact that in the United States moral rights do not exist like those of a continental law system, can bring a justified explanation to this matter. The employee in the continental system will always be the author of the work, mainly because the employee is the owner of the moral rights in the work that are not transferable. There are only transfers or licenses of the economic rights in the work, but the employee will retain the moral rights, hence, the author title.

Section 201(B), and 101of the Copyright Act of 1976 and the 1909 Copyright Act

As in the 1909 Act, section 201 (b) of the 1976 Act established that the employer is the author. [124] Likewise it recognized the exception to the general ownership rule, as it gave the possibility to the parties to agree otherwise, meaning that not only the employer or person from whom the work was prepared can be the owner of the copyright, but also others can be designated e.g. the employee.

Section 101 of the 1976 Act created a big change in comparison to the 1909 Act as it was the first time that the *'work for hire'* term was defined. [125] The definition included works created in employment relationships, a topic which was already covered by the 1909 Act. The most significant difference from the 1909 Act is that the definition of 'work made for hire' also included the works ordered or commissioned for use in nine categories of works.

Note that the nine categories of works do not apply to employees. If an Employee creates a different kind of work he can still be considered within the doctrine of work made for hire. The works of section 101 are only applicable to independent contractors, and are the only type of creations by which an independent contractor can be deemed to be considered within the doctrine of work made for hire. In fact, in the case May v. Morganelii-Heumann & Associates, the court stated that the list provided in the section 101 (2) was a closed and exhaustive list. [126]

a work prepared by an employee within the scope of his or her employment; or

a work specially ordered or commissioned for use *as a contribution to a collective work, as a part of a motion picture or other audiovisual work, as a translation, as a supplementary work, as a compilation, as an instructional text, as a test, as answer material for a test, or as an atlas, if the parties expressly agree in a written instrument signed by them that the work shall be considered a work made for hire.* For the purpose of the foregoing sentence, a "supplementary work" is a work prepared for publication as a secondary adjunct to a work by another author for the purpose of introducing, concluding, illustrating, explaining, revising, commenting upon, or assisting in the use of the other work, such as forewords, afterwords, pictorial illustrations, maps, charts, tables, editorial notes, musical arrangements, answer material for tests, bibliographies, appendixes, and indexes, and an "instructional text" is a literary, pictorial, or graphic work prepared for publication and with the purpose of use in systematic instructional Activities*"*.

There is however the two following formalities that the 1976 Act included in the definition, in order to consider a copyrighted work as a work made for hire:

The parties have to agree that the work will be a work made for hire

The agreement of the parties must be in a written instrument and signed by them.[127]

It is important to take into account that in the first hypothesis of section 101 by which the work is created by an employee, there is no transfer of the copyrighted work as the employer is considered the author. However, for some commentators[128] there is in fact a transfer, but in this case the transfer is operated by law as section 101 gives the ownership of the copyright to the employer. The discussion about whether there is a transfer or not is, however, impractical as the consequence will always be that if the employee and employer do not agree otherwise, the ownership of the copyright will vest on the employer. By contrast, in the majority of the countries with author's right systems the discussion of the transfer of rights is of extreme importance, as at first glance the employee is considered the author, and the employer can be the owner of the economic rights in virtue of a transfer of rights. As we already see, the German case is even more oriented to protect the author as the transfer of economic rights is not possible, and only by licensing an employed author can transfer his rights.

A recommended formality to be fulfilled is the record of the transfer document in the Copyright office[129] to give third parties notice of the transfer.[130] Despite the fact that registration is not a requirement for the existence of a work made for hire, this is a step by which owners of the right can easily prove the ownership of the work and claim rights over third parties (i.e. priorities).[131] In countries like Colombia, as we will see in Chapter vii, the registration requirement has the same effect.

Regarding the duration of the right in the United States for works made for hire, the duration of the copyright will be 95 years from the first publication or 120 years from creation, whichever of the two terms is shorter.[132] By contrast, in other countries under analysis, as we already saw in Germany, the copyright term is considerably different. Likewise, as it will be mentioned in the following Chapter, the term that Colombia has differs from Germany and United States.

The Remaining Problem of the Independent Contractor after the Copyright Act Of 1976

The fact that the Copyright Act defined the term ‘work made for hire’ do not solve the problem of determining when a work created by an independent contractor was considered a work for hire. After the expedition of the 1976 Act, Garlock states that three different interpretations of the ownership of the works created by an independent contractor were made. [133]

The first interpretation was the so-called “Conservative Approach”, and it consisted in applying the previously mentioned instance and expense test, and the right to control test used by courts when the 1909 Act was in force.[134] If the independent contractor made the work by the instance and expense of the buyer, and by his control, the work was considered as a work for hire.[135] However, under this first approach the instance and expense and control tests were not enough. The works produced must fall also within the categories established in the section 101 (2) and there must be a written agreement in which the parties agreed that there was a work for hire.[136] In opinion of O’Meara this first approach was intended to protect independent contractors from the expansive common law doctrine of 1909 by which the instance and expense test and the control test were enough to consider an employer as the copyright owner.[137]

The second interpretation[138] was made in the Aldon Accessories vs. Spiegel case.[139] The court ruled in this case that if an independent contractor is controlled and supervised by the party who ordered the work, then an employer/employee relationship exists, and section 101 of the 1976 Act has to be applied.[140] This ruling was followed in two other cases: Evans Newton Inc v. Chicago Systems software[141] and Brunswick Beacon v. Schoch-Hopchas Publishing Co.[142] As in the Aldon v. Spiegel case, in these two cases the courts ruled that if supervision and direction were present, the relationship between the two parties will be deemed to be an employee/employer relationship and section 101 (1) will be applied. This interpretation is broader than the conservative interpretation and can be considered as very similar to the common law that existed during the 1909 Act. In this second interpretation courts did not take into account subsection (2) of section 101 and gave most importance to the traditional elements of an employer/employee relationship, that is, control and supervision. This issue will be explained in chapter vii when explaining the labor law principle of reality over forms. However, it is important to take into account that a similar situation comes into play here. Although an independent contractor is not an employee and in the formal legal language is not included within the labor law lexicon, the presence of control and supervision are realities that turn the formality (the independent contractor title) into an employee. In other words, the existence of control and supervision during the creation of a work will prevail over the fact that the person who created a work was called an 'independent contractor'. Thus, the independent contractor will be under the work made for hire doctrine because he will be considered an employee.

The third interpretation for the application of work made for hire in the independent contractor hypothesis[143] was given by the Fifth Circuit in the so called Easter Seal Society case.[144] The fifth circuit stated that section 101 (1) of the Act will be applied to the independent contractor only if he is an employee within the terms of agency law. Regarding section 101 (2) it will be applied only if the works fall into the ten categories of works and there was a written instrument signed by the parties stating that the work was considered to be for hire. The change of this third interpretation was that to determine who was an employee the fifth circuit remitted the question to the section 220 of the restatement of agency law of 1958 that defined the term servant and do not use the previous tests of instance and expense nor the control test. In words of Garlock: "In support of its own literal interpretation, the fifth circuit relies primarily on the Actual language of the statute." [145] Further, Garlock states: "The court also favors this literal interpretation because it unites the work made for hire doctrine with the comparatively settled law of agency*". [146]

Summarizing the third approach, the definition of employee was determinative to establish an answer for the problem with the independent contractor. If the elements of the definition of servant were present, the independent contractor will be deemed to be an employee for purpose of the work made for hire. It is interesting how the fifth circuit in this case used agency law and not the pure IP statute, the Copyright Act of 1976. Should the ownership of the copyright created by employees be regulated by an IP statute or a labor statute? This is a policy question that we will see later in the Colombian analysis.

The CCNV Case

The Çommunity for Creative Non Violence (ccnv) v. Reid case[147] has become the most important decision on the topic of 'work made for hire' in the United States. After this case, the previous three different interpretations were no longer used and the ccnv decision became the applicable law.[148] For Nimmer, with this case "*a definitive method of construing the 1976 Act on point became cast in concrete*".[149]

As this is an important case for our analysis, the following short mention of its facts will be made:

The ccnv ordered the production of a sculpture for James Earl Reid. The order stated that the sculpture must depict homelessness with precise words on the work. Furthermore, the order suggested variations during the process of elaboration and it also proposed humans as models from the sculpture. The legal problem began when the parties did not agree to whom the copyright would belong. Thus, the ccnv sued Reid claiming for a work made for hire on the production of the sculpture.[150]

In the ccnv judgment the Supreme Court did not use the exact elements of the definition of employee given in the Second Restatement of Agency law[151] that were used in the Easter Seal case.[152] By contrast, the Supreme Court did not tied up with the Restatement of Agency law to determine the definition of Employee, as the Supreme Court said that the elements provided in section 220 (2) of the Restatement were not determinative.[153] In the words of the Supreme Court:

In determining whether a hired party is an employee under the general common law of agency, we consider the hiring party's right to control the manner and means by which the product is accomplished. Among the other factors relevant to this inquiry are the skill required; the source of the instrumentalities and tools; the location of the work; the duration of the relationship between the parties; whether the hiring party has the right to assign additional projects to the hired party; the extent of the hired party's discretion over when and how long to work; the method of payment; the hired party's role in hiring and paying assistants; whether the work is part of the regular business of the hiring party; whether the hiring party is in business; the provision of employee benefits; and the tax treatment of the hired party. See Restatement ' 220(2) (setting forth a no exhaustive list of factors relevant to determining whether a hired party is an employee).31 *No one of these factors is determinative.*[154]

The ratio decidendi of the present case ruled on Reid's benefit as the work was not considered for hire. Thus, it concluded that Reid was an independent contractor and not an employee.[155]

The United States Copyright office in the Circular # 9, by using the ccnv decision has classified the following three factors to determine when a work is made for hire:

Control by the employer over the work (e.g., the employer may determine how the work is done, has the work done at the employer's location, and provides equipment or other means to create work)

*Control by employer over the employe***e** (e.g., the employer controls the employee's schedule in creating work, has the right to have the employee perform other assignments, determines the method of payment, and/ or has the right to hire the employee's assistants)

Status and conduct of employer (e.g., the employer is in business to produce such works, provides the employee with benefits, and/or withholds tax from the employee's payment).[156]

Nonetheless, the Copyright Office in the said circular states that in the ccnv decision the Court do not settle on which factors were determinative in order to prove an employment relationship.[157]

Coming back to the ccnv case, the Supreme Court also studied the second approach made in the case Aldon Accessories v. Spiegel case already mentioned. The Supreme Court said that the control and supervision arguments that were made in that case, were not sufficient to determine if there was a work made for hire. In words of the Supreme Court:

The Actual control test, articulated by the Second Circuit in Aldon Accessories, fares only marginally better when measured against the language and structure of section 101. Under this test, independent contractors who are so controlled and supervised in the creation of a particular work are deemed "employees" under section 101(1).[158]

Thus, for the Supreme Court it was not enough that the employer had a formal control over the employee. There must be a direction and supervision like the one that was used later in the case of *Quintanilla v. Texas Television* case, meaning that the employer must supervise the manner and means in which the creator performs his job.[159]

Finally, despite the fact that the Supreme Court reached the conclusion that Reid's sculpture was not a work made for hire, this did not mean that the only owner of the work was Reid. The court, however, suggested that that this could be a case of joint authorship as the ccnv also contributed in the creation of the work.[160]

It is important to point out that when American courts conclude that there are not works made for hire, the joint authorship solution is not always the outcome. There are cases in which the authorship can be deemed only on the independent contractor or the employee.[161] In some countries, like Mexico, there is a especial situation as the result is not joint authorship, the general rule is that the employee is the author, but the economic rights are shared equally between the employer and the employee.[162] Thus, another question for debate will be whether it is fairer to rule the ownership question by creating a 50/50 rule and give both employer and employee economic benefit from the work.

After the ccnv decision, the case law on the work made for hire has not gone through major changes as in previous times. In fact, there are cases that back up the ccnv decision like *Carter v. Helmsley Spear.* In this case it was said that despite the parties having signed a labor law contract, it is important that the elements of the works made for hire determined in the ccnv decision are present.[163] We can see here, how the already mentioned principle of the 'reality over the forms' comes into play again. Earlier, we talked about the situation in which an independent contractor can be considered an employee. In the previously cited case we find the opposite situation. The formality would be that the parties agreed there was a labor law contract, and the reality would be that there was not an employee/employer relationship for the purpose of the work made for hire, since its elements were not present.

Critics after the CCNV Case

The legal uncertainty of what is considered a work made for hire was minimized with the ccnv case. However, there are still questions and critics of the work made for hire doctrine. In fact, the Copyright office in the already mentioned Circular 9, stated that as there is "no precise standard for determining whether or not a work is made for hire under the first part of the definition, consultation with an attorney for legal advice may be advisable".[164] This shows that the definition of the work made for hire term is not definitely clear.

497. In this case the appellant (Quintanilla) claimed that he was the exclusive owner of the copyright in a videotape because he supervised the work that Texas TV

made for the creation of this work. See complete background of the case at 495 & 496.

Some commentators, like Assaf, say that the elements of determining a work made for hire fixed in the ccnv decision, have caused legal uncertainty. The main reason for this conclusion is that the test used by the Supreme Court is based on Tort Law principles which are not compatible with the philosophy of Copyright Law.[165]

Furthermore, Assaf does not only criticize the current test fixed on the ccnv decision. He also proposes the following ideas to transform the work made for hire doctrine using arguments focused on copyright principles rather than agency law:

My proposal is that the 'work made for hire' doctrine should be applied from the vantage point of Copyright Law. The test should focus on incentives to create on the one hand and public access to created works on the other. These are the goals of Copyright Law as stated in the Constitution. Thus, the new test should re-interpret the term 'employee' in a manner that complies with the needs of Copyright Law. Most importantly, 'employee' should be interpreted to give the first entitlement to the party most apt to achieve the goals of the Constitution: Instead of using agency test factors such as employee benefits and tax treatment, the courts should consider factors such as the parties' relative incentive to create new works, public accessibility, transaction costs, and the parties relative ability and motivation to disseminate works to the public. The partnership of individual creativity with the employer's resources yields a significant engine for creative production in society. Revising the 'work made for hire' test would re-align this important issue with the rest of intellectual property law.[166]

As we can see, despite the existence of the ccnv decision, there are however some critics in the United States regarding the 'work made for hire' doctrine. We would be right in stating that the general topic under study, in some cases when the law applies, the outcome is not entirely certain in the United States. The reason is mainly because finding a consensus between the definitions and principles of Copyright Law and Labor Law has not been an easy task. This conflict between the two fields of law is not only present in the United States. As we will see in the next Chapter, the Colombian situation can be seen as even more ambiguous, as there is a legal gap on the ownership point that has created a series of positions, some coming from the labor law side and others coming from the author's rights side.

Common Examples of Works That Fall Under the Work for Hire Doctrine

The Copyright office in the cited Circular 9, states that nowadays, the common examples of works of hire are the following: A newspaper article written by a staff journalist for publication in the newspaper that employs him.

A musical arrangement written for xyz Music Company by a salaried arranger on its staff.[167]

The first example proposed by the Copyright Office is of extreme importance and relevant around the world. As we already see in the German Chapter, the European legislator gave the ownership of the economic rights to the employer in this particular kind of works. Despite the fact that the directive only gives economic rights to the employer, this is the most similar provision to the work made for hire system in relation to countries which have a continental law system (e.g. Germany). The question will be whether the author's rights system is becoming more similar to the copyright system or if the situation is vice versa, with the copyright system creating more traditional author's right provisions. In our analysis we will continue to see more similarities between the two systems to finally determine which the prevailing one is.

The Importance of the Scope of Employment Element to Determine a Work Made For Hire

In the William vs. Weisser case the court ruled that if a professor writes his lecture during business hours and without any kind of supervision, that work is not considered to be for hire, despite the fact the professor is an employee of the University working in business hours.[168] The requirement that the created work be bound within the scope of the labor law contract, is put into practice in this case. On this point Nimmer says that: "*Given the requirement that works for hire fall within the scope of employment, it follows that if an employer and employee agree that even works prepared outside such scope will be considered works for hire, those provisions of the contract are invalid.*"[169] Thus, if an employer wants to allege the rights on a work created by an employee, it is a mandatory requirement that the work falls within the scope of the contract. The protection of the employee's rights that Nimmer suggests would prevail over the freedom of the parties. At a first glance, the copyright system in comparison to the author's rights system can be considered as less protective to the employed author. Thus, this kind of protection is paradoxical and we could ask ourselves whether there are similar commentators in line with Nimmer, applying this argument to the author's right system.

Salary as an Element in Determining the Employment Relationship

In the ccnv decision, one of the elements in determining the employment relationship was the "method of payment to the hired party".[170] Thus, as in the continental labor law traditional doctrine, not only the existence of control and supervision, but also the fixation of a salary is considered an indication of the existence of the labor law contract. However, in *Brown v. Cosby*[171], it was stated that despite the presence of a fixed salary, if an employer does not pay the salary to an employee, there is a breach of contract that will not give the ownership of the copyright to the employer.[172] This case was ruled before the ccnv decision. Thus, it would be interesting to ask ourselves if, under current law, the same consequence would apply or the employee will simply have to enforce the right to get paid and loose the right on the created work. As we can see, this is another ruling in order to protect the employed author, which at first glance would be more likely found in an author's right system. In the law of continental systems, however, there are no labor or IP law provisions like this. The stated common law rule can be considered not only as a fair price to an employee that do not get paid, but also as a method of penalizing the employer for not fulfilling his labor law obligations, despite the fact that there are in each country other ways to punish the employer for not paying the employee.[173]

COLOMBIA. LEGAL RULES AND ANALYSIS

we begin the Colombian legal analysis by stating that the two topics of study under examination, employment and copyright, are protected under the Colombian Constitution of 1991. The constitution of Colombia guarantees a right of employment and protection of one's ip.

The term 'employment' is defined in article 25 of the Constitution. Under this provision employment is a constitutional right, and it is an obligation for the state to protect all forms of employment. The first question that we have to raise after reading the previous provision is: what does the Constitution meant by '*all forms of employment'?*[174] The answer for this is the same as in Germany and in the

United States; *employment* is a generic term, encompassing labor law contracts and private law contracts.[175]

In addition, article 61[176] of the Constitution creates an obligation for the Colombian state to protect Intellectual Property rights. This provision does not distinguish between the three traditional IP rights of copyrights, patents and trademarks, but the legal doctrine includes these concepts under the generic concept of Intellectual Property rights.

With referal to the Copyright tradition that has been used in Colombia, the same analysis that was made in Germany applies here, as Colombia is a continental law system. Thus, the proper way to name the right which an employee may have for the works created is *author's' right* and not copyright. However, as it was previously said, in the German analysis, for practical reasons the term copyright may be used here as well.

Although the aim of this analysis is not to consider what constitutes an employment contract in the analyzed countries, some generalities of the Colombian law can be pointed out:

As mentioned, the traditional three main elements of the labor law contract that have been analyzed in United States and Germany are present also in Colombian law in the article 22 of Labor Law Code.[177]

Likewise, as stated above, the term *employment* is a generic term in civil law relationships, in which is included the situation where persons provide services to others. In Colombia the most common civil legal law relationship in which copyrighted works are created is the so called *contract to provide services* or *contract of services* , a literal translation from the Spanish term: *Contrato de prestación de servicios*. The elements of this type of contracts are not defined in a specific provision, but it is of frequent application as it is a legal way by which the one that orders a work is not legally obliged to pay different sums usually related to the Colombian Social Security Regime. However, it is important to take into account that the person who wants to receive the services does not treat the provider as an employee, otherwise he will run the risk of being under a labor law contract even without even signing one as the substantive reality prevails over the practice.[178]

The contract to provide services is not specifically defined in a legal provision; however, there are rules that explain its origin and its philosophy. The first rules especial protección del Estado. Toda persona tiene derecho a un trabajo en condiciones dignas y justas". that mentioned the topic were Articles 2053 and 2063 of the civil code.[179] The first refers to the lending of services to create a tangible work and the latter refers to intangible forms.

The Colombian Commercial Code also includes provisions related to contracts for services. The most important is article 968.[180] However, the only legal norm that has an approximate definition of the contract to provide services can be found in article 32 paragraph 3 of the Law of States' Contracts. For our purpose, the important element of this definition is the express exclusion of labor law contracts when it states: "*in any case, these contracts do not create labor law relationships*".[181] The cited provision clearly shows the legislator's intention to differentiate this contract from labor law contracts.

The previous rules are the basic legal provisions by which a person in Colombia can create work for an employer or for someone that has not the title of employer, but receives the services under a non-labor law relationship.

The Gap in Colombian Law Regarding the Ownership of Economic Rights in Works Created In Employment Relationships

None of the Colombian legal rules above provide a clear answer regarding the ownership of the copyright of works created by employees. The only reference that can be found in the Labor law code in relation to IP is related to the employee obligation to maintain confidentiality.[182] the civil code nor did the commercial code establish a legal rule that provides a clear answer about the ownership of the copyright in Works created by employees.

The Colombian Author's Right Law number 23 of 1982 has in its article 20[183] a specific rule concerning the ownership of the copyright in contracts to provide services, however, the law does not mention any express rule about the situation under an employment contract.

A literal translation of article 20 will be:

When one or more authors during a contract to provide services make a work under the directions of a natural or legal person, the author or authors will only receive the fees that they agreed by contract. Just by this fact, the author or authors transfer their rights on the work, without prejudice of article 30 letters a) and b).[184]

Two consequences will derive from this provision:

That just by signing the contract, the provider of the services will transfer the economic rights.

As Colombia is an Author's Right system, the dualistic theory of rights by which the law differentiates between Moral and Economic rights will be applied here. Thus, the author in this case will retain the moral rights of integrity (a) and paternity (b).[185]

In spite of the previous provision, according to some commentators, like Fernando Zapata lópez, article 183 of the law under study, fixes a formal requirement to make the transfer of the economic rights effective in the course of the contract to provide services.[186]

Article 183 states that every act, in which there is a partial or total transfer of the author right, must be made by public instrument or by a private document certified by a Notary.[187] In addition, to have effect on third parties, the documents have to be registered in the National Office of Author's Right.[188] On this regard there is a big difference with United States and Germany. As previously mentioned on these two countries, the registration of a transfer or a grant at the respective Copyright Office is not a mandatory requirement for the validity of the transfer.

In Zapata´s opinion, article 20 does not establish a legal presumption of transferal of the economic rights.[189] The argument that he relies on to reach this conclusion is that legal presumptions are formed by facts, and in the present case this legal presumption is created by a contract (the contract of services) but not by a fact, so technically it is improper to talk about a legal presumption under this analysis.[190] Moreover, he states that what article 20 is establishing is the effect of signing a contract to provide services, but this does not mean that the parties do not have to fulfill the formalities established under article 183.[191]

Thus, the questions to ask after reading these two legal provisions are:

Why does the law mention in article 20 that simply by signing the contract to provide services, the economic rights will be transferred, if later, in article 183 it establishes an extra requirement for the economic rights transfer?

Does articles 20 and 183 have to be used in order to solve the economic rights problem, or other legal arguments can be used?

There has been different interpretations to resolve this question. However, for the purpose of the study, only the following 4 main approaches are going to be mentioned:

1. The application of the Latin maxim the special law prevails over the generic law 'lex specialis generalem deroga'

The author Carlos Hernán Godoy states that article 183 does not apply to contracts to provide services.[192] He uses the legal principle by which the special law prevails over the generic law *lex specialis generalem deroga* in order to solve the ambiguity.[193] The special provision is Article 20 by which the lawmaker was only regulating the contract to provide services. Thus, in Godoy's opinion there will be no need to require a public instrument or other formalities for a transfer of economic rights in the course of a contract to provide services.[194] Notwithstanding the need for the requirements of article 183 in a contract to provide services, Godoy emphasizes the importance that the three following conditions of article 20 are fulfilled in order to transfer the economic rights:

The contract has to include a clear work plan. The reason for this is to avoid situations in which undefined rights shall be transferred. This is of importance because if the author agreed to broad work, then he may run the risk of lost economic ownership on works that were not meant to be transferred.

The elaboration of the work should be under the risk of the person that orders it.

The price that the parties agree must be clearly specified in the contract.[195]

If as Godoy says, the lawmaker is referring to contracts different from the agreement to provide services in article 183, the question for our purpose will be, what if one of these types of contracts was a labor law contract?

Regarding this question Godoy states that article 20 is not applicable to the labor law agreement,[196] because of the following two arguments:

– In spite of the fact that the text of article 20 is ambiguous because it refers to contract of services, the word fees (*honorarios* in Spanish) marks a clear distinction between the contract of services and the labor law contract, as in the latter the money that the employer pays to the employee is by essence called a wage, but never fees. If the law maker distinguished the word fees, it should be inferred that it was referring to service contracts.[197]

[a] There is not a specific rule for the labor law agreement on the Author's right law. This fact means that we have to apply the general provision of article 183. The wording of Article 183 states that "every act" ("*Todo acto*" in Spanish) of transfer must fulfill the requirements established herein. When the law refers to 'every act' it must be interpreted as every act different from the contract of services where there is a specific rule.[198] Thus, in Godoy's opinion article 183 applies to the labor law agreement, and if the employer wants to receive the economic rights, the agreement will have to fulfill the two requirements already mentioned, that is: it has to be made by public instrument or in a private document certified by a notary, and will have to be registered in the Author's Right National Office to have effects on third parties.

To summarize Godoy's approach: There is no specific provision in the civil, commercial and author's right law that will tell us to whom the economic rights should belong in an employment relationship. As there is no special provision, article 183 is the general rule that we will have to apply for the labor agreement.

2. Transferability of the economic rights in virtue of Article 20 of the author's right law.

The Colombian Consejo de Estado[199] in the year 2003 provided an opinion[200] to the question of the application of articles 20 and 183 in the employment relationships. The opinion can be considered as opposite to Godoy's interpretation mentioned above. This is because the *Consejo de Estado* avers that article 20 is enough to say that the employee transfers the economic rights to the employer. By the sole fact

The following are some of the main reasons that the Consejo de Estado uses to justify the opinion:

Despite the fact that there is no internal law that refers to the situation in the labor law contract, there must be an harmonious interpretation with the following articles of the author's right law: Article 4 of the author's right law permits in some situations that a legal or natural person has the economic rights when he, she or it orders the production of the work at his own risk. Article 92 establishes that if in the course of an employment contract, a collective work is created, and if it is impossible to determine the ownership, the property of the economic rights will belong to the person that ordered the work. Thus, the said harmonic interpretation will apply if the lawmaker regulates the situation in these rules; they have to be applied to the employment contract too without seeing if the created work is collective or not. The result is that the economic rights of the employee are transferred to the employer with the sole act of signing the labor contract[202].

The Colombian Constitutional Court in the judgment C- 278 of 1996 said that article 20 of the author's right law was enough to transfer the economic rights to the natural or legal person who ordered the work. This judgment was confirmed in a later case (C- 155 of 1998). These judgments must be also extended to the labor law contract.[203]

The Andean decision # 351 of 1993 in its article 10 provides the same legal presumption of transfer of economic rights, not only when there is a work that is ordered in the course of a civil relationship, but also in a labor law agreement.[204]

Regarding the application of the previously mentioned article 183 of the author's right law, the *Consejo de Estado* states that this norm could be a mistake by the lawmaker, because the truth of the matter is that the transfer of economic rights in civil law and labor law agreements by which an employer or non employer orders a work, do not require the formalities established in article 183.[205]

3. The favorability principle of the labor law and Author's Right Law

This approach does not use articles 20 or 183. On the contrary, under these interpretations the favorability principles established in the Author's right law and the labor law code are the legal arguments that give the employee the ownership of the economic rights.

Regarding the favorability in the labor law code, Riveros states that the gaps of the legislation may not be interpreted in a manner which is contrary to the interests of the employee who produced the work in an autonomous way or produced the work in accordance with a given plan.[206] The favorability principle protected under labor law bestows on the employee a claim over the economic rights of a work when there is no agreement in which the employee has transferred such rights to the employer.[207]

Likewise, article 257 of the Author's Right Law establishes that any doubt regarding the application of the law will be interpreted in favor of the author. As this is clearly a case where there is not a specific rule that gives an answer, and as the employee in Colombia is the author, he will be the one that benefits from this principle.[208] By contrast, as it was explained in the previous Chapter, the author in the United States is the employer. Thus, there will be an important difference in this point as the application of the said principle in the United States will be in favor of the employer.[209]

4. Labor law approach in favor of the Employer

As the previous interpretation this approach does not use article 20 or 183, it states that the philosophy under the labor law norms implies that every work created by an employee should be property of the employer.

One of the proponents of this philosophy is the Argentinean professor Delia lipzyc who recognizes that despite the difficulty of finding an answer to the question of ownership of works created in employment contracts, the principles of labor law should prevail over the principles of author's law.[210] According to the general principles of labor law, every fruit produced by an employee must belong to an employer, although the moral rights will be always remain the property of the employee.[211] The Colombian Professor Arcadio plazas, shares Lipzyc's approach, and adds that one must differentiate between authorship and what he calls title of rights[212]. The authorship of a work can only vest with the employee, as he is the one who creates the work. The second element, title of rights, belongs to the employer, so the employer will be the direct owner of the economic rights unless the employer agrees differently with the employee.[213] Moreover, Plazas states that employer and employee both satisfied their immediate economic interests because, on the one hand, the employee received a wage for his work and, on the other hand, the employer received the fruits of the works for which he was paying.[214] Another

justification that Plazas uses to support the idea of the ownership of the economic right residing with the employer, is the fact that the employees create copyrighted works, not only according to instructions given by the employer, but also with material tools provided by the employer. Thus, the effort of the employer should be recognized by giving him the ownership of the economic rights.[215]

The previous four theories concerning the ownership of the copyright in works created in employment relationships created can be summarized as follows:

Article 20 of the author's right law is not enough to transfer the economic rights to the employer. For an employer in order to be the owner of the economic rights, he has to fulfill the requirements provided in article 183 of the author's right law. By contrast, in the contract to provide services there is no need to fulfill the requirements fixed on article 183. However, some commentators like Zapata[216] argue that even in the contract to provide services the formal requirements of article 183 have to be fulfilled in order to transfer the right to the person that ordered the work.

In virtue of article 20 of the author's right law, it is clear that an employee is an author that retains the moral rights, however the economic rights are automatically transferred to the Employer. The same conclusion applies to the contract to provide services.

The principles of favorability of the labor law code and the author's right law give the employee the economic rights on its creation. The employer will only have the ownership of the economic rights if the employee decides to transfers them to him.

The labor law should prevail over the author's right in this case, and the economic rights should belong to the employer for the sole fact of signing a labor contract with an employee.

Works Created by Public Servants

Notwithstanding that the Author's right law did not provide a legal answer for the ownership of the economic rights in works created in private employment relationships, Article 91 regulates the subject in works created by public servants.

In this situation, we are under the hypothesis that an employee from the state creates a protected work. The legal consequence is that the State is the owner of the economic rights. This provision can probably contains one of the few exceptions of the moral rights in the law, as it says that "the moral rights will belong to the authors (the employees) as long as their exercise is compatible to the legal duties and rights of the public offices involved".[217] The philosophy under the norm is protecting the public interest of the state, however, there are no known cases related to this matter in which a public company has claim something from an employee because of an incompatible exercise of the moral right.

The situation in Colombia regarding works created by public servants is more similar to the Anglo America Copyright System as the State is the owner at least of the economic rights. By contrast, and despite the fact that Germany is an author's right system like Colombia. The ownership in works created by public servants in Germany is different, as the economic and moral rights vest with the public servants.[218]

CONCLUSIONS

Main Differences in the Law of the Analyzed Countries

As Germany and Colombia are countries based on the author's right system, the employee will always be considered the author of a work created under the scope of employment. Likewise, the employed author will always be a natural person. By contrast, in the United States, the employer is considered the author of a work created under the scope of employment, and he can be a legal entity or a natural person.[219]

With respect to the issue of ownership, since Germany and Colombia are both based on the author's right system, the employee will always be the owner of the inalienable moral rights in these countries. Since there is no express recognition of moral rights in the United States, the employees cannot enjoy such types of rights.

Since Germany is a monistic author's right system, the moral rights and the economic rights are represented in one sole right that belongs to the employee.[220] Consequently, an employee in Germany can only grant the right to use the economic rights, since he will always be considered the owner of economic rights , and no transfer will be possible. By contrast, Colombia is classified under the dualistic theory of moral rights by which moral and economic rights are not merged into a unitary right, and thus, the employee can transfer or license the economic rights to the employer.[221]

The silence of the employer and employee regarding the ownership of the copyrighted works may also bring different results in each country. In the United States, the general rule is that if the parties did not agree to anything otherwise, the employer will be the author and owner of the work. In Germany, if the parties were silent, the employee will exercise the economic rights. However, an important exception to the general rule in Germany can be found in computer programs created by employees.[222] In this case, the silence of the parties will give the exercise of the economic rights to the employer. In Colombia, the law does not tell where an employee and employer are silent on the topic of economic rights, resulting in different interpretations by commentators. Some commentators prefer to give the ownership of the economic rights to the employer while others aim to vest the employee with these rights.

Finally, regarding the duration of the copyright, Colombia has the longer protection, since the economic rights last 80 years after the death of the employee or 80 years after the death of the employer if the economic rights were transferred to him and the employer is a Natural person.[223] With respect to the moral rights, since Colombia follows the dualistic author's right system, the duration of these rights is perpetual. The monistic theory of author's rights in Germany has a different result, whereby the moral and economic rights last 70 years after the employee's death.[224] The United States provides the minimum protection, as the right lasts 95 years from the publication of the work or 120 years from the creation of the work, without taking into account the death of the employer.[225] This can be considered as one clear difference revealing how important is for an author's right system to observe the interests of the authors by giving them longer terms than in a copyright system.

The Tendency of the Author's Right Law Systems like Germany and Colombia to Become Similar to the Anglo American Copyright Systems

The fact that the German law recognizes the employer's ability to exercise economic rights in computer programs, leads to a clear approximation to the American work made for hire doctrine. The employer in Germany is not the author, but the power to exercise the economic rights in these works is enough to reveal a similarity to the Anglo American system, as the economic interests of the employer prevail over those of the employee, who in most cases is the natural person creating the copyrighted work. Likewise, for other types of works, the usual practices in Germany can lead to the same conclusion. In most of the cases, not only have employees granted the use of the economic rights to the employer, but by "implied clauses" or presumptions, the employer finds a means of exercising the economic rights.[226]

Despite the fact that the E.C. computer programs directive leaves the regulation of moral rights to the national law of each member state, the reality in Germany is that the use of the moral rights in software created by employees is being diminished,[227] revealing another similarity to the Anglo American Copyright system where these types of rights are not recognized.

The E.C. computer programs directive also left another issue to the member states, that of computer programs created by independent contractors. On this regard, Germany gave the exercise of the economic rights to the person that orders the work,[228] highlighting another similarity to the Anglo American Copyright system in which the copyright vests in the person that ordered the work, if the conditions of a work made for hire are present.

In the case of Colombia, it is difficult to take a position regarding an approximation to the Anglo American copyright system regarding works created by employees serving private companies. This is due to the fact that the law does not provide a clear answer, and legal commentators have expressed different interpretations about the ownership of the economic rights in employment contracts. By contrast, in works created by public servants, the law in Colombia is clear and shows an approximation to the Anglo American Copyright system, since the economic rights vest in the Nation. Likewise, the moral rights in such public employment contracts are limited, as their exercise is permitted if they do not conflict with the normal exploitation of the work.[229]

Thus, it can be considered paradoxical that two author's right systems like Colombia and Germany do not have uniform rules on the topic, and by contrast, both countries have strong similarities to the Anglo American copyright system. If the Colombian lawmakers decide to amend the law and fill the legal lacunae, the philosophy of the author's right system should not be forgotten. The economic and moral interests of the employed authors have to be conserved. Otherwise, it would be inconsistent to call the system an author's right system which was created to protect the original creation of the human being. Likewise, lawmakers should consider solutions to protect the interests of the authors in industries where employees cannot freely exercise moral and economic rights (i.e. computer programs). Some solutions may lie in creating mechanisms that give extra remuneration to the employees for their work, as is the practice in Germany with inventions created by employees.[230] Another fair and probable solution that can balance the interests of employees and the employers in these kinds of works may consist of dividing the ownership of the economic rights by half, as is the practice in countries like Mexico.[231] One must not forget that it is not every day that an employee is creating works that are protected under copyright. The creation should be rewarded, and in most of the cases the salary is not a great enough incentive. Mechanisms to simultarneously reward authors and stimulate creation are necessary.

Other Types of Similarities between the Countries under Study: Scope of Employment, Employment Relationships and the Use of IP Statutes

In the three countries analyzed, one may conclude that the expression "scope of employment" has a similar meaning. The important indicator in considering whether a work was created under the scope of employment lies in whether the employee created the work in execution of his duties. Other factors, such as the creation of the work in the place of work or during working hours, are subsidiary facts that are not clear indicia to prove that a work is created in an employment relationship.

Likewise, the understanding of a labor law relationship is similar in Colombia, Germany, and the United States. The element of dependency, characterized by the fact that the employer gives orders to the employee in how to do their work or fulfill a schedule, is present in all three countries. Similarly, the principle of reality over the forms[232] is applied in the three countries, as it does not matter if one party uses a different formality from a labor contract to order another party to produce work. If elements such as supervision, control, or dependency are present, the reality shows that there is in fact a labor relationship.

Naturally, in all the countries, it is mandatory to observe labor law provisions such as labor law contracts, labor law codes, and union agreements. This fact has created critics in the United States who believe it is a mistake of courts to take into account agency law in the "work made for hire" doctrine.[233] Nonetheless, one may affirm that the tendency at least in Germany and in the United States has been to regulate the issue of ownership mostly by using Copyright justifications and the National Copyright acts. Since Colombia has not provided a clear answer to the ownership question, if the lawmakers decide to fill in the legal gap, it would be recommendable to follow the legal trend and amend the Copyright provision, that is, the author's right law

NOTES

Goldstein, paul: International Intellectual property law. Cases and Materilas - New York : Foundation. 2D. 2008, at 214.

Christine Kirchberger, Ulrika nyh, Silvina penaloza, Hanna Sepanen and Kerli Tults. Ownership of the Copyright and the Patent Right in Works Created by Employees. Finland, Sweden, Austria, UK, Estonia, and Argentina. Sanna Wolk (ed.) 2002, at 1.

Yu Du and Matthew Murphy. mmlc Group. *Intellectual Property in the Employer and Employee Relationship in China*. at: *http://www.hg.org/article.asp?id=5341.*

oit. Contratos de Trabajo, at http://www.ilo.org/public/spanish/dialogue/themes/ce.htm#ci.

Efren Cordova, Naturaleza y Elementos del Contrato de Trabajo. México. unam, Série B, Estudios Doctrinales Núm 188. 1997. Chapter 16, at 302.

Likewise, the employee has to be free on his decision to work, there cannot be any form of forced labor. On this point see id, at 306.

Cordova, supra note 5 at 306.

Original text of Article 22 reads: "Art. 22. – Definición. 1. Contrato de trabajo es aquél por el cual una persona natural se obliga a prestar un servicio personal a otra persona natural o jurídica, bajo la continuada dependencia o subordinación de la segunda y mediante remuneración (Código sustantivo del trabajo*)".* Text translated by the author.

The theory by which the presence of the three said elements form a labor law contract was born in Germany in the first quarter of the previous century, soon after the first labor laws were enacted. For further information See El derecho del Trabajo en España. Ideologías Jurídicas y Contrato de Trabajo. Madrid, Instituto de Estudios Sociales, 1981. at 127, 128, 129 & 130.

For further information see supra note 5, at 309.

Id, at 312.

For instance, as it will be mentioned in Chapter VII, in Colombia, to solve the legal gap on the ownership point, there are some theories who by way of analogy translate the ownership rules of the contract to provide services to the labor law contract.

martin Valverde, F. Rodríguez- Sañudo y J. García murcia. Derecho del Trabajo. Madrid. Ed. Tecnos, 14 Edición, 2005, at 642.

Id, at 642.

National Labor Law Profile: Federal Republic of Germany. Contributed by Liliane Jung. Last update, April 2001. at http://www.ilo.org/public/english/dialogue/ifpdial/info/ national/ger.htm

Id.

Schricker. Urheberrecht Kommentar (2006) 3. Auflage, at 887 section 13.

Id. at 887 section 13.

Goldstein. supra note 1, at 214.

Id. at 214.

Adolf dietz, German Chapter of the book Compilated by Nimmer, Melville. International Copyright Law and Practice. b. volume 2 1997/2000, at 19.

Juan Pablo Riveros Lara. Derecho de Autor en Colombia.. Ed Hojas e Ideas, at 38.

dietz, supra note 21, at 19.

Id, at 19.

German Copyright Act of 1965 Article 11:

dietz, supra note 21 at 20.

Goldstein, supra note 1, at 214.

Id. at 214.

dietz, supra note 21 at 47,48

Id, at 51. Not only the German law predicts the indivisibility of these two rights, but the term of both rights are the same, 70 years after the death of the author. By contrast, in others authors right tradition Countries like Colombia and France, the moral rights are perpetual, and the term of the economic rights last with time.

Id, at 51.

Goldstein, supra note 1, at 214.

dietz, supra note 21, at 51.

The courts usually have decided if the licensee has the right to sue third parties for infringement. One of the examples by which the court gave the right to sue to a licensee is in one decision of the bgh of June 17 of 1992, (vgl. hierzu bgh grur 1992, 697, 698 F-Alf.). Despite the plaintiff in this case was not an employer. General rules of contracts will apply also if the plaintiff were an employer.

German Copyright Act. See also supra note 25.

dietz, supra note 21, at 52.

Id, at 52.

Id, at 53.

Id, at 54.

See supra note 35.

Dietz, supra note 21, at 54.

Id, at 53.

See supra note 35.

We have to bear in mind that despite referring to registration of transfers in the citation.

The proper term to be use in Germany would be registration of the grants of the contractual right to use the exploitation rights.

dietz, supra note 21 at 55.

Article 43 German Copyright Act. See supra note 35.

Article 69b German Copyright Act. See supra note 35.

dietz, supra note 21, at 50.

Id, at 54.

Id, at 50.

Kirchberger, supra note 2, at 14.

Schricker, supra note 17, at 890 Section 23.

dreier, Schulze. Urheberrechtsgesetz 2 auflage (2006), at 54 lines 24 to 25.

Schricker, supra note 17, at 905 section 65

Id, at 902 section 64.

German Employees' Inventions Act of January 18 2002.

Kirchberger, supra note 2, at 14.

dreier, Schulze, supra note 53, at 56 Lines 22 to 30.

The German Supreme Court have said that the there is a presumption to an implicit transfer of economic rights. Case Reference: rgz 153,1/8. For further information see Schricker, supra note 17.

Schricker, supra note 17, at 894 sect. 38.

Id, at 921 section 101.

Id, at 921 section 101.

Id, at 894 sect 41

Kirchberger, supra note 2, at 14.

Rojahn, Urheber In Arbeits – Oder Dienstverhaeltnissen In Urheberrecht Kommentar, at 683

olenhusen v., a. G., der Urheber- und Leistungsrechtsschutz der Arbeitehmeraehnlichen Personen, grur 2002, book 1at 15.

dietz, supra note 21, at 50.

Id, at 50.

Id, at 50.

Krasser, Urheberrecht in Arbeits-, Dienst- und Aufragsverhaeltnissen (1999), at 97.

dreier, Schulze, supra note 53, at 53 lines 20 to 25. contract comes to an end, the grant is concluded. This will depend on the negotiation of both parties.

dreier. The international Development of Copyright protection for Computer programs. 1993, at 225.

dietz, supra note 21, at 33.

dreier, supra note 72 at 221.

Id, at 227.

Scholz, Implementation of the European Community Software Directive in Germany. (1993) 34 Copyright World, at 36 .

Article 1 E.C. Directive for the legal protection of Computer Programs, at http://eurlex.europa.eu/smartapi/cgi/sga_doc?smartapi!celexapi!prod!CELEXnumdoc&numdoc=31991L0250&model=guichett&lg=en.

dietz, supra note 21 at 33.

For further information regarding originality requirements and the E.C. Directive see Scholz, supra note 76, at 36.

Article 2 E.C. Directive for the Legal Protection of Computer Programs. supra note 77.

Kirchberger, supra note 2, at 15.

dreier. The Council Directive of 14 May 1991 on the Legal Protection of Computer Programs. [1991] 9 eipr, at 3.

Id, at 2.

However, as already mentioned the German Copyright Act does not refer to the term license, and the nearer English translation is a grant of the contractual right to use.

The implied arguments that the employer may alleged are in other words the determination of the scope of employment that was previously analyzed. On this regard, it was said that the labor law contract, the unions agreements and the main area of business of the employer are factors to take into consideration.

Kirchberger, supra note 2, at 15.

dreier, Schulze, supra note 53 Line 15 to 17 at 53.

Lowenheim. Schricker Urheberrecht Kommentar 3. Auflage at 1353 section 15.

Id. at 1351 sect. 11.

dreier, supra note 72, at 221.

Alberto Valdés Alonso. Propiedad Intelectual y Relación de Trabajo: La Transmisión De Los Derechos de Propiedad Intelectual a través del Contrato de Trabajo: Artistas, Programadores Informáticos Y Producción Audiovisual De, Civitas, 2001, 1ª ED. at 32.

dietz, Supra note 21, at 87.

dreier, supra note 82 at 2.

There are other moral rights on the copyright act such as the right of revocation for non exercise (article 41) and Right of revocation for changed conviction (article 42) however, in the chapter of moral rights, the mentioned 3 previous rights are the three rights classified as moral for the act.

Supra note 2, at 15.

Id. at 15.

lehman. The legal protection of Computer Programs in Germany: A Summary of the present situation. (1988) 19 iic 473, at 478.

dreier, Schulze, supra note 53, at 54 Lines 8 to 10.

dietz, supra note 21, at 90.

Id, at 88.

Id, at 88

dreier, supra note 72 at 221.

French Copyright Law of 29/03/1972.

For further Information see supra note 21, At 89, 90, 94, 95 & 96.

Edited By peter Ganea, Christopher Heath and Hiroshi Saito, Japanese Copyright Law. Writings in honour of Gerhard Schricker.. Kluwer Law International (2005) at 36.

id, at 36.

dietz, supra note 21 at 48.

For instance in the case of the bgh of October 9 of 1976 an informational pamphlet published by a government organization was protected by copyright, as it was not under the list covered in article 5.

German translation: Arbeitsverhaeltnis.

German translation: Dienstverhaeltnis.

dietz, supra note 21, at 35.

On chapters vi & vii the American and Colombian provisions will be analyzed.

See. dillman v. White, 102 Fed. 892 (c.c.d. Mass 1900).

Steve E Garlock. The work made for hire doctrine under the copyright Act of 1976: What about the independent contractor? 1988. Washington University Law Quarterly vol 66.423. at 423. 115. Id, at 423.

Bratlleboro Publishing Co. v. Winmill Publishing Corp, 369 F.2d 565 (2d Cir) (1966).

Garlock, supra note 114, at 424.

Siegel v. National Periodical Publications, Inc., 508 F.2d 909 (2d Cir. 1974). 119. Garlock, supra note 114, at 424 120. Id, at 424.

murray v. Gelderman 566 F. 2d 1307 (5th Cir. 1978).

Garlock, supra note 114, at 424.

nimmer, melville, International Copyright Law and Practice. B. Volume 2 1997/2000. United States Chapter, at 48.

"Works Made for Hire. — In the case of a work made for hire, *the employer* or other person for whom the work was prepared *is considered the author* for purposes of this title, and, unless the parties have expressly agreed otherwise in a written instrument signed by them, owns all of the rights comprised in the copyright".

"A 'work made for hire' is —

126. may vs morganelii-Heumann & Associates. 618 F2D 1363 C.A.Cal., (9th Cir. 1980) see at 1368. In this case the appellant (May) was considered by Court as an independent contractor per-se. The drawings that he created were not works included in the list of section 101 (2) see at 1369.

nimmer, supra note 123, at 54.

Id, at 54.

On this regard section 205 (c) of the 1976 Copyright Act requires that the document adequately identifies the work which it relates and that a registration has been made for a work.

us Copyright Office. Circular 1. Notice of Copyright, at http://www.copyright. gov/circs/circ1.html#noc.

Id.

Circular 15 (a) of the United States Copyright office provides a summary of the provisions related with the duration of the copyright under the Copyright Act of 1976, see at: http://www.copyright.gov/circs/circ15a.html.

Garlock, supra note 114, at 425.

Id, at 425.

Id, at 425. 136. Id, at 426.

William o'meara "Works made for Hire" under the Copyright Act of 1976..

Aus: Creighton Law Review. Vol. 15, 1981 - 1982, 2, at 533.

Garlock, supra note 114, at 426.

Aldon Accessories Ltd. v. Spiegel, Inc. 738 F. 2d 548 (2d Cir. 1984).

Garlock, supra note 114, at 426.

Evans Newton Inc. v. Chicago Systems Software, 793 F.2d 889 (7th Cir. 1986).

Brunswick Beacon v. Schock-Hopchas Publishing Co. 810 F. 2d 410 (4th Cir. 1987).

Garlock, supra note 114, at 429.

Easter Seal Society for Crippled Children and Adults of Louisiana, Inc v. Playboy Enterprises. 815 F. 2d 323 (5th Cir. 1987).

Garlock, supra note 114 at 431& 432.

Id, at 431& 432.

Community for Creative Non-Violence vs.Reid. 490 U.S. 730. 109 S.Ct. 2166, U.S.Dist. Col., (1989) (Hereinafter ccnv case).

Nimmer, supra note 123, at 49.

Id, at 49.

ccnv case, supra note 148. See facts of case at 733.

It is important to take into account that since 2006 the current Agency Law is the third Restatement that replaced the Second Restatement of 1958. The ccnv case only analyzed the Second Restatement from 1958. See Third Restatement at http://74.125.39.104/ search?q=cache:Cphn2VXToxQJ:www.wmitchell.edu/academics/curriculum/courses/assignments/Restatement%2520Third%2520of%2520Agency.pdf+restatement+third+of+agency

+law&hl=en&ct=clnk&cd=2&client=firefox-a

As already see in Germany and as will be explained in the Colombian Chapter, the definition of employee that the law used is only establish by a labor law regulation. The fact that in the United States the Court creates a specific definition for employee for purpose of the work made for hire is a big difference between the countries under analysis.

ccnv case, supra note 148, at 751 154. Id, at 751.

The italicized part shows how the Supreme Court did not use the exact definition of the restatement of agency law.

ccnv case, Supra note 148, at 742.

US Copyright Office Circular 9. See at: http://www.copyright.gov/circs/circ9.html.

Id. The circular also underline that as the ccnv decision states; supervision alone is not enough to establish a work made for hire, and that if all or mostly all the elements are proved there is a work made for hire.

ccnv case, supra note 148, at 742.

Quintanilla v. Texas Television 139 F.3d 494C.A.5 (Tex.), (5th Cir. 1998), at

ccnv Supra note 147, at 2168 & 732.

For instance, in the case William v. Weisser, the ownership of the work was only for the employed professor. See infra note 169.

Mexican Federal Author's right Law Art 84.

Carter v. Helmsley Spear 71 F. 3d, C.A.2 (n.y.), 1995. (2nd Cir. 1995). See at 85 & 86.

Circular 9, See supra note 156.

Assaf Jacob. 2008. tort made for hire - reconsidering the ccnv case. Preliminary Draft, Later version pending. See at 1. Available at: http://works.bepress. com/assaf_jacob/1.

Id. at. 1 & 2.

A software program created within the scope of his or her duties by a staff programmer for Creative Computer Corporation.

Circular 9, supra note 156.

William v. Weisser, 273 Cal. App. 3d 726 Cal. Rptr. 542, (Cal. Ct. App. 1969) at 739, 742.

Nimmer, supra note 123, at 50.

ccnv case, supra note 148, at 151.

Brown v. Cosby 433 F. Supp. 1331 d.c.Pa. 1977. (Distr. Ct. 1977) see at 1343 & 1344.

nimmer, supra note 123 at 51.

In comparative labor law, the employer usually has to pay high interests for not paying salaries. For instance, In Colombia if an employer does not pay the employees its monthly salary, the law 789 of 2002 establishes that the employer will have to pay the employee two times of the salary and for two years, and after that time a financial interest will be charged. Thus, another policy question for debate is if labor law illegal behaviors can be punished by affecting other type of rights, like in the present cases, IP rights.

Art. 25 of the Colombian Constitution reads: *"Art. 25* - El trabajo es un derecho y una obligación social y goza, *en todas sus modalidades* (All forms of employment), de la

e.g. In the United States what is known as '*work for commission*' may be included within the work made for hire 101 provision. See supra note 125.

"Art. 61.- El Estado protegerá la propiedad intelectual por el tiempo y mediante las formalidades que establezca la ley".

Colombian Labor Law Code, See supra note 8.

The real conditions of a legal relationship prevail over the forms that the parties select. Thus, it is a recognized principle of labor law that even if parties sign other types of agreements, if the three elements mentioned above are present, the contract is deemed to be a labor law contract. See supra note 5, at 302.

Colombian Civil Code of 1873

Colombian Commercial Code of 1971

Law of State's Contracts # 80 of 1993. Art "3. Contrato de prestación de servicios… En ningún caso estos contratos generan relación laboral ni prestaciones sociales y se celebrarán por el término estrictamente indispensable".

Colombia Labor Law Code in its Articles 58 provides an obligation for the employee of not disclosing confidential information to third parties. In Article 62 (8) it is stated that revealing trade secrets and confidential information can lead to termination of the labor law contract. It is important to clarify that trade secrets and know-how are different concepts, but the Colombian provision refers to both. Thus, the employee will have to show loyalty to his employer by not revealing to third parties this kind of information.

Article 20 Author's Right Law number 23 of 1982.

It is important to note that article 20 starts with the word 'authors', this is without doubt an example of an author's right provision where there is no need to distinguish the transfer of the moral rights as it is implied that the moral rights are inalienable and the author or authors will retain them.

Despite the fact that the Author's right Law recognizes other types of Moral Rights, these are the only moral rights that the law recognizes to the author that creates a work under a contract to provide services.

Zapata lópez Fernando. El derecho de Autor y la Marca. Universidad Externado de Colombia. Revista de Propiedad Intelectual. Centro de Porpiedad Intelectual Primer

Semestre 2001. Revista 2, at 21

Article 183 Colombian Author's Right Law number 23 of 1982.

Id.

Zapata, supra note 187, at 9

Id, at 9. This opinion has been criticized in the opinion of the Colombian Consejo de Estado stating that a contract is a fact, so a presumption can exist. See infra note 201 at 14

Zapata, supra note 187 at 9.

Carlos Hernán Godoy. El Contrato Laboral y de Prestacion de Servicios ¿Herramienta Idónea Para La Transferencia de Derechos?. Conferencia para el Semniario Internacional organizado por la pontificia Universidad Javeriana, at 7.

Id, at 7. The law 57 of 1887, is the Colombian law to solve conflicts between laws. Article 5 (1) states that when there are incompatible provision within the law codes, the legal provisions that refer to an specific matter will prevail over the ones that have a general character.

Id, at 7.

Id, at 9.

Id, at 13.

Id, at 15. 198. Id, at 14.

The literal translation in English of *Consejo de Estado* will be *State adviser.* This organ is the head of the administrative Jurisdiction in Colombia. One of its functions is to give opinions on legal questions that the government makes. The initiative to consult this issue came from the Minister of Justice. It is important to clarify that despite the fact that usually the citizens, courts and other institutions follow these opinions, they are not binding and only constitute recommendations. See Juan Carlos Galindo Vácha, Lecciones de Derecho Procesal Administrativo, Publicado por Pontificia Universidad Javeriana, 2006. See at 190.

Consejera Ponente Susana montes, consultancy number 1538 of October 23 of 2003.

of having a labor agreement the employer can receive the economic rights on the work, and there is no need to fulfill the requirements of article 183.[201]

Id, at 7.

Id, at 10.

Id, at 15.

Id, at 18.

Id, at 13.

Riveros, supra 22, at 124.

Id. at 124.

dnda, Consultancy # 12879 2001. at 56.

For the application of this Principle in the United States, see supra 1, at 222.

lipzyc, delia, Derechos de Autor y Derechos Conexos. Ediciones unesco at 93. 211. Id. at 93.

plazas, Arcadio, Estudio sobre derecho de autor, reforma legal Colombiana, Bogotá, Temis, 1984, at 220.

Id. at 220.

Id, at 220.

Id, at 220.

Zapata, supra note 187.

Article 91 Colombian Author's Right Law # 23 of 1982.

See works created by public servants in Germany in Chapter V (H).

See supra note 124.

See supra note 31.

See art 20 Colombian Author's Right Law. 222. See article 69 (b) German Copyright Act.

See articles 29 & 30 Colombian Author's Right Law. Regarding Legal Persons article 27 establishes a term of 30 years after the first publication of the work.

See article 64 German Copyright Act.

See supra note 132.

See dietz, supra note 48.

See Kirchberger, supra note 95.

See dietz, supra note 29.

See supra note 218.

See supra note 56.

See supra note 163.

See supra 179.

See supra note 166.

LIST OF WORKS CITED

List of Cited Statutes, Agreements, Conventions and Court Cases

German Civil Code of 18 of August of 1896.

German Copyright Law of 9 September 1965.

German Employees Inventions Act of January 18 2002.

E.C. Directive 91/250 on the legal Protection of Computer Programs.

Spanish Employees' Statute of 1995. Real Decreto Legislativo 1/1995, de 24 de marzo, por el que se aprueba el texto refundido de la Ley del Estatuto de los Trabajadores.

French Copyright Law of 1972.

United States Copyright Act of 1909.

United States Copyright Act of 1976.

United States Restatement of Agency law of 1958.

Mexican Federal Author's right Law of 1996.

Colombian Constitution of 1991.

Colombian Civil Code of 1873.

Colombian Commercial Code of 1971.

Colombian Labor Law Code. Decreto Ley No 2663 del 5 de agosto de 1950.

Colombian Law of State's Contracts number 80 of 1993.

Colombian Author's Right Law number 23 of 1982

Decision of the German Federal Court of Justice (bgh) of June 17 of 1992, (vgl. hierzu bgh grur 1992, 697, 698 F Alf).

Decision of the German Supreme Court (rgz). Case reference: 153,1/8.

Decision of the German Federal Court of Justice bgh grur 1974, 480/483.

Dillman v. White, 102 Fed. 892 (C.C.D. Mass 1900).

Bratlleboro Publishing Co. v. Winmill Publishing Corp, 369 F.2d 565 (2d Cir 1966).

Siegel v. National Periodical Publications, Inc., 508 F.2d 909 (2d Cir. 1974).

Murray v. Gelderman 566 F. 2d 1307 (5th Cir. 1978).

Scherr v. Universal Match Corp., 417 F.2d 497 (2d Cir. 1969).

Evans Newton Inc. v. Chicago Systems Software, 793 F.2d 889 (7th Cir. 1986).

Brunswick Beacon v. Schock-Hopchas Publishing Co. 810 F. 2d 410 (4th Cir. 1987).

Easter Seal Society for Crippled Children and Adults of Louisiana, Inc v. Playboy Enterprises. 815 F. 2d 323 (5th Cir. 1987).

Quintanilla v. Texas Television 139 F.3d 494 C.A.5 (Tex.), (5th Cir. 1998).

Carter v. Helmsley Spear 71 F. 3d, C.A.2 (N.Y.) (2nd Cir. 1995).

William v. Weisser, 273 Cal. App. 3d 726 Cal. Rptr. 542, (Cal. Ct. App. 1969).

May vs Morganelii-Heumann & Associates. 618 F2D 1363 C.A.Cal., (9th Cir. 1980).

Brown VS Cosby 433 F. Supp. 1331(Distr. Ct. 1977).

Consultancy Colombian Consejo de Estado, Consultancy number 1538 of October 23 of 2003. Consejera Ponente Susana montes.

Consultancy of the Colombian Direction of Author's Right (dnda), Consultancy

n.º 12879 2001.

list of cited articles and books

Assaf Jacob (2008). Tort Made for Hire - Reconsidering The ccnv Case. Preliminary Draft, Later version pending. Available at: http://works.bepress.com/ assaf_jacob/1.

Christine Kirchberger, Ulrika nyh, Silvina penaloza, Hanna Sepanen and Kerli Tults (2002). Ownership of the Copyright and the Patent Right in Works Created by Employees. Finland, Sweden, Austria, UK, Estonia, and Argentina. Sanna Wolk (ed.).

Cordova, Efrén (1997). Naturaleza y Elementos del Contrato de Trabajo. México. unam, Serie B, Estudios Doctrinales Núm. 188. dietz, Adolf (2000). German Chapter of the book. Compilated by Nimmer, Melville. International Copyright Law and Practice. b. volume 2 1997/2000.

dreier (1991). The Council Directive of 14 May 1991 on the Legal Protection of Computer Programs. 9 eipr.

dreier (1993). The international Development of Copyright protection for Computer programs.

dreier, Schulze (2006). Urheberrechtsgesetz 2 auflage.

El derecho del Trabajo en España. Ideologías Jurídicas y Contrato de Trabajo. Madrid, Instituto de Estudios Sociales (1981).

Galindo Vácha, Juan Carlos (2006). Lecciones de Derecho Procesal Administrativo. Bogotá: Pontificia Universidad Javeriana.

Ganea, peter; Christopher Heath and Hiroshi Saito (ed.) (2005). Japanese Copyright Law. Writings in honour of Gerhard Schricker. Kluwer Law International.

Godoy, Carlos Hernán (s.f.). "El Contrato Laboral y de Prestacion de Servicios ¿Herramienta Idónea Para La Transferencia de Derechos?", en Conferencia para el Seminario Internacional organizado por la pontificia Universidad Javeriana.

Goldstein, paul (2008). International Intellectual property law. Cases and Materilas. New York: Foundation. 2D.

Krasser (1999). Urheberrecht in Arbeits. Dienst- und Aufragsverhaeltnissen.

lehman (1988). The legal protection of Computer Programs in Germany: A Summary of the present situation.

lipzyc, delia (1993). Derechos de Autor y Derechos Conexos. Ediciones unesco.

lowenheim (2002). Schricker Urheberrecht Kommentar 3. Auflage at 1353 section

15.(2002) martín Valverde, A.; F. Rodríguez- Sañudo y J. García murcia (2005). Derecho del Trabajo. Madrid: Ed. Tecnos, 14 Edición.

National Labour Law Profile: Federal Republic of Germany. Contributed by liliane Jung. Last update, April 2001. At http://www.ilo.org/public/english/ dialogue/ifpdial/ info/national/ger.htm.

Nimmer, melville (2000). International Copyright Law and Practice. B. Volume 2 1997/2000. United States Chapter. o'meara, William (1982). "Works made for Hire" under the Copyright Act of 1976.

Aus: Creighton Law Review. Vol. 15, 1981 - 1982, 2. oit. Contratos de Trabajo, at http:// www.ilo.org/public/spanish/dialogue/themes/ ce.htm#ci.

olenhusen v., a. G. (2002). der Urheber- und Leistungsrechtsschutz der Arbeitehmeraehnlichen Personen, grur 2002, book 1. plazas, Arcadio (1984). Estudio sobre derecho de autor, reforma legal Colombiana. Bogotá: Temis.

Riveros lara, Juan pablo (1995). Derecho de Autor en Colombia. Ed Hojas e Ideas.

Rojahn, Urheber (2002). In Arbeits – Oder Dienstverhaeltnissen In Urheberrecht Kommentar.

Scholz (1993). Implementation of the European Community Software Directive in Germany. Copyright World.

Schricker. (2006) Urheberrecht Kommentar 3. Auflage.

Garlock, Steve E (1988). The work made for hire doctrine under the copyright Act of 1976: What about the independent contractor? Washington University Law Quarterly vol 66.423.

United States Copyright Office Circular 9. See at http://www.copyright.gov/circs/circ9.html.

United States Copyright Office, Circular 15 (a), Duration of Copyright, see at: http://www.copyright.gov/circs/circ15a.html.

United States Copyright Office. Circular 1. Notice of Copyright, at http://www.copyright.gov/circs/circ1.html#noc.

Valdés Alonso, Alberto (2001). Propiedad Intelectual y Relación de Trabajo: la transmisión de los Derechos de Propiedad Intelectual a través del Contrato de Trabajo: Artistas, Programadores Informáticos y Producción Audiovisual De. Civitas, 1ª ed.

Yu du and matthew murphy. mmlc Group. Intellectual Property in the Employer and Employee Relationship in China. At: http://www.hg.org/article. asp?id=5341.

Zapata lópez Fernando (2001). "El derecho de Autor y la Marca", en Revista de Propiedad Intelectual. Universidad Externado de Colombia. Centro de Porpiedad Intelectual Primer Semestre 2001. Revista2

4
CHAPTER

COMPANIES ON THEIR PATHS TO JUSTICE: HOW SMALL AND MEDIUM-SIZED ENTERPRISES IN THE NETHERLANDS DEAL WITH POTENTIAL LEGAL PROBLEMS

Marnix T. Croes

Keywords: Small and medium-sized enterprises, paths to justice, legal service providers

INTRODUCTION

The late CEO of Apple, Steve Jobs, took Apple's business very personally. Walter Isaacson, Jobs' biographer, relates in his book how this exceptionally influential innovator of the computer and communications industry never got over his anger when Microsoft's Bill Gates, with whom he was working at the time to develop software for Apple's Macintosh computer, simply copied the basic ideas of the Macintosh graphical user interface – with windows, icons and point-and-click navigation – and turned it into Windows. It was November 1983, the dawn of a new computer age, and Jobs gave Gates a piece of his mind: '"You're ripping us off!" he shouted. "I trusted you, and now you're stealing from us!"'[1] Given that Apple had based the Macintosh operating system on ideas first developed by Xerox PARC, this was a rather bold claim to make. Nevertheless, a string of lawsuits was soon to follow.[2] In 2010 more or less the same thing happened with Apple's iPhone, this time with Google as the proverbial bad

Citation: Croes, M.T., (2012). Companies on their Paths to Justice: How Small and Medium-Sized Enterprises in the Netherlands Deal with Potential Legal Problems. Utrecht Law Review. 8(1), pp.51–77. DOI: http://doi.org/10.18352/ulr.180.

guy. Isaacson recounts how Jobs told him about a lawsuit that Apple had just started against smart phone maker HTC for copying several features as well as the look and feel of the iPhone. This lawsuit was in no small part indirectly aimed at Google, the company that produces Android, the operating system for smart phones and tabloid computers that HTC used. 'Our lawsuit is saying, "Google, you fucking ripped off the iPhone, wholesale ripped us off." Grand theft. I will spend my last dying breath if I need to, and I will spend every penny of Apple's $ 40 billion in the bank, to right this wrong. I'm going to destroy Android, because it's a stolen product. I'm willing to go to thermonuclear war on this.' When Google's CEO Eric Schmidt tried to settle the matter a few days later, Jobs told him in colourful language that Google was in the thieving business: '"We've got you red-handed," he told Schmidt. "I'm not interested in settling. I don't want your money. If you offer me $ 5 billion, I won't want it. I've got plenty of money. I want you to stop using our ideas in Android, that's all I want."'[3]

In the two cases presented above, the business conflicts Apple had with other companies quickly turned into lawsuits. Jobs was not interested in settling, nor in money, but he wanted his competitors to stop using his ideas, probably also because he was infuriated by the ugliness with which he thought they were implementing them. At the same time Jobs was not shy in risking lawsuits in his own dealings with other companies. Isaacson: 'When he decided that a division of Airborne Express wasn't delivering spare parts quickly enough, he ordered an Apple manager to break the contract. When the manager protested that doing so could lead to a lawsuit, Jobs replied, "Just tell them if they fuck with us, they'll never get another fucking dime from this company, ever."'

Taking a step back to see the bigger picture, one wonders if the story of Apple's troubles is exemplary. Do companies have their potential legal problems usually with other companies and is the legal recourse a common remedy? And if not, in what way do companies find solutions to these problems? What kind of conflicts do companies have anyway, with whom, and what do their CEOs think of the options they have to solve them? For sociologists of law, these kinds of questions are the gist of their professional life. Perhaps because they are neither numerous nor influential, the relevance of asking these questions is not self-evident. This is especially the case when one considers that the more numerous and more influential lawyers often seclude themselves from the murky world of the subjects of the law, choosing instead the esoteric sphere of the law and how judges apply it to the cases they decide. Nonetheless, knowledge about how subjects of the law use or do not use the regulations that lawmakers devise to influence their behaviour is useful for lawyers as well. To understand what drives the demand for court cases, for instance; or to recognize why the effects of certain legal arrangements (threaten to) turn out differently than hoped for or expected, sometimes compelling subjects of the law to ignore it, lawmakers to change it, or judges to apply it in a different way; or to understand what the effects of verdicts are and in what way they influence the future behaviour of subjects of the law.

In the case of private citizens and the potential legal problems that they face, the interest of scientists who are not sociologists of law is growing. Since the American Bar Association conducted a survey on the legal needs of American citizens in 19946 a wealth of information has been gathered worldwide on the problems that citizens face and the ways they chose to deal with them.[7] Unfortunately, this is not yet the case when it comes to the different kinds of problems that companies face when doing business. The literature on this topic is sketchy at best, which is quite remarkable when one considers the amounts of money involved. There is some research into the costs of litigation, which shows that the average Fortune 200 company spent $ 133 million on litigation in 2008, excluding awards and settlements.[8] Including these costs the Fortune 500 companies are supposed to have spent an estimated total of $ 210 billion on litigation in 2006, an amount that equals about one third of their annual after tax profits.[9] In spite of these amounts of money involved, little is still known about what kinds of problems companies have, with which type of opponent, and how they resolve those problems. That the Fortune 500 companies settle 98.2% of their problems and obtain a verdict in only 1.8% of them,[10] makes one aware of the fact that simply studying judicial decisions to learn more about the problems companies face will give one a highly selective view. To learn more, we have to choose another approach.

This article aims to answer some of the questions raised above by dealing with the conflicts that Dutch small and medium-sized enterprises (SMEs) have. SMEs are companies that employ at most 99 employees. Jointly they make up a little over 99% of the companies in the Netherlands. In 2009, the Scientific Research and Documentation Centre (WODC) of the Dutch Ministry of Safety and Justice published a study into the kinds of problems Dutch SMEs experience and the ways they deal with them.[11] The study was based on two surveys among the members of the SME panel of EIM Business & Policy

Research[12] in 2006. A total of 2,300 decision makers (mostly managers) in as many SMEs participated in this panel. The first survey concerned the extent to which companies engaged the services of legal assistance providers in 2006 and the serious problems they faced in that year. By serious problems were meant difficulties such as conflicts over working conditions, conflicts over sold products or services, or conflicts over permits or taxes. It was up to the decision maker involved to decide whether their company's problem could be categorized as 'serious' or not. After it became clear that the decision makers reported many problems that appeared to be of minor importance, it was decided to focus the second survey entirely on the potential legal problems they had experienced in 2006. This group of problems was explicitly identified as the subgroup of serious problems that, based on the subjective evaluation of the decision maker, could have resulted or actually did result in legal procedures. Besides, this second survey also inquired into the nature of the opposing party in the conflict and the kind of legal assistance that the decision makers relied upon.

The article is organized as follows. Below, the second section will provide a brief overview of the empirical research into the kinds of problems companies encounter and the ways they choose to solve them. The third section introduces the SMEs in the Netherlands; the fourth section deals with the incidence and frequency of serious problems that SMEs in the Netherlands experience. The fifth section deals with the incidence and frequency of potential legal problems, while the sixth section will examine the nature of the opposing parties. The seventh section deals with the co-occurrence of serious and potential legal problems. The eighth section examines the background characteristics of SMEs and the incidence of serious and potential legal problems encountered. The ninth section deals with the engagement of legal assistance in case of serious and potential legal problems; the tenth section with the SMEs that suffered problems but did not engage legal service providers. The eleventh section examines the customary way of terminating potential legal problems, while the twelfth section will deal with the experiences with the legal service providers. The thirteenth and concluding section will draw attention to some similarities and dissimilarities between the Dutch study and the other previously introduced empirical studies.

COMPANIES ON THEIR PATHS TO JUSTICE

What we do know about the kinds of problems companies encounter and the ways they deal with them is limited. It is clear, however, that large companies try to avoid bringing their problems to court,[13] especially when their business relations are (meant to be) long term.[14] In addition, they base their international business policies – in part – on differences in the choice of contract law and jurisdiction.[15] Some of the literature further suggests that family companies deal with problems in a different way than non-family companies, relying less on the courts and official Alternative Dispute Resolution (ADR) procedures and more on informal forums and arrangements.[16] There are a few modern exceptions to this general rule of sketchiness and three of them will be introduced below: a survey-based report on intellectual property enforcement in smaller UK firms,[17] dealing with the kinds of problems that Apple faced and faces with Microsoft and Google; a survey-based report on the demand for and the supply of legal and related services in Hong Kong;[18] and a survey-based report on the disputes experienced by small businesses in Australia.[19]

Intellectual property disputes in the UK

The report on intellectual property enforcement in British firms dates from 2010. In total, 1,858 micro firms (0-9 employees) and SMEs (in this report: 10-249 employees) that could be characterized as patentees, trade markers, non-patentees (from patent-intensive industries), non-trade markers (from trademark-intensive industries) or firms in copyright/design-intensive industries were contacted. The online survey received 170 responses, representing a 9.1% response rate. The final response rate was raised to 20.1% through the addition of 225 responses to the follow-up telephone survey.

Of the respondents 25% indicated that they had been involved in intellectual property disputes, defined as any infringement, whether or not this ended in legal proceedings, during the previous five years. The possibility of problems was not evenly spread: 40% of patent-holding firms had experienced a dispute in the previous five years, while the same was true of 34% of firms with trade marks. By contrast, firms that did not use patents or trade marks were much less likely to have a dispute (estimated at only 7% of firms in patent-intensive and 5% of firms in trade mark-intensive industries). In the creative industries, which are more likely to use copyright or design rights, around 20% had experienced an intellectual property dispute

Respondents to the online survey gave information on 46 intellectual property disputes. To solve the problem, an exchange of letters between solicitors was the most common solution attempted. This was done in 37 cases, resolving 15 of them (40%). Subsequent studies of Patents Court listings showed that the total number of intellectual property cases that come to court is small (less than 40 per year on average from 2003 to 2009). This number is tiny compared to the number of firms operating in the economy. Many cases never come to court.[20] Apart from that, a settlement occurs in about 40% of all listed cases. The court only adjudicates in 50% of the cases listed.

High-level negotiation between firms was used in 15 instances. Other methods such as mediation, the use of the UK Intellectual Property Office (IPO), and small claims or county courts were rarely used. Only 6 of the 46 disputes ended up in the High Court. Overall, when firms were asked whether they were 'satisfied' with the outcome of the dispute, 80% said they were

SME disputes in Hong Kong

For the Chinese study into the demand for and the supply of legal and related services in Hong Kong a representative sample of 3,337 SMEs (companies with less than 100 employees) was drawn from the Central Register of Establishments maintained by the Census and Statistics Department. The companies were questioned by mail and face to face about problems or disputes which were difficult to solve and that they encountered in 2005 or, when they did not encounter any during that year, they were questioned about the problems in the time period 2001-2004. A total of 1,813 companies participated in the research

On the whole, 30.1% of the responding companies experienced at least one problem or dispute which was difficult to solve in 2005. Another 15.8% did not experience such problems or disputes in 2005, but did so during 2001-2004. This brings the total of companies that experienced problems during the time period of 2001-2005 to 45.9%.[21] These companies reported on average 4.7 problems for the time period under scrutiny.[22] About two thirds (67.2%) of these problems were, according to the respondents, actually unimportant. Another 10.4% was deemed important without any action being taken while in the remaining 22.3% the problem or dispute was deemed important and action was taken. Table 1 provides an overview of the kinds of problems and disputes, the percentage of companies that encountered them (incidence) during the time period under scrutiny, the relative frequencies of all them and only the important problems or disputes.

Slightly less than one third (31.3%) of the important problems or disputes involved consumers of the companies under study. A further 20.6% involved business acquaintances. Employees accounted for 18.6% of these problems, business corporations for 14.5%, private individuals for 8.5% and government departments for 3.6%. In 48.5% of the important problems or disputes the Chinese companies engaged the help of legal service providers.

Table 1: Incidence and relative frequency of problems and disputes among Hong Kong SMEs (N=881).

Type of problem	Incidence (N=881)	Relative frequency of all problems (N=4,311)	Relative frequency of important problems (N=1,452)
Labour disputes or related problems	19.8	11.4	10.6
Renting of premises by company	13.2	4.4	6.0
Renting out of company properties	4.3	2.0	2.1
Properties owned by company	6.5	3.7	2.7
Business-related matters	43.9	35.3	30.0
Other money matters	53.9	25.5	34.7
Intellectual property	10.1	4.1	3.8
Injuries and health problems suffered by employees	15.1	6.5	5.6
Government departments/government officials	11.1	5.4	3.9
Others	2.5	1.8	0.7
Total		100	100

Source: Asia Consulting Group Ltd., Study on the Demand for and Supply of Legal and Related Services, 2008.

SME disputes in Australia

The research in Australia was initiated by the Australian Government's Department of Innovation, Industry, Science and Research. The aim of the project was to investigate to what extent small businesses (less than 20 employees) in Australia have an unmet demand for dispute resolution procedures. To answer this question, a telephone survey and interviews were held to determine the incidence of businessto-business disputes experienced by small businesses and to identify the mechanisms to resolve them. A total of 2,007 companies were questioned, about one seventh (15.1%)[23] reported having had serious business disputes during the past 5 years. Of all the companies 1.5% reported having had routine and minor problems, not something to be concerned about; 2.3% reported having had potentially serious but easily resolved problems without any escalation; 6.6% reported having had potentially serious problems but escalation was avoided due to potential costs; 2.0% reported having had problems that were serious enough to consider utilising third-party intervention, but they did not actually do so; 1.8% reported having been faced with problems that required intervention by a third party or self-representation in formal proceedings; 4.6% reported having had problems which were sufficiently serious to result in legal action being taken by either business involved in the dispute

Regarding the nature of the disputes, of the 9% of respondents which had experienced a serious disagreement (that necessitated the use of a third party or legal action, or having to consider such action) 65% indicated that it had been a disagreement over payment for goods or services; 30% indicated that it was over other contractual obligations (excluding payment, retail tenancy and franchising issues); and 7% indicated that it was another issue. Of the 131 companies which had a dispute and sought third party support, 58% engaged a lawyer for either advice (32%), to initiate legal proceedings (28%) or to defend against initiated proceedings (8%).[24] A quarter

(26%) of the companies that underwent legal proceedings had their case heard in court.

SMEs, disputes and empirical research

Common themes in the three empirical studies are the incidence and frequency of the problems that (small) businesses encounter and the way they try to solve them. In a research field where empirical research is scarce, these are sensible topics to start with. At the same time the three studies show, however, that they have limitations: they are focused on one kind of problem, like the UK study; they have a research design that makes it difficult to say anything about the frequency of the problems encountered, like the Chinese study;[25] or they focus on just one kind of opposing party, like the Australian study. The Dutch study that is presented below is not the first of its kind, but it does a better job in reporting on the incidence and frequency of problems that SMEs experience: it deals with all kinds of problems which SMEs encounter, with all opposing parties that SMEs can face and its research design makes it possible to draw clear conclusions also regarding the frequency of the problems encountered.

SMEs in the Netherlands

In the Netherlands, more than 99% of all companies are SMEs. They are, however, not evenly spread over all sectors of the economy. Table 2 below shows the number of companies in the Netherlands as of 1 January 2006, subdivided by their number of workers and the sector of the economy in which they are active. This table makes clear that more than 91% of all companies in the Netherlands have up to 9 workers and that companies with more than 99 workers are actually not numerous: only 6,615 companies met this criterion The companies in the SME panel of EIM did not come from every sector of the Dutch economy. In Table 2, the numbers relating to the sectors and size categories from which they came are printed in bold type. As the table makes clear, important sectors of the economy that are missing in our research groups are agriculture, education and health care. For the latter two sectors, many of the companies involved would have turned out to be state-owned or state-financed organizations. That is not what we are really interested in here, since we will focus on the private, not the public segment of the economy. The most important economic sector to which the results of the WODC study do not pertain is therefore agriculture.

Table 2: Number of companies in the Netherlands by size and sector, 2006.

Sector	Number of companies	Up to 9 workers	Between 10 and 99 workers	More than 99 workers
Agriculture	93,365	91,600	1,735	30
Fishing	720	685	30	0
Mining	215	130	70	10
Industry	46,605	**36,170**	**9,130**	1,300
Public service corporations	550	480	25	45
Building sector	81,690	**74,465**	**6,885**	340
Repair sector, trade	164,590	**149,465**	**14,310**	810
(Hotel and) catering (industry)	36,650	**33,105**	**3,465**	85
Transportation, storage, communication	27,925	**23,605**	**3,945**	370

Sector	Number of companies	Up to 9 workers	Between 10 and 99 workers	More than 99 workers
Finance	14,665	**13,525**	**1,020**	125
Rental services, business services	158,650	**147,895**	**9,865**	875
Public administration	1,065	330	275	460
Education	20,500	18,060	1,585	850
Health care	42,870	39,320	2,525	1,030
Culture, recreation, other services	56,320	**52,580**	**3,460**	270
Totals	*746,365*	*681,430*	*58,325*	*6,615*

Source: WODC data file.

Since the members of the SME panel are not representative with regard to their size and the sector of the economy in which they are active, weighting was used to correct the disproportion this generates. All figures mentioned below are therefore weighted.

INCIDENCE AND FREQUENCY OF SERIOUS PROBLEMS

Many SMEs face serious problems. A total of 1,298 (61.9%) of the 2,097 surveyed companies experienced serious problems in 2006. In addition, many SMEs face these problems quite regularly: per company that experienced serious problems, the number of these serious problems averaged 12.7 in 2006. For all companies, including the ones that did not experience problems in 2006, this average is 7.9 serious problems. Table 3 presents an overview of the kinds of serious problems that SMEs experienced in 2006 and the frequency with which they encountered them. A distinction is made between nine kinds of problems: problems relating to the payment for goods and services sold; problems relating to the quality, quantity and delivery time of goods and services sold; problems relating to working conditions, wages and the laying off of staff; problems relating to applying for permits; problems relating to taxes, customs and duties; problems relating to the payment for goods and services bought; problems relating to the quality, quantity and delivery time of goods and services bought; problems relating to environmental pollution, stench and noise; and other kinds of problems. Regarding this last-mentioned category of problems, we only know whether companies encountered them, not the frequency with which this occurred. As Table 3 shows, the most frequently experienced serious problems were problems concerning the payment for goods supplied or services provided by the SME (45.4% of the serious problems); the quality, quantity or delivery time of goods or services purchased (16.5% of the serious problems); and the quality, quantity or delivery time of goods supplied or services provided by the SME (9.2% of the serious problems).

Yet, when we focus on the percentage of companies that experienced different kinds of serious problems, the order is slightly different. Serious problems regarding the payment for goods and services sold (experienced by 36.7% of the SMEs) and serious problems regarding the quality, quantity and delivery time of goods and services purchased (experienced by 12.6% of the SMEs) still rank first and second. But in third place, we find serious problems regarding the payment for goods and services bought (experienced by 13.9% of the SMEs). In both cases, however, the first and second positions in the ranking order are taken up by what amounts to problems caused by the 'other' party. This either concerns the unsatisfactory behaviour of the trading partner regarding payment for deliveries by the SME of the respondent, or the unsatisfactory behaviour of the trading partner regarding the quality, quantity and delivery time for goods or services that the SME of the respondent has ordered.

Table 3: Incidence and frequency of serious problems in 2006 (N=2,097, weighted).[26]

Kind of problem	Percentage of companies	Percentage of problems	Average number of problems per company (N=2,097)	Average experienced problem frequency (N=1,298)
Payment for goods and services sold	36.7	45.4	3.6	10.1
Quality, quantity and delivery time of goods and services sold	8.3	9.2	0.7	9.4
Working conditions, wages and the laying off of workers	10.8	2.2	0.2	1.6
Applying for permits	11.9	4.3	0.3	2.9
Taxes, customs and duties	11.5	8.8	0.7	6.3
Payment for goods and services bought	13.9	8.8	0.7	5.3
Quality, quantity and delivery time of goods and services bought	12.6	16.5	1.3	11.1
Environmental pollution, stench and noise	5.2	3.8	0.3	6.0
Other problems	7.5	(at least) 1.0	0.1	1.0
Totals	61.9	100	7.9	12.7

Source: WODC data file.

Table 4 provides a further insight into the spread of the frequency with which the SMEs experienced serious problems in 2006. Apparently, several kinds of these problems were experienced by the majority of the SMEs not more than once a year. This is true for problems regarding working conditions, wages and the laying off of staff; regarding environmental pollution, stench and noise; and regarding applying for permits. Other kinds of serious problems occurred much more often, especially problems relating to the quality, quantity and delivery time of goods and services bought. About one fifth of the 245 SMEs encountered them more than ten times during 2006. Given that, comparatively speaking, the number of companies that did experience this kind of problem was not very high, the average number of problems per company had to be high. And with 11.1 problems per company it was. Another type of serious problem that companies experienced often concerned the payment for goods and services sold. With an average number of problems per SME of 10.1 and 15.1% experiencing them more than ten times, this type of problem ranks second. However, since many more companies faced this kind of problem, 741 to be precise, the total number of these problems is much higher.

Table 4: Percentage of serious problems experienced by SMEs in 2006 (N=1,298, weighted)

Type of problem	Number of problems experienced by percentage of SMEs							Average experienced problem frequency
	1	2	3	4	5	6-10	>10	
Payment for goods and services sold	25.8	19.2	12.4	7.8	7.7	12.1	15.1	10.1
Quality, quantity and delivery time of goods and services sold	27.9	16.3	12.5	2.1	10.8	12.4	18.0	9.4
Working conditions, wages and the laying off of workers	71.7	17.8	6.4	0.8	0.7	2.4	0.1	1.6
Applying for permits	51.1	18.1	15.5	3.0	4.0	6.3	2.0	2.9
Taxes, customs and duties	40.5	25.9	10.3	2.9	9.9	4.4	6.1	6.3
Payment for goods and services bought	31.1	25.2	9.5	7.2	13.3	8.1	5.7	5.3
Quality, quantity and delivery time of goods and services bought	16.9	16.2	11.0	5.1	12.2	19.0	19.6	11.1
Environmental pollution, stench and noise	66.9	14.9	4.9	6.2	0.9	0.8	5.3	6.0

Source: WODC data file.

INCIDENCE AND FREQUENCY OF POTENTIAL LEGAL PROBLEMS

Regarding the potential legal problems, the subgroup of serious problems that, based on the subjective evaluation of the decision maker, could have resulted or actually did result in legal procedures, it is striking that only 37.0% of the SMEs reported them. The frequency with which they had to deal with them is also considerably lower: 5.7 problems for the companies that had to deal with them and 2.1 for all the companies in our sample

Table 5: Incidence and frequency of potential legal problems (N=1,784, weighted).[27]

Kind of problem	Percentage of companies	Percentage of problems	Average number of problems per company (N=1,784)	Average experienced problem frequency (N=660)
Payment for goods and services sold	21.9	46.8	0.98	4.8
Quality, quantity and delivery time of goods and services sold	4.9	6.7	0.14	4.0
Working conditions, wages and the laying off of workers	6.8	4.4	0.09	1.5
Applying for permits	3.6	2.6	0.05	1.7
Taxes, customs and duties	3.5	2.2	0.05	1.5
Payment for goods and services bought	3.6	3.3	0.07	3.6
Quality, quantity and delivery time of goods and services bought	5.6	17.8	0.37	8.3
Liability for and settlement of damage	5.2	5.0	0.10	2.6
Serious kinds of crime and fraud	7.6	11.3	0.24	3.4
Totals	37.0	100	2.1	5.7

Source: WODC data file.

Table 5 gives an overview of the kinds of serious problems that SMEs experienced in 2006 and the frequency with which they were confronted with them. The distinction that has been made between kinds of problems is similar to the division presented above regarding the serious problems. There are, however, a few differences. We added 'liability for and settlement of damage' and 'serious kinds of crime and fraud' instead of 'environmental pollution, stench and noise' and 'other problems', because the first survey had clarified that few companies were confronted by serious problems belonging to the last two categories.

The largest group of potential legal problems relates to the payment for goods supplied or services provided (46.8% of the potential legal problems), followed by problems related to the quality, quantity or delivery time of goods or services purchased (17.8% of the potential legal problems), and problems related to serious forms of crime or fraud (11.3% of the potential legal problems). However, as was the case with the serious problems, when we focus on the percentage of companies that experienced the different kinds of potential legal problems, the order is slightly different. Potential legal problems regarding the payment for goods supplied or services provided still ranks first (experienced by 21.9% of the SMEs). Yet, the second position in this ranking order is taken up by serious kinds of crime and fraud (experienced by 7.6% of the SMEs). The third place is occupied by potential legal problems relating to working conditions, wages and the laying off of workers (experienced by 6.8% of the SMEs). Again, problems caused by 'other' parties dominate.

Table 6: Number of potential legal problems experienced by SMEs in 2006 (N=660, weighted).

Type of problem	Number of problems experienced by percentage of SMEs							Average experienced problem frequency
	1	2	3	4	5	6-10	>10	
Payment for goods and services sold	39.9	18.4	13.4	6.1	5.1	9.5	7.6	4.8
Quality, quantity and delivery time of goods and services sold	45.0	11.6	10.2	3.7	2.0	27.0	0.5	4.0
Working conditions, wages and the laying off of workers	72.9	16.0	7.8	0.6	2.7	0.1	0	1.5
Applying for permits	69.1	13.6	5.7	4.5	6.8	0.3	0	1.7
Taxes, customs and duties	70.0	21.7	1.0	4.0	3.1	0.3	0	1.5
Payment for goods and services bought	35.1	9.9	11.9	13.1	8.2	21.8	0	3.6
Quality, quantity and delivery time of goods and services bought	38.4	19.5	6.1	0.6	9.9	12.1	13.4	8.3
Liability for and settlement of damage	69.0	13.7	13.0	0.2	2.2	0.9	0.9	2.6
Serious kinds of crime and fraud	43.7	22.2	11.0	3.5	9.0	8.3	2.3	3.4

Source: WODC data file.

Table 6 provides a further insight into the spread of the frequency with which the SMEs experienced potential legal problems in 2006. As was the case with the serious problems, there are several kinds of potential legal problems where the majority of companies encountered them only once during 2006. This is true for potential legal problems relating to working conditions, wages and the laying off of staff; relating to taxes, customs and duties; relating to applying for permits, and relating to the liability for and settlement of damage. On average, the potential legal problems concerning the quality, quantity and delivery time of goods and services bought showed the highest average problem frequency, while 13.4% of the companies that experienced them encountered them more than ten times that year. It should be stressed, however, that only 12.1% of the SMEs reported having these problems. Although experienced less frequently per company that encountered them, potential legal problems regarding the payment for goods and services sold were reported by 55.2% of the SMEs that had problems.

With respect to both the serious and the potential legal problems, about three quarters of the problems concern the (payment for the) delivery or purchase of goods or services. This means that the 'normal' economic exchange is the most important source of the problems.

OPPOSING PARTIES

In Section 4 we stated that, according to our respondents, problems caused by 'other' parties dominate. In the second survey, more attention was paid to this opposing party. In most cases, a distinction was made between companies, private persons, the government and other organizations. In cases of specific potential legal problems that limit the kinds of potential opponents, such as problems regarding applications for permits or problems regarding taxes, duties and customs, which only allow for the government as the opposing party, no other parties were distinguished. In other cases, such as potential legal problems regarding working conditions, wages and the laying off of staff, or regarding serious kinds of crime and fraud, alternative opposing parties were distinguished. Table 7 presents an overview of the different types of potential legal problems that were experienced per opposing party.

Of the 3,597 potential legal problems reported in 2006 by the respondents, 54.6% consisted of problems with other companies; 19.5% of problems with private citizens; 6.7% of problems with the government; 4.9% of problems with employees; and 14.2% of problems with other parties (other organizations and the overlapping category 'legal entities other than the company's own employees', which relates exclusively to crime and fraud). Apart from the kinds of potential legal problems for which a company as an opponent does not apply, in Table 7 companies are always the most frequently met opposing party. Besides, companies also continuously rank first as the opposing party when we look at the incidence of the potential legal problems encountered. We can therefore conclude that companies are by far the most important source of potential legal problems for SMEs.

Table 7: Incidence and frequency of a potential legal problem per opposing party (N=1,784, weighted).

Type of problem	Opposing party	Companies with at least one problem in 2006 (N=660)	Potential legal problems (N=3,597)
		Percentage	Percentage
Payment for goods and services sold			
	Companies	14.1	28.5
	Private persons	7.4	16.5
	The government	0.5	1.2
	Other organizations	0.3	0.3
Quality, quantity and delivery time of goods and services sold			
	Companies	2.2	4.4
	Private persons	1.1	1.8
	The government	0.2	0.1
	Other organizations	0.1	0.6
Working conditions, wages and the laying off of workers			
	Employees	6.3	4.5
	Staff representatives	0.0	0
	Union	0.0	0
	The government	0.1	0.1
Applying for permits	The government	3.3	2.7
Taxes, customs and duties	The government	3.0	2.3
Payment for goods and services bought			
	Companies	1.8	3.1
	Private persons	0.1	0.1
	The government	0.2	0.3
	Other organizations	0	0
Quality, quantity and delivery time of goods and services bought			
	Companies	4.4	16.7
	Private persons	0.0	0
	The government	0.0	0
	Other organizations	0.1	1.8
Liability for and settlement of damage			
	Companies	2.0	1.8
	Private persons	1.5	1.1
	The government	0.2	0.1
	Other organizations	0.4	0.3
Serious kinds of crime and fraud			
	Employees	0.7	0.4
	Other legal bodies	6.0	11.3
Totals		37.0	100

Source: WODC data file.

RELATIONSHIPS BETWEEN SERIOUS AND POTENTIAL LEGAL PROBLEMS

As regards the incidence and frequency of the serious or potential legal problems with which they are faced, there are significant differences between SMEs. To a certain extent, these differences in encountering problems can be explained by the fact that the SMEs already had certain problems, which gave rise to new problems. For example, there is, statistically speaking, a significant relationship between the incidence of serious ($r=0.09$; $p< 0.01$; N=1,263) as well as potential legal ($r=0.34$; $p< 0.01$; N=660) problems about the quality, quantity and delivery time of goods or services purchased and payment for these goods or services. This relationship also exists between the frequency of these serious ($r=0.13$; $p< 0.05$; N=1,263) and potential legal ($r=0.21$; $p< 0.01$; N=660) problems. These relationships appear to be a matter of common sense: if an SME is not satisfied with a delivery, the likelihood that it will pay for it (in full and on time) decreases

Another example is the relationship between the incidence (r=0.27; p< 0.01; N=1,298) and frequency (0.35; p< 0.01; N=1,263) of serious problems concerning the quality, quantity and delivery time of both supplied and purchased goods and services. This relationship also exists between the incidence (r=0.18; p< 0.01; N=660) and frequency (r=0.10; p<0. 05; N=660) of potential legal problems regarding the quality, quantity and delivery time of supplied and purchased goods and services. This relationship is conceivable as well. After all, for the production of its goods or services, an SME depends on the performance of its suppliers. If there is a disruption in the performance of these suppliers, this will have consequences for the performance of the SME as well.

Below, four tables present the relationships between the different serious and potential legal problems. Tables 8 and 9 show the incidence and frequency of serious problems; Tables 10 and 11 the incidence and frequency of potential legal problems.

Table 8: Correlation matrix for the incidence of serious problems of SMEs in 2006 (N=1,298, weighted).[1]

Problem type	P2	P3	P4	P5	P6	P7	P8	P9
P1 Payment for goods and services delivered	0.14**	-0.05	-0.17**	-0.14**	-0.01	0.03	-0.10**	-0.08**
P2 Delivered goods and services, other	X	0.12**	-0.02	-0.05	0.07*	0.27**	-0.04	0.02
P3 Working conditions, wages, laying off		X	-0.01	-0.00	-0.04	0.04	-0.06*	0.03
P4 Applying for permits			X	-0.01	-0.06*	0.02	0.12**	0.02
P5 Taxes, customs and duties				X	-0.06*	-0.05	-0.05	-0.04
P6 Payment for goods and services sold					X	0.09**	-0.06*	0.02
P7 Sold goods and services, other						X	0.00	0.07**
P8 Environmental pollution, stench, noise							X	0.01
P9 Other								X

Source: WODC data file.

[1] Pearson correlation coefficients.

* = statistically significant at the 0.05 level (two-sided).

** = statistically significant at the 0.01 level (two-sided).

Table 9: Correlation matrix for the frequency of serious problems of SMEs in 2006 (N=1,263, weighted)[1]

Problem type	P2	P3	P4	P5	P6	P7	P8
P1 Payment for goods and services delivered	0.24**	0.07*	-0.09**	-0.01	0.13**	0.14**	-0.06*
P2 Delivered goods and services, other	X	0.21**	-0.02	0.02	0.06*	0.35**	-0.02
P3 Working conditions, wages, laying off		X	0.06*	0.05	-0.06	0.05	-0.01
P4 Applying for permits			X	0.00	-0.06*	0.06*	0.05
P5 Taxes, customs and duties				X	-0.03	-0.04	-0.05
P6 Payment for goods and services sold					X	0.13**	-0.05
P7 Sold goods and services, other						X	0.01
P8 Environmental pollution, stench, noise							X

Source: WODC data file.
[1] Pearson correlation coefficients.
* = statistically significant at the 0.05 level (two-sided).
** = statistically significant at the 0.01 level (two-sided).

Table 10: Correlation matrix for the incidence of potential legal problems of SMEs in 2006 (N=660, weighted).[1]

Problem type	P2	P3	P4	P5	P6	P7	P8	P9
P1 Payment for goods and services delivered	0.07	-0.25**	-0.03	-0.22**	0.02	-0.04	0.05	-0.18**
P2 Delivered goods and services, other	X	-0.08*	-0.00	0.04	0.05	0.18**	0.10*	-0.07
P3 Working conditions, wages, laying off		X	-0.03	-0.09*	-0.06	-0.11**	-0.01	0.01
P4 Applying for permits			X	0.05	0.11**	0.12**	0.04	0.05
P5 Taxes, customs and duties				X	0.05	0.05	-0.01	-0.01
P6 Payment for goods and services sold					X	0.34**	0.10*	-0.07
P7 Sold goods and services, other						X	0.06	-0.00
P8 Liability for damage							X	-0.02
P9 Crime and fraud								X

Source: WODC data file.
[1] Pearson correlation coefficients.
* = statistically significant at the 0.05 level (two-sided).
** = statistically significant at the 0.01 level (two-sided).

Table 11: Correlation matrix for the frequency of potential legal problems of SMEs in 2006 (N=660, weighted).[1]

Problem type	P2	P3	P4	P5	P6	P7	P8	P9
P1 Payment for goods and services delivered	0.03	-0.08*	0.03	-0.11**	0.03	0.06	0.05	0.03
P2 Delivered goods and services, other	X	-0.06	-0.06	-0.00	-0.05	0.10*	0.02	0.02
P3 Working conditions, wages, laying off		X	0.13**	-0.09*	0.02	-0.06	-0.01	-0.02
P4 Applying for permits			X	0.03	0.00	-0.03	0.01	0.01
P5 Taxes, customs and duties				X	-0.05	-0.03	0.03	0.07
P6 Payment for goods and services sold					X	0.21**	0.00	-0.07
P7 Sold goods and services, other						X	-0.02	-0.02
P8 Liability for damage							X	-0.49
P9 Crime and fraud								X

Source: WODC data file.
[1] Pearson correlation coefficients.
* = statistically significant at the 0.05 level (two-sided).
** = statistically significant at the 0.01 level (two-sided).

The four tables make it clear that the incidence and frequency of some kinds of serious or potential legal problems are more likely than others to be correlated. This is especially true for the incidence and frequency of problems, whether serious or potentially legal in nature, concerning the quality, quantity and delivery time of goods and services sold. As noted above, the fact that the production of goods and services by the SMEs depends on the behaviour of trading partners and can easily be disrupted is probably the reason why we see relatively many correlations here. On the other hand, a potential legal problem like crime and fraud shows few relationships with other problems. Only the incidence of this category of potential legal problems correlates statistically significantly with the incidence of potential legal problems regarding the payment for delivered goods and services. This relationship is negative, which probably means that some respondents had some difficulties in choosing whether their potential legal problem ought to be seen as a case of crime and fraud or as a case of deferred payment.

BACKGROUND CHARACTERISTICS AND THE INCIDENCE OF SERIOUS AND POTENTIAL LEGAL PROBLEMS

In order to gain more insight into the likelihood of the incidence of serious and potential legal problems, the role of some characteristics of companies was researched as well. These characteristics were: the sector of the economy in which the SME was active; the number of employed persons in 2006; the age of the company; the number of establishments of the SME; the degree of independence of the SME (whether or not the company was a branch or a franchise); its legal form; and whether the SME was a member of a trading association or not. With respect to these characteristics, Table 12 presents an overview of all the responding SMEs in the panel of EIM and the responding SMEs experiencing at least one serious problem in 2006. For the latter, the percentage of the category of the characteristics is given as well. Whether or not belonging to this category meant that the SME ran a statistically significant higher or lower risk of encountering serious problems is indicated as well.

Table 12: Characteristics of SMEs and the incidence of serious problems in 2006 (N=2,097, weighted).

Characteristics of the SME	Category	All SMEs (N=2,097)	SMEs with at least one serious problem in 2006 (N=1,298)	
		Percentage	Percentage	As a percentage of the category
Sector	Industry	8.2	9.0	68.0
	Building sector	14.4	16.0	68.6**
	Repair sector, trade	30.1	30.0	61.6
	(Hotel and) catering (industry)	6.8	6.2	57.0
	Transportation, storage, communication	5.0	4.5	56.2
	Finance	2.7	2.8	64.3
	Rental services	27.1	27.3	62.5
	Culture, recreation, other services	5.7	4.1	44.2**
	Totals	100	100	61.9
Number of employed persons in 2006	1	20.7	16.2	48.4**
	2	21.8	18.8	53.5**
	3-4	24.3	26.0	66.3*
	5-9	24.9	28.1	69.7**
	10 and above	8.3	10.9	81.0**
	Totals	100	100	61.9
Company age	less than 5 years	11.1	10.8	59.6
	5 to 10 years	20.2	21.5	65.1
	10 to15 years	30.6	27.8	55.6**
	15 to 25 years	19.8	21.7	67.2**
	25 to 40 years	8.9	9.2	63.4
	40 and above	9.1	8.9	60.3
	Totals	100	100	61.3
Number of establishments	1	90.1	87.9	59.8**
	2	6.6	7.6	71.3*
	3-4	1.8	2.6	86.1**
	5 and above	1.5	1.9	79.3
	Totals	100	100	61.3
Degree of independence	Entirely independent	95.9	94.4	60.3**
	Other	4.1	5.6	85.0**
	Totals	100	100	61.3
Legal form	Private limited company	28.3	32.7	70.8**
	Partnership (firm)	34.7	33.2	58.7
	One-man business	34.9	31.6	55.6**
	Other	2.1	2.4	70.7
	Totals	100	100	61.3
Membership of a trade association	Yes	52.1	54.5	64.2
	No	47.9	45.5	58.2
	Totals	100	100	61.3

Source: WODC data file.

* = the difference in chance is statistically significant ($p<0.05$, Fischer exact test, two-sided)

** = the difference in chance is statistically significant ($p<0.01$, Fischer exact test, two-sided)

Table 12 makes clear that SMEs that were confronted with relatively few types of serious problems in

2006 were companies:

- That were active in the business sector 'culture, recreation, other services';
- That employed one or two employees;
- That had been in business for 10 to 15 years;
- That consisted of a single establishment;
- That were entirely independent;
- Whose legal form was a one-man business?

Companies that were faced with relatively many types of serious problems in 2006 were companies:

- That were active in the business sector 'construction';
- That employed three or more employees;
- That consisted of two or more establishments;
- That were not entirely independent;
- Whose legal form was a private company with limited liability.

Regarding the incidence of potential legal problems, the role of the same characteristics was researched.

Table 13 presents the results of this analysis.

Table 13: Characteristics of SMEs and the incidence of potential legal problems in 2006 (N=1,784, weighted).

Characteristics of the SME	Category	All SMEs (N=1,784)	SMEs with at least one potential legal problem in 2006 (N=660)	
		Percentage	Percentage	As a percentage of the category
Sector	Industry	8.2	8.6	39.0
	Building sector	14.4	15.8	40.5
	Repair sector, trade	30.0	30.6	37.7
	(Hotel and) catering (industry)	6.8	3.9	21.5**
	Transportation, storage, communication	5.0	5.9	43.8
	Finance	2.6	2.4	34.0
	Rental services	27.1	28.6	39.1
	Culture, recreation, other services	5.8	4.2	26.9*
	Totals	100	100	37.0
Number of employed persons in 2006	1	21.0	13.7	24.2**
	2	20.2	15.5	28.5**
	3-4	23.9	25.0	38.9
	5-9	25.2	29.2	43.0**
	10 and above	9.8	16.6	62.8**
	Totals	100	100	37.0

Characteristics of the SME	Category	All SMEs (N=1,784)	SMEs with at least one potential legal problem in 2006 (N=660)	
		Percentage	Percentage	As a percentage of the category
Company age	Less than 5 years	15.0	16.5	40.9
	5 to10 years	20.9	21.4	37.9
	10 to 15 years	26.3	23.7	33.5
	15 to 25 years	17.8	18.1	37.7
	25 to 40 years	9.8	9.5	36.0
	40 and above	10.3	10.7	38.7
	Totals	100	100	37.0
Number of establishments	1	90.1	86.5	35.6**
	2	6.5	7.3	41.4
	3-4	2.2	3.8	62.5**
	5 and above	1.2	2.4	72.7**
	Totals	100	100	37.0
Degree of independence	Independent	96.0	94.1	36.3**
	Other	4.0	5.9	54.9**
	Totals	100	100	37.0
Legal form	Private limited company	32.8	40.5	45.7**
	Partnership (firm)	31.1	28.5	33.9
	One-man business	34.5	29.4	31.5**
	Other	1.6	1.7	37.9
	Totals	100	100	37.0
Membership of a trade association	Yes	53.0	58.3	40.8**
	No	47.0	41.7	32.9**
	Totals	100	100	37.1

Source: WODC data file.

* = the difference in chance is statistically significant (p<0.05, Fischer exact test, two-sided)

** = the difference in chance is statistically significant (p<0.01, Fischer exact test, two-sided)

Table 13 makes clear that SMEs that were faced with relatively few potentially legal types of problems were companies:

- That were active in the business sectors '(hotel and) catering (industry)' or 'culture, recreation, other services';
- That employed one or two employees;
- That consisted of a single establishment;
- That were entirely independent;
- Whose legal form was a one-man business;
- That were not affiliated with any trade association.

Companies that were faced with relatively many types of potential legal problems were companies:

- That employed five or more employees;
- That consisted of three or more establishments;
- That were not entirely independent;

- Whose legal form was a private company with limited liability;
- That were affiliated with a trade association.

ENGAGING LEGAL ASSISTANCE IN CASE OF SERIOUS AND POTENTIAL LEGAL PROBLEMS

Companies that are faced with problems have various options for dealing with them. An important choice is whether or not to engage legal assistance and, if so, what kind of legal assistance. This does not exclusively involve the legal profession: legal service providers also include accountants, advisors, mediators, dispute committees, the courts, legal expenses insurance companies, industry associations, bailiffs, collection agencies and the police. As Table 14 shows, in 2006 industry associations were most often engaged by the companies, irrespective of the question whether this was for a serious problem or merely for advice: 25.9% of all SMEs did so in 2006. Lawyers were engaged by 25.8% of all SMEs, legal advisors by 20.3% and court bailiffs by 17.6% of all SMEs.

Table 14: Incidence of SMEs making use of legal service providers in 2006 (N=2,097, weighted).[28]

Legal service provider	Percentage
Industry Association	25.9
Lawyer	25.8
Legal advisor	20.3
Bailiff	17.6
Police	17.2
Courts	9.5
Legal expenses insurance	8.7
Other	3.6
Mediator	2.3
Arbitrator	1.8
Conciliation service	1.2

Source: WODC data file.

When we look at Table 15, which presents the frequency of engaging legal assistance, irrespective of whether this assistance was relied upon for advice or help with a serious problem, the order looks different. In that case, the main service providers are court bailiffs: in 2006, they were engaged in 23.5% of all engagements. They are followed by the industry association (21.9% of all engagements), lawyers (16.9% of all engagements), and legal advisors (13.1% of all engagements). When we look at the average number of times the legal service provider was called in per SME that engaged the said provider, the ranking is again different. The court bailiff again ranks first (on average engaged 6.5 times), but this time he is followed by ‘other’ legal service providers (on average engaged 6.1 times), the industry association (on average engaged 4.1 times) and the courts (on average engaged 3.3 times). A combination of a relatively low percentage of the total number of times a legal service provider was called in with a relatively high average number of times of being called in per SME that called in the provider indicates that a relatively small number of companies used this provider frequently. This is the case with the 'other' legal service providers. A combination of a relatively high percentage and a relatively low average means that the legal service provider was called in by many SMEs, but not time after time. This is, for instance, the case with lawyers.

Table 15: Frequency of SMEs using legal service providers in 2006 (N=2,097, weighted).

Legal service provider	Frequency of being called in							Percentage of times of being called in	Average number of times called in per SME that called in the legal service provider
	1	2	3	4	5	6-10	>10		
Bailiff	35.7	18.2	8.7	8.6	9.3	12.2	7.1	23.5	6.5
Industry association	25.5	26.9	12.8	8.2	11.2	9.4	6.0	21.9	4.2
Lawyer	40.9	22.1	12.5	8.2	4.5	10.4	1.5	16.9	3.2
Legal advisor	38.1	25.2	12.8	9.4	5.0	7.1	2.4	13.1	3.1
Police	53.6	21.9	9.9	3.9	3.9	5.6	1.2	8.9	2.5
Courts	62.0	20.8	9.4	1.3	0.7	4.8	1.0	6.5	3.3
Other	15.9	18.8	12.9	16.7	11.0	14.4	10.3	4.3	6.1
Legal expenses insurance	64.2	23.4	5.7	3.4	0.2	2.8	0.3	3.0	1.7
Mediator	61.4	15.6	17.7	4.5	0	0.8	0	0.8	1.7
Arbitrator	78.6	9.1	7.5	0	0	4.8	0	0.6	1.5
Conciliation service	75.8	6.7	16.7	0	0.8	0	0	0.4	1.4

Source: WODC data file.

In some cases, it is obvious that the legal service provider was called in for help and not to provide information: the courts, arbiters, mediators and conciliation services are engaged to obtain a decision, not to enlighten SMEs about their legal position. For the other legal service providers this was, however, less clear, so the respondents that engaged them were asked to indicate why they did so: for help with a serious problem, for information, or for both? Table 16 presents the results. In the majority of cases, the court bailiff, police, legal expenses insurance and the lawyer are approached to provide help, while the industry association is mainly approached to provide information.

The aforementioned figures relate to all companies in the first survey, irrespective of whether they had serious problems. The group of companies that did not experience serious problems but nevertheless engaged legal assistance is considerable: 37.9% of the 799 companies without serious problems in our research did so. The trade associations are engaged the most by this group of companies (31.0% of the engagements by this group), followed by legal advisors (18.2% of the engagements), the police (16.8% of the engagements) and lawyers (13.3% of the engagements). Exactly why they relied on these service providers varies; however, trade associations and legal advisors are usually engaged to provide information and not to help with a serious problem.

Table 16: SMEs and their reason for using different kinds of legal services in 2006 (N=2,097, weighted).

Legal service provider	Help	Information	Help and information
Bailiff	90.0	2.9	7.1
Police	85.9	7.9	6.1
Legal expenses insurance	73.7	11.1	15.2
Lawyer	60.8	10.1	29.1
Other	47.1	17.9	34.9
Legal advisor	30.1	45.1	24.8
Industry association	13.2	68.3	18.5

Source: WODC data file.

The incidence and frequency of engaging legal assistance providers look different when the focus shifts to the potential legal problems. In part this is caused by the fact that the legal service providers that we distinguished during the second survey, based on the experiences with the first survey, is slightly different. The arbiter and the conciliation service were removed from the list, while the debt collection agency and the accountant were added. But there are other differences that cannot be explained by differences in the questionnaire. In the case of potential legal problems (Table 17), 12.4% of all SMEs engaged the services of a lawyer, followed by 8.9% that engaged the services of a collection agency, 8.5% that engaged the services of a judge and went to court, and 7.0% that engaged the services of a court bailiff.

Table 17: Incidence of using legal service providers by SMEs with potential legal problems in 2006 (N=660, weighted).

Legal service provider	Percentage
Lawyer	12.4
Debt collection agency	8.9
Courts	8.5
Bailiff	7.0
Accountant	5.2
Legal expenses insurance	5.0
Industry association	4.9
Police	4.4
Legal advisor	3.9
Other	1.9
Mediator	1.6
Total	25.8

Source: WODC data file.

As regards the frequency of an engagement in the event of potential legal problems in 2006, the collection agency was the most important legal service provider (20.9% of all engagements), followed by lawyers (18.2% of all engagements), court bailiffs (18.1% of all engagements) and the courts (9.0% of all engagements). Table 18 gives an overview of the frequency of engaging the different legal service providers. Apart from the court bailiff and the debt collection agency, the SMEs engaged the legal service providers in the majority of the cases only once during 2006. The average number of times a legal service provider was engaged by the SMEs makes clear that, on average, only the police, the debt collection agency and the bailiff were engaged more than three times.

Table 18: Frequency using legal service providers by SMEs with potential legal problems in 2006 (N=660, weighted).

Legal service provider	Frequency of being called in by SMEs							Average number of times called in per SME that called in the legal service provider
	1	2	3	4	5	6-10	>10	
Bailiff	39.5	24.7	14.3	6.7	2.7	5.2	6.9	4.6
Debt collection agency	46.6	10.2	13.3	7.5	6.5	10.3	5.6	4.2
Police	50.6	17.5	15.7	5.0	4.6	4.3	2.5	3.2
Legal expenses insurance	61.5	16.5	7.6	4.0	3.3	4.5	2.6	2.8
Lawyer	54.2	18.7	7.9	3.2	4.0	5.2	2.8	2.6
Accountant	58.1	13.2	16.7	5.0	2.0	4.8	0.2	2.1
Industry association	51.3	28.4	8.6	6.7	1.4	2.4	1.3	2.0
Courts	64.4	19.0	8.1	3.0	2.0	0.8	2.6	1.9
Legal advisor	69.9	11.1	8.2	6.8	2.8	0.1	1.1	1.8
Other	79.5	2.1	12.0	6.4	0.2	0	0	1.5
Mediator	82.6	13.4	3.5	0.6	0	0	0	1.2

Source: WODC data file.

LEGAL SERVICES NOT ENGAGED

In the event of potential legal problems, some SMEs chose not to engage legal service providers. The potential legal problems for which SMEs did not seek the help of legal service providers were problems with other companies regarding the quality, quantity or delivery time of purchased goods or services: three quarters of the SMEs confronted therewith did not engage legal service providers at all. What were the reasons for not engaging the providers? Table 19 gives an overview, distinguishing between 'did not think of it'; 'the problem was too unimportant'; 'engaging legal service providers costs too much time', 'the opponent is penniless', therefore he cannot be forced to pay; 'engaging legal service providers costs too much money'; 'engaging legal service providers would not change anything'; 'the problem with the opponent was already solved' and 'other' reasons.

The most common reason for not engaging legal service providers was that the parties had solved the potential legal problems themselves: 33.9% of the reasons provided related to this solution. In the case of potential legal problems regarding the quality, quantity and delivery time of goods and services sold or the payment for goods and services bought, both problems that are 'caused' by the SMEs themselves, the majority of the reasons given for not engaging legal service providers was that the problem had already been solved. However, Table 19 also makes clear that solving the problems is less likely with some potential legal problem categories. Unsurprisingly, this is the case with serious kinds of crime and fraud, not just because in many cases the perpetrator will be unknown, but also because these problems are likely to result in criminal prosecutions, proceedings in which the victimized party only plays a minor role. This is also the case, however, with problems regarding applications for permits and taxes, customs and duties.

Other relatively often mentioned reasons for not engaging legal service providers in case of potential legal problems were the costs (time and money) involved in such an engagement. That nothing could be recovered from the other party or that the problem could not be resolved were less important reasons. It also did not often occur that the respondents indicated that they considered the matter to be unimportant: only 7.5% of the explanations could be interpreted as such. This is emphasized by the fact that the respondents only rarely indicated that they had not considered engaging legal assistance providers.

Table 19: Frequency of reasons for not using legal service providers while having potential legal problems (N=580, weighted).

Kind of problem	Reason not to use legal service (row percentages)								
	Did not think of it	Too unim-portant	Costs too much time	Opponent is penniless	Costs too much money	Useless	Problem already solved	Other	Total
Payment for goods and services sold	0.5	6.6	14.4	13.7	15.8	7.1	30.3	11.6	100 (31.0)
Quality, quantity and delivery time of goods and services sold	2.5	7.5	14.0	3.8	6.8	9.7	52.4	3.3	100 (11.7)
Labour conditions, wages and the laying off of workers	0	7.5	14.8	0.6	14.2	1.8	41.5	19.6	100 (5.1)
Applying for Permits	0	12.3	17.6	0	2.0	21.4	24.3	22.4	100 (7.7)
Taxes, customs and duties	0	4.3	8.0	0	6.4	13.7	27.9	39.7	100 (4.4)
Payment for goods and services bought	0	3.4	13.2	8.0	18.8	2.9	50.4	3.4	100 (6.4)
Quality, quantity and delivery time of goods and services bought	1.1	12.0	13.5	0	9.0	5.4	41.6	17.4	100 (13.2)
Liability for and settlement of damage	0	0.3	12.0	5.3	14.9	5.0	44.8	17.7	100 (8.5)
Serious kinds of crime and fraud	3.9	11.2	18.4	8.3	6.7	21.6	5.3	24.7	100 (12.1)
Totals	1.1	7.6	14.4	6.7	11.3	9.6	33.9	15.4	100 (100)

Source: WODC data file.

CUSTOMARY TERMINATION OF PROBLEMS

When asked about the way in which companies usually resolve their potential legal problems, 58.7% of the SMEs stated that they do so by means of an agreement with the other party. However, this does not mean that 58.7% of the potential legal problems result in an agreement, because the underlying number of problems has not been taken into account. It nevertheless provides an indication of the importance of the agreement as a way to wrap up potential legal problems. This is especially the case with the potential legal problems relating to taxes, customs and duties, and to the quality, quantity and delivery time of goods and services sold. A court decision appears to be the second most important way of ending potential legal problems. Table 20 gives an overview.

Table 21 uses the same numbers, but this time it distinguishes between the different opponents that the SMEs with potential legal problems are confronted with. This table makes clear that especially problems with the government, individuals and also other companies are usually terminated with an agreement. The examples of Apple's way of doing business at the beginning of this article are therefore not exemplary. A court verdict is the most common way of ending problems with employees. However, since the court has to permit the SMEs to terminate employment contracts, this is not much of a surprise.

Table 20: Ways generally used to terminate potential legal problems I (N=734, weighted).

Kind of problem	Ways of terminating problems (row percentage)				
	Verdict by Judge	Other verdict	Agreement	Other	Totals
Payment for goods and services sold	24.5	2.2	59.7	13.6	100 (41.8)
Quality, quantity and delivery time of goods and services sold	4.7	0	82.6	12.7	100 (7.1)
Labour conditions, wages and the laying off of workers	34.4	6.9	47.0	11.7	100 (14.3)
Applying for permits	8.9	6.0	58.5	26.6	100 (4.5)
Taxes, customs and duties	11.9	0.4	83.3	4.3	100 (5.1)
Payment for goods and Services bought	16.9	0	71.8	11.3	100 (3.6)
Quality, quantity and delivery time of goods and services bought	8.2	0	67.3	24.6	100 (8.3)
Liability for and settlement of Damage	12.4	4.4	61.8	21.4	100 (7.1)
Serious kinds of crime and Fraud	22.3	6.6	20.2	50.9	100 (8.2)
Totals	20.5	3.0	58.7	17.8	100 (100)

Source: WODC data file.

Table 21: Ways generally used to terminate potential legal problems II (N=734, weighted).

Kind of opponent	Ways to terminate problems (row percentage)				
	Verdict by judge	Other verdict	Agreement	Other	Totals
Companies	20.4	2.0	60.8	16.8	100 (45.2)
Individuals	15.3	1.5	69.2	14.0	100 (18.9)
The government	13.4	2.5	72.0	12.1	100 (11.7)
Other organizations	15.5	2.1	64.8	17.6	100 (2.0)
Employees	31.3	6.3	50.1	12.2	100 (15.6)
Other legal entities	24.1	8.1	8.4	59.5	100 (6.6)
Totals	20.5	3.0	58.7	17.8	100 (100)

Source: WODC data file.

EXPERIENCES WITH LEGAL SERVICE PROVIDERS

The respondents were finally asked about their general opinion concerning the operation of the service providers engaged by them. Table 22 presents the results. The average valuation of the functioning of the legal assistance providers, in general or with respect to the role they played in ending the potential legal problems, is quite high: 3.5 to 3.6 out of 5. This does not detract from the fact that there are considerable differences in the valuations of each legal assistance provider, and also in the spread of the opinions per legal assistance provider. The trade organizations and the dispute committees (valued with a 3.9 each) and the legal advisors (valued with a 3.8) score relatively highly with respect to the general question about their operation. In particular the courts, the police and arbiters score relatively lowly (each scoring a 3.2).

Table 22: Opinions about the functioning of legal service providers (N=2,808, weighted).

Legal service provider	Opinion (row percentage)							
	Very negative	Negative	Neutral	Positive	Very positive	No opinion	Total	Average
Industry association	1.8	4.0	6.2	73.7	13.6	0.7	100 (19.4)	3.9
Conciliation service	2.0	3.9	9.6	68.1	11.5	14.9	100 (1.0)	3.9
Legal advisor	2.0	4.8	15.2	66.4	8.9	2.8	100 (15.1)	3.8
Other	2.8	8.8	13.8	56.3	7.2	11.1	100 (2.7)	3.6
Lawyer	4.2	14.5	16.6	57.3	6.4	1.0	100 (19.2)	3.5
Legal expenses insurance	7.6	12.8	15.0	54.0	10.1	0.4	100 (6.5)	3.5
Mediator	5.4	14.9	20.4	49.9	7.0	2.3	100 (1.7)	3.4
Bailiff	5.7	20.5	13.7	54.0	4.6	1.4	100 (13.1)	3.3
Arbitrator	6.2	17.0	25.7	45.4	3.8	1.8	100 (1.4)	3.2
Police	7.9	20.4	15.8	49.8	5.2	0.8	100 (12.9)	3.2
Courts	7.5	23.2	16.1	42.5	7.0	3.7	100 (7.1)	3.2
Totals	4.5	12.8	13.8	59.0	8.1	1.8	100 (100)	3.5

Source: WODC data file.

When asked about their opinion regarding the role of the legal service providers in ending the potential legal problems which the SMEs were dealing with, the results are slightly different. Table 23 present the results. The accountant (4.2), the mediator and the trade organizations (both 4.0) score relatively highly. The police (2.9) and debt collection agencies (3.4) score fairly lowly.

Table 23: Opinions about the role of the legal service provider in ending potential legal problems (N=707, weighted).

Legal service provider	Opinions (row percentage)							
	Very dissatisfied	Dissatisfied	Neutral	Satisfied	Very satisfied	No opinion	Total	Average score
Accountant	0.2	7.6	6.0	51.2	32.8	2.2	100 (13.2)	4.2
Industry association	2.5	9.4	10.5	45.0	30.9	1.7	100 (12.3)	4.0
Mediator	3.0	6.1	13.6	47.9	27.7	1.7	100 (4.0)	4.0
Lawyer	2.6	10.4	5.6	54.8	25.7	1.0	100 (31.4)	3.9
Legal advisor	3.9	2.1	10.0	68.9	14.4	0.6	100 (10.0)	3.9
Legal expenses insurance	5.2	11.3	12.5	47.5	23.3	0.2	100 (12.6)	3.7
Bailiff	5.5	16.3	15.1	47.1	11.7	4.1	100 (17.5)	3.6
Courts	7.4	12.5	15.2	46.3	11.4	7.2	100 (21.4)	3.6
Debt collection agency	9.4	16.6	15.1	43.7	13.6	1.3	100 (22.2)	3.4
Police	20.0	23.5	13.2	33.6	9.5	0.2	100 (11.2)	2.9
Total	7.5	13.5	13.3	42.7	19.9	3.1	100 (100)	3.6

Source: WODC data file.

DISCUSSION

In this article, we have given an overview regarding the serious and potential legal problems that SMEs encounter in the Netherlands and the ways in which they deal with these problems. Based on two surveys pertaining to 2006, the incidence and frequency of the different kinds of problems have been presented; the concurrence of problems; the association of characteristics of companies with the likelihood that they are presented with problems; the nature of the opponents; the incidence and frequency of resorting to legal service providers by the SMEs, and their evaluation of the performance of these legal service providers. To conclude, some of the results presented above will be compared to the results of the empirical research summarized in Section 2 to point out similarities and dissimilarities and avenues for further research.

In the case of the British companies that were party to an intellectual property dispute, many problems never came to court. Even when this was the case, a settlement was reached in 40% of the cases listed in the Patents Courts. In only 50% of the cases listed did the court deliver a verdict? That potential legal cases do not result in a verdict but are settled instead, with or without the help of a lawyer, is not only the case with intellectual property disputes. As the previous pages have shown, an agreement with the opponent is for SMEs the most common way to terminate potential legal problems. This was especially the case when the problem concerned the quality, quantity and/or delivery time of goods or services that the SME itself was selling or when the opponent was either the government or a private individual. This does not mean, however, that court decisions are not important because in the shadow of the law the threat of a verdict is always there. This does not mean, however, that this threat is the same and carries the same weight in each and every problem with each and every opposing party. It would be interesting to know to what extent potential outcomes of potential legal procedures play a role in different kinds of problems with different kinds of opponents, especially in a context where governments, like the Dutch government, aim to reduce the costs of justice by selectively limiting access to justice.[29]

When the results of the Chinese research are compared to the Dutch one, it is striking that the Dutch companies report for one year a much higher problem incidence than the Chinese companies for five years: 61.9% of the Dutch companies reported having experienced serious problems in 2006 while only 45.9% of the Chinese companies reported problems for the five years from 2001-2005. Limited to just one year, the problem rate for the Chinese companies would go down to 30.1%: less than half of what the Dutch SMEs reported having experienced in 2006. When on the Dutch side of this last comparison the focus would be on just the potential legal problems that, according to the respondents, could have resulted or did result in legal procedures, while on the Chinese side we still include all reported problems, the figures are more similar: 37.0% for the Dutch SMEs against 30.1 % for the Chinese SMEs. These results raise several questions. Are Dutch SMEs more prone to report problems and to consider legal procedures than their Chinese colleagues? Is the access to justice in Hong Kong perhaps less favourable than in the Netherlands? This could mean that Chinese SMEs seek to prevent or defuse potential problems at an earlier stage than Dutch SMEs, resulting in a smaller number of SMEs reporting problems. Or are Dutch SMEs, even according to Chinese standards, really more likely to encounter problems?

When one would consider the Australian study into the business problems of small companies (with less than 20 employees) this appears to be the case. Although the analyses above have shown that the smaller Dutch SMEs are less often confronted with serious or potential legal problems, the percentage that still encounters them is still considerable. When it comes to size, the one-person company is the SME with the lowest risk of serious or potential legal problems: 48.4% and 24.2% per year respectively. Compared to the Australian serious business dispute risk for small companies of 15.1% per five years, this is remarkably high. Even when one would take into account that the Dutch risks refer to problems with all possible opposing parties and the Australian study only refers to problems with other businesses it remains high: the majority (54.6%) of all the potential legal problems that Dutch SMEs reported for 2006 concerned disputes with another company.

This difference in problem incidence rates is not only intriguing, but also quite fundamental. When comparing the results of different jurisdictions and legal cultures, it appears appropriate to start with the incidence and frequency of problems encountered, and try to explain them before turning to a comparison of relying on legal service providers. In the case of Australia the access to justice for small companies does not appear to be an immediate concern[30] so a search for an explanation of the remarkable difference in problem incidence rates would not start there.

A final word of caution. Although the results are representative, apart from the

SMEs in the agricultural sector, it should be noted that they pertain to only one year, 2006. This year was, economically speaking, a good year. The effects of the financial crisis that started in 2007 and of the subsequent recession, which might still develop into a full-blown depression, had not yet been felt. It therefore appears likely that the results would be different if the survey was repeated today. When it concerns naked survival, it is not unlikely that more managers would be inclined to act like Steve Jobs at the beginning of this article. Further research will have to make that clear.

NOTES

1 W. Isaacson, Steve Jobs, 2011, p. 115.

2 Apple lost the lawsuits and in the aftermath a settlement was reached in 1997.

3 See Isaacson, supra note 1, p. 284.

4 Ibid., pp. 116, 284.

5 Ibid., p. 207. Sure enough a lawsuit was the result.

6 American Bar Association, Legal needs and civil justice. A Survey of Americans. Major Findings from the Comprehensive Legal Needs

Study, 1994.

7 See for an overview of the non-American literature: B.C.J. van Velthoven & C.M. Klein Haarhuis, Geschilbeslechtingsdelta 2009. Over verloop en afloop van (potentieel) juridische problemen van burgers, 2010, pp. 31-35. For the American legal needs literature, see <http:// www.nlada.org/Civil/Civil_SPAN/SPAN_Library> (last 1 visited June 2011).

8 Searle Center on Law, Regulation, and Economic Growth, Litigation Cost Survey of Major Companies, 2010, p. 7.

9 J.B. Henry, 'Fortune 500: The Total Cost of Litigation Estimated at One-Third Profits.' 2008 The Metropolitan Corporate Counsel, February, p. 28.

10 Ibid.

11 M.T. Croes & G.C. Maas, Geschilbeslechtingsdelta midden- en kleinbedrijf. Over het optreden en afhandelen van (potentieel) juridische problemen in het midden- en kleinbedrijf, 2009.

12 <http://english.eim.nl/> (last visited 1 June 2011).

13 See Henry, supra note 9, p. 28.

14 A. Jettinghof, Het komt zelden voor. Beheersing van klachten en geschillen in relaties tussen bedrijven, 2001

15 S. Vogenauer, Civil Justice Systems in Europe: Implications for Choice of Forum and Choice of Contract Law. A Business Survey. Final Results, 2010, pp. 13-33.

16 M.A. Gomez, 'All in the family: the influence of social networks on dispute processing (a case study of a developing economy)' 2008 Georgia journal of international and comparative law 36. no. 2, pp 291-353.

17 C. Greenhalgh et al., Intellectual property enforcement in smaller UK firms. A report for the Strategic Advisory Board for Intellectual Property Policy (SABIP), 2010.

18 Asia Consulting Group Ltd., Study on the Demand for and Supply of Legal and Related Services, 2008.

19 Orima Research, Small Business Dispute Resolution, 2010.

20 See also J.O. Lanjouw & M. Schankerman, 'Protecting intellectual property rights: are small firms handicapped?' 2004 Journal of Law and Economics 47 no. 1, pp. 45-74. Their results pertaining to US firms from 1978 to 1999 confirm this. They furthermore stress that the possibility of litigation is considerably higher for smaller companies.

21 Asia Consulting Group, supra note 18, p. 89. On the same page the number of companies that reported having experienced problems during this five-year period is 881, which is 48.6% out of a total of 1,813. It is unclear which percentage is correct.

22 For about two thirds of the respondents, this was one year, for the remainder 5 years. General statements in this report relating to the (relative) frequency with which companies encountered problems are seriously hampered by adding these two groups together.

23 Orima research, supra note 19, p. 5. On page 6 the report claims that 80% of the companies did not report any dispute or disagreement during the last five years. Which percentage is correct, is unknown.

24 Orima research, supra note 19, p. 18. Numbers are taken from figure 9; the appendices that are supposed to be part of the report and contain the figures have not been published, unfortunately.

25 See note 21, supra.

26 Of the SMEs, 1,298 (61.9%) indicated that they had encountered at least one potential legal problem in 2006. However, the number of companies that were able to tell with what frequency they had encountered the different kinds of serious problems was slightly smaller. This last number was used to calculate the number of problems per company. The total average number of problems per company is calculated by taking the total number of mentioned problems and dividing that number by 2,097 and 1,298, respectively

27 660 SMEs (37.0%) indicated that they had encountered at least one potential legal problem in 2006. However, the number of companies that were able to tell with what frequency they encountered the different kinds of potential legal problems was slightly smaller. This last number was used to calculate the number of problems per company. The total average number of problems per company is calculated by taking the total number of mentioned problems and dividing that number by 1,784 and 660, respectively

28 This percentage relates to the number of companies that reported having engaged a legal service provider. The number of companies that were able to indicate how often this happened was in some cases slightly lower. The incidence rate in table 27 in M.T. Croes & G.C. Maas, Geschilbeslechtingsdelta midden- en kleinbedrijf. Over het optreden en afhandelen van (potentieel) juridische problemen in het midden- en kleinbedrijf, 2009, p. 60 is based on this slightly lower number of companies and

therefore provides slightly lower percentages in some cases.

29 Kamerstukken II 2008-2009, 31 758, no. 3.

30 Orima research, supra note 19, p. 24.

5
CHAPTER

CHANGING INTERNATIONAL 'SUBJECTIVITY' AND RIGHTS AND OBLIGATIONS UNDER INTERNATIONAL LAW – STATUS OF CORPORATIONS

Merja Pentikäinen

Keywords: Subjects of international law, international (legal) personality, international (legal) capacity, corporations, human rights protection

DOCTRINE OF THE SUBJECTS OF INTERNATIONAL LAW

Broadening the circle of subjects

Introductory textbooks on public international law invariably include a section on the subjects of international law appearing as part of the fundamentals of this branch of law.[1] The doctrine of international 'subjectivity'[2] is also among the international law topics that have attracted the attention of a number of scholars who have entered the debate on the content and reach of this 'subjectivity'. The subject of international law has been defined, for instance, in the following way: it is an entity capable of possessing international rights and duties and having the capacity to maintain its rights by bringing international claims;[3] it is capable of independently bearing rights and obligations under international law.[4] The idea of subjects of the international legal system is often linked – even conflated – with the notion of international legal personality.[5] It has been suggested that international legal personality arises in three principal contexts: capacity

Citation: Pentikäinen, M., (2012). Changing International 'Subjectivity' and Rights and Obligations under International Law – Status of Corporations. Utrecht Law Review. 8(1), pp.145–154. DOI: http://doi.org/10.18352/ulr.185.

to make claims in respect of breaches of international law; capacity to make treaties and agreements valid on the international plane; and the enjoyment of privileges and immunities from national jurisdictions.[6] A review of the literature addressing the issue of international 'subjectivity' suggests that varying kinds of links are made between international (legal) 'subjectivity', international (legal) capacity and international (legal) personality.[7] In the past, when international law was viewed as regulating solely inter-state relations, states were the only subjects of international law. Departure from this exclusively state-centric model of the international legal system in the course of the years – thus recognising the changes in the dynamic of the international system – has also resulted in the widening of the group of entities labelled as international law subjects. An important step was taken in 1949 when the International Court of Justice (ICJ) gave its advisory opinion concerning the international rights and duties of international organisations, more specifically the UN in the case at hand. In the case of Reparation for Injuries Suffered in the Service of the United Nations the UN was characterised as an international person and as a subject of international law, capable of possessing international rights and duties and capacity to maintain its rights by bringing international claims.[8] Subsequently, international 'subjectivity' of international organisations has been widely recognised, and the capacities of international organisations are regarded as also encompassing the capacity to become parties to international agreements and the capacity to enjoy certain privileges and immunities.[9]

While states have the status of primary subjects of international law with the most extensive capacities (full legal capacity),[10] the 'subjectivity' of international organisations is limited and determined by the powers vested in them.[11] The scope of this 'subjectivity' does give rise to various interpretations. Among other things, the issues of human rights obligations of international organisations and the accountability of international organisations for human rights violations have sparked vivid debates.[12] While it has been concluded that universally recognised human rights are binding upon international organisations, international law is still in a state of flux, e.g. where it concerns the division of responsibilities between international organisations and their Member States.[13] The contemporary literature on international law also lists other actors among the subjects of international law, including insurgents, national liberation movements, and certain sui generis or state-like entities. [14] Even individuals have appeared on some of these lists of subjects.[15] Those who challenge this view of seeing individuals as subjects of international law underline the fact that individuals are under the exclusive control of states. When treaties provide for the rights and duties of individuals, this would mean that each state only undertakes (by agreement vis-à-vis the other Contracting States) to confer such rights and impose duties on individuals solely within its own legal system. Individuals' rights to file complaints with international judicial or quasi-judicial bodies are just exceptional, being no more than a procedural right which lacks any attendant substantive right or the power to enforce a possible decision of an international body.[16] However, developments in international law over the years have made the international position of individuals complex and multifaceted. Under modern international law, individuals have gradually come to be regarded not only as holders of material interests acknowledged at the international level, but they are also capable of infringing fundamental values of the world community. The development of international human rights law and the doctrine of individual criminal responsibility under international law have introduced important changes in the international legal system. The most recent affirmation of individual criminal responsibility at the international level is to be found in the 1998 Statute of the International Criminal Court (ICC) which provides for criminal jurisdiction over individuals accused of genocide, crimes against humanity, war crimes and the 'crime of aggression'.[17] These changes have influenced the debate on the international 'subjectivity' of individuals. As a result of both granting individuals legal rights and placing obligations on them that are operational at the international level, there are scholars who are of the opinion that individuals possess international legal status as subjects of international law.[18]

Multinational corporations – contested subjects

If there are different scholarly views on the international 'subjectivity' of individuals, the status of corporations as subjects of international law is even more contested. The debate on the international 'subjectivity' of corporations revolves around the business entities that operate across national borders, labelled 'multinational corporations', for instance.[19] Debates on this matter are characterised by a strong resistance to include corporate entities among the subjects of international law, and until recently suggestions that corporations be considered as having international legal personality were exceptional. Many authors have simply left the question open.[20]

Those scholars who have addressed the issue have noted, for instance, that multinational corporations have 'controversial candidatures' which in principle have no international legal personality.[21] According to some views, these entities are sometimes counted among the subjects of international law.[22] It is acknowledged that the situation becomes more complex when a corporation is closely controlled by a government so that it could be considered as a state agency, with or without some degree of autonomy. Additionally, ownership of shares may give a state a controlling interest in a 'private law corporation'.[23] The rights and responsibilities of corporations that are state-owned or otherwise controlled by a state raise important questions from the viewpoint of human rights protection. The prevailing state of affairs appears to enable the state to escape its human rights obligations when the state operates in the business context as a company actor.

As regards the broader question of whether corporations have rights and obligations under international law, they are viewed as possessing rights, for instance, under international investment law, including the right not to be discriminated against vis-à-vis national firms and a right to receive compensation in the event of expropriation. Under human rights law, corporate entities enjoy such rights as the right to a fair trial, the right to privacy, the right of freedom of expression, and property rights.[24] Corporations have been granted locus standi before some international tribunals.[25] A corporate entity can be an applicant even before a human rights supervisory body. This possibility was created under the European Convention on Human Rights.[26] In one of the seminal judgments of the European Court of Human Rights, i.e. in the case of The

Sunday Times v United Kingdom, the first applicant was Times Newspapers Ltd.[27] In some cases, the legal person may be the only appropriate victim that can complain to the Strasbourg Court.[28] In a recent case in which the Strasbourg Court ruled, the applicant was a publicly-traded private open joint-stock company.[29]

There are scholars who consider that it is at least theoretically possible that international law could impose some human rights obligations directly on corporations.[30] Some of the existing general rules of international human rights law found in public international law, and traditionally applicable only to states, can be said to apply also to non-state actors. This is to recognise the importance of non-state actors and their influence without suggesting that they have achieved the role of legislator. The situation has been described as states having fixed non-state actors with some rights and duties, whereby these actors have become subjects of interest without any automatic legitimising effect.[31] It is worth noting that corporate accountability was actively discussed in the preparatory process of the Statute of the ICC, and that references to the prosecution of corporate entities were even inserted in the draft Statute. Eventually, however, these references were left out from the final text of the Statute.[32] It has been pointed out that the lack of international jurisdiction does not mean that corporations are under no international legal obligations, nor does it prevent us from speaking about corporations breaking international law. International human rights obligations can fall on states, individuals and other non-state actors. Where obligations exist, different jurisdictions may or may not be able to enforce them. In the absence of in-ternational enforcement mechanisms open to claims against corporate actors, international law is being used to hold corporations accountable for human rights violations at the national level.[33] Among the most notable national context to hold corporations accountable for the violations of international human rights is the Alien Tort Claims Act (ATCA) in the USA.[34]

The debate on the status of corporations in the international legal system has features similar to that on the 'subjectivity' of individuals, including whether rights and obligations stipulated in international documents apply directly to corporations under international law or indirectly through national legal systems. The traditional way of seeing the human rights regulation of corporations is as 'indirect' regulation through national law when, on the basis of states' international obligations, states are obligated to ensure that human rights norms are not breached by private actors.[35] Based on states' obligation to protect human rights, states are obliged to take steps to ensure protection against human rights abuses by private actors operating under or within their jurisdiction. Under this traditional 'indirect' form of regulation and state-centred framework, human rights standards are imposed on corporations at national level and states may be held responsible for human rights violations if these violations result from their failure to regulate corporate activity effectively. In these situations states' performance is assessed on the basis of the standard of due diligence.

There are strong arguments as to why human rights law should be applied directly to corporations, i.e. why international law should 'directly' regulate corporate activities: corporations can and do affect enjoyment of human rights, and they enjoy considerable rights and benefits flowing from international law.[36] Additionally, in practice, states have different capacities to regulate corporate activities effectively at the national level. For instance, developing host states that are highly dependent on foreign investment may face particular problems to effectively regulate the activities of multinational corporations. In these situations when it is not possible to depend exclusively on host states to hold multinational corporations accountable for human rights violations, attention has been drawn to the regulatory potential of corporations' home states.[37] This state of affairs has also strengthened demands to render corporations directly accountable under international law.

However, for the time being any agreement on the direct applicability of international human rights law on corporations is lacking.[38] The traditional 'indirect' regulation model according to which states are the only bearers of human rights obligations under international law still appears to be the prevailing standpoint. In defence of this traditional view, it is claimed that attempting to extend legal duties under human rights law to non-state actors bestows on such actors an unfortunate legitimacy, which will undermine the authority of the state and dilute the responsibilities of states with respect to their human rights obligations. Changing the original course would allegedly cause the unravelling of the whole human rights project.[39]

The role of corporations in the area of human rights protection has recently acquired considerable attention when the Special Representative of the UN Secretary General on the issue of human rights and transnational corporations and other business enterprises (the Special Representative of the UN Secretary General on Business and Human Rights (SRSG)) submitted his reports, and the final one in the spring of 2011.[40] These reports have sparked an unprecedented debate on the responsibilities of corporate actors for human rights violations. The SRSG introduced the 'Protect, Respect and Remedy' Framework, underlining the crucial and primary role of states to protect human rights but also drawing attention to the role of corporations in the area of human rights protection. The Framework underlines different roles and duties of states and corporate actors[41] and calls for corporate responsibility to respect human rights.[42] The 'Remedy part' of the Framework draws attention to the need to strengthen effective access to remedies with respect to human rights violations linked to corporate activities. The SRSG's proposals have been vividly discussed – also criticised – by academics.[43] The business community appears to have welcomed them since they are viewed to clarify the situation on the responsibilities of business actors in the area of human rights protection.[44] In his reports the SRSG neither expressly calls for changing the international law system on responsibilities nor touches upon the issue of international 'subjectivity' (nor personality or capacity), but he labels his approach as 'principled pragmatism'.[45] Obviously the SRSG's proposals cannot result in changes in international law as such, but actions of states are crucial for any substantive modifications of the existing international law system. However, the SRSG's reports are of great significance because they have set off an extremely useful debate, e.g. on the existing gaps in human rights regulation and responsibilities of corporate actors under international law. Furthermore, the reports have been instrumental in putting the spotlight on the role of business actors in conflict situations when human rights are at particular risk – often left unprotected to a great extent –[46] and on the operation of corporations that are state-owned or otherwise state-controlled.[47] Although the question of whether the SRSG's remarks and proposals will have any concrete effects on the international legal system remains to a great extent in the hands of states, it is nevertheless notable that the 'Protect, Respect, Remedy' Framework has already influenced legislation at the national level and practices of international organisations, e.g. in the area of responsible supply chain management of business actors. These effects have been concretised in the context of the minerals originating from conflict-ridden Eastern Congo resulting, among other things, in the introduction of a piece of national legislation in the USA (the Dodd-Frank Act). The SRSG's proposals have also influenced UN and OECD practices.[48]

'SUBJECTIVITY' AS A RELATIVE NOTION; CRITICISM OF THE DOCTRINE OF 'SUBJECTIVITY'

Whatever is viewed to be the exact group of subjects of international law, apart from states, the other subjects possess limited legal capacity under international law: they have a limited capacity to be granted international rights and powers or to be under international obligations, or a limited capacity to act, i.e. to put into effect their rights and powers in judicial and other proceedings (to enforce their rights) at the international level.[49] Already in its Reparation for Injuries opinion, the ICJ noted that there is neither a uniform nature nor content for the subjects of international law.[50] In general, there is no standard set of rights and obligations for each and every subject of international law, but 'subject' is a relative notion, the precise contents of which may differ from subject to subject and even between various subjects of the same category.[51] At best, the legal situation can be characterised as complex, and the number of entities with personality for particular purposes is considerable. A great deal depends on the relation of the particular entity to the various aspects of the relevant substantive law. For instance, while the individual is in certain contexts regarded as a legal person, he/she has no treaty-making capacity under international law.[52] In light of the debates revolving around the question of international 'subjectivity', it is hardly surprising that many scholars view the very idea of 'subjects' in the international legal system as confusing, even misleading.[53] The confusion is seen to stem in part from the doctrine of 'subjectivity' being conflated with the notion of international legal personality and international capacity.[54] Some authors see 'subjectivity' and legal personality as being the same, while others do not equate these concepts. It has been underlined that the elements of international legal personality, international legal capacity and international 'subjectivity' should not be tightly linked.[55]

Andrew Clapham has discussed the issue of international 'subjectivity' under the heading of 'subjects as prisoners of doctrine'.[56] He considers the traditional treatment of the question regarding subjects of international law both confusing and incomplete. According to him, it makes complete sense to talk about limited international personality of corporations, but the problem is that the question of international legal personality has remained entangled with the misleading concept of subjects of international law and the related question of attributions of statehood under international law. Increasing the categories of international legal persons recognised under international law is assumed to lead to an expansion of the possible authors of international law. This is seen to threaten the viable development of a decentralised, state-centred international legal order.[57] In Clapham's view, the concept of a subject of international law is often useless. While the role of non-state actors on the international plane cannot be ignored, the doctrine of 'subjectivity' developed to explain the framework of rights and duties under international law constrains the debate. Therefore, scholars are increasingly rejecting the whole notion of subjects and exposing the fact that there seem to be no commonly agreed rules to determine who can be classed as a subject. Clapham suggests concentrating on the rights and obligations of entities rather than their personality and moving from the debate on 'subjectivity' to the capacity of the entity to enjoy rights and bear obligations. Rights and obligations under international law should not depend on the 'mysteries of subjectivity'.[58]

Jennifer A. Zerk points to the fact that the development of human rights law and international economic law has dramatically increased the scope for participation in international law by non-state actors. According to her, rather than dividing participants into 'subjects' and 'objects' of international law, as has traditionally been done, a more useful approach would be to consider the degree to which international law recognises the existence of different kinds of participants in the international legal system.[59] Rosalyn Higgins' criticism of the division of 'subjects' and 'objects' of international law is perhaps the most compelling. She has concluded that 'the whole notion of "subjects" and "objects" has no credible reality, and, in my view, no functional purpose. We have erected an intellectual prison of our own choosing and then declared it to be an unalterable constraint'. Higgins notes that it is more helpful, and closer to perceived reality, to view international law as a particular decision-making process including a variety of participants.[60]

Jan Klabbers has referred to the non-existence of any agreement among international lawyers about the identity of international law subjects.[61] He describes the 'subjectivity' of international law as a status conferred by the academic community: a subject of international law is the legitimate subject of international research and reflection. Personality, in turn, is a status conferred by the legal system. The confusion results from the circumstance that the international legal system has no single authority endowed with the power to confer personality. Consequently, the very notion of subjects of international law is characterised by fluidity. Given the circumstance that different subjects may have different sets of rights and obligations under international law, the precise degree of rights and obligations is a matter of analysis. Klabbers concludes that personality in international law, like 'subjectivity', is but a descriptive notion: useful to describe a state of affairs, but normatively empty, as neither rights nor obligations flow from it automatically. Personality is by no means a threshold that must be crossed before an entity can participate in international legal relations; instead, once an entity does participate, it may be described as having a degree of international legal personality.[62]

RETHINKING 'SUBJECTIVITY' IN INTERNATIONAL LAW – DISCARDING THE DOCTRINE ALTOGETHER?

The creation of large multinational corporations and the ensuing increase in corporate power have made corporations increasingly visible actors in international relations. Presently, corporate entities enjoy a considerable number of rights and obligations deriving from international law. The role of corporations has also resulted in including multinational corporations among the subjects of international law. However, it appears that the doctrine of international 'subjectivity', at least in its present form, has difficulties accommodating non-state entities.[63] In the background one can detect states' hesitancy to broaden the circle of subjects and the fear of weakening the state-centric system of international regulation.64 As discussed in this article, the doctrine of subjects of international law has also come under critical scrutiny by a number of scholars. Combining 'subjectivity' with such notions as personality and capacity in various – often vague – ways has rendered the doctrine confusing, even misleading, and out of step with the present-day needs of the international community. Many authors have suggested shifting the focus from the debate on the subjects of international law to the participants in international legal relations, concentrating on the capacity of an actor to enjoy rights and incur obligations under international law. A number of remarks appear to favour discarding the very doctrine of international 'subjectivity'.

If the doctrine of international 'subjectivity' were discarded and, for instance, the doctrine of participants in international legal relations introduced in its stead, it would still be necessary to ask if this 'trick' helps to solve the problems linked to the former. Perhaps the doctrine of participants in international legal relations is not as empty and 'mysterious' as that of 'subjectivity', but in order to move forward from the confusion created by the 'subjectivity' doctrine, any doctrine introduced to replace it would also need to be clarified. Who are the relevant participants, what kinds of rights and obligations do they have under international law, and how accountability and responsibilities to be concretised are some of the questions that would need to be answered. However, before we discard old concepts and introduce new ones, it may be worthwhile to consider if the existing doctrine of subjects of international law could be clarified and modified in such a way as to make it workable. It is quite possible that after some proper academic brainstorming the doctrine of international 'subjectivity' may well function as an umbrella concept for the roles of different participants in international legal relations, also pointing to their rights and obligations as well as making sense of accountability and responsibilities of various actors.

The Special Representative of the UN Secretary General on Business and Human Rights (SRSG) chose – and undoubtedly wisely so – to adopt the approach of 'principled pragmatism' in his work that enabled him to avoid entering endless debates on theories and interpretations of international law, including international 'subjectivity' characterised by disagreements and even deadlocks. The 'Protect, Respect and Remedy' Framework proposed by the SRSG provides a good basis for the development of the international legal system in the direction of increasing its ability to accommodate the accountability of corporations for human rights violations. Strengthening this accountability is crucial in filling the existing gaps in the area where the system of international law, including the allocation of responsibilities, does not correspond to reality. Far too often corporations escape any accountability, for instance, in situations when the host state is unwilling or unable to protect human rights. Furthermore, as the SRSG pointed out, there are serious gaps in the protection of human rights in conflict situations and in contexts having a state-business nexus.

What further complicates the issue of responsibilities nowadays is the privatisation of many functions, such as medical care, that in many states have been taken care of by the public sector. This privatisation development also concerns armed conflicts, when many states contract private firms to carry out direct military activities or activities supporting them. In these circumstances of the privatisation of conflicts the very question of state responsibility for violations of international law has become complicated and blurred.[65] This has also brought to the fore the question of the accountability of private corporations participating in activities in conflict situations.[66] Furthermore, it is not uncommon that many corporations working and investing in conflict zones or having other business links to conflicts are state-owned or otherwise state-controlled. These are just a few examples to highlight how challenging many presentday situations may be from the viewpoint of human rights protection which also have links to the debates on international 'subjectivity' and participation in international legal relations. There are major gaps in human rights protection when various state interests (such as economic and military ones) come into play. To fill these gaps the existing norms of international law on accountability and responsibilities require thorough rethinking and redirecting, and, in general, more responsible thinking particularly on the part of governments.

Paying attention to the roles and duties of various actors that are relevant to human rights protection is crucial, regardless of labels, i.e. whether they are called subjects, participants or something else. The role and duties of states are of the utmost importance, as is underlined by the SRSG in his reports. While it is crucial to strengthen accountability of all actors affecting the protection of human rights, the role of corporations as profit-creating actors and their different roles and capacities vis-à-vis states should be paid due regard in considerations of 'translating' human rights obligations for corporate actors.[67] Furthermore, there are compelling reasons for maintaining the international legal system in which states retain their principal position as the drafters of international law norms. States are – if not always in practice, at least potentially – more democratic actors than corporations. Governments must be able to assess competing public interests and freely discharge their regulatory responsibilities for achieving social welfare objectives. It is precisely this capacity for performing important filtering functions that justifies the state-centric fiction of international law-making.[68]

NOTES

1 See e.g. I. Brownlie, Principles of Public International Law, 1999, pp. 57-68; A. Cassese, International Law, 2005, pp. 71-150; M. Dixon, Textbook on International Law, 2007, pp. 111-141.

2 The word 'subjectivity' is probably not a very eloquent English expression. It is said to be a Germanism (J. Klabbers, An Introduction to International Institutional Law, 2009, p. 40, fn. 10), but since it does appear in the literature on international law addressing the subjects of international law, the author feels it is appropriate to use it.

3 See Brownlie, supra note 1, p. 57. Brownlie's definition echoes the elements put forth in the ICJ's advisory opinion on Reparation for Injuries Suffered in the Service of the United Nations. See the remarks on this case below. Brownlie considers this conventional definition to be circular when it recognizes the capacity to act at the

international level of an entity that is already capable of acting at the international level. See also A. Clapham, Human Rights Obligations of Non-State Actors, 2006, p. 64. Challenging this circularity, see A. Meijknecht, Towards International Personality: The Position of Minorities and Indigenous Peoples in International Law, 2001, p. 24.

4 See Klabbers, supra note 2, p. 38.

5 Ibid., p. 39. Klabbers points out that hypothetically entities can possess legal personality under any legal system, p. 44.

6 See Brownlie, supra note 1, p. 57.

7 See also Meijknecht, supra note 3, pp. 23-63; Clapham, supra note 3, p. 64; J. Wouters et al., 'Introductory Remarks', in J. Wouters et al. (eds.), Accountability for Human Rights Violations by International Organisations, 2010, pp. 1-18, at p. 6. In his publication from the 1970s C.N. Okene considers international 'subjectivity' through treaty-making capacity. See C.N. Okene, Controversial subjects of contemporary international law. An examination of the new entities of international law and their treaty-making capacity, 1974.

8 Reparation for Injuries Suffered in the Service of the United Nations, Advisory Opinion, (1949) ICJ Reports 174, at p. 179. The advisory opinion arose out of the establishment of the state of Israel. The resulting unrest in the Middle East forced the UN to nominate a mediator, the Swedish Count Folke Bernadotte, to consider the issue. Count Bernadotte and a number of his associates were killed in Jerusalem in September 1948, allegedly by a private gang of terrorists. After this incident the UN General Assembly sought an advisory opinion from the ICJ. The question was raised as to whether the UN, as an organisation, could claim reparation for these injuries from the responsible state.

9 See Brownlie, supra note 1, p. 58. See also Klabbers, supra note 2, pp. 40-42, 131-152, 251-270; D.E. Arzt & I.I. Lukashuk, 'Participants in International Legal Relations', in C. Ku & P.F. Diehl (eds.), International Law. Classic and Contemporary Readings, 1998, pp. 155-176, at p. 155.

10 Cassese refers to states as fundamental subjects of international law. See Cassese, supra note 1, p. 71.

11 For remarks on attributed and implied powers of international organisations, see Klabbers, supra note 2, pp. 53-73. Brownlie calls states and international organisations the 'normal types' of legal person on the international plane. See Brownlie, supra note 1, p. 58.

12 See e.g. the publication by Wouters et al., supra note 7.

13 For discussion of whether or not international organisations are bound by international human rights obligations under international law, see O. De Schutter, 'Human Rights and the Rise of International Organisations: The Logic of Sliding Scale in the Law of International Responsibility', in J. Wouters et al. (eds.), Accountability for Human Rights Violations by International Organisations, 2010, pp. 51-128, at pp. 55-73, 104, 125.

14 See Cassese, supra note 1, pp. 124-150. Insurgents and national liberation movements

are noted to have special links to states since they are entities potentially on their way to becoming states. The former come into being through their struggle against the state to which they previously belonged. The latter group is viewed as consisting of organised groups particularly fighting against colonialism, racist regimes or alien domination. This legitimisation is based on the principle of self-determination. Cassese labels the Holy See, the sovereign order of Malta and the International Committee of the Red Cross as being sui generis entities. Clapham calls de facto regimes, the Holy See and the Order of Malta as the entities with state-like qualities also often counted among the subjects of international law. See Clapham, supra note 3, p. 59. For Brownlie, 'established legal persons' include states, political entities legally proximate to states, condominiums, internationalised territories, international organisations, agencies of states and agencies of organisations. Non-self-governing peoples, states in statu nascendi, legal constructions, belligerent and insurgent communities, entities sui generis and individuals he describes as having 'special types of personality'. See Brownlie, supra note 1, pp. 59-66.

15 See ibid., pp. 58, 66; Cassese, supra note 1, pp. 142-150; Clapham, supra note 3, p. 61.

16 See Cassese, supra note 1, pp. 144-150. For the denial of international 'subjectivity' of individuals (in earlier literature), see e.g. H. Lauterpacht, International Law and Human Rights, 1968, pp. 6-9.

17 See Art. 5 of the Statute of the ICC, Rome, 17 July 1998, in force 1 July 2002, UN Doc. A/CONF.183/9, United Nations Treaty Series, Vol. 2187. Nowadays individual criminal responsibility under international law also extends to such international crimes as slavery, disappearances and torture. See Clapham, supra note 3, p. 29.

18 For remarks on the status of individuals in international law, see Cassese, supra note 1, pp. 142-150. See also Arzt & Lukashuk, supra note 9, pp. 157-166.

19 These entities have been described using different combinations of the terms multinational, transnational, business and enterprise. Regardless of the exact term used, this kind of entity is characterised by its ability to operate across national borders and outside the effective supervision of domestic and international law that makes them important actors from the viewpoint of international law. M.T. Kamminga & S. Zia-Zarifi, 'Introduction', in M.T. Kamminga & S. Zia-Zarifi (eds.), Liability of Multinational Corporations under International Law, 2000, pp. 1-15, at pp. 2-3. For the remarks on defining multinational corporations, see also C. Wells & J. Elias, 'Catching the Conscience of the King: Corporate Players on the International Stage', in P. Alston (ed.), Non-State Actors and Human Rights, 2005, pp. 141-175, at pp. 148-150. Clapham has opted for the term transnational corporations. See Clapham, supra note 3, pp. 76-80, 199-201. Arzt & Lukashuk refer to transnational enterprises, supra note 9, pp. 166-173.

20 See Clapham, supra note 3, pp. 76-77.

21 See Brownlie, supra note 1, p. 66. Brownlie notes that although corporations can make agreements with foreign governments, a concession or contract between a state and a foreign corporation is not governed by the law of treaties. See also Arzt &

Lukashuk, supra note 9, pp. 167, 173.

22 See Klabbers, supra note 2, p. 38. See also Kamminga & Zia-Zarifi, supra note 19, p. 4; S. Tully, Corporations and International Lawmaking, 2007, p. 323.

23 Brownlie notes that legal persons created by states by treaty nowadays perform important functions, and the status of the bodies is regulated by the national law of one or more of the parties. Brownlie calls these bodies 'intergovernmental corporations of private law' and 'établissements publics internationaux'. A corporation may receive a privileged status in (even independence from) national law, and it may have both a considerable quantum of delegated powers and organs with autonomy in decision- and rule-making. In this case, the body concerned has the characteristics of an international organisation. Despite this, Brownlie does not view it as representing a distinct species of legal person on the international plane. See Brownlie, supra note 1, pp. 67-68.

24 J.A. Zerk, Multinationals and Corporate Social Responsibility. Limitations and Opportunities in International Law, 2006, p. 75. See also Clapham, supra note 3, pp. 80-81.

25 This is the case before the International Convention for the Settlement of Investment Disputes (ICSID) Tribunals. Corporations may also submit amicus briefs to WTO panels. See Tully, supra note 22, p. 323. The Iran-United States Claims Tribunal was established in the aftermath of the Iranian Islamic revolution of 1979 to resolve claims between Iran and the United States as well as between Iranian and US nationals, including corporations. Arzt & Lukashuk, supra note 9, pp. 167-168. A corporation could be a respondent in the Seabed Disputes Chamber of the Law of the Sea Tribunal. See Arts. 187 and 291(2) of the UN Convention on the Law of the Sea (1982), United Nations Treaty Series, Vol. 1833. See also Clapham, supra note 3, p. 31.

26 See Clapham, supra note 3, p. 81.

27 [1979] ECHR, Ser. A. No. 30.

28 See Clapham, supra note 3, p. 81. Clapham refers to the case of Agrotexim and Others v Greece, judgment of 24 October 1995. The Strasbourg Court interpreted the concept of 'non-governmental organisations', regarded as possible victims of violations of the rights stipulated in the Convention, as extending to legal persons more broadly, hence also corporations. See Clapham, supra note 3, pp. 81-82.

29 Case of OAO Neftyanaya Kompaniya Yukos v Russia, judgment of 20 September 2011, [2011] ECHR 1342. Among other things, the Court found that the respondent state had violated the company's rights under Art. 6 of the European Convention on Human Rights (right to a fair trial). For remarks on the standing of corporations before the Strasbourg Court, see S. Joseph, 'Scope of Application', in D. Moeckli et al. (eds.), International Human Rights Law, 2010, pp. 150-170, at p. 153.

30 See Zerk, supra note 24, pp. 76-79.

31 See Clapham, supra note 3, p. 28. In his earlier writings Clapham noted that non-state bodies, including corporations, have long been subject to human rights obligations, as implemented and enforced under domestic and regional law. See A. Clapham, Human Rights in the Private Sphere, 1993. It is worth noting that corporate actors can contribute

to international law making through the work of the International Labour Organization (ILO) in which 'tripartism' enables the representation of employers' interests and thereby can incorporate corporate contributions in the work of the organisation. See also Tully, supra note 22, p. 321. For some remarks on historical developments of corporate contributions to international law making, see pp. 320-321.

32 This is noted to be a result of concern over the practicalities of prosecuting corporate defendants, rather than doubt as to whether international criminal law actually applies to companies. See Zerk, supra note 24, p. 76. See more elaborately A. Clapham, 'The Question of Jurisdiction under International Criminal Law over Legal Persons: Lessons from the Rome Conference on an International Criminal Court', in M.T. Kamminga & S. Zia-Zarifi (eds.), Liability of Multinational Corporations under International Law, 2000, pp. 139-195, at pp. 143-160. Several international treaties have expressly included corporate crimes, including the Apartheid Convention, and treaties governing corruption and bribery, hazardous wastes, and other environmental violations. B. Stephens, 'The Amorality of Profit: Transnational Corporations and Human Rights', 2002 Berkeley Journal of International Law 20, pp. 45-90, at p. 77.

33 See Clapham, supra note 3, pp. 31, 58.

34 Ibid., p. 237. For regimes of domestic regulation (including civil liability) of corporate behaviour, see R.G. Steinhardt, 'Corporate Responsibility and the International Law of Human Rights: The Next Lex Mercatoria', in P. Alston (ed.), Non-State Actors and Human Rights, 2005, pp. 177-226, at pp. 187-202.

35 See Zerk, supra note 24, pp. 76-93.

36 Corporations acquired benefits under international law when a huge number of international treaties contributed to a conducive business environment. See also Zerk, supra note 24, pp. 76-79. The Special Representative of the UN Secretary General on Business and Human Rights (SRSG) points to a far-reaching role of bilateral investment treaties and host government agreements. See SRSG 2010, infra note 40, p. 6. For advantages of direct regulation of multinational corporations, see S. Joseph, 'An Overview of the Human Rights Accountability of Multinational Enterprises', in M.T. Kamminga & S. Zia-Zarifi (eds.), Liability of Multinational Corporations under International Law, 2000, pp. 75-93, at pp. 87-88.

37 See Zerk, supra note 24, pp. 83-91. The SRSG draws attention to the use of extraterritorial jurisdiction. See e.g. SRSG 2010, infra note 40, p. 11; SRSG 2011, infra note 40, p. 7.

38 The existing international regulation of business conduct in the area of human rights is characteristically of a non-binding nature. See Steinhardt, supra note 34, pp. 202-213. See also D. Weissbrodt & M. Gruger, 'Human Rights Responsibilities of Businesses as Non-State Actors', in P. Alston (ed.), Non-State Actors and Human Rights, 2005, pp. 315-350.

39 See Clapham, supra note 3, p. 25. For remarks on states' reservations about upgrading the status of multinational corporations (transnational enterprises) at the international level, see also Arzt & Lukashuk, supra note 9, pp. 168-169.

40 The UN Secretary General appointed Professor John Ruggie from Harvard University as his Special Representative on this matter. The most important reports summarizing the work of the SGSR are the reports published in 2008, 2009 and 2010, as well as the final report of 2011: Reports of the SRSG on the issue of human rights and transnational corporations and other business enterprises, John Ruggie: Promotion and protection of all human rights, civil, political, economic, social and cultural rights, including the right to development. Protect, Respect and Remedy: a Framework for Business and Human Rights, A/HRC/8/5, 2008 (SRSG 2008); Promotion and protection of all human rights, civil, political, economic, social and cultural rights, including the right to development. Business and human rights: Towards operationalizing the 'protect, respect and remedy' framework, A/HRC/11/13, 2009 (SRSG 2009); Business and human rights: Further steps towards the operationalization of the 'protect, respect and remedy' framework, A/HRC/14/27, 2010 (SRSG 2010); Guiding Principles on Business and Human Rights: Implementing the United Nations 'Protect, Respect and Remedy' Framework, Advanced edited version, A/HRC/17/31, 2011 (SRSG 2011).

41 Among other things, the SRSG refers to the lack of democratic legitimacy of companies. See SRSG 2010, supra note 40, para. 64.

42 The SRSG's Framework is intended to apply to all states and to all business enterprises, both transnational and others, regardless of their size, sector, location, ownership and structure. See SRSG 2011, supra note 40, Annex, p. 6.

43 Note e.g. the critical remarks of Radu Mares.

44 For the remarks on the positive reception of the proposal on the Framework, see e.g. SRSG 2011, supra note 40, Introduction to the Guiding Principles, Para. 8.

45 The SRSG notes that the normative contribution of his proposal does not lie in the creation of new international law obligations but 'in elaborating the implications of existing standards and practices for states and businesses; integrating them within a single, logically coherent and comprehensive template; and identifying where the current regime falls short and how it should be improved'. See SRSG 2011, supra note 40, Introduction to the Guiding Principles, Para. 14. See also Annex, p. 6.

46 See e.g. SRSG 2010, supra note 40, Paras. 12, 44-45, 61, 69.

47 See e.g. SRSG 2011, supra note 40, Annex, Paras. 4-6. According to the SRSG, where a business enterprise is controlled by the state, or where its acts can be attributed otherwise to the state, an abuse of human rights by the business enterprise may entail a violation of the state's own international law obligations. Ibid., Para. 4.

48 M. Rajavuori, Corporate Human Rights Due Diligence and Congolese Conflict Mineral Supply Chains, Master of Laws thesis, Law Faculty of the University of Turku, 2011.

49 See Cassese, supra note 1, pp. 72, 150. The 'subjectivity' of non-state entities is characterised as derivative. J. Klabbers, '(I Can't Get No)

Recognition: Subjects Doctrine and the Emergence of Non-State Actors', in J. Petman & J. Klabbers (eds.), Nordic Cosmopolitanism. Essays

in International Law for Martti Koskenniemi, 2003, pp. 351-369, at p. 361.

50 The Court held: 'The subjects of law in any legal system are not necessarily identical in their nature or in the extent of their rights, and their nature depends on the needs of the community'. Reparation for Injuries Suffered in the Service of the United Nations, supra note 8, p. 178.

51 See Klabbers, supra note 2, p. 39.

52 See Brownlie, supra note 1, p. 68.

53 See e.g. Clapham, supra note 3, p. 80; Klabbers, supra note 2, p. 39.

54 See Klabbers, supra note 2, p. 39.

55 Meijknecht points out that international legal personality and international (legal) 'subjectivity' are not identical, but rather they are two different aspects of the fact that an entity enters the field of international law. See Meijknecht, supra note 3, pp. 24-25, 34.

56 See Clapham, supra note 3, pp. 59-63.

57 Ibid., p. 59. Clapham mentions two fears that create resistance to the recognition of international legal personality for corporations. First, the fear that foreign corporations would somehow more easily be able to interfere in the political and economic affairs of states if they were acknowledged as possessing a degree of international personality. Second, the fear that these foreign corporations would be able to trigger excessive diplomatic protection for national companies of the host state where the foreign nationals are controlling shareholders in those companies, p. 78.

58 Ibid., pp. 60-62, 68-69, 83.

59 See Zerk, supra note 24, pp. 73-74.

60 R. Higgins, Problems and Process. International Law and How We Use it, 1994, pp. 49-50. Remarks on the subject-object dichotomy in international law, see also Meijknecht, supra note 3, pp. 46-48.

61 See Klabbers, supra note 49, p. 352.

62 See Klabbers, supra note 2, pp. 39, 51-52. Klabbers refers to views according to which the very metaphor of personality (in this case as regards international organisations) is misleading, p. 52. Also Arzt & Lukashuk deem it more important to concentrate on actual participation in the process of creating, making claims under, and enforcing international law, rather than focusing on the formal issues of international 'subjectivity' or international legal personality. See Arzt & Lukashuk, supra note 9, p. 156. R. Urueña puts forth interesting views on 'subjectivity' and participation in international law in R. Urueña, No Citizens Here: Global Subjects and Participation in International Law, Centre on Excellence in Global Governance Research, Faculty of Law, University of Helsinki, 2010.

63 See also Klabbers, supra note 49, p. 369.

64 See also ibid., pp. 362, 364-365, 367; and Meijknecht, supra note 3, p. 551.

65 These challenges are elaborated upon in K. Creutz, Transnational Privatised Security and the International Protection of Human Rights, publications of the Erik Castrén Institute of International Law and Human Rights, University of Helsinki, the Erik

Castrén Institute Research Reports 19/2006.

66 For instance, it has been pointed out that in these contexts private security forces have often become part of the problem instead of becoming part of the solution. One of the solutions offered to this challenge is to consider private security firms as (modern) mercenaries in armed conflicts or agents of the state. At the same time it has been stated that this legal analysis fails to capture the full picture. See Clapham, supra note 3, p. 302.

67 See also Zerk, supra note 24, pp. 76-79.

68 See also Tully, supra note 22, pp. 330-332, 345.

6

CHAPTER

THE EUROPEAN PRIVATE COMPANY, ITS SHAREHOLDERS AND ITS CREDITORS

Sandra van den Braak

Keywords: Company law, European Private Company, SPE, creditors, shareholders, buy-out

INTRODUCTION

In June 2008, the European Commission presented a Proposal for a Council Regulation on the Statute for a European Private Company (*Societas Privata Europaea*, SPE).[1] The SPE will be a new legal form for small and medium-sized companies, allowing them to set up the same European legal entity across the Member States. The SPE will n be the first legal entity based on a European Regulation. There are already three others: the European Economic Interest Grouping, the European Public Company (*Societas Europaea*, SE) and the European Cooperative Society.[2]

The history of the SPE goes back to the 1990s. In the beginning it was an initiative by academics but over time it gained support in Brussels and it ended up as a 'priority initiative' of the European Commission's 2008 Work Programme.[3] The SPE project is not to be confused with a project of a group of company law experts from different Member States. This group is working on a Model Company Law Act for Europe (EMCLA).[4] whereas after its adoption the Council Regulation on the SPE Statute is directly applicable in all Member States, the EMCLA will only present Member States with a model which they may or may not use when drafting their own national company law. This paper deals with the Commission's SPE Proposal, not with the

Citation: Van den Braak, S., (2010). The European Private Company, its shareholders and its creditors. Utrecht Law Review. 6(1), pp.1–21. DOI: http://doi.org/10.18352/ulr.111.

EMCLA.

According to the SPE Proposal, the SPE Statute shall apply from July 2010 onwards. However, the adoption of the Proposal is not without problems. The Proposal is based on Article 308 EC Treaty, which means that its adoption requires the unanimous consent of all 27 Member States. As the Proposal is not undisputed, it may be difficult to reach unanimity.[5] In March 2009, the European Parliament adopted a legislative resolution with regard to the SPE proposing quite a few amendments to the Commission's Proposal. At present, in September 2009, it is still unclear whether the Commission will come up with an official revised compromise proposal. Whatever the outcome of the discussions will be, in any case the date of July 2010 seems to be a little optimistic.[7]

In this paper I will try to answer the question whether we need the SPE and whether the SPE Proposal provides for adequate protection for two important categories of stakeholders: shareholders and creditors.[8] In Section 4 below I will examine the potential need for the SPE. Section 5 concentrates on the position of shareholders and Section 6 on the position of creditors.[9] Section 7 contains a brief analysis and the final Section 8 makes some final remarks. Before examining the need for the SPE, it is wise to take a closer look at what the SPE is. Therefore the focus will first be on the requirements for the establishment of an SPE (Section 2) and the rules which are applicable to an SPE (Section 3). The various sections not only deal with the Commission's Proposal, but also with the relevant amendments by the European Parliament

On Friday, 26th June 2009, a conference on the SPE was held in Utrecht, organized by Utrecht University's Molengraaff Institute for Private Law. At the basis of this conference was a book on the SPE written by experts of the Ius Commune research programme.[10] This book as well as the report on the conference[11] have proved to be important sources for my research

REQUIREMENTS FOR THE ESTABLISHMENT OF AN SPE

Article 3 SPE Proposal

According to Article 3(1) SPE Proposal, an SPE shall comply with the following requirements. Firstly, its capital shall be divided into shares. Secondly, a shareholder shall not be liable for more than the amount he has subscribed or agreed to subscribe. Thirdly, an SPE shall have legal personality. Fourthly, its shares shall not be offered to the public and shall not be publicly traded.[12] finally, an SPE may be formed by one or more natural persons and/or legal entities.[13]

Minimum capital requirement?

The five requirements mentioned in the previous section seem to have the consent of all those involved with the SPE. However, there are also a number of issues that are not undisputed. The first one relates to the capital of the SPE.

The requirement of a minimum capital when incorporating a private company is present in many continental European jurisdictions. For instance, in the Netherlands there is a minimum capital requirement of € 18,000 for the Besloten Vennootschap and in Germany the minimum for a Gesellschaft mit beschränkter Haftung is € 25,000. However, in the wake of the case law of the European Court of Justice (ECJ) with regard to the freedom of establishment,[14] there is a tendency towards abolishing the minimum capital requirement. Germany has recently introduced the Unternehmergesellschaft with a minimum capital of € 1 and the Netherlands is in the process of abolishing the minimum capital requirement for the Besloten Vennootschap. [15] Among the arguments for abolishing it are that its amount is arbitrary and that there is no guarantee that it is still available at the time the creditor wishes his claim to be settled.[16]

In line with the tendancy at a national level, Paragraph 11 of the preliminary considerations to the SPE Proposal points out that the SPE should not be subject to a high mandatory capital requirement since this would be a barrier to the creation of SPEs. Accordingly, Article 19(4) SPE Proposal states that the capital of the SPE shall be at least € 1. However, the European Parliament is of a different opinion. It sticks to the requirement of a certain amount of capital and therefore it has proposed an amendment to Article 19(4) which, in certain circumstances, provides for a minimum of € 8,000.[17] For Dorresteijn and Uziahu-Santcroos, this amendment illustrates the difficulties in positioning the SPE in relation to domestic companies.[18]

Size restriction?

The SPE Statute is one of the measures of the Small Business Act (SBA), a Commission policy document designed to assist small and medium-sized enterprises (SMEs).[19] The objective of the SBA is to improve the framework conditions for SMEs, which account for more than 99 % of companies in the European Union, to do business in the Single Market and to improve their market performance. The SPE Statute is supposed to meet this objective by allowing entrepreneurs to set up an SPE following the same, simple, flexible company law provisions across the Member States.[20] However, as the SPE Proposal does not contain any company size restriction, large companies and groups may also benefit. The question whether the SPE should be limited to SMEs only has been discussed on several occasions, the main concern being that the SPE may be used by large companies to avoid the application of (rigid) rules of national company law.[21]

Cross-border element?

Another issue to be addressed is whether the accessibility of the SPE should depend on the presence of a cross-border dimension of the business. There is no cross-border requirement in the Proposal, which means that also in the case of purely national economic activities entrepreneurs may establish an SPE.[22] According to the Explanatory Memorandum to the SPE Proposal, an initial cross-border element would significantly reduce the potential of the instrument, it could easily be circumvented and would be difficult to monitor and enforce.[23]

The observation has been made that due to the lack of a Community dimension as a prerequisite for the incorporation or the existence of the SPE, the adoption of the SPE Proposal might not be reconcilable with the subsidiarity principle of Article 5 EC

Treaty.[24] However, according to the Commission the objective of the SPE to enable SMEs to use the same company form across the EU cannot be sufficiently achieved by the Member Sates themselves and therefore action at EU level is necessary.[25] In this context it is noteworthy that the European Parliament has proposed to add cross-border conditions to the Proposal. According to the proposed amendment of Article 3 SPE Proposal, an SPE shall have a cross-border element demonstrated by one of the following: a cross-border business intention or corporate objective; an intention to be significantly active in more than one Member State; establishments in different Member States, or a parent company registered in another Member State. However, the observation has been made that the cross-border requirements proposed by the European Parliament take a different approach from the requirements relating to other supranational legal forms[26] and, moreover, that they are very easy to circumvent.[27] On the other hand, without a cross-border requirement, the SPE may enter into competition with national legal forms and thus force Member States to adjust their own private limited company forms to the SPE model.[28]

RULES ON THE LAW WHICH IS APPLICABLE TO AN SPE

Article 4 SPE Proposal

Article 4 SPE Proposal provides for a hierarchy of rules applicable to the SPE. According to this hierarchy, the SPE is first to be governed by the directly applicable mandatory provisions of the Regulation. However, as the SPE not only intends to have a uniform legal form, but also a flexible one, the Regulation does not provide for an entirely autonomous mandatory regime. Annex I to the Regulation provides a list of matters in respect of which the shareholders of the SPE are obliged to lay down rules in their articles of association. Hence the articles of association constitute the second level. The third level in the hierarchy of applicable rules is the national law related to private companies of the Member State where the SPE is registered. The national law of this Member State only comes into play where a matter is not covered by the articles of the Regulation or by Annex I.

Regulation

The SPE Proposal comprises ten chapters entitled successively General provisions (I), Formation (II), Shares (III), Capital (IV), Organisation of the SPE (V), Employee participation (VI), Transferring the registered office of the SPE (VII), Restructuring, dissolution and nullity (VIII), Additional and transitional provisions (IX), Final provisions (X). The Proposal also provides for two Annexes. Annex I relates to the articles of association of the SPE and Annex II to the registration of the transfer of the registered office of the SPE. In total the SPE Proposal contains forty-seven articles.

Articles of association

According to the general provision of Article 4 SPE Proposal, an SPE shall also be governed, as regards the matters listed in Annex I to the Regulation, by its articles of association. The matters covered by Annex I are numerous – the list covers over forty issues – but they have in common that they notably concern the internal organisation of the SPE. As Annex I only prescribes what should be regulated in the articles of association and not how it should be regulated, the shareholders of the SPE are free to determine in their articles of association the internal organisation which is best suited to their needs.

The point has been made that although the contractual freedom of the shareholders to regulate the internal relations of the company may enhance the desired flexibility of the SPE, the flexibility thus achieved comes at a price because the search for tailor-made rules involves high transaction costs.[29] It is admitted that the inclusion in the SPE Regulation of model articles of association which could be adopted and/or adapted will meet this objection. However, no model articles have yet been drafted.[30]

The SPE Proposal does not regulate what happens if a matter listed in Annex I is not or is only partly regulated in the articles of association. The lack of default provisions is generally considered to be a serious problem and the observation has been made that it leads to inacceptable legal incertainty.[31]

Applicable national law

According to Article 4 SPE Proposal, where a matter is not covered by the Regulation or by Annex I, an SPE shall be governed by the law which applies to private limited companies in the Member State in which the SPE has its registered office.

It is admitted that the legal technique of Article 4 SPE Proposal aims to set aside national company law as much as possible. However, one may argue that it will be difficult to reach this goal. To begin with, the Regulation does not cover matters like insolvency, employment and tax,[32] which are important issues for the operation of the company. Secondly, there are quite a few matters that the Regulation itself assigns to the national law of the Member States.[33] Thirdly, upon further reflection the legal technique of Article 4 SPE Proposal is not as clear as it may seem at first glance. In the legal structure of the SPE as laid down in Article 4 SPE Proposal, the applicability of the national law is triggered by the words 'not covered by' the Regulation or Annex I. Thus the uniformity of the SPE will to a large extent depend on the interpretation of the wording 'not covered by'. Is this wording to be interpreted narrowly as advocated by, for instance, De Kluiver and Roest[34] or broadly as advocated by, for instance, Drury who fears 'extreme diversification' in the varieties of the SPE if it would become dependent on the national laws of the Member States?[35] Moreover, as pointed out by De Kluiver and Roest[36] and also by Lennarts,[37] even if a matter is to be considered exclusively covered by the Regulation or its articles of association, disputes will have to be settled before national courts which are influenced by their own national company law backgrounds. I do agree that even a broad interpretation is not an antidote to diversification but, on the other hand, over time preliminary proceedings before the ECJ may have a harmonising effect.

POTENTIAL NEED FOR THE SPE

Cross-border group structures

Companies wishing to expand across borders can in theory do so by creating either foreign branches which do not have a separate legal personality or foreign subsidiaries that do have legal personality. As a matter of fact cross-border activities are mostly organized through subsidiaries, which have the benefit of limited tax exposure and which are more trusted by local creditors and customers.[38] Once the choice has been made to establish a subsidiary abroad instead of a branch, a second question arises: which legal form will the subsidiary have? At this stage of the decisionmaking process, there are again two options.

The first option is to use the national legal form of the Member State where the subsidiary is to be established. However, this option has the disadvantage that this legal form may be unfamiliar to the parent company.[39] As a result, there may be high transaction costs upon the formation of the subsidiary. Besides, a difference in the legal form between the parent company and the subsidiary may also lead to compliance costs associated with the operation of the subsidiary. Moreover, every time the parent company wishes to establish a new subsidiary in another Member State, the disadvantage reappears

The second option is to use the national legal form of the Member State of the parent company. In this scenario the subsidiary would have a legal form that is familiar to the parent company, but that qualifies as 'foreign' in the Member State where it is set up. In theory, however, due to the freedom of establishment it could rely on recognition as a separate legal subject.[40] Though this option has the advantage of a familiar and similar legal form for all group members, it also has serious disadvantages. At the 2009 conference on the SPE in Utrecht, Teichmann asserted that because of these disadvantages, this option is in fact not an option at all. Among the disadvantages he mentioned were mistrust in the minds of the business partners and the authorities of the Member State of the subsidiary. They may wonder why the parent company has not used a local legal form for its subsidiary and the authorities may tend to respond to the supposed evasion of their domestic law with 'poisoned arrows'.[41] Whether or not these arrows are reconcilable with the freedom of establishment, in any case they constitute a legal uncertainty that business does not want to face.

The rationale for the SPE

From the foregoing it may be clear that the facility to incorporate subsidiaries in different Member States that are governed by the same set of rules is an important advantage of the SPE. In cross-border group structures this could save considerable costs. In fact, the advantage of a uniform structure for establishing subsidiaries throughout the EU is commonly accepted as an important rationale for the SPE.[42] The European label of the SPE is also often mentioned, particularly as a marketing tool for entrepreneurs from the 'new' Member States or for those who are considering trading outside the EU or who are considering running a cross-border joint venture.[43] The purpose of setting up the

SPE for enabling easy start-ups seems to lose weight since due to the recent reforms of national company law the current national legal forms are also more easily accessible.[44]

SHAREHOLDERS

Introduction

Shareholders' rights can be divided into two main categories: participation rights and financial rights. Participation rights, often referred to as voice rights,[45] relate to the possibilities that shareholders have to influence the company's policy; financial rights relate to the financial benefits that shareholders can derive from the company. In this section, the focus will be on the voice rights provided for by the SPE Proposal.[46] In Sections 5.2 to 5.6 I will successively introduce the right to be informed, the right to be consulted, the right to challenge resolutions, the right to request a resolution and the right to request an independent expert.

Disputes between shareholders or between shareholders and the company may have a negative impact on the company. In public companies those conflicts can come to an end when the dissatisfied shareholder sells his or her shares on the market. However, in private limited companies there is no market for shares[47] and that is why shareholders in private limited companies usually have exit rights, e.g. the right to expel another shareholder or the right to leave the company oneself. Considering that the private company is an environment with a high risk potential for conflicts because it is ipso facto unstable, exit rights are of the utmost importance.[48] In Sections 5.7 and 5.8 I will deal with the exit rights provided for by the SPE Proposal and in Section 5.9 the focus will be on the role of the applicable national law

As a starting point for my further research on this issue I will use a joint venture SPE with its registered seat in the Netherlands and with a Dutch shareholder A as one of four shareholders who each hold 25 % of the shares and the voting rights.[49]

The right to be informed

The right of shareholders to be informed is of great importance. In fact, it is on the basis of information that shareholders determine their position and exercise their rights. According to Article 28(1) SPE Proposal all shareholders shall have the right to be duly informed and to ask questions to the management body about resolutions, annual accounts and all other matters relating to the activities of the SPE. Article 28(2) provides that the management body may only refuse to give access to information if doing so could cause serious harm to the business interests of the SPE.

For our shareholder A these provisions are good news. He will get all the information he asks for, unless 'serious harm' will occur. However, if the focus is on the details, there are at least two questions that remain unanswered. The first one relates to the duty of management to supply the information. To whom is this duty owed? Of course it is owed to the individual shareholders who asked for the information, but is it also owed to all shareholders alike because otherwise they would be treated unequally?[50] The second question relates to procedural issues. Imagine our shareholder A not getting the information he asked for. What remedy is available to him and which court has jurisdiction? Should Article 22(2) of the Brussels I Regulation apply by analogy, which would lead to the Dutch courts having jurisdiction (the court of the registered seat)?[51] Our Dutch shareholder A would probably favour the jurisdiction of the Dutch court, but what if shareholder B, living in the UK, would like to exercise his right to information? Would B also be enthousiastic? I agree with Lennarts who points out that the SPE Proposal should contain an explicit jurisdiction rule, because otherwise the right to information risks being nothing more than a 'paper tiger'.[52]

The right to be consulted

Article 27(1) SPE Proposal provides for a list of matters that shall be decided by a resolution of the shareholders. These matters include, amongst others, a variation of rights attaching to shares, the expulsion of shareholders, the withdrawal of shareholders, distribution to the shareholders, the aquisition of own shares, a reduction of share capital and the appointment and removal of directors

According to Article 27(1), the shareholders' resolution shall be taken by a majority as defined in the articles of association. However, according to Article 27(2) for a number of key resolutions (for example, with regard to a variation of rights attaching to shares) the majority may not be less than two-thirds of the total voting rights attached to the shares issued by the SPE.[53] For our 25 % shareholder A this means that it depends on the articles of association whether these key resolutions can be taken without his consent. If the articles require a majority between twothirds (the minimum with regard to these resolutions) and three-quarters, he can be overruled

The observation has been made that the SPE Proposal, by not forbidding it, allows for the imposition of obligations on shareholders against their will. However, opinions differ on the required majority for such a resolution.[54] A broad interpretation of the wording 'rights' in Article 27(1)(a) (the variation of rights attaching to shares) will also include obligations and thus, according to Article 27(2), a qualified majority will be mandatory for imposing a variation of the obligations attaching to shares. On the other hand, a narrow interpretation of Article 27(1)(a) will lead to the conclusion that even a simple majority resolution would suffice. But whatever the correct interpretation might be, in both scenarios a shareholder can be confronted with additional obligations against his will. I do agree with Lennarts that this issue merits (re)consideration.[55] Imagine our shareholder A voting against a resolution imposing the obligation on all shareholders to grant a loan to the SPE and imagine the other three shareholders voting in favour of this resolution. The outcome is that our shareholder A is confronted, against his will, with the imposition of this obligation. This may make a minority position in the SPE very unattractive.

The right to challenge resolutions

According to Article 27(4) SPE Proposal resolutions shall comply with the SPE Regulation and with the articles of association of the SPE. Thus, according to the Proposal, resolutions can be declared ineffective due to an infringement of the SPE

Statute or an infringement of the articles of association. However, according to the proposed amendment to this provision by the European Parliament, resolutions may be declared ineffective also due to an infringement of the applicable national law. Together with Lennarts I note that the amendment introducing a reference to the applicable national law as a ground for annulment is not without importance for minority shareholders.[56] Imagine the three fellow shareholders of our shareholder A having abused their majority power to enforce a resolution that gravely violates his (A's) interests. Under the SPE Proposal this would not be a ground for an annulment of the resolution since neither the Proposal nor the articles of association (necessarily) refer to the issue of abuse of power. Under the amendment this is different because the reference to the applicable national law brings into play Article 15 Dutch Companies Act, which refers to the principle of reasonableness and fairness. According to this Dutch provision, a resolution that violates the principle of reasonableness and fairness may be annulled and this will be the case when the interests of a minority shareholder have been gravely violated. The proposed amendment by the European Parliament will thus constitute better protection for our shareholder A.

As for the procedural side of the matter: according to Article 27(4) SPE Proposal this issue is governed by the applicable national law. For our shareholder A this would mean that Article 15(3) and (5) Dutch Companies Act would apply. According to these Dutch provisions he would have one year to bring an action before the Dutch court (the court of the registered seat). However, under the proposed amendment by the European Parliament his position would be less strong because the amendment reduces the time available for challenging the resolution to one month from the date of the resolution.[57]

The right to request a resolution

Pursuant to Article 29(1) SPE Proposal shareholders holding 5 % of the voting rights attached to the shares of the SPE shall have the right to request the management body to submit a proposal for a resolution to the shareholders. The request must state the reasons and indicate the matters that should be subject to such a resolution. If the request is refused or if the management body does not submit a proposal within 14 calendar days of receiving the request, the shareholders concerned may then submit a proposal for a resolution to the shareholders regarding the matters in question. The threshold of 5 % is not a barrier for our shareholder A, who holds 25 % of the voting rights. He will be able to make his voice heard.[58]

The right to request an independent expert

The right to request an independent expert can be characterized as a special information right.[59] According to Article 29(2) SPE Proposal, if there is any suspicion of a serious breach of the law or of the articles of association of the SPE, shareholders holding 5 % of the voting rights attached to the shares of the SPE shall have the right to request the competent court or administrative authority to appoint an independent expert to investigate and report on the findings of the investigation to the shareholders. The expert will be allowed to have access to the documents and records of the SPE and to require information from the management body.

For our shareholder A holding 25 % of the voting rights, the threshold of 5 % is not a problem. He has the right to request an independent expert. Clear as this may seem, there are also issues that remain unclear. Without going into details, I would like to mention three questions raised by Lennarts.[60] First, which court is the competent court? Is Article 22(2) of the Brussels I Regulation to be applied by analogy once again? Secondly, how should the wording 'serious breach of law' be interpreted? Does the 'law' also include the applicable national company law (which in the case of our 'Dutch' SPE would imply the applicability of the principle of reasonableness and fairness)? Thirdly, who pays? Without a clear answer to these questions, A's right to request an independent expert is likely to remain latent.

Expulsion

Article 17 SPE Proposal deals with the situation where a majority of the shareholders want to expel a minority. The expulsion implies the acquisition of the shares of the expelled shareholders by either the SPE or the other shareholders.[61] Article 17(1) reads as follows: 'On the basis of a resolution of the shareholders and on an application by the SPE, the competent court may order the expulsion of a shareholder if he has caused serious harm to the SPE's interest or the continuation of the shareholder as a member of the SPE is detrimental to its proper operation. An application to the court shall be made within 60 calendar days of the resolution of the shareholders'. Article 17(2) deals with the temporary suspension of the rights of the shareholder to be expelled and Article 17(3) with the acquisition of his shares. Hereafter, I will concentrate on the first step towards expulsion, the shareholders' resolution. For an analysis of the second and third step, successively an application by the SPE to the court and a court order, I would like to refer to De Kluiver and Roest, who are very critical in their evaluation of the procedure.[62]

According to Article 27 (1)(b) and 27(2) SPE Proposal, the resolution of expulsion requires a qualified majority of two-thirds of the total voting rights attached to the shares issued by the SPE. For our 25 % shareholder A, this means that if his three fellow shareholders want him out, he may be expelled from the SPE. Presuming that A himself will not be in favour of his own expulsion, he will probably try to challenge the resolution on his expulsion. In Section 5.4 above it was shown that A can bring an action for the annulment of the resolution before the Dutch court. Consequently, the Dutch court will verify whether there is a valid ground for expulsion. According to Article 17(1) SPE Proposal, there is a ground for expulsion if A has caused serious harm to the SPE's interest or when the continuation of his membership is detrimental to the SPE's operation. Admittedly, whether or not A's action for annulment will succeed depends on the facts of the case. What was A's behaviour and does it qualify for expulsion? However, the outcome of the action is not only a matter of facts but also a matter of interpretation. As is clearly shown by De Kluiver and Roest, different national courts may have different views as to how broadly or narrowly the grounds for expulsion are to be interpreted. Besides, under the proposed amendment by the European Parliament, the Dutch courts may also take into account the principle of reasonableness and fairness.[63]

In addition to his right to challenge the resolution, A seems to have a second possibility to try to block his expulsion. Because his expulsion will be based on a court order, he will have the right to plead his case before the court that has to decide upon the application by the SPE. Assuming that the competent court in this respect is once again the Dutch court,[64] from a procedural point of view this does not seem to be very efficient.

Withdrawal

Article 18 SPE Proposal deals with the situation where a shareholder wants to withdraw from the SPE. His withdrawal implies the acquisition of his shares by either the SPE or the other shareholders. Article 18(1) contains the grounds for withdrawal and Article 18(2) to 18(6) provide for the procedure to be followed. Hereafter, I will concentrate on the grounds for withdrawal. For a critical analysis of the procedure I would like to refer once again to De Kluiver and Roest, who conclude that with regard to the procedure there are too many open issues.[65]

According to Article 18(1) the right to withdraw is based on two requirements. First, the activities of the SPE are being or have been conducted in a manner which causes serious harm to the interests of the shareholder. Secondly, the serious harm is a result of one or more of the following events: (a) the SPE has been deprived of a significant part of its assets; (b) the registered office of the SPE has been transferred to another Member State; (c) the activities of the SPE have changed substantially; (d) no dividend has been distributed for at least 3 years even though the SPE's financial position would have permitted such a distribution. It is interesting to note that the European Parliament has proposed to amend Article 18(1) rather fundamentally. According to the amendment, the first requirement of 'serious harm' no longer applies.[66] As a consequence, the four events mentioned in the Proposal always imply the possibility of a withdrawal for those who did not subscribe to the resolution relating to one of the events. Since these events are of such a nature that their sole occurrence against the will of a shareholder may qualify as 'serious harm', to me this seems to be a valid approach. De Kluiver and Roest are more critical with regard to this amendment, but I doubt whether all their arguments are convincing.[67] Their main concern seems to be that if the four events mentioned in Article 18(1) SPE Proposal in any case provide for a right to be bought out, the financial consequences for the SPE might be too heavy to bear. I do not share this concern because, first, the right to be bought out does not necessarily have financial consequences for the SPE (the shares may be acquired by the other shareholders), and, secondly, if the SPE acquires the shares of the withdrawing shareholder the rules relating to share buy-backs (see Section 6.2 hereafter) will apply.

Another change proposed by the European Parliament is to no longer limit the grounds for withdrawal to the four events mentioned in the Proposal. According to the amendment the articles of association may also provide for grounds for withdrawal. Since, in practice, the situations in which withdrawal is an appropriate solution for intra-company conflicts may vary, it seems to be a good idea to broaden the scope of the right to withdraw. However, in the opinion of De Kluiver and Roest the best solution would be to introduce a general clause in the Proposal itself, granting a buy-out remedy 'at will', whereby shareholders would have a right to be bought out provided that an appropriate notice period is observed and that the level of payments associated with the exit takes into account the additional costs of refinancing the company as well as, in the case of oppression or unfair conduct on the side of the continuing shareholders, additional payments by the continuing shareholders [68]

It will be clear from the foregoing that our shareholder A will be better off with the amendment than with the Proposal in situations where he does not agree with his three fellow shareholders and would like to withdraw. Under the amendment he will not have to meet the 'serious harm' requirement and, in addition, the articles of association may provide for additional grounds for withdrawal.

Applicable national law

As we have seen in Section 3 above, according to Article 4 SPE Proposal the SPE is governed first by the Regulation, secondly by its articles of association and thirdly by the applicable national law. In Sections 5.2 to 5.8 an overview was given of the voice rights and the exit rights of an SPE's shareholder as provided for by the proposed Regulation and we have seen what our shareholder A can do when he does not agree with his fellow shareholders. Now the question is whether or not the provisions in the Regulation and the articles of association fully cover all his voice and exit rights. If so, Dutch law has no autonomous role in this context. However, in a more narrow interpretation of the scope of the Regulation, A may also benefit from rights and/or mechanisms provided by Dutch national law. In this context there are (at least) three matters that merit our attention.

In Dutch law there is a distinction between resolutions being null and void and resolutions qualifying for annulment by the court. This distinction is fundamental because in the former case the resolution is null and void ab initio and in the latter case the resolution remains valid until it is annulled. As Lennarts observes, the text of the SPE Proposal does not mention the possibility of resolutions being null and void ab initio. [69] Does this mean that nullity ab initio on the basis of national law is ruled out? It has to be noted that according to the proposed amendment to Article 27(4) SPE Proposal by the European Parliament, shareholders' resolutions may be declared ineffective only by means of a court action. Although, on the one hand, it is difficult to imagine a legal system without nullity ab initio; on the other hand, the reference to a court action might be an indication of the exclusion of nullity ab initio. A second matter that needs attention is Dutch inquiry proceedings as laid down in Articles 344 to 359 Dutch Companies Act. Does the right to request an independent expert as provided for by Article 29(2) SPE Proposal leave room for the applicability of these proceedings? The aim of the Dutch proceedings is not only to gather information, but it may also be to put an end to intra-company conflicts. In order to attain this aim, the court may order measures such as the annulment of resolutions or the dismissal of directors and it is because of these measures that the Dutch inquiry proceedings are commonly seen as a very important source of minority shareholder protection.[70] Is the difference in aim and scope sufficient to conclude, as Lennarts does, that the Dutch proceedings do apply to an SPE registered in the Netherlands?[71]

With regard to exit rights there seems to be no room for the application of national provisions. But as we have seen in the previous section of this paper, according to the amendment by the European Parliament additional grounds for withdrawal may be introduced in the articles of association and thus national provisions may apply by placing them in the articles of association. However, the applicability of Articles 17 and 18 SPE Proposal cannot be excluded, which is highly regretted by De Kluiver and Roest. Because of the high risk of intra-company conflicts in private limited companies, these authors attach heavy weight to a well developed and detailed mechanism of shareholder dispute resolution including buy-out remedies and therefore they prefer the possibility of opting out of the Regulation and opting in for a certain national jurisdiction.[72] Attractive as their approach may seem – it certainly provides for legal certainty – it will also have a negative effect on the uniformity of the SPE throughout the European Union. In my view, the suggestion to introduce a general clause in the Proposal granting a buy-out remedy 'at will'[73] is a better one

In a discussion on the rights of shareholders and the applicable national law some attention should also be paid to derivative actions, an issue that is not dealt with in the SPE Proposal. The SPE Proposal does not give individual shareholders the right to directly sue directors of the SPE who have not acted in the best interests of the company and therefore have caused damage to the company. According to the Explanatory Memorandum, the directors' duty to act in the best interest of the company is a duty owed to the SPE and therefore a duty that may only be enforced by the SPE itself.[74] However, the national company law of some Member States does allow individual shareholders to enforce a company's claim by way of a derivative action.[75] The rationale for this derivative action is to resolve the problem of conflicting interests that arises when the SPE itself will have to initiate litigation against a director. As is shown by Olaerts, there are arguments to assume that it depends on the applicable national company law whether or not an SPE shareholder will have a derivative action.[76] Since Dutch law seems to rule out derivative suits,[77] our shareholder A has no action against the directors of the SPE if they have violated their duties towards the company.[78]

CREDITORS

Introduction

Traditionally, the creditors of a company have found protection in capital protection rules, which intend to ensure that shareholders pay a certain amount into the company and to ensure also that this amount is maintained. However, lately the traditional approach has been losing ground to a new one, according to which the creditors of a company are protected by rules that aim to ensure that there shall be no withdrawals of assets from the company to the benefit of the shareholders and at the detriment of the creditors.[79] In view of the abandonment of a minimum capital requirement in the SPE Proposal, it is obvious that the Commission takes the progressive approach.[80] In Section 6.2 I will consider the rules that guarantee that there will be no unlawful withdrawals of assets from the SPE.

A prudent creditor who is considering dealing with a company will probably be interested not only in protection against unlawful withdrawals, but he may also ask himself under what circumstances the directors can be held liable for misconduct and what his position will be if the company becomes insolvent. In Section 6.3 I will focus on the liability of the directors of the SPE and in Section 6.4 I will make some remarks on the position of creditors if the SPE becomes insolvent. As a starting point for my research in this section I will use an SPE with its registered seat in the Netherlands. Before dealing with the matters I have just mentioned, I would like to make a brief comment on the idea of creditor self-help. According to this notion, creditors are supposed to take care of their own protection by negotiating, for instance, for immediate payment, personal guarantees of directors or retention-of-title clauses.[81] It is admitted that the better the creditor self-help system is supposed to work, the less protection creditors need from company law.[82]

Unlawful withdrawals

The SPE Proposal contains three mechanisms for providing for a flow of assets from the SPE to the shareholders: distribution of dividend (Article 21), share buy-backs (Article 23) and capital reduction with repayment on shares (Article 24). According to the relevant provisions, these mechanisms have three common features. First, they are based on a resolution of the shareholders (Article 27(1)(e), (f) and (i)).[83] Secondly, they have to satisfy a mandatory balance-sheet test (Articles 21(1), 23(2) and 24(1)) and thirdly, there is an optional solvency test (Articles 21(2), 23(2) and 24(1)).[84] The balance-sheet test guarantees that after withdrawal from the SPE, the assets of the SPE fully cover its liabilities and that reserves that may not be distributed under its articles of association remain untouched. The solvency test includes a solvency certificate certifying that the SPE will be able to pay its debts as they become due in the normal course of business within one year of the date of the distribution. The solvency certificate is only mandatory if the articles of association so require. However, in the opinion of Barneveld, the absence of the requirement of a solvency certificate does not imply the absence of the requirement of the solvency test itself. In his view, the general duties and liabilities of directors as laid down in Article 31 SPE Proposal also cover the duty of a solvency test.[85]

According to the proposed amendment by the European Parliament to Article 19(4) SPE Proposal, where the articles of association of the SPE do not require a solvency certificate, the capital of the SPE shall be at least € 8,000. To prevent a distribution from this capital, the European Parliament also proposes an amendment to the balance-sheet test, providing that the remaining amount of the deposit shall not fall below the amount of the minimum capital.[86]

However reassuring these provisions may be, for a creditor it is also important to know what happens if a distribution of dividend, a share buy-back or a repayment on shares leaves the SPE's liabilities uncovered. Is the unlawful distribution to be compensated by the shareholders and/or the directors? With regard to the shareholders, the SPE Proposal contains a specific provision. According to Article 22, any shareholder who knew or should have known that the distribution did not satisfy the balance-sheet test or the required solvency test must return to the SPE what he has received. The proposed amendment to this provision by the European Parliament goes even further by stating that all unlawful distributions must be returned, irrespective of any subjective element.

The SPE Proposal does not contain a specific provision with regard to directors who have participated in an unlawful withdrawal. However, according to Barneveld, the general provision of Article 31 SPE Proposal, stating that a director shall have a duty to act in the best interests of the SPE and that he shall be liable to the company for any act or omission in breach of his duties which causes loss or damage to the SPE, also covers the duty and liability in the case of an unlawful withdrawal. In Barneveld's view, if a director proposes a distribution that does not satisfy the balance-sheet test or the solvency test, he can be held liable by the SPE on the basis of Article 31(4) SPE Proposal.[87] In this view, the proposed amendment of Article 31(5) SPE Proposal by the European Parliament, stating, among other things, that the directors shall pay compensation in particular where payments have been made in breach of Article 21 SPE Proposal, qualifies as a specification of Article 31(4).

Although the protection of creditors can be seen as the rationale for the provisions in the SPE Proposal relating to the recovery of unlawful withdrawals by shareholders and to the compensation to be paid by directors, these provisions do not provide for a claim against the shareholders and/or the directors by the creditors themselves. It is up to the SPE to request recovery by the shareholders or compensation by the directors. However, in case of the insolvency of the SPE, the trustee in bankruptcy can claim on behalf of the SPE. I will come back to this in Section 6.4. Besides, the creditors may have other instruments at their disposal to act against the shareholders and/or the directors. As for the shareholders, under certain circumstances they may be held liable on the basis of the rules of tort.[88]

Liability of directors

With regard to the liability of directors a distinction can be made between the internal liability of directors towards the company and the external liability of directors towards creditors. Article 31 SPE Proposal contains a general provision with regard to internal liability. Article 31(1) contains the duty to act in the best interests of the SPE, Article 31(2) states that duties shall be owed to the SPE, Article 31(3) relates to conflicts of interest, Article 31(4) states that if a director acts in breach of his duties, he shall be liable to the SPE for the loss or damage he has caused,[89] and Article 31(5) states that without prejudice to the provisions of the Regulation, the liability of directors shall be governed by the applicable national law. The articles of association may provide for any other specific duties of directors.[90] As is clearly shown by Olaerts, the interpretation of Article 31 entails several questions that the national courts will probably answer along the lines of their own national rules on directors' liability, thus threatening the desired uniformity of the SPE.[91] However, Olaerts also notes that at the same time the introduction of a general standard may turn out to be a valuable step towards bottom-up harmonization in an area that is currently far from harmonised.[92] Against this background it is noteworthy that the European Parliament has proposed two amendments to Article 31 that contain top-down harmonization. First, the European Parliament proposes an addition to Article

31(4), stating that liability shall not extend to directors who are able to demonstrate their blamelessness and who made known their disagreement with the failure to fulfil duties. Secondly, the European Parliament proposes a new Article 35(5a), stating that any right of action pursuant to this article shall lapse within four years of the date when it arose. Without these two additions, the issues of blamelessness and the time frame will remain subject to national law and hence be subject to bottom-up harmonization. Besides, Dorresteijn and Uziahu-Santcroos note that since the amendments place the SPE at an advantage or a disadvantage in comparison to companies under national law, the amendments may have the side-effect of enhancing intra-state competition.[93]

The SPE Proposal does not provide for rules relating to the external liability of its directors. Considering this, on the basis of Article 4 SPE Proposal one may argue that the external liability of the directors of an SPE shall be governed by the applicable national law.[94] For the directors of an SPE with its registered office in the Netherlands this means that with regard to the issue of their external liability, Dutch company law applies.

The Dutch Companies Act offers several grounds for directors' external liability. It contains provisions for liability in the context of the registration of the company (Article 180(2)(a)), minimum capital (Article 180(2)(b) and (c)), share buy-backs (Articles 207a, 207d), insolvency (Article 248) and misrepresenting the company's condition towards third parties (Article 249). However, one can hardly argue that all these provisions apply to the directors of an SPE. It is obvious that the provision of Article 180(2)(a) is not suitable to apply to the directors of an SPE. While in the Dutch system the company acquires legal personality before its registration, the SPE shall acquire legal personality on the date on which it is entered in the register. As a consequence the Dutch system of directors' liability for acts of the company in the time frame between the formation of the company and its registration as provided for in Article 180(2)(a) is without relevance in the context of the SPE. With regard to the Dutch liability of Article 180(2)(b) and (c), there is a similar argument for not applying them to the directors of an SPE, at least under the Commission's Proposal. Because the SPE Proposal does not contain a minimum capital requirement, the Dutch system of directors' liability for the acts of the company in the time frame between the formation of the company and the moment the minimum capital is fully paid up, once again seems without relevance in the context of the SPE. However, if there is to be a minimum capital as provided for by the amendment by the European Parliament, these Dutch provisions may apply – though probably not for long because under the Bill amending Dutch private company law[95] they will be abolished. Matters are more complicated with regard to the Dutch provisions under Article 207a and 207b Companies Act (liability for unlawful share buy-backs). According to Article 4 SPE Proposal, matters shall be governed by the applicable national law only where they are not covered by the Regulation or the articles of association. As we have seen in the previous Section 6.2, one may argue that Article 31 SPE Proposal covers the matter of the internal liability of the directors for unlawful share buy-backs. Besides, Article 23(5) SPE Proposal states that shares acquired by the SPE in contravention of the Regulation or the articles of association shall be sold or cancelled within one year of their acquisition. Is this supposed to exclude external liability based on national company law or not? If not, Article 207a and 207b of the

Dutch Companies Act may apply.

Among the provisions of the Dutch Companies Act with regard to the external liability of directors there are also two provisions that do not need Article 4 SPE Proposal in order to apply to the directors of an SPE. As for Article 248 (liability in insolvency), in the following Section 6.4 we will see that its application is triggered by mechanisms outside the SPE Proposal and as for Article 249 (liability for misrepresenting the condition of the company), its applicability is triggered by the reference in Article 25 SPE Proposal to the applicable national law.[96] Another thing which must be kept in mind is that not only company law can serve as a basis for a claim against a company's director but also tort law.[97] According to the relevant Dutch case law, a director is liable towards a creditor of the company if he has entered into a contract on behalf of the company with the creditor while knowing that the company will not be able to pay its debts and that in the end the creditor will be left empty-handed.[98] It is evident that this liability also applies to the directors of an SPE, provided, of course, that according to the rules of private international law Dutch tort law will apply.[99]

Insolvency of the SPE

The effectiveness of any system of creditor protection is ultimately tested when the company becomes insolvent. What is the position of the creditors of an insolvent SPE with its registered seat in the Netherlands? According to Article 40(3) SPE Proposal, insolvency shall be governed by the applicable national law and by Council Regulation (EC) No. 1346/2000.[100] As a result, the creditor of an SPE with its registered seat in the Netherlands is not in a different position than the creditor of any other private limited company declared bankrupt before a Dutch court. Here it is not as such necessary to discuss the position of an SPE's creditor. However, in the light of the foregoing it is noteworthy that the Dutch trustee in bankruptcy has at his disposition several ways of reconstructing the estate of the SPE. In the context of this paper, three of these possibilities deserve our attention. First, the trustee may exercise any right of action that the SPE may have with regard to the internal liability of the directors, including the internal liability for unlawful withdrawals. Secondly, the trustee may challenge any legal acts of the SPE that are detrimental to the general body of creditors,[101] under certain circumstances also including unlawful withdrawals.[102] Thirdly, he may have a claim against the directors of the SPE, based on Article 248 Dutch Companies Act. If the insolvency of the company has been caused by the apparent negligence of the board of directors, the directors and also the shadow-directors are liable for the deficit. These three mechanisms show that the protection of creditors is not only a matter of company law, but also and perhaps even more a matter of insolvency law.[103]

BRIEF ANALYSIS

The second section of this paper has shown that with regard to the requirements for the establishment of an SPE, there are still some political decisions to be taken. Do we want a minimum capital requirement or not? Do we want a size restriction or not? Do we want a cross-border requirement or not? The third section of this paper has illustrated that with regard to the rules applicable to an SPE, the hierarchy of applicable rules proposed in Article 4 SPE Proposal entails questions that are difficult to answer. In the fourth section of this paper we have seen that the potential need for the SPE can be reduced essentially to its advantage of offering a uniform structure for establishing subsidiaries throughout the EU.

Considering the issues raised with regard to the applicable rules, two comments can be made with regard to the need for the SPE. To start with, it is not likely that business communities need something whose form and shape is still to be determined. As long as there is uncertainty about the applicable rules, business communities might not be interested in the SPE at all. Secondly, the aim of the uniformity of the SPE does not seem to have been fully attained because the applicable national law seems to play a considerable role. Although the applicable national law is supposed to come into play only at the third level of the hierarchy of applicable rules presented in Article 4 SPE Proposal, it is difficult to imagine the functioning of the first two levels without any help from the applicable national law. As for the Regulation, it will be interpreted by the national courts and it may take some time before preliminary proceedings before the ECJ will have a harmonising effect. As for the matters to be regulated by the articles of association, the question arises what will happen if a matter is not or only partly covered by the articles of association. Most probably, the answer will be found in the applicable national law. Moreover, the third level of applicable rules itself seems to be fairly broad. As we have seen, the applicable national law covers, for instance, the thorny issue of directors' liability.

The fifth section of this paper has highlighted the position of the shareholder of an SPE and we have seen which voice rights and exit rights the Regulation offers him. However, we have also seen that his position is not as clear as it may seem at first glance. Not only are there procedural issues that need clarification, but also the role of the applicable national law entails legal uncertainty. As long as the position of the shareholder remains unclear, one can hardly argue that the SPE Proposal provides for adequate protection. Some comments can be made, though. As we have seen in Sections 5.3, 5.4 and 5.8, a minority shareholder may face additional obligations or other oppressing resolutions, without the possibility to challenge these resolutions and without the possibility of a withdrawal. In my view, this is something that certainly qualifies as inadequate protection. Considering this, the question of how to prevent a shareholder finding himself in this position will inevitably arise. In theory, his protection can be organised at each of the three levels of applicable rules. Protection at the third level of the applicable national law does not seem to be a good idea, since the legal technique of Article 4 SPE Proposal is already full of problems. In this respect the issues raised in Section 5.9 – for instance the uncertainty with respect to the applicability of Dutch inquiry proceedings – are illustrative. As for protection at the second level of the articles of association, one of the proposed amendments by the European Parliament fits within this option. As we have seen in Section 5.8, the European Parliament has proposed an amendment allowing for grounds for withdrawal in the articles of association. Although I support the idea of broadening the scope of the right to withdraw, I am not convinced that the proposed amendment is the best solution. According to this amendment, the protection of the minority shareholder depends on what the shareholders themselves are willing to put into the articles of association. I doubt whether this is a wise idea because I think that when starting a business, partners simply do not think of everything that can go wrong.[104] Therefore I agree with De Kluiver and Roest who advocate the introduction of a buy-out remedy at will in the Regulation

Another thing is that for an adequate protection of shareholders, the availability of the principle of reasonableness and fairness seems to be essential. As we have seen in Section 5.4, the European Parliament has proposed an amendment stating that resolutions may be declared ineffective also on the grounds of an infringement of the applicable national law. Considering that the principle of reasonabless and fairness (or a similar principle) is present in the private company laws of most Member States, the amendment in this respect seems to offer adequate protection. On the other hand, by leaving protection to the applicable national law, the amendment does not contribute to the desired uniformity of the SPE. The sixth section of this paper has concentrated on the position of the creditors of an SPE. We have seen that the SPE Proposal offers protection against unlawful withdrawals from the SPE. Shareholders must return to the SPE what they received and directors have to pay compensation to the SPE. We have also seen that the protection of the creditors of an SPE is not only a matter of company law, but also a matter of tort law and of insolvency law. As a consequence, in some respects the position of the creditors of an SPE is no different from the position of the creditors of any other company.

FINAL REMARKS

As for the first central question in this paper – whether we need the SPE – the following can be concluded. As long as we do not know what the form and shape of the SPE will be, the answer will probably be in the negative because what business communities need above all is legal certainty. As a consequence, what we first need is certainty about the role of the applicable national law. Moreover, when looking for certainty, we have to keep in mind that the bigger the role for the applicable national law, the less uniform the SPE will be. Since the need for the SPE corresponds to its uniformity, it will be wise to exclude the applicability of the national law as much as possible. On the other hand, a complete disconnection of the SPE from the applicable national law may be an unrealistic expectation.

As for the second central question in this paper – whether shareholders and creditors are adequately protected – the following can be concluded. Considering that the SPE in its current shape and form is an adventure with an open ending, one can hardly argue that the protection of shareholders and creditors deserves the designation 'adequate'. So the real question is whether we are willing to go for the SPE anyhow, despite the legal uncertainty of that journey. From the perspective of the creditor, the adventurous nature of the journey is not likely to be a problem. The creditor might even be unaware of what kind of adventure he is in because the legal uncertainty does not concern him. Besides, he has other means at his disposal to protect himself. However, for the shareholder the SPE adventure might contain elements of a nightmare. He might find himself stuck in a situation that was not in his tour guide and without the instruments to find a way out. My conclusion is therefore that the shareholder should not be allowed to embark on the SPE adventure unless he is equipped with an adequate buy-out remedy. Adequate protection calls for a buy-out remedy that is not limited to specific events because it is impossible to foresee all the events that may occur along the way. Adequate protection also calls for a remedy in the SPE Regulation because at the beginning of the adventure the shareholder might have forgotten to organise self-help along the way or he might not have been in a position to do so. In that case we simply cannot leave him out in the cold.

NOTES

1 COM(2008)396, Interinstitutional File 2008/0130 (CNS).

2 See respectively Council Regulation (EEC) 2137/85 of 25 July 1985, Council Regulation (EC) 2157/2001 of 8 October 2001, and Council Regulation (EC) 1435/2003 of 22 July 2003.

3 For an overview of the history and background of the SPE see O. Uziahu-Santcroos, 'The SPE: A Necessary Tool for SMES?', in: D.F.M.M. Zaman et al. (eds.), The European Private Company (SPE). A Critical Analysis of the EU Draft Statute, 2009, pp. 4-6.

4 On this project see T. Baums & P. Krüger Andersen, The European Model Company Law Project, and ECGI Working Paper Series in Law, No. 097/2008, March 2008. In the group of experts the Netherlands is represented by Harm-Jan de Kluiver, who apparently does not fully support the SPE Proposal. See H.J. de Kluiver, '(Re) Considering the SPE', 2008 European Company Law, no. 3, pp. 112-113.

5 A conference on the SPE, held by the European Commission in Brussels on 10th March 2008, revealed several controversial issues. For the report on this conference see M.L. Lennarts & O. Uziahu-Santcroos, 'Report on the Conference on the European Private Company, Societas Privata Europaea (SPE), held in Brussels, 10 March 2008', 2008 Ondernemingsrecht, no. 7, pp. 263-268.

6 European Parliament legislative resolution of 10 March 2009 on the Proposal for a Council Regulation on the Statute for a European Private Company, P6_TA (2009)0094.

7 Just to compare: the birth of the SE in 2001 had taken thirty years and at that time the EU consisted of only 15 Member States. On the other hand, the birth of the European Cooperative Society in 2003 was a very quick one.

8 Of course employees are also to be considered important stakeholders. For their position see R. van het Kaar & I. Zaal, 'Employee Participation', in: D.F.M.M. Zaman et al. (eds.), The European Private Company (SPE). A Critical Analysis of the EU Draft Statute, 2009, pp. 159-174.

9 For specific issues relating to the transfer of the registered office of the SPE to another Member State I refer to S.M. van den Braak, 'Transferring the Registered Office', in: D.F.M.M. Zaman et al. (eds.), The European Private Company (SPE). A Critical Analysis of the EU Draft Statute, 2009, pp. 175-196.

10 D.F.M.M. Zaman et al. (eds.), the European Private Company (SPE) – A Critical Analysis of the EU Draft Statute, 2009.

11 O. Uziahu-Santcroos, 'Report on the Conference on the European Private Company

(Societas Privata Europaea) on Friday 26th June 2009 in Utrecht, the Netherlands', 2009 Tijdschrift voor Ondernemingsbestuur, no. 4, pp. 106-112.

12 This requirement emphasizes the closely held character of the company and thus distinguishes the SPE from the SE.

13 This requirement allows for a single shareholder SPE. In the light of the 12th EC Company Law Directive on the single member company this is not a new phenomenon in the European context.

14 In this context, there are several milestone judgments by the European Court of Justice: ECJ, 10 July 1986, Case 79/85, Segers; ECJ, 9 March 1999, Case 212/97, Centros; ECJ, 5 November 2002, Case 208/00, Überseering; ECJ, 30 September 2003, Case 167/01, Inspire Art.

15 The Bill amending Dutch private company law is pending before Parliament. Kamerstukken II 2006-2007, 31 058 (Wet vereenvoudiging en flexibilisering BV-recht).

16 H. Boschma, L. Lennarts & H. Schutte-Veenstra, 'the Reform of Dutch Private Company Law: New Rules for the Protection of Creditors', 2007 European Business Organization Law Review 8, p. 573.

17 Those advocating that a minimum capital requirement should be maintained see it as an entry price for limited liability and a demonstration of seriousness. See P. Hommelhoff & C. Teichmann, 'Auf dem Weg zur Europäischen Privatgesellchaft (SPE)', 2008 DstR, no. 19, p. 931.

18 A.F.M. Dorresteijn & O. Uziahu-Santcroos, 'The Societas Privata Europaea under the Magnifying Glass (Part 2)', 2009 European Company Law, no. 4, p. 159. For objections against the abolishment of a minimum capital requirement see P. Hommelhoff, 'Die Europäische Privatgesellschaft (SPE): Auswirkungen auf die nationale GmbH', 2008 Der Gesellschafter, no. 6, p. 345.

19 Think Small First – A 'Small Business Act' for Europe, Brussels 19 June 2008, COM (2008) 394 (SEC (2008) 2101, SEC (2008) 2102).

20 Explanatory Memorandum to the SPE Proposal, p. 2.

21 See O. Uziahu-Santcroos, 'the SPE: A Necessary Tool for SMES?' in: D.F.M.M. Zaman et al. (eds.), the European Private Company (SPE). A Critical Analysis of the EU Draft Statute, 2009, p. 13, who also remarks that this has already been experienced with the SE, as is illustrated by the formation of Allianz SE, formerly Allianz AG, a large German insurance firm. By opting for an SE, Allianz managed to reduce the number of representatives on the Supervisory Board. At the same time, according to M.L. Lennarts & O. Uziahu-Santcroos, 'Report on the Conference on the European Private Company, Societas Privata Europaea (SPE), held in Brussels, 10 March 2008', 2008 Ondernemingsrecht, no. 7, p. 265, the SE runs the risk of becoming obsolete if the SPE will be available to large companies. The size issue was also raised at the conference in Utrecht in 2009. See O. Uziahu-Santcroos, 'Report on the Conference on the European Private Company (Societas Privata Europaea) on Friday 26th June 2009 in Utrecht, the Netherlands', 2009 Tijdschrift voor Ondernemingsbestuur, no. 4, p. 109.

22 This is not the case for the SE. See Article 2 SE Regulation, which includes cross-

border conditions.

23 Explanatory Memorandum, p. 3.

24 The issue of subsidiarity was discussed on several occasions. See the presentation by J. Bloemarts, 'Presentations Held at the Public Hearing before the Committee on Legal Affairs of the European Parliament in Brussels, 22 June 2006, on the European Private Company', 2006 European Company Law, no. 6, pp. 265-267. See also M.L. Lennarts & O. Uziahu-Santcroos, 'Report on the Conference on the European Private Company, Societas Privata Europaea (SPE), held in Brussels, 10 March 2008', 2008 Ondernemingsrecht, no. 7, p. 265. For the position of the Dutch Government see Kamerstukken II 2007-2008, 31 543, no. 1-7.

25 Explanatory Memorandum, p. 3.

26 This observation was made by Professor Zaman at the conference in Utrecht in 2009. See O. Uziahu-Santcroos, 'Report on the Conference on the European Private Company (Societas Privata Europaea) on Friday 26th June 2009 in Utrecht, the Netherlands', 2009 Tijdschrift voor Ondernemingsbestuur, no. 4, p. 107.

27 A.F.M. Dorresteijn & O. Uziahu-Santcroos, 'The Societas Privata Europaea under the Magnifying Glass (Part 2)', 2009 European Company Law, no. 4, p. 159.

28 H.E. Boschma & J.N. Schutte-Veenstra, 'De Europese BV: het voorstel voor een SPE-Statuut', 2008 Ondernemingsrecht, no. 17, p. 604.

29 This observation was made by Professor Drury at the conference in Brussels in 2008. See M.L. Lennarts & O. Uziahu-Santcroos, 'Report on the Conference on the European Private Company, Societas Privata Europaea (SPE), held in Brussels, 10 March 2008', 2008 Ondernemingsrecht, no. 7, p. 266. See also P. Hommelhoff, 'Die Europäische Privatgesellschaft (SPE): Auswirkungen auf die nationale GmbH', 2008 Der Gesellschafter, no. 6, p. 340; A.F.M. Dorresteijn & O. Uziahu-Santcroos, 'The Societas Privata Europaea under the Magnifying Glass (Part 1)', 2008 European Company Law, no. 6, p. 282.

30 This issue was also raised at the conference in Utrecht in 2009. See O. Uziahu-Santcroos, 'Report on the Conference on the European Private Company (Societas Privata Europaea) on Friday 26th June 2009 in Utrecht, the Netherlands', 2009 Tijdschrift voor Ondernemingsbestuur, no. 4, p. 109. See also A.F.M. Dorresteijn & O. Uziahu-Santcroos, 'The Societas Privata Europaea under the Magnifying Glass (Part 2)', 2009 European Company Law, no. 4, p. 153.

31 See for instance H.J. de Kluiver, '(Re)Considering the SPE', 2008 European Company Law, no. 3, pp. 112-113; A.F.M. Dorresteijn & O. Uziahu-Santcroos, 'The Societas Privata Europaea under the Magnifying Glass (Part 1)', 2008 European Company Law, no. 6, p. 282; H.E. Boschma & J.N. Schutte-Veenstra, 'De Europese BV: het voorstel voor een SPE-Statuut', 2008 Ondernemingsrecht, no. 17, pp. 604 and 610 suggest that the applicable national law should function as a safety net.

32 Explanatory Memorandum to the SPE Proposal, p. 2.

33 S. Rammeloo, 'Matters Related to Private International Law', in: D.F.M.M. Zaman et al. (eds.), the European Private Company (SPE). A Critical Analysis of the EU Draft

Statute, 2009, p. 35, provides for an overview of no less than fourteen provisions in the Proposal that refer to the applicable national law.

34 H.J. de Kluiver & J.Roest, 'Expulsion and Withdrawal of Shareholders', in: D.F.M.M. Zaman et al. (eds.), The European Private Company (SPE). A Critical Analysis of the EU Draft Statute, 2009, p. 69.

35 R. Drury, 'The European Private Company', 2008 European Business Organization Law Review 9, pp. 131-132. See also the observation by Teichmann that there should preferably be no reference to national law at all as reported by M.L. Lennarts & O. Uziahu-Santcroos, 'Report on the Conference on the European Private Company, Societas Privata Europaea (SPE), held in Brussels, 10 March 2008', 2008 Ondernemingsrecht, no. 7, p. 265.

36 H.J. de Kluiver & J.Roest, 'Expulsion and Withdrawal of Shareholders', in: D.F.M.M. Zaman et al. (eds.), The European Private Company (SPE). A Critical Analysis of the EU Draft Statute, 2009, p. 70.

37 M.L. Lennarts, 'Voice Rights of Shareholders', in: D.F.M.M. Zaman et al. (eds.), The European Private Company (SPE). A Critical Analysis of the EU Draft Statute, 2009, p. 126.

38 This observation was made by J. Simon, 'Presentations Held at the Public Hearing before the Committee on Legal Affairs of the European Parliament in Brussels, 22 June 2006, on the European Private Company', 2006 European Company Law, no. 6, p. 274. For the reasons for setting up group structures see also A. Dorresteijn et al., European Corporate Law, 2009, pp. 281-282.

39 Because private company law has not been affected by harmonization as much as the law regulating public companies, there are considerable differences between the different national private company forms.

40 ECJ, 30 September 2003, Case 167/01, Inspire Art.

41 See O. Uziahu-Santcroos, 'Report on the Conference on the European Private Company (Societas Privata Europaea) on Friday 26th June 2009 in Utrecht, the Netherlands', 2009 Tijdschrift voor Ondernemingsbestuur, no. 4, pp. 107-108.

42 R. Drury, 'The European Private Company', 2008 European Business Organization Law Review 9, p. 126; P. Hommelhoff, 'Die Europäische Privatgesellschaft (SPE): Auswirkungen auf die nationale GmbH', 2008 Der Gesellschafter, no. 6, p. 338.

43 M.L. Lennarts & O. Uziahu-Santcroos, 'Report on the Conference on the European Private Company, Societas Privata Europaea (SPE), held in Brussels, 10 March 2008', 2008 Ondernemingsrecht, no. 7, p. 264; H.E. Boschma & J.N. Schutte-Veenstra, 'De Europese BV: het voorstel voor een SPE-Statuut', 2008 Ondernemingsrecht, no. 17, p. 602.

44 This point was made by Professor De Kluiver at the conference in Utrecht. See O. Uziahu-Santcroos, 'Report on the Conference on the European Private Company (Societas Privata Europaea) on Friday 26th June 2009 in Utrecht, the Netherlands', 2009 Tijdschrift voor Ondernemingsbestuur, no. 4, p. 108.

45 See for instance M.L. Lennarts, 'Voice Rights of Shareholders', in: D.F.M.M. Zaman

et al. (eds.), The European Private Company (SPE). A Critical Analysis of the EU Draft Statute, 2009, pp. 117-134.

46 The financial benefits that shareholders can derive from the company are included in Section 6.2 of this paper.

47 See Article 3(1)(d) SPE Proposal.

48 H.J. de Kluiver, '(Re) Considering the SPE', 2008 European Company Law, no. 3, p. 112.

49 An SPE may issue non-voting shares. For the rights attached to these shares and the possible complications see M.L. Lennarts, 'Voice Rights of Shareholders', in: D.F.M.M. Zaman et al. (eds.), The European Private Company (SPE). A Critical Analysis of the EU Draft Statute, 2009, p. 120.

50 On the principle of equality see L. Timmerman & A. Doorman, Rights of Minority Shareholders in the Netherlands, A Report written for the XVth World Congress of the International Academy of Comparative Law, section 4. Available at.

51 This suggestion is made by M.L. Lennarts, 'Voice Rights of Shareholders', in: D.F.M.M. Zaman et al. (eds.), The European Private Company (SPE). A Critical Analysis of the EU Draft Statute, 2009, p. 128. See also S. Rammeloo, 'Matters Related to Private International Law', in: D.F.M.M. Zaman et al. (eds.), The European Private Company (SPE). A Critical Analysis of the EU Draft Statute, 2009, p. 40.

52 M.L. Lennarts, 'Voice Rights of Shareholders', in: D.F.M.M. Zaman et al. (eds.), The European Private Company (SPE). A Critical Analysis of the EU Draft Statute, 2009, p. 129.

53 Lennarts, supra note 52, p. 119 notes that this threshold in fact includes a quorum, because it takes into account the total voting rights attached to all shares and not only the votes cast.

54 Lennarts, supra note 52, p. 120.

55 Lennarts, supra note 52, p. 120.

56 Lennarts, supra note 52, pp. 124-125.

57 A.F.M. Dorresteijn & O. Uziahu-Santcroos, 'The Societas Privata Europaea under the Magnifying Glass (Part 2)', 2009 European Company Law, no. 4, p. 156 note that this time frame seems to be too short for a shareholder who is unaware of the resolution and therefore they suggest that the time should start to run on the date when the shareholder becomes aware of the resolution.

58 M.L. Lennarts, 'Voice Rights of Shareholders', in: D.F.M.M. Zaman et al. (eds.), The European Private Company (SPE). A Critical Analysis of the EU Draft Statute, 2009, p. 127 observes that compared to Dutch law A seems to have a relatively strong position.

59 Lennarts, supra note 58, p. 129.

60 Lennarts, supra note 58, pp. 130-131.

61 H.J. de Kluiver & J.Roest, 'Expulsion and Withdrawal of Shareholders', in: D.F.M.M.

Zaman et al. (eds.), The European Private Company (SPE). A Critical Analysis of the EU Draft Statute, 2009, p. 74 are afraid that the acquisition of the shares by the SPE might harm the interests of the creditors of the SPE. I do not share their concern because I think that the rules relating to share buy-backs (see Section 6.2 of this paper) also apply in the context of expulsion and withdrawal.

62 De Kluiver & Roest, supra note 61, p. 65.

63 De Kluiver & Roest, supra note 61, p. 72.

64 Compare Section 5.6 of this paper.

65 De Kluiver & Roest, supra note 61, p. 78.

66 It has to be noted that the requirement of serious harm is still part of Article 18(6) SPE Proposal. According to De Kluiver & Roest, supra note 61, p. 74 footnote 22, the only logical explanation for this is that the European Parliament has overlooked the matter in its resolution.

67 De Kluiver & Roest, supra note 61, p. 74.

68 De Kluiver & Roest, supra note 61, p. 78. For an elaboration of this exit model see H.J. de Kluiver, 'Private Ordering and Buy-Out Remedies within Private Company Law: Towards a New Balance between Fairness and Welfare?' 2007 European Business Organization Law Review 8, pp. 103-119. See also M.L. Lennarts, 'Voice Rights of Shareholders', in: D.F.M.M. Zaman et al. (eds.), The European Private Company (SPE). A Critical Analysis of the EU Draft Statute, 2009, p. 132. See also the presentation by Professor Roest at the conference in Utrecht as reported by O. Uziahu-Santcroos, 'Report on the Conference on the European Private Company (Societas Privata Europaea) on Friday 26th June 2009 in Utrecht, the Netherlands', 2009 Tijdschrift voor Ondernemingsbestuur, no. 4, p. 110. This report also makes clear that Professor Teichmann was not very enthousiastic concerning the idea of a buy-out remedy at will.

69 M.L. Lennarts, 'Voice Rights of Shareholders', in: D.F.M.M. Zaman et al. (eds.), The European Private Company (SPE). A Critical Analysis of the EU Draft Statute, 2009, p. 122.

70 L. Timmerman & A. Doorman, Rights of Minority Shareholders in the Netherlands, A Report written for the XVth World Congress of the International Academy of Comparative Law, available at .

71 M.L. Lennarts, 'Voice Rights of Shareholders', in: D.F.M.M. Zaman et al. (eds.), The European Private Company (SPE). A Critical Analysis of the EU Draft Statute, 2009, p. 132.

72 H.J. de Kluiver & J.Roest, 'Expulsion and Withdrawal of Shareholders', in: D.F.M.M. Zaman et al. (eds.), The European Private Company (SPE). A Critical Analysis of the EU Draft Statute, 2009, p. 68 and p. 79.

73 See Section 5.8 of this paper.

74 Explanatory Memorandum to the SPE Proposal, p. 9.

75 See D. Latella, 'Shareholder Derivative Suits: A Comparative Analysis and the Implications of the European Shareholders' Rights Directive', 2009 European

Commercial and Financial Law Review, no. 3, pp. 307-323.

76 M. Olaerts, 'Directors' Duties and Liabilities', in: D.F.M.M. Zaman et al. (eds.), the European Private Company (SPE). A Critical Analysis of the EU Draft Statute, 2009, p. 148. See also M.L. Lennarts & O. Uziahu-Santcroos, 'Report on the Conference on the European Private Company, Societas Privata Europaea (SPE), held in Brussels, 10 March 2008', 2008 Ondernemingsrecht, no. 7, p. 268, who believe that the introduction of a derivative suit should be accompanied by the introduction of the business judgment rule.

77 HR 2 December 1994, NJ 1995, 288 (Poot/ABP).

78 Of course he may have an action based on the general principles of tort law, but in that case it is a duty towards A himself that is at stake. See Section 6.3 of this paper.

79 J. Barneveld, 'Legal Capital and Creditor Protection – Some Comparative Remarks', in: D.F.M.M. Zaman et al. (eds.), the European Private Company (SPE). A Critical Analysis of the EU Draft Statute, 2009, p. 83; H. Boschma, L. Lennarts & H. Schutte-Veenstra, 'The Reform of Dutch Private Company Law: New Rules for the Protection of Creditors', 2007 European Business Organization Law Review 8, p. 603.

80 By raising the minimum capital to € 8,000 the European Parliament confesses to the more traditional view.

81 H.E. Boschma & J.N. Schutte-Veenstra, 'De Europese BV: het voorstel voor een SPE-Statuut', 2008 Ondernemingsrecht, no. 17, p. 607; J. Barneveld, 'Legal Capital and Creditor Protection – Some Comparative Remarks, in: D.F.M.M. Zaman et al. (eds.), The European Private Company (SPE). A Critical Analysis of the EU Draft Statute, 2009, p. 85.

82 A point made by Professor Neville at the conference in Utrecht in 2009. See O. Uziahu-Santcroos, 'Report on the Conference on the European Private Company (Societas Privata Europaea) on Friday 26th June 2009 in Utrecht, the Netherlands', 2009 Tijdschrift voor Ondernemingsbestuur, no. 4, p. 109.

83 According to Article 27(2) SPE Proposal, a resolution on the reduction of share capital shall be taken by a qualified majority. For the other resolutions a simple majority may suffice, unless the articles of association provide otherwise.

84 It should be noted that in addition to this, in the case of capital reduction the creditors shall have the right to ask for adequate safeguards. See Article 24(3) SPE Proposal.

85 J. Barneveld, 'Legal Capital and Creditor Protection – Some Comparative Remarks', in: D.F.M.M. Zaman et al. (eds.), the European Private Company (SPE). A Critical Analysis of the EU Draft Statute, 2009, p. 91.

86 According to Barneveld, supra note 85, p. 90 it is of minor importance whether or not € 1 or perhaps even € 8,000 may be distributed.

87 Barneveld, supra note 85, p. 98.

88 In HR 9 November 1991, NJ 1992, 174 (Nimox) the shareholder was deemed to have committed a tort against the creditors by voting in favour of a distribution that satisfied the balance-sheet test but nevertheless endangered the company's continuity.

See also H. Boschma, L. Lennarts & H. Schutte-Veenstra, 'The Reform of Dutch Private Company Law: New Rules for the Protection of Creditors', 2007 European Business Organization Law Review 8, pp. 573-574.

89 In Section 6.2 of this paper we have seen that this general provision may also cover directors' liability in the specific case of an unlawful distribution.

90 See Annex I to the SPE Proposal.

91 M. Olaerts, 'Directors' Duties and Liabilities', in: D.F.M.M. Zaman et al. (eds.), the European Private Company (SPE). A Critical Analysis of the EU Draft Statute, 2009, pp. 144-149. See also A.F.M. Dorresteijn & O. Uziahu-Santcroos, 'The Societas Privata Europaea under the Magnifying Glass (Part 1)', 2008 European Company Law, no. 6, p. 281, who also expect that national courts will apply the standards for national companies.

92 Olaerts, supra note 91, p. 157. See also M.L. Lennarts & O. Uziahu-Santcroos, 'Report on the Conference on the European Private Company, Societas Privata Europaea (SPE), held in Brussels, 10 March 2008', 2008 Ondernemingsrecht, no. 7, p. 266, who note that since bottom-up harmonisation may take years, this is not very attractive for the business community.

93 A.F.M. Dorresteijn & O. Uziahu-Santcroos, 'The Societas Privata Europaea under the Magnifying Glass (Part 2)', 2009 European Company Law, no. 4, p. 157. See on this issue also H.E. Boschma & J.N. Schutte-Veenstra, 'De Europese BV: het voorstel voor een SPE-Statuut', 2008 Ondernemingsrecht, no. 17, p. 610 who note that the absence of a cross-border requirement may enhance competition between the SPE and a company under national company law.

94 J. Barneveld, 'Legal Capital and Creditor Protection – Some Comparative Remarks', in: D.F.M.M. Zaman et al. (eds.), the European Private Company (SPE). A Critical Analysis of the EU Draft Statute, 2009, p. 98.

95 See note 15, supra.

96 With regard to Article 249 Dutch Companies Act see M. Olaerts, 'Directors' Duties and Liabilities', in: D.F.M.M. Zaman et al. (eds.), The European Private Company (SPE). A Critical Analysis of the EU Draft Statute, 2009, p. 151.

97 Article 162 of Book 6 of the Dutch Civil Code.

98 HR 6 October 1989, NJ 1990, 286 (Beklamel).

99 See in this context also S.M. van den Braak, 'Vestigingsvrijheid en misbruik van de (buitenlandse) vennootschap', 2006 Ondernemingsrecht, no. 5, p. 176.

100 For international cases see Articles 3 and 4 of this Regulation (European Insolvency Regulation), according to which in the case of a Dutch SPE the Dutch courts shall have jurisdiction to commence insolvency proceedings and the applicable insolvency law shall be Dutch law.

101 See Articles 4(2) (m) and 13 European Insolvency Regulation and Article 42 et seq. Dutch Insolvency Act.

102 M.L. Lennarts, De Twilight zone, 2006.

103 See also S.M. van den Braak, 'Creditor Protection at the Crossroads of Company and Insolvency Law: The Dutch Example', 2008 European Company Law, no. 5, pp. 229-236.

104 Just to compare: which partners think of separation at the moment of their marriage?

7
CHAPTER

JURISDICTION BY NECESSITY AND THE REGULATION OF THE TRANSNATIONAL CORPORATE ACTOR

Chilenye Nwapi

Keywords: Jurisdiction, necessity jurisdiction, transnational corporations, human rights violations, extraterritorial regulation

INTRODUCTION

When a court lacks territorial jurisdiction to adjudicate a dispute, it may turn to an emerging doctrine in jurisdictional law, which allows the court to assume jurisdiction over the dispute where the court considers that there is no other forum in which the dispute may be adjudicated or in which the plaintiff may reasonably be expected to initiate the suit. A court exercising such jurisdiction is said to be acting as a forum of necessity or, as it is called in civil law parlance, forum necessitatis. Such jurisdiction serves as 'a safety valve' to avoid a total denial of access to justice.[1] The rationale provides that there could be extraordinary circumstances where the normal jurisdictional standards would be impractical, because the insistence on the satisfaction of their requirements might totally bar the adjudication of the dispute anywhere in the world.[2] The dominant concern is therefore the need to avoid a denial of access to justice – a fundamental objective of modern international law.[3]

The purpose of this article is to examine the possibilities for the utilization of this doctrine to promote the accountability of transnational corporations (TNCs) for extraterritorial human and environmental rights violations. The nature and reach of the operations of TNCs have rendered them almost impervious to traditional standards of

Citation: Nwapi, C., (2014). Jurisdiction by Necessity and the Regulation of the Transnational Corporate Actor. Utrecht Journal of International and European Law. 30(78), pp.24–43. DOI: http://doi.org/10.5334/ujiel.cb.

jurisdiction. So far, few countries have been the destination for such suits. Foremost among them is the United States, where, using the Alien Tort Statute,4 many victims of human rights abuses in Africa, Asia and Latin America have brought suits in US courts against corporations. Other countries that have seen such litigation include the Netherlands,[5] the UK[6] and Canada.[7]

After an analysis of the inadequacy of existing jurisdictional doctrines for the effective regulation of the transnational corporate actor, this article explores the origin of the jurisdiction by necessity doctrine and indicates which countries have adopted it. Then follows a critical analysis of the elements of the doctrine to see how the doctrine may be applied to the regulation of the transnational corporate actor. The last section concludes the discussion. The central argument of this article is that with the emergence of the jurisdiction by necessity doctrine, victims of transnational corporate human rights violations in countries with weak accountability mechanisms now have a new jurisdictional tool with which they may seek justice in foreign countries. It should be noted, however, that this article is concerned with civil jurisdiction alone and does not extend to criminal jurisdiction.

THE INADEQUACY OF EXISTING JURISDICTIONAL DOCTRINES FOR THE REGULATION OF THE TRANSNATIONAL CORPORATE ACTOR

The Growth of Corporate Power

It is well-settled that TNCs have become such powerful global actors that many individual countries lack the resources and will to regulate them.[8] Many TNCs have grown into entities of such 'astonishing magnitude' that, in terms of economic power, they fully measure up to individual countries.[9] Crucial to the growth in their power is their ability to incorporate in one country and operate in many other countries simultaneously through a complex web of subsidiaries.[10] The nature and grasp of their operations are such that 'they often operate in jurisdictions in which human rights violations occur, obtain benefits from subsidized arrangements with governments that commit human rights violations, provide goods and services that result in human rights violations, or organize in ways that violate the rights of workers.'[11] The Canadian Lawyers Association for International Human Rights (CLAIHR) cites four ways in which a corporation's activities may 'bolster the repressive capacity and the staying power of a regime that systematically violates human rights':

It can provide goods and services that support the regime's despotic capability;

It can be a main source of revenue that reinforces the despotic capability of the regime;

It can provide the regime infrastructure (like roads, railways, power stations, et cetera) that increases its repressive capability; and

Its presence there may provide the repressive regime international credibility.[12]

In many instances, TNCs operate in countries that are split by violent conflicts and sometimes fall 'prey to one faction or another.'[13]

In other instances, their operations generate opposition that sparks violent unrest. When violence erupts, some have responded by 'tapping directly into the military expertise and firepower of both state and private armies.'[14]

Orthodox methods of regulation through host-countries' domestic laws have proved ineffective to regulate TNCs. This is because the developing countries where virtually all of the violations occur are concerned that severe regulation of TNCs might drive TNCs away to other countries and thereby hamper the countries' economic development. As the editors of Liability of Multinational Corporations under International Law observe:

With foreign direct investment replacing intergovernmental aid as the most important means of transferring capital and technical know-how from the developed to the developing world, governments in developing countries are tempted to – and in some cases compelled to – attract investors by minimizing the potential costs facing investing MNCs. This desire, compounded in many instances by the relative weakness of host States compared to the larger and more experienced MNCs, means that injured citizens of these host States are left without any legal recourse [in their country].[15]

Professor Forcese cites a US State Department Report that observes that in some of the developing countries where such corporate abuses occur, the courts are short-staffed. Judges are often absent from court, frequently because they are pursuing other means of livelihood to supplement their meagre salary. Courtrooms lack modern equipment and court officials often lack the proper training and motivation for work, due also to inadequate salary and poor work environment.[16]

Jonathan Clough has summarised the key features of the scenarios that make exclusive host-country regulation of TNCs difficult: The defendant is a large, well-resourced transnational corporation.

The alleged human rights abuses occurred in a country (the 'host jurisdiction') other than the transnational corporation's country of incorporation (the 'home jurisdiction').

The host jurisdiction is unable and/or unwilling to investigate and prosecute the alleged abuses.

The transnational corporation is alleged to be complicit in the human rights abuses either directly or, more commonly, indirectly through the interposition of subsidiaries or other intermediaries such as independent contractors.[17]

For their part, Western countries – the 'birthplace' of most of the TNCs – have shown strong reluctance, even opposition, to the regulation of the activities of their corporations abroad. A notorious example was the George W Bush administration's relentless efforts to eviscerate the Alien Tort Statute – the major legal recourse for most victims of corporate human rights abuses in the developing world.[18] In 2003, following the US-UK invasion of Iraq and the ousting of President Saddam Hussein, President Bush issued Executive Order 13303 immunising US corporations from any suit arising from any activity, including environmental damage and human rights violations, undertaken by a US corporation in furtherance of the Iraq invasion.[19] The order prevented lawsuits by US citizens against corporations and precluded foreigners from invoking the statute. Such acts of corporate protectionism by Western countries symbolize, arguably, the extent of the influence of TNCs even within their home countries.

The Current State of International Law

The current state of international law offers little to no assistance to victims of corporate human rights abuses in developing countries without effective accountability mechanisms. Traditionally, international law applies to States alone, although, since the Nuremberg trials that followed World War II, international law has been held to apply also to individuals.[20] All other non-State actors, such as corporations, are still held to relate indirectly with international law via their national governments.[21] Attempts by victims of egregious corporate human rights abuses to frame their claims in terms of international law violations always meet with the almost insurmountable challenge that corporations are 'incapable of violating international law' or 'cannot be held accountable for international law violations' – depending on the intellectual sensitivity of the particular challenger. In a 2008 report to the UN Human Rights Council, Professor John Ruggie noted that the international community had yet to adapt the human rights regime to protect individuals and communities against corporate human rights abuses.[22]He decried the 'governance gap created by globalization' as 'the root cause of the business and human rights predicament today.'[23] Thus while the international community condemns violations of international fundamental norms, 'it provides limited effective remedies for individual victims of [those violations].'[24] Yet the need for accountability is readily apparent and compelling. As Professor Naomi Roht-Arriaza puts it, '[a]ccountability [for corporate human rights violations] is now routinely demanded ... in part due to a recognition that the seeds of future violations are sown, in part, in the failure to come to terms with past cycles of violations.'[25] Necessity jurisdiction may have partially come to the rescue.

Existing Jurisdictional Doctrines

Beyond executive efforts by home-countries to block corporate accountability for human rights violations committed by their corporations in developing countries, the aforementioned features of transnational corporate conduct have rendered existing jurisdictional doctrines ineffective to allow litigation in the courts of home-countries. First, jurisdiction is traditionally based on territorial considerations aimed at establishing the existence of some link between the forum country and the dispute. Depending on the jurisdiction, such link is described as 'a real and substantial connection'[26] or as 'minimum contacts'[27] between the dispute and the forum seized. The connection or contacts may relate to the subject matter of the litigation (the tort, contract or the property that is the subject matter of the litigation) or to the parties (especially the defendant). But what exactly amounts to the requisite connection depends on the specific facts of each case. The rules serve as a check upon excessive jurisdiction. In some jurisdictions, such as Canada and the US, they are regarded as constitutional imperatives, preventing courts and legislatures from derogating from them.[28]

In addition, there are other jurisdictional standards that are usually considered independently of the above connection tests, although they do reflect the spirit of the tests. Especially in common law jurisdictions, the presence of the defendant within the forum, consent or attornment to the jurisdiction of the forum court, can serve as independent bases of (in personam) jurisdiction. In some civil law jurisdictions, such as France, jurisdiction is tied to the nationality of the parties, especially that of the defendant.[29] In many other civil law countries, such as Austria,[30] Germany,31Denmark,[32] Sweden[33] and Switzerland,[34] it is even tied to the existence of the defendant's property within the forum. The rules thus differ jurisdiction to jurisdiction.

Some regional treaties have however been created to establish uniform jurisdictional rules for the State parties to them. There is, for instance and perhaps most notably, Regulation (EU) No 1215/2012 of the European Parliament and of the Council of 12 December 2012 on jurisdiction and the recognition and enforcement of judgments in civil and commercial matters (recast) (Brussels I Regulation)[35] which applies to EU member States. Difficulties encountered in the recognition and enforcement of foreign judgments due to differing jurisdictional rules between national borders necessitated the emergence of the regulation. The effect of the differing rules was that States denied recognition and enforcement to foreign judgments that arose from jurisdictional assumptions that were based on standards that were inconsistent with the jurisdictional standards of the recognising State. As one scholar puts it, this had the practical effect of 'one hand taking back what the other hand conferred.'[36] To ensure 'decisional harmony', 'predictable and easily administered jurisdictional norms' and 'free movement of judgments'[37] regional jurisdictional rules were conceived. The collapse of negotiations of the Hague Conference on Private International Law for a Convention on Jurisdiction and Foreign Judgments in Civil and Commercial Matters[38] thwarted international efforts to create a treaty with world-wide application.

Brussels I Regulation established the defendant's domicile as the primary jurisdictional standard.[39] This is regardless of the defendant's nationality and regardless of the plaintiff's domicile. But a member State reserves the right to assert jurisdiction, in accordance with its national law, over a defendant who is not domiciled within its territory.[40] In cases of multiple defendants, jurisdiction over one defendant automatically confers on the court jurisdiction over all the other defendants, provided there is a close relationship among the claims against the defendants, rendering it pragmatic to adjudicate all the claims together to avoid the risk of conflicting decisions from separate proceedings.[41] Jurisdiction over original proceedings equally triggers jurisdiction to adjudicate third party proceedings relating to the same facts.[42] The same applies to counterclaims.[43] In situations where there are parallel proceedings, however, the first-seized rule applies, enabling the court first-seized of jurisdiction to take precedence over the court later seized.[44]

Besides domicile, alternative bases of jurisdiction are established under Article 7 of the Regulation. In matters relating to contracts, the court of the Member State where the contract is to be performed is the valid jurisdictional forum.[45] In matters relating to tort, the court of the Member State on whose territory the wrong occurred has jurisdiction, provided the defendant is domiciled in the territory of a member State.[46] Where the civil claim relates to an act over which a court is exercising criminal jurisdiction, the same court can assert jurisdiction over the civil claim as well.[47]

But these jurisdictional rules have not always met the dictates of justice. In an increasing number of cases, strict adherence to them has resulted in denials of access to justice. Such denials violate fundamental international principles of justice. Article 6(1) of the ECHR, for instance, provides that 'in the determination of his civil rights and obligations or of any criminal charge against him, everyone is entitled to a fair and public hearing within a reasonable time by an independent and impartial tribunal established by law'. This provision has been construed as granting a right of access to justice or a right of access to a court.[48] The provision speaks to the need for exceptional jurisdictional policies that, serving as safety valves, cater for cases in which the established jurisdictional standards would be unworkable from an access-to-justice standpoint. Jurisdiction by necessity may represent such a safety valve.

Indeed, Canadian courts have explicitly recognized the inadequacy of the real and substantial connection test to meet the demands of justice in civil proceedings for extraterritorial human rights violations. In Bouzari v Islamic Republic of Iran[49] – a case in which the plaintiff claimed to have been tortured in Iran by the Islamic Republic of Iran – the Ontario Court of Appeal found that Iran had no connection with Ontario beyond its diplomatic presence. Finding that this did not suffice for jurisdiction under the real and substantial connection test, the Court looked to international law and found 'no broadly shared international practice among states to assume jurisdiction over civil actions in similar circumstances.'[50] The Court then opined:

> [36] [T]here are several circumstances that make the presumptive conclusion of no jurisdiction troubling. First, the action is based on torture by a foreign state, which is a violation of both international human rights and peremptory norms of public international law. As the perpetrator, Iran, has eliminated itself as a possible forum, although it otherwise would be the most logical jurisdiction. This would seem to diminish significantly the importance of any unfairness to the defendant due to its lack of connection to Ontario.
>
> [37] Second, if Ontario does not take jurisdiction, the appellant will be left without a place to sue. Given that the appellant is now connected to Ontario by his citizenship, the requirement of fairness that underpins the real and substantial connection test would seem to be of elevated importance if the alternative is that the appellant cannot bring this action anywhere.[51]

The Court did not however proceed to determine how the real and substantial connection test should be applied to meet the requirements of justice and fairness that are embedded in it, because the doctrine of state immunity would bar suit against Iran in any case. But the above statements speak clearly to the need for something more in jurisdictional considerations to meet the demands of justice in transnational human rights cases. As McConville has argued, 'transnational human rights torts litigation … does not easily fit into the framework of territorial jurisdiction.'[52] Although the Bouzaricase involved a State defendant, rather than a corporate defendant, cases involving corporate defendants present similar – perhaps even more – jurisdictional difficulties (with the exception of the doctrine of immunity).

In 2010, the Ontario Court of Appeal took the matter further. In Van Breda v Village Resorts Ltd[53] – a consolidated appeal from two separate tort claims for damages for personal injury suffered by Canadian tourists during scuba diving accidents that occurred when they were vacationing at resorts in Cuba – the Court explicitly recognised the inadequacy of the real and substantial connection test and went on not only to reformulate the doctrine to meet the demands of justice, but also to adopt the doctrine of 'forum of necessity' as a jurisdictional corrective applicable to cases 'where there is no other forum in which the plaintiff could reasonably seek relief'.[54] The Court wrote: The forum of necessity doctrine recognizes that there will be exceptional cases where, despite the absence of a real and substantial connection, the need to ensure access to justice will justify the assumption of jurisdiction. The forum of necessity doctrine does not redefine real and substantial connection to embrace 'forum of last resort' cases; it operates as an exception to the real and substantial connection test. Where there is no other forum in which the plaintiff can reasonably seek relief, there is a residual discretion to assume jurisdiction. In my view, the overriding concern for access to justice that motivates the assumption of jurisdiction despite inadequate connection with the forum should be accommodated by explicit recognition of the forum of necessity exception rather than by distorting the real and substantial connection test.[55] This acknowledgement marked a remarkable development in the law of jurisdiction in Ontario. Although on appeal, the Supreme Court declined to pronounce on the doctrine's validity within the Canadian legal system because the case was not argued on that term, this has not restrained the courts of other provinces from citing the decision, usually with explicit approval.[56] A leading Canadian scholar has stated: '[a] flexible approach to jurisdiction that takes into account and gives appropriate weight to the particular subject matter of the proceedings and that does not insist on direct territorial connections in cases where none could ever exist is surely a welcomed development.'[57] Jurisdiction by necessity may fulfill this important role.

THE PROVENANCE OF THE DOCTRINE OF JURISDICTION BY NECESSITY

The provenance of the doctrine of jurisdiction by necessity is credited to civil law traditions, although there is some probability that the doctrine appeared at an earlier time in US jurisprudence than it did in the law or jurisprudence of any other country.[58]The doctrine has roots in Article 6(1) of the ECHR which establishes a right of access to justice. Early adoptions of the doctrine were not based on statutory authority. In the Netherlands, for instance, where the doctrine was statutorily adopted at a relatively early time, even before the statutory adoption Dutch courts avoided jurisdictional injustices by extensively interpreting jurisdictional statutes 'or by assuming jurisdiction as forum necessitatis', where there was a sufficient connection with the Netherlands.[59] The doctrine's first formal adoption may be found in the 1985 Inter-American Convention on Jurisdiction in the International Sphere for the Extraterritorial Validity of Foreign Judgments, Article 2 of which provides:

The requirements for jurisdiction in the international sphere shall also be deemed to be satisfied if, in the opinion of the judicial or other adjudicatory authority of the State Party in which the judgment is to be given effect, the judicial or other adjudicatory authority that rendered the judgment assumed jurisdiction in order to avoid a denial of justice because of the absence of a competent judicial or other adjudicatory authority.[60]

Switzerland was among the first countries to statutorily adopt the doctrine. Article 3 of its Federal Code on Private International Law provides: 'If this Code does not provide for jurisdiction in Switzerland and if proceedings abroad are impossible or cannot reasonably be required to be brought, the Swiss judicial or administrative authorities at the place with which the facts of the case are sufficiently connected shall have jurisdiction.' In 1991, it was adopted under Article 3136 of the Civil Code of Quebec[61](Canada), and in the late 1990s and early 2000s, a number of Canadian common law provinces adopted it under the Uniform Court Jurisdiction and Proceedings Transfer Act (UCJPTA).[62] Some of the provinces that have yet to adopt the UCJPTA have referred approvingly to the doctrine. In Ontario, for instance, the Court of Appeal referred to the doctrine in Van Breda as 'a significant jurisdictional doctrine'63 and explicitly recognised it as a residual basis for assuming jurisdiction in the absence of the real and substantial connection test and as an exception to it.64 Other jurisdictions where the doctrine has been adopted, either implicitly through case law or explicitly by statute include: Belgium,[65] Mexico,[66] the Netherlands,[67] Uruguay,[68] Argentina, Austria, Costa Rica, Estonia, Finland, Germany, Iceland, Japan, Lithuania, Luxembourg, Poland, Portugal, Romania, Russia, South Africa, Spain, and Turkey.[69] In the UK, the following statement of the Privy Council in AK Investments CJSC v Kyrgyz Mobil70 speaks to the application of the doctrine:

But the practical reality of the matter is that if the KFG Companies are confined to their remedies against the Appellants in Kyrgyzstan they will not in fact be able to pursue any of their claims there. Consequently, although this is in form a case about the appropriate forum, in reality it is a case in which, if the Isle of Man is not the appropriate forum, the KFG Companies will have no practical remedy at all.[71]

A 2007 study commissioned by the EU to provide a comparative analysis of residual jurisdiction in the twenty-seven EU member States and to recommend ways of harmonising the rules reported that in States where there was no basis (case law or statutory) for assuming jurisdiction by necessity, jurisdiction by necessity would not automatically be denied should an appropriate case come before them. The study noted that some national reporters believed that while there was no statute or case law in their countries adopting jurisdiction by necessity, there was no theoretical basis to say that a party would be denied access to a court if access to a court was essential to uphold his/her rights.[72] The study concluded that jurisdiction by necessity was a 'general principle of public international law'.[73]

At the regional level, the doctrine is explicitly adopted in the EU Council Regulation (EC) No 4/2009 on Jurisdiction, Applicable Law, Recognition and Enforcement of Decisions and Cooperation in Matters relating to Maintenance Obligations,[74] Article 7 of which provides: Where no court of a Member State has jurisdiction pursuant to [the Regulation] the courts of a Member State may, on an exceptional basis, hear the case if proceedings cannot reasonably be brought or conducted or would be impossible in a third State with which the dispute is closely connected. The dispute must havc a sufficient connection with the Member State of the court seised.

The doctrine has also been included in a proposed EU regulation that seeks to establish uniform rules throughout Europe for the regulation of matrimonial property proceedings.[75] Article 7 of the proposal provides: 'Where no court of a Member State has jurisdiction under [the Regulation], the courts of a Member State may, exceptionally and if the case has a sufficient connection with that Member State, rule on a matrimonial property regime case if proceedings would be impossible or cannot reasonably be brought or conducted in a third State.'[76] Lastly, the doctrine's adoption was included in the proposed recast of Brussels I Regulation but was deleted in the version that was finally agreed to by the member States.[77] It has been suggested that the earlier inclusion in, and subsequent deletion from, the recast Regulation does not destroy the view that the doctrine is not incompatible with international law.[78] Rather, the obligatory nature of the Regulation might have worried member States that have not yet adopted the doctrine.[79]

ANALYSIS OF THE DOCTRINE AND ITS APPLICATION TO TRANSNATIONAL CORPORATE WRONGS

The jurisdictions where the doctrine has been adopted may be divided into three categories: (1) those explicitly requiring some connection between the dispute and the forum; (2) those that are silent on the requirement of a connection; (3) and those in which absence of fair trial, even though not explicitly contained in the relevant statute, has already been recognised in case law as a basis for the exercise of jurisdiction under the doctrine. Of note, no case has been found in which absence of fair trial was, as a matter of principle, rejected as a basis. These categories of jurisdictions all have identified three common elements: (1) the absence of jurisdiction in the forum court; (2) the impossibility of the plaintiff bringing proceedings abroad; and (3) the reasonableness of requiring the plaintiff to bring the proceedings abroad. Article 3136 of the Civil Code of Quebec belongs to the first category. It states:

Even though a Quebec authority has no jurisdiction to hear a dispute, it may hear it if the dispute has a sufficient connection with Quebec, where proceedings cannot possibly be instituted outside Quebec or where the institution of such proceedings outside Quebec cannot reasonably be required.

To the second category – silence on a connection requirement – belong the common law provinces of Canada that have adopted the CJPTA. Section 6 thereof provides:

A court that under section 3 lacks territorial competence in a proceeding may hear the proceeding despite that section if it considers that (a) there is no court outside British Columbia in which the plaintiff can commence the proceedings, or (b) the commencement of the proceeding in a court outside British Columbia cannot reasonably be required.

In this category of jurisdictions, it is doubtful that the courts would fail to insist on the existence of some connection with the forum.80 In both Belgium and the

Netherlands, although their Codes do not explicitly recognise absence of fair trial as a valid basis for necessity jurisdiction, their courts have read absence of fair trial into their Codes.81 Both Codes also contain a requirement of some connection with their territory. However, it is doubtful that, in jurisdictions where absence of fair trial has not been considered, their courts would reject the absence of fair trial in the foreign forum as a valid basis for jurisdiction under the doctrine. Granted, the degree of unfairness of trial that is likely to be considered sufficient to warrant assertion of necessity jurisdiction may vary from jurisdiction to jurisdiction.

Five elements of the doctrine thus emerge. Stated in more logical order, they include: (1) the absence of jurisdiction in the forum seized of the matter; (2) the requirement of some connection with that forum; (3) the impossibility of bringing the proceedings in the forum with jurisdiction; (4) the reasonableness of requiring that the proceedings be brought in the forum with jurisdiction; and (5) the absence of fair trial in the foreign forum. The first element may be regarded as an indicium (rather than a requirement as such of the doctrine) in that it is a circumstance which tends to suggest that the application of the doctrine is likely, or, perhaps put more accurately, which prompts thoughts about the possible application of the doctrine in order to avoid a denial of justice. The other elements are not to be regarded as mere indicia of the doctrine but as requirements that the plaintiff must establish before the court can ultimately invoke the doctrine. As will be seen in the discussion that follows, these requirements are not to be cumulatively present before the court can apply the doctrine, except of course the second element – the requirement of some connection with the forum, which must be shown to exist – particularly in jurisdictions where it is explicitly required – before the court can apply the doctrine and before even any of the remaining three elements can be considered. Thus, where elements (1) and (2) are present, the presence of either (3), (4) or (5) can ground the assumption of jurisdiction by necessity. The relationship of these elements to the doctrine is that they are intended to show that refusal to adjudicate the action would result in an unacceptable denial of access to justice. The most basic of all the elements is the first element – the absence of jurisdiction in the forum seized of the matter – and it would be easy to apply because the plaintiff asking the court to invoke jurisdiction by necessity would be implicitly conceding that the court lacks jurisdiction in the matter. It would be inconceivable that the defendant would insist that the court has jurisdiction and should not even consider jurisdiction by necessity. Thus, arguably, the 'absence of jurisdiction' referred to therein relates to the absence of ordinary or normal jurisdiction to adjudicate the dispute based on well-established jurisdictional rules. It cannot relate to absence of jurisdiction by necessity. This first element of the doctrine is thus non-contentious and does not require further discussion. The following discussion therefore addresses the other four elements.

The Requirement of a Connection with the Forum

The national statutes explicitly requiring a connection with the forum have used such concepts as 'sufficiently connected',[82] 'sufficient connection',[83] 'close connections',[84]'adequate relation',[85] or 'strong linking factor'.[86] But they do not define what constitutes such connections. Nuyts writes that in Belgium, the 'close contacts' requirement is not applied stringently.[87] The Belgian nationality or domiciliary or habitual residence of the plaintiff satisfies the requirement, as do cases where the parties have assets in Belgium.[88] In jurisdictions, such as France, Austria and Germany, where assets in the province constitute a valid ground for jurisdiction, the existence of such assets would obviate the need to consider necessity jurisdiction. In Austria, there is an explicit requirement that the plaintiff be an Austrian national, domiciliary or resident.[89]In Quebec, because the doctrine applies as an exception to the real and substantial connection test due to 'the impossibility of having access to a foreign court in a litigation that has a sufficient link with Québec',[90] a 'sufficient connection' with Quebec must be understood as a lesser degree of connection than the real and substantial connection test requires. This must be so because the Quebec Code permits jurisdiction 'even though a Quebec authority has no jurisdiction to hear a dispute'. The requirement of a 'sufficient connection' may thus not be applied stringently, as otherwise, jurisdiction by necessity may become indistinguishable from the real and substantial connection test. Hence, it has been suggested that temporary residence of one of the parties in Quebec, or the fact that 'a juridical act is to be used here,' or the existence of any of the parties' property in Quebec, may supply the required 'sufficient connection'.91 What is not clear, however, is whether the residence or property in the forum must be shown to have existed when the cause of action arose. Given the exceptional nature of the doctrine, however, and the fact that the doctrine aims at avoiding a denial of access to a court, it would appear that a cause of action threshold would not be required.

Applying this to litigations concerning transnational corporate wrongs, the plaintiffs can establish that the action has a connection with the chosen forum by showing that any of the plaintiffs resides within the forum. A majority of the transnational human rights cases that have been litigated against corporations have this feature.[92] The existence of the corporation's parent or subsidiary within the forum may also supply the needed connection even if that parent or subsidiary is not implicated in the alleged violations. Normal jurisdictional doctrines would generally not regard the mere existence of the corporation's parent or subsidiary in the forum as a sufficient link where the parent or subsidiary is not also implicated in the violations,[93] but there is no reason why a court should not regard it as sufficient for the purpose of asserting jurisdiction by necessity, as a stronger link would most likely give the court normal jurisdiction and thereby render jurisdiction by necessity unnecessary.

Impossibility of Bringing Proceedings Abroad

None of the statutes adopting jurisdiction by necessity define the meaning of impossibility of bringing proceedings abroad. It is therefore not clear whether it refers to legal impossibility or to practical impossibility or to both. In the absence of statutory clarification, the general practice has been to interpret impossibility as both legal impossibility and practical impossibility.94 But given the existence of the fourth element – the reasonableness of requiring proceedings abroad – it makes more sense to regard this element as speaking to legal impossibility alone, as otherwise the two elements will inextricably overlap. Thus, in Anvil – a case involving allegations of human rights abuses in the Democratic Republic of Congo by a company incorporated under the laws of the Northwest Territories of Canada but with its headquarters in Australia – the Quebec Court of Appeal rejected the plaintiff's claim that difficulties in getting Australian lawyers to take up the case in Australia met the impossibility requirement.95

It has been suggested that legal impossibility arises 'where no foreign court has jurisdiction,' or where 'only a court which has annulled a clause choosing the forum' has jurisdiction,96 or 'when there is a legal obstacle to accessing the foreign court'97 or when 'the foreign court lacks jurisdiction under the foreign law or has already dismissed the claim for lack of jurisdiction'.98 In Germany and, debatably, in France, the fact that the foreign judgment is unenforceable in the forum has been accepted as a valid ground.99But a court cannot decide that it is not impossible to bring the action elsewhere simply by showing that another forum might exercise necessity jurisdiction. In other words, the existence of necessity jurisdiction in another forum cannot defeat the successful application of the impossibility element. Legal impossibility would also include cases where the claim is non-justiciable in the forum that otherwise has jurisdiction. The non-justiciability could be due to the existence of a legal immunity protecting the defendant from liability. Cases in which particular types of claims are ousted from the jurisdiction of the courts in the foreign forum are also included. In the former case, however, policy considerations might call for respect for certain immunity clauses, specifically, where the immunity clause was created as part of an amnesty mechanism – as was the case in Phillips v Eyre100 – to promote peace in countries recovering from conflicts. Disregard of such clauses might do irreparable harm to such countries and cannot be regarded as consistent with international public policy. Given the typical nature of transnational corporate wrongs litigation, the legal impossibility element is not likely to be relied upon, for it would rarely be the case that the country where the conduct occurred would lack jurisdiction in the matter or bar legal proceedings. It is to the 'reasonableness of requiring proceedings abroad' element that the plaintiffs would more likely turn.

The Reasonableness of Requiring Proceedings Abroad

Unreasonableness has been expressed in different ways. In Belgium, requiring foreign proceedings must be considered 'unreasonable'; in Austria, it must be 'unacceptable'; in Portugal it must involve an 'unreasonable difficulty'; and in Estonia the plaintiff 'cannot be expected' to bring proceedings in the foreign forum.[101] This requirement thus speaks to non-legal or practical difficulties in bringing the suit in the foreign forum. Minus those practical difficulties, there is no legal barrier to bringing the action in the foreign forum. Such practical difficulties must be so onerous that it would be unreasonable to require the plaintiff to bring the suit in that foreign forum. The problem then in the application of this element is how to determine what amounts to an unreasonable requirement.

An undoubted example is the existence of war or other violent conflicts in the foreign forum, causing a shutdown of the legal system or making it unsafe for the plaintiff to travel there to initiate the action. Such a situation constitutes a genuine obstacle rendering it unreasonable to require the plaintiff to risk his/her life to initiate the proceedings in the foreign forum. A plaintiff's well-founded fear that he/she might be politically persecuted if found in that foreign forum, or might lose his/her life or be subjected to torture or other inhuman treatment if he/she is found there, should be respected. In a case of unlawful imprisonment and torture in Libya brought by a Libyan plaintiff in 2012 during the Libyan crisis that resulted in the killing of Muammar Gaddafi, a Dutch court held that in view of the situation in Libya, the plaintiff could not reasonably be required to bring the action in Libya.102 It may also happen that asking the plaintiff to wait for the end of the war or conflict to bring the suit in the foreign forum might result in the suit becoming statute-barred under the laws of the foreign forum.

Also in Solvochem v Rasheed Bank,[103] the Hague Court of Appeal affirmed the Hague District Court's assumption of jurisdiction in a case that should have been brought in Iraq, because at the time the claim was initiated in the Netherlands, the Dutch plaintiff could not have been expected to bring the action in Iraq at a time when the Iraqi crisis was still raging.

In Kiefer v Canada (Minister of Justice), the Quebec Superior Court of Justice (Canada) stated that '[m]ere inconvenience' is not enough.[104] In Lamborghini, the Court considered the relative inconvenience of accessing the foreign court as not meeting the reasonable requirement test.105 In Obégi v Kilani,106 the Ontario Superior Court of Justice (Canada) relied on the defendant's 'past conduct and ability to evade potential future obligations'107 to rule that the plaintiff could not reasonably be required to bring proceedings abroad, although it found that the case met the requirements of the real and substantial connection test and so did not ultimately base its jurisdiction on necessity.

Other circumstances have been suggested: (1) the fact that the country is affected by natural disasters;108 (2) where the exercise of jurisdiction in the foreign forum is 'discretionary';[109] (3) where 'the defendant benefits from a certain immunity';[110] (4) where the plaintiff is 'a refugee who cannot act in the country he has fled';1[11] (5) 'cases of superior force such as war';[112] (6) where there is a defect in the foreign proceedings, such as delay in the administration of justice, corrupt judiciary or an 'ideological imperative';[113] (7) where the remedy sought is 'specific to the domestic purposes' of the forum and 'an effective decision can be achieved by [that forum] alone';1[14] (8) where 'an unacceptable risk' to the plaintiff is involved if he is to litigate in the foreign forum, and if the plaintiff is financially incapable of litigating the suit there.[115]

Some of the above suggestions are however problematic. For instance, where the foreign court's jurisdiction is discretionary, it is not clear how that makes it unreasonable to require the plaintiff to initiate the proceedings there. There is no reason to speculate on how the foreign court would exercise its discretion. The plaintiff should be required to give the foreign court an opportunity to exercise its discretion before it can be said that it would be unreasonable to require the plaintiff to initiate the suit in the foreign court. But even this would appear to give rise to a case of legal impossibility rather than practical impossibility to which the reasonable requirement test speaks, since, if the foreign court exercises its discretion negatively, it becomes legally impossible for the plaintiff to litigate there.116 Similarly, where the defendant would benefit from a certain immunity in the foreign forum, it becomes a matter of legal impossibility rather than practical impossibility.117 In addition, claims that the foreign judiciary is corrupt, or what McEvoy calls an 'ideological imperative' – such as in commercial transactions where the parties entered into a choice of court agreement in favour of a capitalist State that subsequently transformed into a Marxist State – may raise imperialism concerns where the foreign country is a former colony of any Western country.118 Lastly, factors like delays in the administration of justice may create too low a threshold for the application of the doctrine.

In Belgium, the reasonableness requirement covers cases where fair trial is not guaranteed in the foreign forum.119 This however does not include cases where the foreign jurisdiction 'would declare the plaintiff's claim inadmissible or would dismiss it on the merits.'120 In Olney v Rainville, the British Columbia Supreme Court (Canada) stated that necessity jurisdiction 'refers to the ability [of the plaintiff] to commence an action, not to barriers to success.'121 This means that that the plaintiff may not be successful in the competent forum cannot render it unreasonable to require him/her to litigate in that forum.

But, in Belgium, the fact that bringing the action in the foreign forum would be 'out of proportion' with the financial interests involved would suffice, provided its practical effect would deprive the plaintiff of effective access to the court.122 By contrast, in the Netherlands, poverty alone, or the fact that the costs of bringing the foreign proceedings would be prohibitively high, is not enough.123

To apply the doctrine in a balanced manner, in jurisdictions where the plaintiff's financial incapacity to bring the suit in the foreign jurisdiction is accepted as a valid ground, the financial capacity of the defendant to litigate in the plaintiff's chosen forum ought to be considered as well. For if the defendant cannot reasonably be expected to afford to defend the suit in the plaintiff's chosen forum, the essence of jurisdiction by necessity would be missed, which is to ensure that a forum is provided where the plaintiff can ventilate his/her grievances and the defendant present his/her defence. Justice is for both parties. 'Even in times of war, where the plaintiff cannot reasonably be expected to institute the suit in the warring State, the ability of the defendant to travel out of that warring State (assuming the defendant resides there) to the plaintiff's chosen forum is an important consideration.'[124]

The court must thus endeavour to balance the relative capacity of both parties to litigate in the forum,[125] although care must be taken to avoid the analysis reverting into a forum non conveniens analysis.126 That the plaintiff cannot reasonably be expected to bring the action in the foreign forum does not mean that just any other forum should take up the adjudication of the dispute based on jurisdiction by necessity. There could be several other forums permitting jurisdiction by necessity. In fact, it may be desirable for the court to invoke the doctrine of forum non conveniens to decide whether it should proceed to adjudicate the dispute where there exists another forum that allows jurisdiction by necessity and the dispute at bar is shown to meet the requirements of jurisdiction by necessity under the laws of that other forum – that is, where that other forum is deemed more suitable for the litigation. It is fair to not unreasonably require the plaintiff to litigate in the foreign forum; but the plaintiff cannot be given an absolute right to decide the forum of necessity.

Attempts to use statutes of limitation as the basis to invoke the necessity jurisdiction of the court have been made in Canada. In Wolfe v Wyeth,[127] the requirements of the real and substantial connection test were met, but the Ontario Superior Court of Justice ignored this finding and resorted to the 'exceptional doctrine of Forum of Necessity.'[128] The court appeared to suggest that the expiration of the limitation period in the natural forum for the litigation (Pennsylvania) was a relevant consideration in the application of the doctrine.[129] On appeal, the Ontario Court of Appeal affirmed the finding that the real and substantial connection test was met and declined to consider necessity jurisdiction.[130] In Jordan v Schatz,[131] the British Columbia Supreme Court stated that 'simple fairness and justice' justified the exercise of jurisdiction where the action had become statute-barred in the foreign forum.[132] The learned trial judge appeared to have been persuaded by the plaintiff's claim that the defendant 'lulled' him to sleep until the limitation periods in the forums where the action might have been brought expired. Although the defendant denied lulling the plaintiff to sleep, the British Columbia Court of Appeal overturned the decision, stating that 'jurisdiction simpliciter cannot be founded on the simple fact that the Alberta and Saskatchewan limitation periods expired, whether or not the plaintiff was lulled to sleep by the defendant.'[133] In Josephson v Balfour Recreation Commission[134] – a case where a claim for contribution and indemnity was made against a third party defendant – the limitation period in Idaho where the action should have been brought had expired, but the British Columbia Supreme Court either inadvertently overlooked or did not want to consider its significance and assumed necessity jurisdiction on the basis that it was not reasonable to require the defendant to proceed against the third party defendant in Idaho since any suit filed there would not be recognized under Idaho law.135 It was a case in which, if the defendant failed to join the third party, he would never again be able to bring proceedings against the third party.

The question is whether the consequences of a statute of limitation can be avoided through third party proceedings for contribution and indemnity in another forum. Jurisdiction by necessity does not seem to comprehend a situation like this. Statutes of limitation are well-established legal rules that have sound foundations. They cannot become objectionable merely because the plaintiff has nowhere else to turn to. TheJosephson situation was quite complicated in that case the purpose for which the defendant sought to invoke jurisdiction by necessity was to enable him claim contribution and indemnity against a third party he truly believed was responsible for the harm and against whom he would otherwise not be able to make the claims again. But sad as his situation may be, would it be fair to deny the third party the benefits of a statute of limitation the third party was fully entitled to? The answer is most likely in the negative. However, in cases of gross violations of international fundamental norms, where the limitation period provided under the laws of the foreign country may be described as unreasonably short given all the circumstances of the case, and the party seeking to invoke necessity jurisdiction can show that he/she was unable to bring the action in time due to no fault or negligence on his/her part, it may be just to allow the case to proceed.

To apply the above analysis to the context of the transnational corporate actor, it is useful to observe the features of a typical transnational lawsuit alleging human rights violations by multinational corporations in developing countries. In these cases, the plaintiffs are typically poor villagers in developing countries ravaged by the activities of the corporation. The corporation is often a subsidiary of another corporation headquartered in a country other than where the alleged conduct occurred. In some cases, the parent corporation is implicated. Due to the importance of the corporation to the national economy of the plaintiffs' country, the plaintiffs' government is hardly able or willing to bring the corporation to justice. In some cases, the plaintiffs' government is complicit in the violations. In addition, the cases often present complex evidentiary difficulties that would require expensive means of proof as well as experienced and frequently very expensive lawyers to conduct the case effectively. The plaintiffs are hardly able to afford such expertise. Without financial assistance, they may not be able to bring the action in the first place. Further, legal aid is often not available in the plaintiffs' country, or is generally available, but not for actions of this nature. Contingency fee services may be outlawed. Following protests by the villagers against the conduct of the corporation, the kingpins of the protests (who frequently become the named plaintiffs) are often forced to self-exile in another country by harassments, threats and intimidation from their government, and are often unable to return to their homeland. In exile, they connect with human rights NGOs who help them to initiate the proceedings in the foreign land. The suits are thus brought in the courts of a country other than the country where the alleged violations occurred. This is a typical case; individual cases may not share all of these characteristics.

But with those facts, the plaintiffs stand a chance of being able to establish practical difficulties in initiating the suit in their home country that render it unreasonable to require them to initiate the suit there. Such difficulties may be comprised in their inability to return to their country for the purpose of the litigation. On the relative capacity of the parties to litigate the dispute either in their home country or in their chosen forum, the fact that the defendant is a multinational corporation weighs in favour of litigation in the plaintiffs' chosen forum. For it will hardly be the case that a multinational corporation with offices and businesses in several countries around the world will be financially unable to send one of its officers to any forum to defend the corporation. Moreover, the suits are typically brought where the headquarters of the parent corporation is located. So the issue of the defendant's capacity to litigate in the plaintiffs' chosen forum poses no serious difficulties in transnational corporate wrongs litigation.

Absence of Fair Trial in the Foreign Forum

Fair trial has to do with the prospect that the plaintiff may not receive fair trial in the foreign jurisdiction if compelled to initiate the proceedings there. As indicated earlier, none of the statutes adopting the doctrine explicitly contains a fair trial element. But according to Nuyts, a fair trial element has been read into the statutes in some jurisdictions, Belgium, for example.[136] It is likely that other jurisdictions will follow suit when a proper case comes before them.

The attitude of Dutch courts – in commercial cases – has been to ascertain whether the likelihood of an unfair trial in the foreign jurisdiction was foreseeable to the plaintiff at the time of entering into the transaction and to hold, if it was foreseeable, that the plaintiff must accept that forum as he/she finds it. In Tbilisi Central Plaza BV v JSC

BTA Bank,[137] the parties entered into a contract which stipulated Kazakhstan as the jurisdiction where any dispute arising from the contract would be settled. The plaintiff sought to avoid settlement in Kazakh courts on the basis of systemic corruption in Kazakhstan. The District Court of Rotterdam began by noting that corruption and lack of impartiality were a valid basis of jurisdiction in exceptional circumstances. Those circumstances, the court argued, should in this particular case, take into consideration the fact that the parties freely entered into the choice of jurisdiction agreement stipulating Kazakhstan. While it does not appear that the choice of jurisdiction agreement was the principal theory of the decision, it certainly was considered relevant.[138]

Similarly, in Llanos Oil Exploration Ltd v Republiek Colombia and Ecopetrol SA,139 the plaintiff claimed that it was impossible to obtain fair trial in Columbia, particularly in cases in which the Republic of Columbia was a party, due to pervasive corruption in that country. It furnished documentary evidence showing that Columbia was one of the most corrupt nations in the world where lawyers and judicial officers were frequently under death threats. The case related to an oil concession contract which the plaintiff claimed the defendants – which included the Republic of Columbia and an oil company – illegally terminated. It claimed damages in tort and in contract. In the contract were choice of jurisdiction and choice of law clauses in favour Columbia. The Hague District Court stated that the plaintiff knew the existence of the alleged circumstances in Columbia when it chose Columbian law as the governing law of the contract and Columbian courts as the court to which they shall turn to in the event of a dispute. The court regarded the circumstances as not so unforeseen or exceptional that trial in Columbia ought reasonably not to be required. The court also found that the case lacked a sufficient connection with the Netherlands.[140] This last finding appeared to be a subsidiary issue in the decision while the plaintiff's knowledge of corruption in Columbia was the principal issue. The court thus disregarded a more important element in the application of the doctrine and focused on an element that was only read into the text of the adopting statute. Although the result would have been the same, the court's approach raises questions about the integrity of the decision.

Given that negative judicial pronouncements regarding the justice system of other countries can create international relations problems[141] and can destroy inter-judicial cooperation between the courts of different legal systems, courts should avoid venturing into such pronouncements whenever they can. In fact, such pronouncements may well destroy the doctrine's credibility and honour.

CONCLUSION

The enormous power at the disposal of the transnational corporate actor has rendered traditional regulatory mechanisms in developing countries ineffective to police it and to bring justice to those harmed by its activities. In Western countries that are home to most of these corporations, the complex web of subsidiaries with which the corporations operate have also rendered the transnational corporate actor difficult to regulate. Traditional jurisdictional doctrines hardly reach far enough to bring the actions of a corporation's foreign subsidiaries under the legal watch of the home country. With the emergence of jurisdiction by necessity, however, and its adoption in many legal systems, victims of transnational corporate human rights violations now have a new jurisdictional possibility to assert. In situations where it would be impossible for the plaintiff to initiate the suit in the foreign country where the dispute ought to be decided, or where for practical reasons the plaintiff cannot reasonably be expected to initiate the suit there, a court may assume jurisdiction by necessity where failure to do so might prevent the suit from being heard at all. The application of the doctrine generally requires the existence of five elements: (1) the absence of jurisdiction in the forum seized of the matter; (2) the requirement of some connection with that forum; (3) the impossibility of bringing the proceedings in the foreign forum with jurisdiction; (4) the reasonableness of requiring the plaintiff to bring the proceedings in that foreign forum; and (5) the absence of fair trial in the foreign forum. While each jurisdiction is free to interpret these factors as it deems appropriate, as Nuyts' study shows, the interpretations advanced by most countries so far are reasonably uniform. Given the nature of the factors, the most contentious cases will most likely turn on the reasonableness of requiring proceedings abroad. As shown in this article, plaintiffs in transnational corporate human rights lawsuits stand a good chance of establishing practical difficulties in initiating the suit in their home country that render it unreasonable to require them to initiate the suit there. Jurisdiction by necessity thus has the potential to address some of the jurisdictional difficulties encountered transnational corporate human rights litigation.

NOTES

[1]John P McEvoy, 'Forum of Necessity in Quebec Private International Law: CcQ Article 3136' (2005) 35 Review General 61 at 90 (hereinafter 'McEvoy').

[2]ibid at 64.

[3]See, for instance, the European Convention on Human Rights, 4 November 1950, Europ TS No 5, article 6(1) of (hereinafter 'ECHR').

[4]28 USC §1350 (1988).

[5]See, eg, District Court of The Hague, 30 January 2013, ECLI:NL:RBDHA:2013:BY9854, Friday Alfred Akpan v Royal Dutch Shell; Oguru, Efanga & Milieudefensie v Royal Dutch Shell Plc and Shell Petroleum Development Co Nigeria Ltd, ECLI:NL:RBSGR:2009:BK8616.

[6]See, eg, Bodo Community v Shell Petroleum Dev Co of Nigeria, [2012] EWHC (QB) (a case brought by farmers and fishermen from the Nigerian village of Bodo against oil giant Shell for environmental damage caused by oil spills); Guerrero v Monterrico Metals Plc, [2009] EWHC 2475, [2010] EWHC 3228 (case brought by Peruvian environmental protesters who were allegedly tortured and maltreated by British mining company Monterrico Metals); Lubbe v Cape Plc, [2000] 1 WLR 1545 (HL) (a cases brought by South Africans over damaged caused by a UK company in South Africa); Connelly v RTZ Corporation Plc, [1998] AC 854 (also (a cases brought by South Africans over damaged caused by a UK company in South Africa).

[7]See, eg, Recherches Internationales Québec v Cambior Inc, [1998] QJ No 2554 (a case brought against a Canadian miner over a mining disaster that occurred in Guyana); Yassin v Green Park International Inc, 2010 QCCA 1455 (CanLII) (a case relating to

forced removal of the plaintiffs to pave way for construction work being done by the plaintiff corporation in the Israeli-occupied West Bank); Piedra v Copper Mesa Mining Corporation, 2011 ONCA 191 (CanLII) (a case brought by Ecuadorean plaintiffs against a Canadian mining company for various torts allegedly committed by the mining company); Anvil Mining Ltd v Association canadienne contre l'impunité, 2012 QCCA 117 (CanLII) (a class action brought against a Canadian mining over alleged complicity in war crimes and crimes against humanity in the Democratic Republic of Congo); Choc v Hudbay Minerals Inc, 2013 ONSC 1414 (a case brought by an indigenous group in Guatemala against Canadian mining companies operating in Guatemala for acts of rape, murder and forced removal).

[8]Stephen R Ratner, 'Corporations and Human Rights: A Theory of Legal Responsibility' (2001) 111 Yale Law Journal 461.

[9]Philip Blumberg, 'Accountability of Multinational Corporations: The Barriers Presented by Concepts of the Corporate Juridical Entity' (2001) 24 Hastings International and Comparative Law Review 297. Fiona McLeay adds that '[t]he problem is accentuated by the benefits TNCs receive from the establishment of export processing zones and the guarantees afforded under bilateral investment treaties.' Fiona McLeay, 'Corporate Codes of Conduct and the Human Rights Accountability of Transnational Corporations – A Small Piece of a Large Puzzle', Global Law Working Paper 01/05, at 5, Symposium – 'Transnational Corporations and Human Rights', New York University School of Law. Online, NYU, <http://www.law.nyu.edu/global/workingpapers/2005/ECM_DLV_015787>.

[10]Jonathan Clough, 'Punishing the Parent: Corporate Criminal Complicity in Human Rights Abuses' (2008) 33 Brooklyn Journal of International Law 900.

[11]Patrick Macklem, 'Corporate Accountability under International Law: The Misguided Quest for Universal Jurisdiction' (2005) 7(4) Int Law FORUM du droit international 281.

[12]CLAIHR, 'Backgrounder: Options Available to the Government of Canada in Responding to Canadian Corporate Complicity with Human Rights Abuses' (2000) at 5-6, online, University of Ottawa, <http://aix1.uottawa.ca/~cforcese/other/complicity.pdf>. See also Craig Forcese, Putting Conscience into Commerce: Strategies for Making Human Rights Business as Usual (Montreal: International Centre for Human Rights and Democratic Development, 1997) 18.

[13]Craig Forcese, 'Deterring 'Militarized Commerce': The Prospects of Liability for 'Privatized' Human Rights Abuses' (2000) 31 Ottawa Law Review 173 (hereinafter Forcese, 'Deterring Militarized Commerce').

[14]ibid.

[15]Menno T Kamminga and Saman Zia-Zarifi, 'Liability of Multinational Corporations under International Law: An Introduction' In: MT Kamminga and S Zia-Zarifi (eds), Liability of Multinational Corporations Under International Law (The Hague: Kluwer Law International, 2000) 2. See also Chika B Onwuekwe, 'Reconciling the Scramble for Foreign Direct Investments and Environmental Prudence: A Developing Country's Nightmare' (2006) 7(1) Journal of World Investment and Trade 115 (arguing that the

quest for economic development puts many developing countries' governments under severe pressure to approve foreign direct investment without adequately taking into account its environmental impacts).

[16]Forcese, Deterring Militarized Commerce (n 13) 185.

[17]Jonathan Clough, 'Not-So-Innocents Abroad: Corporate Criminal Liability for Human Rights Abuses' (2005) 11(1) Australian Journal of Human Rights 5. See also Beth Stephens, 'The Amorality of Profit: Transnational Corporations and Human Rights' (2001) 20 Berkeley Journal of International Law 45 at 54 ('A review of the history and focus of the transnational enterprise demonstrates that the multilayered, multinational division of labour and responsibility of the modern corporation, its single-minded focus on economic gain, and its economic and political power all render multinational corporations a difficult regulatory target.')

[18]See EarthRights International, 'In Our Court: ATCA, Sosa and the Triumph of Human Rights', July 2004, online: EarthRights International, <http://www.earthrights.org/publication/our-court-atca-sosa-and-triumph-human-rights>; Human Rights Watch, 'Defend the Alien Tort Claims Act', online: Human Rights Watch, <http://www.hrw.org/campaigns/atca/>; Jim Lobe, 'Attorney-General Attacks Key Law', 15 May 2003, online: Inter Press Service, <http://www.ipsnews.net/interna.asp?idnews=18218>.

[19]See Executive Order No 13303 Protecting Development Fund for Iraq and Certain Other Property in Which Iraq has an Interest, 22 May 2003, 68 Fed Reg, 31,931. See also R Khavari, 'Executive Order 13303: Is the Bush Administration Choosing Corporations over Human Rights Actions Instituted via the Alien Tort Claims Act?' (2006) 14(1) Tulsa Journal of Comparative and International Law 119 at 120; C.R. Kelly, 'the War on Jurisdiction: Troubling Questions about Executive Order 13303' (2004) 46 Arizona Law Review 483-517.

[20]See, eg, the decision of the Trial Chamber of the International Criminal Tribunal for the former Yugoslavia, Prosecutor v Anto Furundzija, Case No IT-95-17/1-T10, para 155 (Judgment of 10 Dec 1998); The Nurnberg Trial (United States v Goering), 6 FRD 69, 110 (International Military Tribunal at Nuremberg 1946) (rejecting the argument that only States could be liable under international law and affirming that international law recognises individual responsibility); Robert H Jackson, Final Report to the President Concerning the Nurnberg War Crimes Trial (1946) 20 Temp LQ 338 at 342; Brigadier General Telford Taylor, USA, Chief of Counsel for War Crimes, Final Report to the Secretary of the Army on the Nurernberg War Crimes Trials Under Control Council Law No 10, 15 August 1949, at 109 online: US Government,http://www.loc.gov/rr/frd/Military_Law/pdf/NT_final-report.pdf> ('[T]he major legal significance of the [Nurernberg] judgments lies, in my opinion, in those portions of the judgments dealing with the area of personal responsibility for international law crimes.'). The establishment of the ICC with jurisdiction to prosecute individuals suspected to have committed crimes of serious concern to the international community is the high point of the recognition of individual responsibility in international law.

[21]Some scholars, however, have challenged this orthodox notion of international law. For instance, Myres S McDougal and Gertrude CK Leighton argue that the notion

that international law deals only with relations among states is a 'nineteenth century canard': Myres S McDougal & Gertruder CK Leighton, 'The Rights of Man in the World Community: Constitutional Illusions Versus Rational Action' (1949) 59(1) Yale Law Journal 74. And Philip Jessup has contended that recent developments have made the notion no longer true: Philip Jessup, A Modern Law of Nations: An Introduction (New York: Macmillan, 1948) 15-16.

[22]See John Ruggie, Protect, Respect and Remedy: A Framework for Business and Human Rights, Report of the Special Representative of the Secretary-General on the Issue of Human Rights and Transnational Corporations and other Business Enterprises, Human Rights Council, Eight Session, A/HRC/8/5, p 3 at para 1, 7 April 2008, online: UN Global Compact, <http://www.unglobalcompact.org/docs/issues_doc/human_rights/Human_Rights_Working_Group/29Apr08_7_Report_of_SRSG_to_HRC.pdf>.

[23]ibid, para 3.

[24]Anne C McConville, 'Taking Jurisdictioin in Transnational Human Rights Tort Litigation: Universality Jurisdiction's Relationship to Ex Juris Service, Forum Non Conveniens and the Presumption of Territoriality' in Craig Scott, (ed.), Torture as Tort: Comparative Perspectives on the Development of Transnational Human Rights Litigation (Portland: Hart Publishing, 2001) at 161 (hereinafter 'McConville').

[25]Naomi Roht-Arriaza, 'Combating Impunity: Some Thoughts on the Way Forward' (1996) 59:4 Law and Contemporary Problems 93.

[26]Morguard Investments Ltd v De Savoye [1990] 3 SCR 1077 (Canada) (hereinafter 'Morguard').

[27]International Shoe Co v Washington, 326 US 310 (1945) (US).

[28]In Canada, it is traced to s 92 of the Constitution Act, 1867, 30 & 31 Vict, c 3. See Hunt v T & N Plc (1993), 109 DLR (4th) 16. In the US it is traced to the Due Process Clause of the Fourteenth Amendment.

[29]French Civil Code, Article 14.

[30]Lother Hoffman, 'Austria' in Christian Campbell, (ed.), International Civil Procedure, vol 1 (Salzburg: Yorkhill Law Publishing, 2007) at 24 (citing s 99 of Jurisdiktionsnorm) (provided the defendant's property within the Austrian forum is not unduly smaller than the amount in dispute). An Austrian court has taken jurisdiction over a French skier based on the skier having left his underwear in his hotel room in Austria. Christopher B Kuner, 'Personal Jurisdiction Based on Defendant's Property in German law: Past, Present and Future' (1992) 5(2) Transnational Law 691 at 693 n 4 (citing Jan Kropholler, 'International Zustāndigkeit' in 1 Hanbuch Des Internationalen Zivilverfahrensrechts 183, 320 n 681 (1982)).

[31]Under the doctrine of Vermögensgerichtstand, defendant's ownership of property within a German forum was sufficient for the exercise of in personam jurisdiction over such defendant regardless of his place of domicile. Kuner, ibid, 692. This doctrine is codified in section 23 of the German Code of Civil Procedure 1877 that remains in force till date: 'For complaints asserting pecuniary claims against a person who has no domicile (Wohnsitz) within the country, the court of the district within which this

person has property (Vermogen), or within which is found the object claimed by the complainant, has jurisdiction.' Under this provision, jurisdiction is not limited to claims having some nexus with the property that is the basis of jurisdiction. Jurisdiction may be asserted against any defendant, natural or legal person. The plaintiff may be German or foreign and need not be domiciled in Germany. Once jurisdiction is established, it continues to inhere in the court even if the defendant ceases to have property in the German forum. The value of the property need not correspond in any particular relation to the value of the claim. Property may be a physical object, debt or some other claim to property or performance but must have an independent value, 'some sort of monetary value on the open market'. Even a debt owed a defendant suffices even though it may not lead to actual payment and even if it is the plaintiff that owes the debt. However, the defendant's property must be owned in good faith, so that, for example, the plaintiff may not rely on the defendant's claim for costs following a previous lawsuit dismissed with costs. See Kuner, ibid, 695-700 (observing that the expansive nature of Vermögensgerichtstand has led to controversial decisions).

[32]Danish Law on Civil Procedure, Article 248.

[33]Under the famous 'Swedish Umbrella Rule', a Swedish court can assume jurisdiction based on the presence of the defendant's property within the Swedish forum. Hans Smit, 'Common and Civil Law Rules of In Personam Adjudicatory Authority: An Analysis of Underlying Policies' (1972) 21 International and Comparative Law Quarterly 335 (observing that '[t]he danger of leaving one's umbrella in Sweden is known the world over. For if a non-resident leaves his umbrella in Sweden, he creates the authority for a Swedish court to cast him in a personal judgment for a debt obligation in any amount.')

[34]Swiss Federal Code on Private International Law, 1987, 8 December 1987: 'If this Code does not provide for jurisdiction in Switzerland and if proceedings abroad are impossible or cannot reasonably be required to be brought, the Swiss judicial or administrative authorities at the place with which the facts of the case are sufficiently connected shall have jurisdiction.'

[35]OJ L351/1, 20 December 2012. This Regulation modified the EU Council Regulation (EC) No 44/2001 of 22 December 2000 on Jurisdiction and the Recognition and Enforcement of Judgments in Civil and Commercial Matters, OJ L 12, 16 January 2001, which itself replaced the 1968 Brussels Convention on Jurisdiction and the Enforcement of Judgments in Civil and Commercial Matters, 27 September 1968, 8 ILM 229 (1969).

[36]Stephen B Burbank, 'Jurisdictional Equilibrium, the Proposed Hague Convention and Progress in National Law' (2001) 49 Am J Comp L 203 at 216.

[37]Arthur T von Mehren, 'drafting a Convention on International Jurisdiction and the Effects of Foreign Judgments Acceptable World-wide: Can the Hague Conference Project Succeed?' (2001) 49 American Journal of Comparative Law 191 at 194 (hereinafter Mehren, 'Drafting a Convention International Jurisdiction').

[38]See the Preliminary Draft Convention on Jurisdiction and Foreign Judgments in Civil and Commercial Matters, 30 October 1999, Prel Doc No 11 (August 2000), online: Hague Conference on Private International Law, <http://www.hcch.net/upload/wop/jdgm_pd26e.pdf> (last accessed 18 May 2011) For a history of the negotiations, see

Mehren, 'Drafting a Convention International Jurisdiction' (n 37) 191-202 (observing, at 195, that the negotiations failed due to fundamental differences in the views of the negotiating states (in particular, between the US and European Union states) regarding a range of issues, including, in particular, the role of adjudication in modern society). There is also the 2005 Hague Convention on Choice of Court Agreements, 30 June 2005, 44 ILM 1294 (2005), which, though not yet into force and which focuses on exclusive jurisdiction clauses, has a section (Article 8) on recognition and enforcement of foreign judgments resulting from such clauses.

[39]Brussels I Regulation (n 35) Article 4(1).

[40]ibid, Article 4(2).

[41]ibid, Article 8 (1).

[42]ibid, Article 8(2).

[43]ibid, Article 8(3).

[44]ibid, Articles 29-32. The court later seised is required to stay its proceedings until the court first-seised has determined its jurisdiction. Where the court first seised has determined that it has jurisdiction, the court later seised shall decline jurisdiction. But this rule applies only as between courts of member States. Where one of the proceedings is in a court of a non-member State, the national rule of the court of the Member State applies.

[45]ibid, Article 7(1)(a).

[46]ibid, Article 7(2).

[47]ibid, Article 7(3).

[48]Airey v Ireland, 32 Eur Ct HR Ser A (1979). See also JJ Fawcett, 'The Impact of Article 6(1) of the ECHR on Private International Law' (2007) 56 International Criminal Law Report 1 at 2.

[49](2004) 71 OR (3d) 675 (hereinafter 'Bouzari').

[50]ibid, para 35.

[51]ibid, paras 36 and 37.

[52]McConville (n 24) 165.

[53](2010), 98 OR (3d) 721 (hereinafter 'Van Breda').

[54]ibid, para 54.

[55]ibid, para 100.

[56]See, eg, Piscedda Mining Construction International Inc v Crew Gold Corp, 2011 YKSC 79 at paras 59-60 (Yukon Territory); Ayles v Arsenault, 2011 ABQB 493 at paras 32-33 (Alberta); Sears Canada Inc v C & S Interior Designs Ltd, 2012 ABQB 573 at para 15 (Alberta); Fewer v Ellis, 2011 NLCA 17 at paras 45-46 (Newfoundland and Labrador).

[57]François Larocque, Civil Actions for Uncivilized Acts: The Adjudicatory Jurisdiction of Common Law Courts in Transnational Human Rights Proceedings (Toronto: Irwin

Law, 2010) at 173.

[58]See Chilenye Nwapi, 'A Necessary Look at Necessity Jurisdiction' (2014) 47:1 UBC Law Review (Forthcoming) (hereinafter 'Nwapi') (exploring the early emanations of the doctrine, and suggesting that the application of the doctrine may be read into the 1950 US Supreme Court decision in Mullane v Central Hanover Bank and Trust Co, 339 US 306 (1950) and a few other subsequent cases).

[59]Mirjam Freudenthal & Frans van der Velden, 'The Netherlands' in JJ Fawcett, ed, Declining Jurisdiction in Private International Law: Reports to the XIVth Congress of the International Academy of Comparative Law, Athens, August 1994 (Oxford: Oxford University Press, 1995) 321 at 322, footnote 3 (citing a 1984 case, HR, 26 October 1984 [1985] NJ 696 as an example).

[60]24 May 1984, 24 ILM 468 (1985).

[61]8 December 1987.

[62]The provinces that have adopted it include Prince Edward Island (PEI) in late 1997: Court Jurisdiction and Proceedings Transfer Act, SPEI 1997, s 23 (although the statute has not yet come into force, but it will come into force on a date to be announced by the provincial cabinet, which has not yet been announced; the Yukon Territory in 2000: Court Jurisdiction and proceedings Transfer Act, SY 2000, c 64a 3136, where, like PEI, the statute has also not yet come into force; British Columbia in early 2003: Court Jurisdiction and proceedings Transfer Act, SBC 2003, c 28; and Nova Scotia in late 2003: Court Jurisdiction and proceedings Transfer Act, SNS 2003, c 2. In Alberta and Manitoba, their law reform commissions have recommended the adoption of the doctrine but the recommendations have not yet been implemented. Saskatchewan was the first province to adopt the UCJPTA, but did not adopt the necessity jurisdiction provision of the Act.

[63](n 53) para 54.

[64]ibid, para 100. As noted earlier, when the case reached the Supreme Court of Canada, the Court declined to consider the doctrines validity within the Canadian legal framework because the appeal was not argued on necessity jurisdiction. Had it been so argued, the Court would not only have decided whether without legislative authority, Ontario courts could assume necessity jurisdiction, but also whether even with legislative adoption, the doctrine would have passed a constitutional test, given the constitutionalisation of jurisdiction in Canadian private international law. See Morguard (n 26).

[65]Article 11 of Belgian Code of Private International Law Code, 15 July 2004, states: 'Notwithstanding the other provisions of the present statute, the Belgian courts will exceptionally have jurisdiction when the subject matter presents close connections with Belgium and proceedings abroad seem impossible or when it would be unreasonable to demand that the action be brought abroad.'

[66]See Jorge A Vargas, 'Enforcement of Judgments in Mexico: The 1988 Rules of the Federal Code of Civil Procedure' (1994) 14:2 Northwestern Journal of International Law and Business 376 at 392 (citing Mexican Federal Civil Procedure Code, 2008, Article 565).

[67]Article 9 of the Dutch Code of Civil Procedure, 2002, provides: When Articles 2 up to and including 8 indicate that Dutch courts have no jurisdiction, then they nevertheless have if: (a) the case concerns a legal relationship that only affects the interests of the involved parties themselves and the defendant or a party with an interest in the legal proceedings has appeared in court, not exclusively or with the intention to dispute the jurisdiction of the Dutch court, unless there is no reasonable interest to conclude that the Dutch court has jurisdiction; (b) a civil case outside the Netherlands appears to be impossible; or (c) the legal proceedings, which are to be initiated by a writ of summons, have sufficient connection with the Dutch legal sphere and it would be unacceptable to demand from the plaintiff that he submits the case to a judgment of a foreign court.

[68]Uruguay Private International Law Act 2009, Article 56(8).

[69]See Mario JA Oyarzábal, 'Jurisdiction over International Electronic Contracts: A View on Inter-American, Mercosur, and Argentine Rules' (2005) 19 Temple International and Comparative Law Journal 87 at 95; Julian Feichtinger & Karin Lehner, 'Comparative Study of 'Residual Jurisdiction' in Civil and Commercial Disputes in the EU: National Reporter: Austria', (2006) p 11, online: EU, <http://ec.europa.eu/civiljustice/news/docs/study_resid_jurisd_austria_en.pdf>; and Ubertazzi, 'Intellectual Property Rights and Exclusive (Subject Matter) Jurisdiction: Between Private and Public International Law' (2011) 15:2 Marquette IP L Rev 357 at 387-388. In Finland, it is 'somewhat unclear' whether jurisdiction by necessity is a valid ground for jurisdiction. But it is believed in Finland that a Finnish court can assume jurisdiction on the basis of the absence of a valid forum abroad. Juci Ikonen, 'Comparative Study of "Residual Jurisdiction" in Civil and Commercial Disputes in the EU: National Report for: Finland', (2006) p 8, online, EU: <http://ec.europa.eu/civiljustice/news/docs/study_resid_jurisd_finland_en.pdf>.

[70][2011] UKPC 7.

[71]ibid, para 6.

[72]Arnaud Nuyts, 'Study of Residual Jurisdiction: Review of the Member States' Rules concerning the 'Residual Jurisdiction' of their courts in Civil and Commercial Matters pursuant to the Brussels I and II Regulations', 3 September 2007 at 64, online: EC, <http://ec.europa.eu/civiljustice/news/docs/study_residual_jurisdiction_en.pdf> (hereinafter 'Nuyts').

[73]ibid, 64.

[74]18 December 2008, 2009 OJ (L7/8).

[75]Proposal for a Council Regulation on jurisdiction, applicable law and the recognition of decisions in matters of matrimonial property regimes' COM (2011) 126 of 16 March 2011.

[76]For a review of the proposed regulation, see CMV Clarkson, 'Matrimonial Property: The Proposed EU Regulation' (2011) 17: 9 Trusts and Trustees 846-854.

[77]Regulation (EU) No 1215/2012 of the European Parliament and the Council of 12 December 2012, on jurisdiction and the recognition and enforcement of judgments in civil and commercial matters (recast), 20 December 2012, OJ L 351.

[78]Nwapi (n 58).

[79]ibid.

[80]Commenting on the absence of a connection requirement in section 6 of the Canadian CJPTA and relating it to the requirement of a sufficient connection under the Civil Code of Quebec, Black, Pitel and Sobkin opine that the drafters of the CJPTA might have thought that the requirement of a connection was implicit in section 6 of the CJPTA. To them, it cannot be assumed that the section was intended to create 'unrestricted authority to hear a case whenever the court was satisfied it was appropriate to do so.' An alternative explanation, according to them is that the drafters might have thought that in light of the connection requirements of the real and substantial connection test, inclusion of a connection requirement under the section, which was intended to provide a distinct basis of jurisdiction from the real and substantial connection test, might 'confuse the analysis' and distract attention from the primary focus of the section, which is to avoid a denial of access to justice. They offer a third alternative, which is that the drafters might have intended that no connection was required. They consider this alternative 'unlikely' because it would go against the caution issued by the Supreme Court of Canada against unrestrained jurisdictional assertions, and favour the first alternative which considers the requirement of some connection implicit in the section. Vaughan Black, Stephen GA Pitel & Michael Sobkin, Statutory Jurisdiction: An Analysis of the Court Jurisdiction and Proceedings Transfer Act (Toronto: Carswell, 2012) at 164-165.

[81]Nuyts (n 72).

[82]Swiss Federal Code of Civil Procedure (n 25).

[83]Civil Code of Quebec (n 58) Art 3136; Dutch Code (n 64).

[84]Belgian Code of Private International Law (n 62).

[85]This is the case in Poland. See Nuyts (n 72), 66.

[86]This is the case in Portugal. See Nuyts, ibid.

[87]ibid.

[88]ibid.

[89]ibid.

[90]Lamborghini (Canada) Inc v Automobili Lamborghini SPA, [1997] RJQ 58 at para 48 (italics mine) (hereinafter 'Lamborghini').

[91]JA Talpis & J-G Castel, 'Interpreting the Rules of Private International Law' in Reform of the Civil Code, vol 5B: Private International Law, translated by Me Susan Altschul, (Montreal: Barreau du Quebec and the Chambre des notaires du Quebec, 1993) 1 at 55.

[92]For instance, in Wiwa v Royal Dutch Petroleum, 226 F 3d 88 (2d Cir 2000) (US), the lead plaintiff was a Nigerian national who relocated to the US. In the Dutch case Akpan v Royal Dutch Shell, supra note 5, the second plaintiff was a corporate personality domiciled in Amsterdam. And in the Canadian case Cambior, the plaintiff was an organisation incorporated in Canada for the purpose of initiating the proceedings on behalf of the foreign victims of the alleged environmental disaster.

[93]In their application of the real and substantial connection test, for instance, Canadian courts routinely require a connection with the province where the proceedings are

initiated. Such a connection may be provided by the occurrence of the activity or part thereof within the territory of the province, or by prima facie evidence that the Canadian arm of the corporation participated in the alleged foreign conduct. See, for instance, Anvil Mining Ltd v Canadian Association Against Impunity, 2012 QCCA 117 at para 85 (CanLII) (hereinafter 'Anvil') (holding that since "Anvil's activities in Quebec had absolutely nothing to do with 'complicity' to commit 'war crimes' or 'crimes against humanity' while operating a mine", Quebec lacked jurisdiction in the matter).

[94]McEvoy (n 1) 107.

[95]Anvil (n 93) paras 102-103.

[96]Talpis and J-G Castel (n 91).

[97]Nuyts (n 72) 65.

[98]ibid.

[99]ibid.

[100]See, generally, Phillips v Eyre (1870), LR 6 QB 1 (UK).

[101]Nuyts (n 72) 65.

[102]See 'Brief of Professor Alex-Geert Castermans (Leiden University), Professor Cees van Dam (Utrecht University), Dr. Liesbeth Enneking (Utrecht University), Dr. Nicola Jaagers (Tilburg University), Professor Menno Kamminga (Maastrcht University), as Amici Curiae in support of the petitioners', in Kiobel v Royal Dutch, 13 June 2012, No 10-1491, p 23-24, online: Chamber Litigation, <http://www.chamberlitigation.com/sites/default/files/scotus/files/2012/Professor%20Alex-Geert%20Castermans%20et%20al.%20Supplemental%20Amicus%20Brief%20in%20Support%20of%20Petitioners%20--%20Kiobel,%20et%20al.%20v.%20Royal%20Dutch%20Petroleum%20REARGUMENT%20(U.S.%20Supreme%20Court).pdf>.

[103]High Court, November 30, 2010, ECLI: NL: GHSGR: 2010:BO6529.

[104]2012 QCCS 5655 at para 52 (CanLII).

[105]Lamborghini (n 90).

[106]2011 ONSC 1636 (CanLII).

[107]ibid, para 116.

[108]According to Nuyts (n 69) 65, this is the case in the Netherlands.

[109]Talpis and Castel (n 91).

[110]ibid.

[111]ibid.

[112]ibid.

[113]McEvoy (n 1) 111.

[114]ibid.

[115]ibid.

[116]Nwapi (n 58).

[117]ibid.

[118]ibid.

[119]Nuyts (n 72) 65.

[120]ibid, 65 (referring to the rule in France).

[121]2008 BCSC 753, 83 BCLR (4th) 182. On appeal, the British Columbia Court of Appeal held that British Columbia had jurisdiction in the matter, but stayed the action in favour of litigation in Quebec on the grounds of forum non conveniens. 2009 BCCA 380, 94 BCLR (4th) 118 at para 34-53.

[122]Nuyts (n 72) 65.

[123]Mourant & Co Retirement Trustees Ltd, Zutphen District Court, 16 January 2008, ECLI: NL: RBZUT: 2008:BC9336.

[124]Nwapi (n 58).

[125]Tracy Lee Troutman, 'Jurisdiction by Necessity: Examining one Proposal for Unbarring the Dorrs of our Courts' (1988) 21 Vanderbilt Journal of Transnational Law 401 at 415; Arthur von Mehren, 'Adjudicatory Jurisdiction: General Theories Compared and Evaluated' (1983) 63 Boston University Law Review 279 at 311.

[126]Nwapi (n 58).

[127]2010 ONSC 2368 (CanLII).

[128]ibid, paras 41-42.

[129]ibid.

[130]Wolfe v Pickar, 2011 ONCA 347 at para 51 (CanLII).

[131]1999 CanLII 6035 (BC SC).

[132]ibid, para 26. The learned trial judge appeared to have been motivated by the fact that the defendant appeared to have 'lulled' the defendant to sleep until the limitation periods in Alberta and Saskatchewan, either of where the action might have been brought, expired.

[133]Jordan v Schatz, [2000] 7 WWR 442 at para 20 (BCCA) (stressing, at para 26, that '[t]he fact that no other forum is available to the plaintiff, due to the lapse of a limitation period in another jurisdiction, unfortunately does not bear upon the question of whether British Columbia has jurisdiction.')

[134]2010 BCSC 603.

[135]ibid, para 102.

[136]Nuyts (n 72) 65.

[137]District Court Rotterdam, 8 June 2011, ECLI: NL: RBZUT: 2008:BC9336.

[138]See Xandra E Kramer, 'Private International Law Responses to Corruption: Approaches to Jurisdiction and Foreign Judgments and the International Fight against Corruption' in HG van de Bunt et al, eds, International Law and the Fight against Corruption: Mededelingen van de Koninklijke Nederlandse Vereniging voor Internationaal Recht, Preadviezen, vol no: KNVIR139 (Advisory Report for the Dutch Royal Society of International Law) (Den Hague: Asser Press,

2012) 92 at 125.

[139]Llanos Oil Exploration Ltd v Republiek Colombia and Ecopetrol SA, District Court The Hague, 30 May 2012, ECLI:NL:RBSGR:2012:BX1740.

[140]Kramer (n 138) 125-126.

[141]Koji at 6 (stating that 'the need to determine whether a claimant will obtain a 'fair trial' in a non-Member State may have an adverse impact on foreign relations').

REFERENCES

1. Black, V, Pitel, SGA & Sobkin, M, Statutory Jurisdiction: An Analysis of the Court Jurisdiction and Proceedings Transfer Act (Toronto: Carswell, 2012)
2. Blumberg, P, 'Accountability of Multinational Corporations: The Barriers Presented by Concepts of the Corporate Juridical Entity' (2001) 24 Hastings International and Comparative Law Review 297
3. Burbank, SB, 'Jurisdictional Equilibrium, The Proposed Hague Convention and Progress in National Law' (2001) 49 Am J Comp L 203
4. CLAIHR, 'Backgrounder: Options Available to the Government of Canada in Responding to Canadian Corporate Complicity with Human Rights Abuses' (2000) at 5-6, online, University of Ottawa, <http://aix1.uottawa.ca/~cforcese/other/complicity.pdf>.
5. Clough, J, 'Not-So-Innocents Abroad: Corporate Criminal Liability for Human Rights Abuses' (2005) 11(1) Australian Journal of Human Rights 5
6. Clough, J, 'Punishing the Parent: Corporate Criminal Complicity in Human Rights Abuses' (2008) 33 Brooklyn Journal of International Law 900
7. EarthRights International, 'In Our Court: ATCA, Sosa and the Triumph of Human Rights', July 2004, online: EarthRights International,http://www.earthrights.org/publication/our-court-atca-sosa-and-triumph-human-rights
8. Feichtinger, J & Lehner, K, 'Comparative Study of 'Residual Jurisdiction' in Civil and Commercial Disputes in the EU: National Reporter: Austria', (2006) p 11, online: EU,http://ec.europa.eu/civiljustice/news/docs/study_resid_jurisd_austria_en.pdf
9. Forcese, C, Putting Conscience into Commerce: Strategies for Making Human Rights Business as Usual (Montreal: International Centre for Human Rights and Democratic Development, 1997) 18
10. Forcese, C, 'Deterring 'Militarized Commerce': The Prospects of Liability for 'Privatized' Human Rights Abuses' (2000) 31 Ottawa Law Review 173
11. Freudenthal, M & van der Velden, F, 'The Netherlands' in JJ Fawcett, ed, Declining Jurisdiction in Private International Law: Reports to the XIVth Congress of the International Academy of Comparative Law, Athens, August 1994 (Oxford: Oxford University Press, 1995) 321
12. Hoffman, L, 'Austria' in Christian Campbell, (ed.), International Civil Procedure, vol 1 (Salzburg: Yorkhill Law Publishing, 2007)

13. Human Rights Watch, 'Defend the Alien Tort Claims Act', online: Human Rights Watch,http://www.hrw.org/campaigns/atca/

14. Ikonen, J, 'Comparative Study of "Residual Jurisdiction" in Civil and Commercial Disputes in the EU: National Report for: Finland', (2006) p 8, online, EU: <http://ec.europa.eu/civiljustice/news/docs/study_resid_jurisd_finland_en.pdf>

15. Jackson, RH, Final Report to the President Concerning the Nurnberg War Crimes Trial (1946) 20 Temp LQ 338

16. Jessup, P, A Modern Law of Nations: An Introduction (New York: Macmillan, 1948)

17. Kamminga, T and Zia-Zarifi, S, 'Liability of Multinational Corporations Under International Law: An Introduction' In: MT Kamminga and S Zia-Zarifi (eds), Liability of Multinational Corporations Under International Law (The Hague: Kluwer Law International, 2000) 2

18. Kelly, CR, 'The War on Jurisdiction: Troubling Questions about Executive Order 13303' (2004) 46 Arizona Law Review

19. Khavari, R, 'Executive Order 13303: Is the Bush Administration Choosing Corporations over Human Rights Actions Instituted via the Alien Tort Claims Act?' (2006) 14(1) Tulsa Journal of Comparative and International Law 119

20. Kramer, XE, 'Private International Law Responses to Corruption: Approaches to Jurisdiction and Foreign Judgments and the International Fight against Corruption' in HG van de Bunt et al, eds, International Law and the Fight against Corruption: Mededelingen van de Koninklijke Nederlandse Vereniging voor Internationaal Recht, Preadviezen, vol no: KNVIR139 (Advisory Report for the Dutch Royal Society of International Law) (Den Haag: Asser Press, 2012) 92

21. Kuner, CB, 'Personal Jurisdiction Based on Defendant's Property in German law: Past, Present and Future' (1992) 5(2) Transnational Law 691

22. Larocque, F, Civil Actions for Uncivilized Acts: The Adjudicatory Jurisdiction of Common Law Courts in Transnational Human Rights Proceedings (Toronto: Irwin Law, 2010)

23. Lobe, J, 'Attorney-General Attacks Key Law', 15 May 2003, online: Inter Press Service, <http://www.ipsnews.net/interna.asp?idnews=18218>

24. Macklem, P, 'Corporate Accountability under International Law: The Misguided Quest for Universal Jurisdiction' (2005) 7(4) Int Law FORUM du droit international 281

25. McConville, AC, 'Taking Jurisdictioin in Transnational Human Rights Tort Litigation: Universality Jurisdiction's Relationship to Ex Juris Service, Forum Non Conveniens and the Presumption of Territoriality' in Craig Scott, (ed.), Torture as Tort: Comparative Perspectives on the Development of Transnational Human Rights Litigation (Portland: Hart Publishing, 2001)

26. McDougal, MS, & Leighton, GCK, 'The Rights of Man in the World Community: Constitutional Illusions Versus Rational Action' (1949) 59(1) Yale Law Journal 74

27. McEvoy, JP, 'Forum of Necessity in Quebec Private International Law: CcQ Article 3136' (2005) 35 Review General 61

28. McLeay, F, 'Corporate Codes of Conduct and the Human Rights Accountability of Transnational Corporations – A Small Piece of a Large Puzzle', Global Law Working Paper 01/05, at 5, Symposium – 'Transnational Corporations and Human Rights', New York University School of Law. Online, NYU,http://www.law.nyu.edu/global/workingpapers/2005/ECM_DLV_015787

29. von Mehren, AT 'Adjudicatory Jurisdiction: General Theories Compared and Evaluated' (1983) 63 Boston University Law Review 279

30. von Mehren, AT, 'Drafting a Convention on International Jurisdiction and the Effects of Foreign Judgments Acceptable World-wide: Can the Hague Conference Project Succeed?' (2001) 49 American Journal of Comparative Law 191

31. Nuyts, A, 'Study of Residual Jurisdiction: Review of the Member States' Rules concerning the 'Residual Jurisdiction' of their courts in Civil and Commercial Matters pursuant to the Brussels I and II Regulations', 3 September 2007 at 64, online: EC,http://ec.europa.eu/civiljustice/news/docs/study_residual_jurisdiction_en.pdf

32. Nwapi, C, 'A Necessary Look at Necessity Jurisdiction' (2014) 47:1 UBC Law Review (Forthcoming)

33. Onwuekwe, CB, 'Reconciling the Scramble for Foreign Direct Investments and Environmental Prudence: A Developing Country's Nightmare' (2006) 7(1) Journal of World Investment and Trade 115

34. Oyarzábal, MJA, 'Jurisdiction over International Electronic Contracts: A View on Inter-American, Mercosur, and Argentine Rules' (2005) 19 Temple International and Comparative Law Journal 87

35. Ratner, SR, 'Corporations and Human Rights: A Theory of Legal Responsibility' (2001) 111 Yale Law Journal 461

36. Roht-Arriaza, N, 'Combating Impunity: Some Thoughts on the Way Forward' (1996) 59:4 Law and Contemporary Problems 93

37. Ruggie, J, Protect, Respect and Remedy: A Framework for Business and Human Rights, Report of the Special Representative of the Secretary-General on the Issue of Human Rights and Transnational Corporations and other Business Enterprises, Human Rights Council, Eight Session, A/HRC/8/5, p 3 at para 1, 7 April 2008, online: UN Global Compact, <http://www.unglobalcompact.org/docs/issues_doc/human_rights/Human_Rights_Working_Group/29Apr08_7_Report_of_SRSG_to_HRC.pdf>

38. Stephens, 'The Amorality of Profit: Transnational Corporations and Human Rights' (2001) 20 Berkeley Journal of International Law 45

39. Takahashi, K, 'Review of the Brussels I Regulation: A Comment from the Perspective of non-Member States (Third States)' (2012) 8(1) Journal of Private International Law 1

40. Talpis, JA, & Castel, J-G, 'Interpreting the Rules of Private International Law' in

Reform of the Civil Code, vol 5B: Private International Law, translated by Me Susan Altschul, (Montreal: Barreau du Quebec and the Chambre des notaires du Quebec, 1993) 1

41. Troutman, TL, 'Jurisdiction by Necessity: Examining one Proposal for Unbarring the Dorrs of our Courts' (1988) 21 Vanderbilt Journal of Transnational Law 401
42. Ubertazzi, B, 'Intellectual Property Rights and Exclusive (Subject Matter) Jurisdiction: Between Private and Public International Law' (2011) 15:2 Marquette IP L Rev 357
43. Vargas, JA, 'Enforcement of Judgments in Mexico: The 1988 Rules of the Federal Code of Civil Procedure' (1994) 14:2 Northwestern Journal of International Law and Business 376

8
CHAPTER

MAPPING JUDICIAL DIALOGUE ACROSS NATIONAL BORDERS: AN EXPLORATORY NETWORK STUDY OF LEARNING FROM LOBBYING AMONG EUROPEAN INTELLECTUAL PROPERTY JUDGES

Emmanuel Lazega

Keywords: European patent judges, collective learning, discussion networks, reading networks, citation networks, lobbying

LEARNING PROCESSES AMONG JUDGES ACROSS BORDERS

Internationalisation in the judiciary is based, in part, on learning what judges across borders do. The modest purpose of this descriptive study is to look at learning processes among judges internationally, including high court judges. If one asks why not all judges in Europe read and cite decisions made in other courts in Europe, several obstacles to exchanges and learning are listed by the judges themselves. Language barriers come first; many judges do not use a second language, and when they do, they have to rely on English. Systemic and procedural differences are also often evoked: in some countries there is no practice of referring to foreign judgments and foreign literature, at least no direct citations, either by judges or by the parties; in others, judges are allowed to do so only if the foreign decisions are translated, or only if reference to foreign sources is first made by the parties themselves. Often there is no political will or decision authorizing or encouraging judges to make references to foreign judicial decisions. Finally, the nature of the task is not routine. This judge illustrates this issue very clearly: 'It is not difficult to look at foreign decisions. The problem is how easy it is to follow them, to really figure out what thinking is behind these decisions. Not all judges express their motives in the same ways; the decision must fit with the way in which it was brought to

---

Citation: Lazega, E., (2012). Mapping Judicial Dialogue across National Borders: An Exploratory Network Study of Learning from Lobbying among European Intellectual Property Judges. Utrecht Law Review. 8(2), pp.115–128. DOI: http://doi.org/10.18352/ulr.198.

the court, with local proceedings and local traditions and history. You have to "construe the claim" as the British would say. But how do you do that? You can read a number of foreign decisions without being able to see how the foreign judge comes to the decision. That is more difficult to do. If the other judge deals with the same patent, it is very interesting to see what he did with it, even if inevitably one comes to different conclusions. It also depends on what parties have argued in this case. If the arguments are the same, the conclusion may be the same. If not, it can be prohibitive to give a decision that you would like to give, given what they have done. It is useful to see what others have done. But it is difficult to analyse. If you are not very well informed about the ins and outs of German law and its applications in that country, you cannot analyse a German decision properly. The most useful thing is (...) to go sit down with the German judges and participate in their decisions, see how they do it, and then compare: would we have done it the same way or not? This is more effective than just reading.'

Looking at the context in which dialogue and learning take place across borders is thus crucial. This context is itself structured by differences, debates and competitions of many kinds, including regulatory competition, in ways of carrying out fundamental tasks, such as building legitimacy, creating coherence and respecting plurality.[1] Our approach in this paper will not deal with these general issues. Instead, in order to understand dialogue and the process of learning across borders, we focus on a case in point and a specific dimension of this context: social exchange among judges. We ask what is the relationship between actors' positions in the structure of international social exchanges among national court judges and their learning behaviour? Are stands taken by individual judges on various issues or controversies in their fields of specialty correlated with their position in this structure? Is this structure highly centralized or rather highly polarized, and what are the consequences of each situation for these processes? These questions lead to an additional issue, that of the capacity of such networks to contribute to the creation of a collective and international frame of reference for the judiciary, including but not exclusively high court judges, for example for judges specialized in the same substantive areas and following each other's work. As part of this wide issue of learning and influence, we wish to map such networks by describing, in an exploratory way, 'How do judges look at the work of other judges at the international level?'

We thus focus on invisible aspects of judicial internationalisation rather than the more visible legal phenomena (e.g. judicial decisions, legislation, or even formal and official associations such as that described by Claes and de Visser.[2] Indeed, essential to this purpose is the mapping of the various means and resources of which courts avail themselves to retrieve and exchange information beyond their own borders. Occasionally such means are formally institutionalised, e.g. in the form of electronic databases or periodic meetings for the exchange of information. Often however they are opaque and implicit, utilized in such a natural and subconscious fashion that one must actively work to identify them. We therefore map out various ways in which judges conduct dialogue with their foreign peers. We also analyse the relevant results and make systematic inferences about the general tenor and character of transjudicial dialogue. Our mapping can thus help study usually invisible 'transjudicial borrowing' and 'transjudicial dialogue'.[3] In particular, based on previous work on the balance between cooperation and competition characterizing collegiality,[4] we add a third dimension to Claes and de Visser's approach to this dialogue. Instead of stressing conversation and deliberation, we put more emphasis on institutional entrepreneurship in which judges can be involved in a bottom-up collegial, regulatory process underlying pluralism,[5] professional and political, as well as regulatory competition.

RESEARCH METHOD

We use social network analysis to map a social network of judges, including High Court judges, that describes the ways in which they look at the work of other judges across borders and learn from each other. Social network analysis is a method that reconstitutes the system of social exchanges among members of a predefined population. In our case, the exchanges are exchanges of information and advice. We would like to explore questions such as 'Where do High Court judges get their information (about decisions made elsewhere) from? Who are the judges talking to, or seeking advice from? Whose work abroad are they aware of? Who cites whom, if at all?' Each of these questions would help reconstitute a separate network; each network can be analysed separately or jointly with others

In this context, learning does not take place as it would at school. It happens in relation to work performance and to common projects raising controversies when judges from different countries and legal cultures have different perspectives on such projects. In addition to the reconstitution of an international social network among judges, we would like – at this exploratory stage – to look at more dependent variables such as position taken in such controversies. This would provide examples of the effect of existing social networks on ongoing debates in learning and influence within this population.

POPULATION AND FIELDWORK: THE EXAMPLE OF INTERNATIONAL PATENT JUDGES

Given the difficulty of asking network questions to justices in general, we used the following strategy[6] for the reconstitution of some of these networks. We focus on an association of specialized judges who meet and exchange across borders, at the European level. We were able to locate the Venice Forum, an international association of strongly committed Intellectual Property (IP) judges, in particular patent judges (35 judges comprising a mix of judges from highest courts and lower courts). They meet annually in Venice, convened by the European Patent Lawyers Association (EPLAW) together with the European Patent Office (EPO) and the Intellectual Property Judges Association (IPJA).[7] It is also a heterogeneous set of judges in the sense that the structure of their career differs in various European countries and legal cultures. Europe has currently 27 jurisdictions and 27 kinds of patents decisions.

The Venice Forum judges represent courts involved in IP litigation. One has to be invited by EPLAW in order to participate. There are country delegations, usually a couple of judges from each country, except for the largest countries or the more active ones in the field. Pre-selection is mainly carried out by EPLAW, whose president picks out the judges who will come and contribute. Four Dutch judges were present in Venice in 2009 whereas in the Netherlands there are about 10 to 12 such judges. They are the same 'kind' of judges from all countries: they are not representatives, but rather activist judges concerned with patent issues and about the emergence of the European Patent Court (EPC). Some come to participate, together with EPLAW, in shaping the procedure of the future EPC; others accept the invitation because they want the voice of their country to be heard.

Indeed, the main background feature of this meeting is the long and tortuous process of creation of the European Patent Court. The meeting itself was part of an ongoing process of lobbying Brussels for the construction of the EPC and definition of its procedure. This lobbying was seen by corporate lawyers and judges alike as important for the European economy, in which entire industries are built on business models with patents at their core. As we shall see, a small number of countries are pushing harder than others in the lobbying process.

The social construction of a European Patent judiciary as a bottom-up process begins with transnational interactions and dialogue between these judges who can be considered to be 'institutional entrepreneurs'. This set of actors is therefore quite specific, closed and selective. We were not allowed to attend their meeting per se but we could see that fierce discussions could take place – although no-one left shaking their head.[8] We carried out the survey nevertheless because we hoped that the heterogeneity of this subset of judges was sufficient to bring out regularities in the pattern of exchanges and show the diversity of approaches towards learning – even if this learning is inextricably linked to controversy with respect to the choice of procedure to be implemented at the EPC.

Many patent judges in this association have more or less frequent bilateral relations, exchanging views and problems. Fieldwork to reconstitute the network that is created by these relations was carried out in Venice in October 2009. We took advantage of the existence of this annual meeting in Venice in order to carry out our interviews. We submitted this survey to all participating judges at the European Judges Forum (San Servolo Conference, 30-31 October 2009). At the beginning of our fieldwork, we did not know if individual patent judges would be prepared to answer our network questions. We received a relatively open attitude in general, once the judges knew that the interviewers were scholars. The survey received a 100% participation rate. The questionnaire is presented in Appendix 1.

MAPS OF DIALOGUE ACROSS BORDERS AS MEASURED BY SOCIAL NETWORKS

Mapping flows of information among judges identified by their country was carried out using social network analysis and qualitative face-to-face interviews. The reconstitution of the network used sociometric questions listed in Appendix 1. We also asked the judges about their preferences in controversial issues regarding the construction of a harmonized procedure for the European Patent Court. In order to understand the learning and influence processes that drive internationalization of law, we then link position in the network and preferences with respect to the controversy.

We find that there is a hierarchy among various forms of network learning across borders. Three networks were measured among IP European judges at the Venice Forum: 'personal discussion network', a 'reading other judges' work' network and an 'explicit reference to other judges' decisions' network. Reconstitution and analysis of these networks shows that the discussion network is denser than the reading network, which is denser than the explicit reference network. There is much more activity in direct personal discussion with colleagues across borders (for example at events such as the Venice Forum), than with actual reading of their work (decisions and articles); there is quite little explicit reference to other foreign judges' decisions in these judges' own decisions. In other words, at this stage, learning across borders occurs more through discussion than through reading, and more through reading than through explicit reference to work of other judges (which is not allowed in some countries).

Some countries are more active in the learning process among this set of judges: Dutch, UK, German, Italian and French judges are the most active in the personal discussion network and in the reading network. UK, German and Dutch judges are the most active in the explicit reference network. Dutch, UK and German judges display the highest activity in all three networks (reading, discussion and explicit reference). Italian and French judges also display high activity in the reading and discussion networks, but not in the explicit reference network. Note that explicit reference to work of other judges is not permitted in some countries (for example France).

The analysis of these networks also shows that learning across borders depends on the existence of highly active and central judges in a core-periphery structure in which the periphery is itself fragmented. A small subset of highly central judges in this system can be identified as opinion leaders among their colleagues. Indeed some networks are more centralized than others. The central judges facilitate learning through personal discussions, through reading other judges' work, and through explicit citation of other judges' work. This highly central subset of opinion leaders also increases transparency by referring to decisions of foreign courts. Colleagues recognized as opinion leaders come from different countries depending on the kind of network: French, Dutch, Italian, German, UK and Swiss judges are among the most central in the personal discussion network. Dutch, German, and UK judges are among the most central in the reading network. UK, German and Dutch judges are the most central in the explicit reference network. Opinion leaders who are central in all three networks tend to be UK, German and Dutch judges

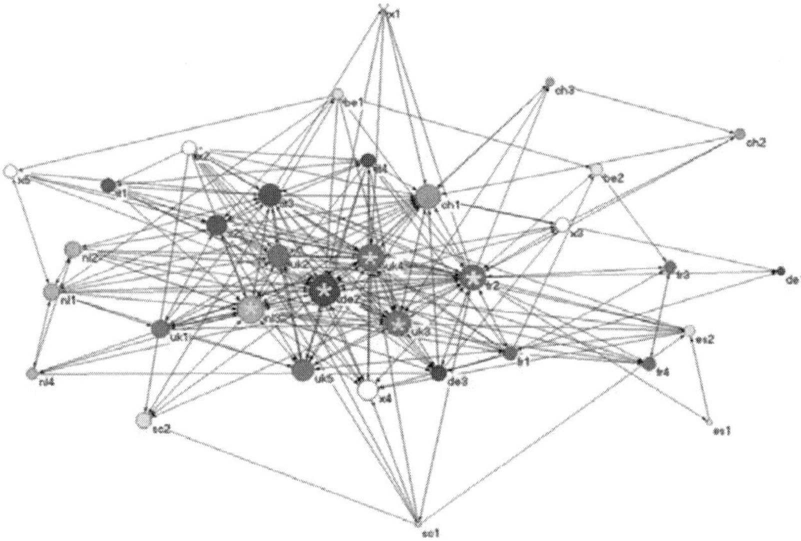

Figure 1a: Visualization of the personal discussion network among European IP judges belonging to the Venice Forum

Legend: Individual judges are identified by their country of origin and countries are colour coded. Circle size represents each judge's centrality. Highly central judges (identified by the symbol *) are those most cited by colleagues (i.e. number of citations above the 90th percentile in at least two networks). To protect anonymity of respondents, individuals who are single representatives of their country in this group are clustered in the white (X) subgroup.

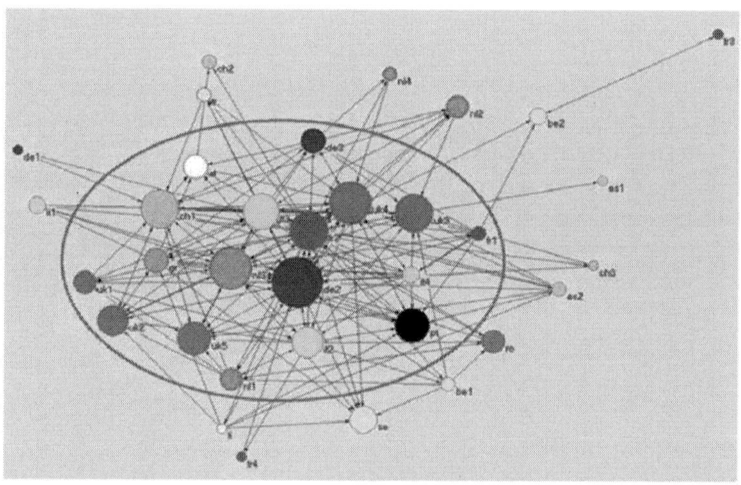

Figure 1b: Visualization of the personal discussion network among European IP judges belonging to the Venice Forum, without ties to judges from one's own country

Legend: This Figure is similar in construction to Figure 1a. The ellipse identifies the core of the network.

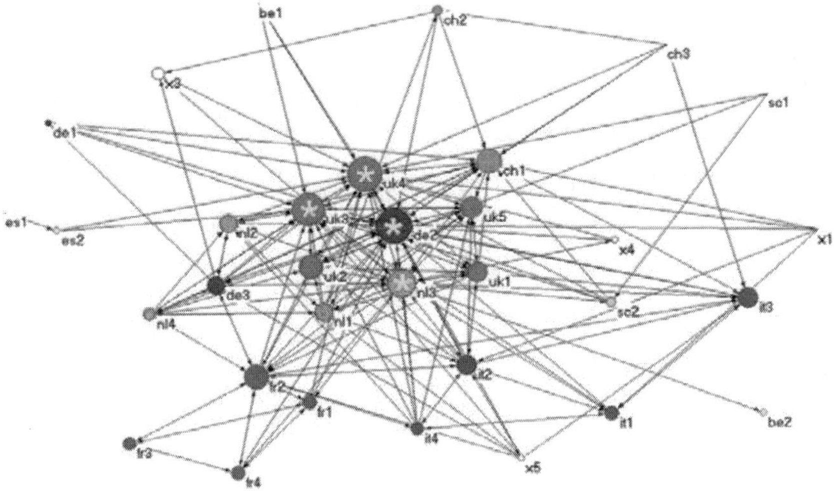

Figure 2: Visualization of the direct reading network among European IP judges belonging to the Venice Forum

Legend: Individual judges are identified by their country of origin and countries are colour coded. Circle size represents each judge's centrality. Highly central judges (identified by the symbol *) are those most cited by colleagues (i.e. number of citations above the 90th percentile in at least two networks). To protect anonymity of respondents, individuals who are single representatives of their country in this group are clustered in the white (X) subgroup.

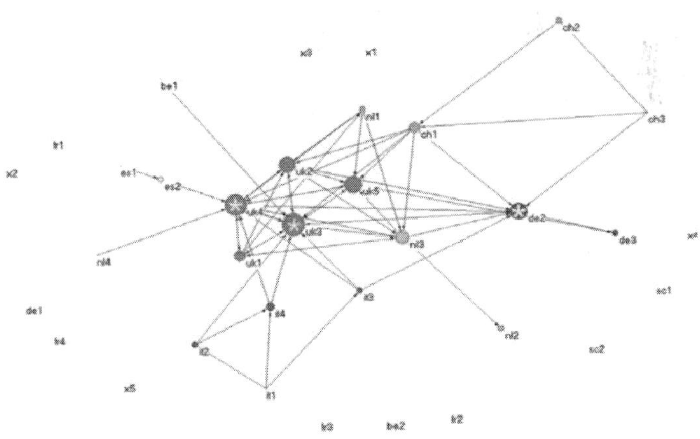

Figure 3: Visualization of the explicit reference network among European IP judges belonging to the Venice Forum

Legend: Individual judges are identified by their country of origin and countries are colour coded. Circle size represents each judge's centrality. Highly central judges (identified by the symbol *) are those most cited by colleagues (i.e. number of citations above the 90th percentile in at least two networks). To protect anonymity of respondents, individuals who are single representatives of their country in this group are clustered in the white (X) subgroup.

DIALOGUE AND CONTROVERSIAL ISSUES AMONG IP JUDGES

In order to measure a possible outcome of this learning process, we look at whether or not there is consensus among these judges with respect to controversial issues concerning patents and procedure for the future EPC: assessment of inventive step, determination of scope of protection, involvement of technical experts, and personal rule applied to define what a patent is.

When assessing inventive step, most judges (76%) declare that they – explicitly or tacitly – apply the same method as the Examining Divisions and Boards of Appeal of the EPO (problem-and-solution approach). Almost all judges (91%) think that decisions of foreign courts in relation to the same patent with which they deal are indeed relevant. A strong majority (67%) also declares that they do refer in their own decisions to decisions of foreign courts. When determining a scope of protection, a majority of judges (64%) considers that the statements of the applicant during the grant procedure before the European Patent Office does play a role. In the mind of 65%, this could only lead to a limitation of the scope of protection. A majority of judges (60%) involves independent technical experts to report on inventive step. Only 49% involve independent technical experts to report on scope of protection. Almost all judges say that the parties have the opportunity to comment on the reports of the experts

For choosing between two different rules to apply when defining patents, 46% of the Venice Forum judges consider patents are exceptions to the freedom of copying. Therefore, they think that the validity of patents and their scope of protection should be critically assessed. 27% of the judges support another definition, for which patents are granted as a reward to the contribution of the inventor to technological development, with the implication that the patent holder is entitled to a mild assessment of the validity of the patent and a broad scope of protection. 21% hesitate. 74% are personally quite happy with their choice

In sum a high level of consensus exists among Venice Forum IP judges on several issues (assessment of inventive step, problem-and-solution approach, relevance of foreign decisions), but strong differences remain: there is a heterogeneous use of judicial discretion in balancing 'patent as exception' and 'patent as reward'. There is great diversity with respect to narrow versus broad scope of protection. A real risk exists that differences among the practices of these judges could lead to diverging decisions. This diversity leads to the question of whether learning across borders leads to uniform positions among judges and to the role of opinion leaders in this harmonization.

DIALOGUE, NETWORKS AND CONTROVERSIES

The analysis shows that, on average, opinion leaders in this learning process have positions different from less central IP judges with respect to five issues.

Figure 4: illustrates these differences. Figure 4 Comparison between average positions of opinion leaders versus average positions of all other judges with respect to five issues

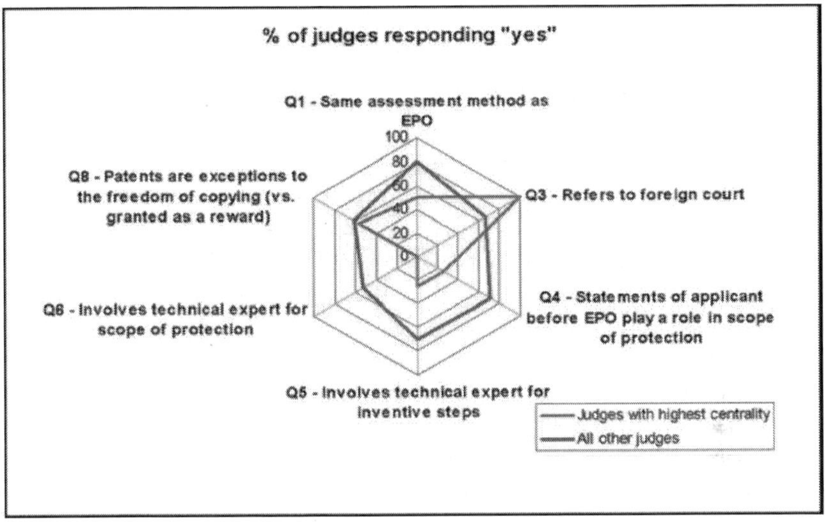

Legend: In blue: average response profile of all judges. In red: response profile of opinion leaders.

1. Assessing inventive step: problem-and-solution approach? 0 = No

3. Reference to decisions of foreign courts? 0 = No

4. Statements of applicant during grant procedure before the European Patent Office play any role when determining the scope of protection? 0 = No

5. Involvement of independent technical experts to report on inventive step? 0 = No

6. Involvement of independent technical experts to report on scope of protection? 0 = No

8. Which rule do you apply? 0 = Patents are exceptions to the freedom of copying.

It shows that highly central judges tend to use the problem-and-solution approach less systematically than all others. They refer to foreign courts in their own decisions (with exceptions, for example, in France, Spain, and Romania) more than all others. They consider that 'statements of applicant during grant procedure play a role when determining the scope of protection' less than all others. They involve independent technical experts to report on inventive step less than all others. They involve independent technical experts to report on scope of protection less than all others. One may therefore hypothesize a future convergence of judges in this network towards a UK-German-Dutch position if judges follow their highly central colleagues (opinion leaders identified above). A final map (Figure 5) represents judges perceived by their peers as closest to a future EU uniform position, i.e. as reflecting in their discourse the future European norm.

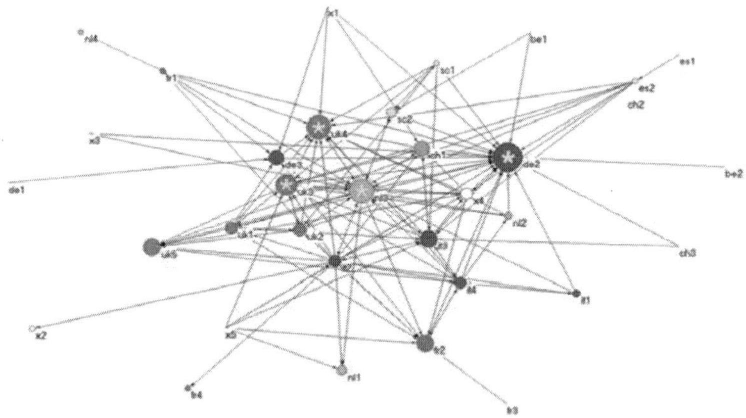

Figure 5: Judges perceived by their peers as closest to future EU uniform position with respect to patents

Legend: Countries are coded by colours, and circle size represents each judge's centrality. In this graph, highly central judges (identified by symbol *) are those most cited by colleagues (i.e. number of citations above the 90th percentile in at least two networks). To protect anonymity of respondents, individuals who are single representatives of their country in this group are labelled X.

Figure 5 shows that the Venice Forum judges perceive among themselves at least six judges, from five countries, as colleagues whose positions on controversial issues are likely to reflect the future EU uniform position. In this network, these judges are Dutch, German, British, Italian and Swiss. Some of them are already central in the social networks mapped above. Others have different ideas with respect to 'harmonization' of positions in Europe, stressing 'circulation' instead of convergence, even if this leads to diverging decisions. Thus, in 2009, convergence towards consensus on the EU uniform position in this network still remained uncertain. We infer from this structure that learning through networks across borders does not necessarily, by itself, lead to convergence of perspectives and uniform positions among IP judges in Europe. As a consequence, our analysis provides some understanding of the process of the social construction of a common frame of reference among them but cannot yet predict the future European norm which will come out of this process

DISCUSSION AND CONCLUSION

This descriptive paper tracks dialogue and collective learning across borders through personal networks of judges in a case in point: patent judges brought together at an annual meeting by corporate lawyers involved in institutional lobbying for the construction of a European Patent Court with a specific procedure. Empirical observation shows that personal networks of discussion with foreign judges, reading of their work and reference to their decisions do exist and can be reconstituted with a degree of approximation. Our network study shows that judges from some countries are more active in this dialogue than judges from other countries. The learning process is driven, to some extent, by a small subset of super-central individuals who frame this dialogue and can be considered to be opinion leaders in this social milieu. We measure a strong level of consensus among these judges on several controversial issues surrounding the procedure of a possible future European Patent Court. But strong differences between them remain. Dialogue and collective learning do not, by themselves, lead to convergence towards a uniform position in these controversies. For example, on average, opinion leaders in this group have different positions from most judges with respect to several issues. In particular, opinion leaders, even if they increase transparency by referring to decisions of foreign courts, are not always considered by their peers to be closest to a future EU uniform position. Dialogue across borders does not mechanically create consensus.

Our descriptive approach is not meant to answer the question why some individual judges and countries are more central than others in the learning process that is intertwined with a regulatory one. Many hypothetical reasons could be listed. One such reason might be that leading legal systems, or strong traditions in legal entrepreneurship in the business sector, structure that network. Another may be that some countries may invest in the patent judiciary more than other countries for institutional, economic and/or political reasons. For example, France has fewer judges specialized in intellectual property than other countries simply because judges in the French judiciary are usually generalists rotated from one specialty to another every three years. Thus highly specialized, stable and central British, German or Dutch judges would tend not to have comparable French alter egos in this network because the structure of judicial careers is different in France. A third reason could be that some senior individuals with staying capacity in this rather closed collegial milieu and with high centrality become particularly important as institutional entrepreneurs, and skilled at helping other colleagues in the network reach a certain level of comfort with specific solutions to common problems – a kind of judgment associated with learning by Bell.[9] Further research should improve the list of hypotheses and test them systematically. This would help disentangle various effects hidden behind the importance of specific individuals in the networks examined here, since these individuals represent various legal orders, legal systems, and positions in their countries and in Europe. This would also bring new insights into the effect of context on the learning process

Our empirical network study of this milieu was also meant to evaluate the feasibility of this approach and provide tentative substantive results. Methodologically, we were able to identify several limitations for this kind of research. If 100% of the judges present in Venice in October 2009 responded to our questionnaire, it is because interviews were carried out face to face with our team of highly skilled colleagues. An online questionnaire, that was meant to extend the study to the judges from the 2008

Venice Forum, failed miserably. As a result, for example, German judges are under-represented in the survey compared with the number of German judges usually attending the meetings. One opinion leader, who was invited and expected at the meeting, did not come and did not participate in the survey.

If transnational dialogue and collective learning do take place among this specific set of IP judges, it is in fact inseparable from two phenomena. First, corporate lawyers, who represent corporate clients, play an important role in gathering the judges because they have an interest in knowing their judges personally, in getting used to their ways of making decisions, and in trying to get a few messages across to promote the interests of their clients. The network examined here was gathered by invitation from corporate lawyers (EPLAW) with help from EPO and IPJA. This in itself both makes measurement possible and raises measurement problems. The IP domain is one in which judges are most heavily courted by large industrial interest groups with patents at the core of their business model. Therefore several well-known IP judges in Europe never come to the Venice events because they consider them to be part of a political process in which they should not participate. Much learning takes place in such settings nevertheless.

Second, in our specific case in point, internationalisation in IP law, and business law in general, can be considered to be more advanced than in other areas of law, and more exposed to institutional changes. Indeed, the judges themselves are involved in a lobbying process in which they are institutional entrepreneurs in the construction of the European judiciary (a European Patent Court), with strong incentives to exchange with their peers and compete for influence on behalf of their country and/or on behalf of their own ideas and sense of professionalism. Some of them come because they fear that if they did not, the voice of their country would not be heard; in a context in which large IP cases are taken by multinational companies to Germany, the UK and the US, they think that it matters whether or not their country is represented in this setting. It remains to be seen whether this very specific process of dialogue and learning across borders – in which the political stakes and process are very present and visible – can be extended to other areas of law. Generalization of results obtained from this set of strongly committed IP judges to the population of all judges making IP decisions in Europe is therefore not established. So we believe that it would be useful to carry on examining bottom-up collegial and judicial dialogue across national borders in its context, while paying attention to the economic, social and political phenomena that drive it.

CONCLUSION

Again your responses will be kept strictly confidential. If your words are quoted in the final report of this survey, they will be so anonymously. In order to better preserve the confidentiality of your own responses and to minimize the possibility that responses by others are biased, we would appreciate it if you would not discuss the details of the interview with your colleagues before the end of the conference.

NOTES

1. A.S. Muller & S. Richards (eds.), Highest Courts and Globalization, 2010; A.

Hol & M. Loth, Reshaping Justice. Judicial Reform and Adjudication in the Netherlands, 2004; A. Hol & P. Langbroek (eds.), 'Special issue on Adjudication in a Globalizing Context', 2007 Utrecht Law Review 3, no. 1, (last visited 27 February 2012); J. Bell, 'Introductory themes to the use of foreign legal materials in judgments', HiiL Workshop, Bologna, 20 November 2009; J. Allard & A. Garapon, Les Juges dans la mondialisation. La nouvelle révolution du droit, 2005; A.-M. Slaughter, A New World Order, 2005.

2. See the paper by Claes & de Visser in this issue (M. Claes & M. de Visser, 'Are You Networked Yet? On Dialogues in European Judicial Networks', 2012 Utrecht Law Review 8, no. 2, pp. 100-114).
3. Slaughter, supra note 1.
4. E. Lazega, The Collegial Phenomenon, 2001. E. Lazega, 'Cooperation among competitors. Its Social Mechanisms through Network Analyses', 2009 SocioLogica, no. 1, (last visited 27 February 2012),
5. Hol & Loth, supra note 1
6. Another strategy is to look at citation networks among judges. However, that is not necessarily much easier, especially because judges do not always have the same citation practices in all countries. We know for example that French judges do not cite foreign statutes or cases for reasons of their own (for example they allegedly do not want to cite statutes that might become obsolete).
7. The European Patent Lawyers Association (EPLAW, formerly EPLA) is a professional association of patent lawyers, with a registered office in Brussels. Its stated object is 'the promotion of efficient and fair handling of patent litigation in Europe and the strengthening of ties between well-established patent lawyers in Europe'. In a conference organized by the EPLAW in October 2005 in Venice, a panel of judges adopted a resolution calling for a single European patent court. In a second conference, called the Second Venice Forum and jointly organized by the EPLAW and the European Patent Office in 2006 in San Servolo, an island in the Venetian Lagoon, a panel of judges approved a Resolution adopting guidelines for the Rules of Procedure of the European Patent Court to be set under the European Patent Litigation Agreement (EPLA), which has yet to enter into force. Since 2001, the EPLAW has also taken a series of resolutions relating to European patent law.
8. We also know of judges who refused to participate in these events. Patent judges are often the targets of groups lobbying on behalf of the previously mentioned industries, and some of them see the Venice Forum as part of such a process,
9. See the paper by John Bell in this issue (J. Bell, 'The Argumentative Status of Foreign Legal Arguments', 2012 Utrecht Law Review 8, no. 2, pp. 8-19).

9
CHAPTER

RETHINKING COMPETITION LAW

Rutger Claassen and Anna Gerbrandy

Keywords: Competition law, non-economic interests, capability approach

INTRODUCTION

To ensure the efficient functioning of markets, European competition law prohibits undertakings from entering into anti-competitive agreements and abusing a dominant position on the market.[1] The standard justification for European competition rules lies in the welfare gains of having competitive markets for consumers. Coordination of behaviour between undertakings drives up prices, which has a negative effect on consumer welfare. Competition law therefore serves to prevent a series of economic benefits (for companies) in order to realize another series of economic benefits (for consumers). However, companies sometimes enter into agreements to further a non-economic goal, such as rendering production facilities more ecologically friendly or strengthening social cohesion in inner-city areas. They may have different motivations for doing so, but in these cases the question arises: should European competition law take these non-economic interests into account? If so, how can this be done?

Since the 1990s the European Commission has increasingly adopted a consumer welfare approach to the interpretation of European competition law. In this paradigm, it is difficult to give non-economic interests their due, as we will show by discussing three recent cases in which economic and non-economic goals clash (Section 2). While the consumer welfare approach has been criticized, it is a challenge to come up with a constructive alternative. In this article, we propose the capability approach as an alternative framework for interpreting competition law. This approach was developed by economist Amartya Sen and philosopher Martha Nussbaum as an

Citation: Claassen, R. & Gerbrandy, A., (2016). Rethinking Competition Law. Utrecht Law Review. 12(1), pp.1–15. DOI: http://doi.org/10.18352/ulr.321.

alternative to utilitarian approaches in welfare economics and theories of justice. We will introduce the main features of the capability approach and propose how it can be applied to competition law, focusing on two key issues: the identification and the weighing of capabilities in a competition case (Section 3). Third, we argue that there are good principled reasons to incorporate non-economic goals into competition law, both in terms of legal interpretation of the relevant EU texts, moral arguments about the appropriate division of labor between private companies and political bodies, and in terms of political considerations about the legitimacy of decision-making by competition authorities (Section 4). Fourth, we compare how both the capability approach and the consumer welfare approach would think about the three illustrative cases in which non-economic goals are at stake. We argue that the capability approach better handles these cases (Section 5). Overall, the capability framework, although not without difficulties of its own, may provide a more legitimate theory for European competition law

The method used is multidisciplinary: we combine law with political philosophy. The aim of our endeavor is to show how a theory which is widely used in political philosophy can show a way out of one of the challenges within European competition law. We link this theoretical exploration with practice and show how combining the capability approach with actual competition cases may lead to quite surprising results.

APPROACHES IN EU COMPETITION LAW

The general aim of competition law, as understood by economists and lawyers alike, is to address the market failure of market power by adding a layer of legal rules to ensure the proper functioning of markets. Although the notion that competition is a cornerstone of market economies is widely accepted, there is no agreement on the more specific aims of competition law. In the European context it has always been understood that perfect competition is an ideal, unreachable in practice. However, there are important unresolved questions about the extent to which unfettered competition may be checked by other public policy interests. Especially with regard to non-straightforward cases there is no clear-cut answer as to which standard should be used. Positions of the European Commission and the European Court of Justice, especially where public interests are involved, seem to diverge.

For our purposes a simplified outline of this debate suffices. The currently dominant approach in European competition law is the consumer welfare approach, especially since it is advocated by the Commission.[2]

This approach focuses on the outcomes of market exchanges, and does so by considering their effects on (aggregate) consumer welfare. Although the concept of consumer welfare itself is not clearly defined, [3] it is understood through the lens of economic efficiency calculations.[4] Economists (and lawyers following their lead) calculate the losses and gains to consumer welfare of allowing a specific agreement between undertakings.[5] Both are expressed in the same monetary units, leading to a simple sum: if costs are greater than benefits, the agreement is contrary to competition law. Under what we will call a narrow consumer welfare approach, as primarily advocated by the European Commission, agreements between undertakings leading to an increase in price, a limitation in output (quantity, quality or range) or a limitation of innovation, are prohibited because they are considered detrimental to consumer welfare. Other interests are assumed to lie outside its scope. This creates a tension between the value of consumer welfare and other public values.[6] Here, we will follow customary terminology and use the terms 'economic interests' (the consumer welfare interests that are the focus of the narrow consumer welfare approach) and 'non-economic interests' (that fall beyond the scope of assessment in this approach) to refer to the difference between these values. Although the boundaries between the two are fuzzy – as our examples below will illustrate – it is generally understood that non-economic interests are benefits that are either not directly included in the consumer welfare standard, or are not (reliably) economically calculable.

In contrast, a broad consumer welfare standard is somewhat more open to including non-economic interests. Such a standard is used for example by the Dutch competition authority in specific cases (as we will see below). It incorporates (easily) calculable non-economic benefits that are not directly related to the product in question but that do accrue to the consumers of these products. Thus it includes these non-economic benefits indirectly, to the extent that they pertain to the same group of consumers as the ones suffering price increases. The example of the Energy Agreement, below, will illustrate such an approach in practice. However, it is unclear just how strongly these benefits need to relate to the same group of consumers, in the same market. Clearly the further this is stretched, the more controversial the interpretation of the consumer welfare standard becomes.

Although not used in competition law, we can imagine the use of a third welfare standard: an inclusive welfare standard (the label is ours).[7] In contrast to the consumer welfare approaches, such an approach takes non-economic interests directly into account, and does not require a link to the same group of consumers. It does so by using a broader conception of 'welfare' and adding (measured and quantified) non-economic benefits to the assessment mix. Such a standard is based on the idea that anything can be expressed in terms of preferences and thus be quantified and compared,[8] by asking about consumers' preferences and using a willingness-to-pay quantification in monetary terms.[9] This does not answer the question of whether one should do so.[10] Although this standard does include non-economic interests, it does so by using a market-based concept (subjective preference satisfaction) as its starting point. We applaud this standard's principled decision to include non-economic interests (see Section 4). Nonetheless, it is our contention that to take full account of the value of public interests when assessing agreements between companies taking responsibility for public interests, we would need to go beyond such an inclusive welfare standard and introduce a non-welfarist standard, such as the one offered by the capability approach. But this is running ahead of the argument.

We will now first illustrate the difficulties of using a consumer welfare approach (narrow or broad), by introducing several competition law cases. In each of these cases non-economic interests present a problem for competition law, and the question is if and how to take them into account. These illustrations will come back in Section 5, where we will further discuss the application of the different standards.

A first illustrative case relates to the Dutch Energy Agreement (Energieakkoord), an agreement on a roadmap towards more sustainable energy in the Netherlands in 2020. Parties to the agreement include energy producers, distributors, the Government, and advisory bodies to the Government (Social Economic Council). They agreed to the (accelerated) closing down of five coal-fired power plants, which leads to less supply of electricity and to lower emissions of noxious gases and particulate matter. It is on this element of the agreement – in isolation – that the Dutch competition authority (Autoriteit Consument en Markt, ACM) provided an 'informal opinion' (a non-binding preliminary assessment), applying (also) European competition law. The ACM labelled the closing of coal-fired power plants a restrictive production agreement in violation of competition law.[11]

Animal welfare cases provide a second class of illustrations of non-economic interests. For example, under ongoing consideration is an agreement in the Netherlands relating to intensive pig farming (the Verbond van Den Bosch).[12] Parties to the agreement include the provincial government, farmers, animal-fodder producers, veterinarians, and supermarkets. This agreement includes lowering the use of antibiotics in animal husbandry, which results in less resistance to antibiotics in humans and provides for greater animal welfare. But it might also lead to higher consumer prices. In this case there are both human health (i.e. consumer welfare) and animal welfare benefits, so that a broad consumer approach would give consideration to some of the benefits (i.e. those relating to humans) of the agreement. But we can easily imagine cases where there are only animal welfare benefits. For example, think of protecting the habitat of a species of birds not even on the brink of extinction. Suppose that dairy farmers, using their grassland for grazing cattle, in collaboration with nature conservation societies, come to an agreement to protect the black-tailed godwit (a protected species). Although not specifically beautiful, it makes an impressive melancholy sound, especially in flocks; but it nor its eggs are generally used as food. The effect of such an agreement might be higher prices of dairy products, but also the flourishing of the black-tailed godwit.[13] How to decide such a case?

A third illustration concerns efforts to combat binge drinking. This phenomenon has become more widespread since the price for alcoholic drinks has decreased relative to other consumptions. Supermarkets in the UK and Ireland have been urged to take responsibility to counteract binge drinking, because of its health risks for young people, but also because it entails healthcare costs and police effort. However, these supermarkets are 'trapped in a downwards spiral of price-centric competition'.[14] Therefore an important chain of supermarkets in the UK – Tesco – proposed to reconsider the pricing of alcohol, but only if done together with its competitors. Such a pricing agreement would clearly go against competition law, at least if the possible benefits (avoided healthcare costs, lower policing costs, and better inner-city atmosphere and liveability) are not taken into the assessment. Legislative action was then considered, by setting a minimum price for alcoholic beverages.[15]

In all of these cases it proves difficult to take non-economic interests into account in a systematic way if a consumer welfare standard is used (see also Section 4). It is for this reason that we will now propose an alternative approach.

A CAPABILITY APPROACH TO COMPETITION LAW

The capability approach as alternative to resourcist and utilitarian approaches

The capability approach was originally developed by economist Amartya Sen and philosopher Martha Nussbaum. The capability approach is a flexible framework, which has been used in a variety of contexts. Sen's aim was to propose an alternative view of welfare, compared to standard welfare economics, which is based on the moral philosophy of utilitarianism.[16] Nussbaum's aim was to propose an alternative to utilitarian and resourcist theories in the area of theorizing about distributive justice. [17] The basic idea of the approach is that we should start from the fact that individuals have 'capabilities to function' in a specific way. A function or functioning is a 'being or doing' of a person. Eating, sleeping, driving, walking, being healthy, being educated etc. are examples of functionings. A capability is an ability or opportunity to function in a certain way. I have the capability to be well-nourished if I have the opportunity (given my income and access to food markets) to consume a nutritious diet. I may decide not to use my capability; I may choose not to eat today but too fast. But, as Sen has often argued, having such a personal choice is important. A fasting person, but not a starving person, has the opportunity to reach a sufficient nutritional intake. He has the freedom to choose how to function. We can then evaluate the level of welfare or the justice of a society by looking at how well it succeeds in guaranteeing each citizen a set of basic capabilities.

This perspective differs from its competitors, resourcism and utilitarianism. Resources are inputs of any person's capability set. We need food to have the capability to eat, we need healthcare services to have the capability to be healthy. Resourcist theories define welfare or justice by looking at each person's possession of a basket of resources. On a macro-level, evaluating countries' performance by looking at the average resource bundle per person (GDP per capita) is an example of a resourcist approach. However, resources do not translate into capabilities in a straightforward manner. Two persons, one healthy and the other disabled, may need to receive different resource bundles to reach the same set of capabilities, given differential personal, social and environmental conversion factors. Therefore it is important to evaluate economic processes by looking at the actual set of functionings individuals are able to realize (i.e. their capability set), instead of merely at their resource bundle.[18]. At the other end of the process, individuals derive a certain utility or well-being from their functionings. However, here too there is no one-to-one correspondence between a capability set and one's utility level. Two persons with the same capability set can experience different levels of well-being. If social policy focuses on utility levels, then it will be held hostage by persons who need champaign and caviar to reach the same level of well-being as their neighbours who are content to have fish and chips; or it can miss the urgency of poverty where people have adjusted their expectations and are happy to live on a low level of functionings achievement. The capability approach avoids these opposite pitfalls, ignores both resource inputs and utility outputs and steers our evaluations to the capabilities people actually have.

Sen and Nussbaum have also stressed that the capability approach can be seen as a human rights approach. People should have rights to basic human capabilities.[19] States are made responsible for the capability level of their citizens. This provides an important connection to the field of law, including competition law

The capability approach in the context of competition law

For the connection between law and the capability approach to work, two important issues need to be resolved. First, which capabilities are the basic capabilities that people should have a right to? Sen and Nussbaum have given different answers, where Nussbaum has formulated a list of ten central capabilities,[20] and Sen thinks this selection process is best left to democratic processes.[21] Second, how to weigh them against each other and make trade-offs? These two questions, as to selection and weighing of capabilities are still very much open to interpretation and further development in the capability approach. They are also key to the application of the approach to competition law.[22]

As a necessary first step, all capability interests of the parties that have a stake in a specific competition dispute would need to be identified. To tailor the approach to the competition-law context we propose to conceptualize these interests as consisting of three distinct types of capability sets: market-constituting capabilities, consumptive capabilities and third-party capabilities.

First, market-constituting capabilities consist of the capabilities to hold property and to contract, i.e. the ability to engage in voluntary exchanges to obtain goods and services. These capabilities are constitutive for the institution of the market; markets could not exist without them.[23] The capability approach can and arguably should recognize the two basic market freedoms – to hold property and to contract – as important capabilities that are valuable for citizens to possess.[24] These capabilities express the value of freedom of choice in the economic context.[25] This does not mean that the capability approach is fanatically pro-market, because as we will see the approach will also recognize other valuable capabilities, which will need to be weighed against these market-constituting capabilities. Nor is the approach anti-market. The capability approach will assess the legitimacy of specific markets on a case-by-case basis.[26]. In a competition case, market-constituting capabilities have a certain weight because they express the producers' freedoms to conclude agreements with each other as they see fit. These freedoms may obviously come into conflict with the two other sets of capabilities, which we will now address.

Second, consumptive capabilities refer to a set of widely different basic capabilities that are essential to human flourishing: capabilities for health, education, nourishment, housing etc. These we call consumptive capabilities because each of these capabilities in turn requires (amongst other things) consumers' ability to purchase those goods and services which are necessary to realize them. The market is instrumental to the production and exchange of these goods: it may, or may not, be the best institution to achieve them. From a capability perspective, given the scarcity of resources, the most efficient system of providing these goods should be chosen, so that the total set of capabilities can be realized at least up to a threshold level.[27] In competition cases, this means that a consumers' interest in consumptive capabilities (say, to heating houses and cooking food) translates into an interest in getting market goods (say, gas and electricity) to be delivered to them at the lowest possible price; given the fact that this will leave them with as much budget as possible to satisfy their other basic capabilities (later in this section this claim will be qualified).

Third, we use the label of third-party capabilities to refer to capabilities of others than consumers or producers. Here non-economic interests enter the capability approach. In the Dutch Energy Agreement, for example, these are capabilities of future generations which stand to be harmed by damage to the climate if CO_2 emissions are not reduced in time.[28] In the case about intensive pig farming, animal capabilities are at stake.[29] In the case of binge drinking we need to deal with capabilities for health of (inter alia) young people, as well as capabilities for security of inner-city inhabitants. These examples are not exhaustive: there is a wide variety of possible third-party capabilities. Now, we do not claim that it is uncontroversial that these third-party capabilities should be recognized. But we do argue that competition law should make room to discuss and possibly incorporate non-economic interests (Section 4) and show how this can be done by conceptualizing these interests in terms of capabilities (Section 5).

The second step in any application of the capability approach to competition law will be to weigh the capability interests at stake. There are three theoretical issues here

A first issue is how much weight every capability should be awarded. Capabilities cannot be weighed using market prices because such prices rely on each individual's purchasing power and willingness to pay. Imagine two different cases. In case X the animal capabilities of a group of chimpanzees must be weighed against consumers' capability to purchase life-saving healthcare medication, while in case Y the same animal capabilities must be weighed against the consumptive capability to purchase a new brand of cosmetics. Quite apart from the size of the respective groups (suppose the numbers of animals and consumers are the same for X and Y), the value of the consumptive capability will be different in a different product market. This is an important methodological difference with an economic approach, which simply counts preferences and is blind to the differential value of different capabilities. This means we need alternative ways to establish weights. In the end, whatever methodology we choose, the actual weighing process needs to be done in an institutional context that is democratically legitimated (see Section 4).

A second issue is the distributive principle guiding such a weighing exercise. The analogy with economic reasoning suggests maximizing the total level of capabilities. Let us assume that in a competition case there are four parties, A & B (producers) and C & D (consumers). We will assume that if we allow an agreement between A & B to stand this raises their capability levels to 15, while C & D's capability levels fall to 10. In the situation where the agreement is prohibited as a violation of competition law, A & B will experience a capability level of 5, and C & D of 25. The second situation, then, realizes a higher total capability level (30), compared to the first situation (25). However, as Nussbaum proposes, each basic capability should be realized up to a threshold level. If the threshold were put at, say, 8, then the second situation is problematic because it allows the capability level of A & B to fall below the threshold. Using a threshold principle means opting for the first situation would be the right choice, because there all parties' capabilities are above the threshold. This principle would be important in competition cases as well, as we will show, and holds that it is more important for each person to have a sufficient level of every basic capability, than to have a maximal aggregate level. For example, the value of the capability to contract is that it allows freedom of choice. The capability to contract is more meaningfully realized to the extent that consumers are able to choose from a larger variety of contract partners. Other things being equal, a choice is more meaningful when there are more alternatives to choose from ('your money or your life!' is not an attractive choice situation to be in). However, at some point, there are diminishing returns. To be able to choose from 50 brands of washing powder arguably is not much more valuable than to be able to choose from 30 brands.

Other basic capabilities exhibit a similar structure of diminishing returns. Most pertinent in the competition context is that thinking in terms of thresholds is antithetical to the economic objective of maximizing consumptive capabilities (and the accompanying effort of competition authorities to ensure the lowest possible price on the market). When the consumers' budgets are sufficient to satisfy all their basic consumptive capabilities then any further protection of consumptive capabilities only works to bring them even higher above the threshold than they already are.[30] Such increases above the threshold are less valuable than increases to bring them (or anyone else) up to the threshold level. When a price-increasing producer agreement serves to protect third-party capabilities (which we imagine have not yet reached the threshold) and thereby increases prices so that it decreases consumer capabilities (but still keeps them above the threshold), then the first may have more weight in the overall judgment than the latter

A final issue is whether the weighing act should take a quantitative form (let us call this type of weighing 'calculation'), based on the model of an economic cost-benefit analysis, or a qualitative form (let us call this type of weighing 'balancing'). Some authors argue that capabilities can be measured.[31] if that is the case, then there are no principled objections to a quasi-economic weighing of capabilities. Other authors, however, follow Nussbaum in stressing the incommensurability of capabilities: each of them is of separate value and these values cannot be compared in terms of a common metric.[32] In the absence of commensurability, we can make choices, but they take the form of a discursive style of reasoning in which different types of interests are roughly balanced against each other. This type of balancing is also familiar in legal literature.[33] our line on this is that we should proceed with care when we try to quantify non-economic interests. It may be possible to quantify where we mainly need to balance price-related consumptive capabilities to price-related market-constituting capabilities. But when non-economic interests come into the picture, quantifying would often present a distorted picture of the nature or magnitude of the interests at stake.

THE ARGUMENT FOR INCLUSION OF NON-ECONOMIC INTERESTS IN COMPETITION LAW

The previous section has argued that if we want to include non-economic interests into competition law assessments, the capability approach provides a good normative framework for doing so. But should we include these interests in the first place?

As the cases mentioned in Section 2 illustrate, undertakings, sometimes co-jointly with pressure groups and/or government bodies, may decide to take responsibility for a public interest and join forces in improving (parts of) their processes. Of course, such initiatives generally will not be against the self-interest of the companies concerned either, resulting in good public relations, a well-known and outstanding reputation or profit in a new market.[34] In competition law this type of cooperation is at odds with the competition law paradigm of individual agents, seeking self-interested profit maximization. In the discussion on the goals of competition law and standards to be used in assessing competition cases, arguments have been made against incorporating non-economic interests in a competition law assessment. We will review the three main arguments, which we have labelled the legal, moral and political argument.[35] We will reject each of them and provide reasons for including non-economic interests in competition law.

First, the legal argument holds that the relevant legal texts do not support inclusion of non-economic interests in a competition law assessment (though often this argument is enmeshed in the moral argument, presented next).[36] In the European context these texts are the Treaty on the Functioning of the European Union (TFEU), secondary legislation and policy documents of the Commission. The reason to focus on consumer welfare is, firstly, because the exception of Article 101(3) TFEU includes the requirement of a fair share of benefits accruing to consumers. Secondly, because in secondary legislation and accompanying guidance the Commission focuses on consumer welfare,[37] and because the Commission is an important actor in shaping and enforcing competition law, these latter documents carry legal and interpretational weight.[38]

These arguments in our view are not convincing. On the contrary, the legal texts at least leave room for, but more importantly require, a broader interpretation. A coherent reading of the Treaty provisions, including its general goals,[39] and its integration clauses,[40] does not lead to any single goal (and therefore: standard) of competition law. Instead, several, sometimes conflicting, goals are possible. The Court's judgments support this view.[41] Therefore there are good legal reasons to include non-economic interests in competition law.[42]

Second, there is the moral argument that private parties should concentrate on profit maximization and not try to realize social ends that lie outside the market. This argument presupposes a particular division of labour between the private and the public realm. Private actors concentrate on their private objectives, and in doing so ensure the optimal functioning of the market mechanism. Public actors legislate in favour of public objectives, and in doing so ensure a level playing field of publicly defined constraints under which market agents pursue their own interests. This argument, then, rests on two related grounds. On the one hand, it is concerned with the optimal economic functioning of the market, in terms of consumer welfare. Collusive agreements between private actors are a threat to this and competition law aims to restore the market's functioning by prohibiting them where they distort competition. On the other hand, the argument is concerned with the coherence of different parts of the legal system. Competition law has a different function from other areas of law. Whereas other areas may constrain market actors in order to realize noneconomic objectives, competition law constrains market actors to make the market function on economic terms. Thus, competition law should not be overburdened and made incoherent by also having to deal with these non-economic objectives.[43]

The reason for calling this a 'moral' argument is that the upshot of this division of labour between private and public actors (and between different parts of the legal system) is that market actors cannot assume their moral responsibility in the same way in which this is possible for private persons operating outside a market context. A group of producers who believe it is their moral responsibility to tackle a social problem – as a group – is unable to do so because they are declared part of a system which is only geared towards one goal, consumer welfare.[44] In the field of business ethics, this position – that firms do not have a moral responsibility – is very controversial, to say the least. Most authors there argue that firms do have at least some moral responsibilities, although of course the exact ground on which this is argued as well as the scope of these obligations are under much debate.[45] The capability approach has been used to this extent as well.[46] One important reason for assuming moral responsibility is that legislators are often too slow or at too far a distance from practice to do be able to effectively regulate social problems.[47] On a global level it is also possible that there effectively is no government that can regulate.[48] The emergence of movements for corporate social responsibility in the last decades is a sign that cooperation and initiatives of private actors are necessary in an era of declining public capacity to tackle problems effectively. To prohibit agreements to reach non-economic goals would mean to drain private actors' responsibility for them.

Perhaps the real reason behind the reluctance to grant moral responsibility to private actors lies elsewhere: with the consequences it would have for the authorities having to evaluate these private actions when being called upon to settle disputes in the context of competition law. This brings us to the third and political argument: that a weighing of these interests which each have a very different character – a market interest against a non-market interest – should not belong to the legitimate authority of administrative agencies.[49] This legitimacy argument is serious: it holds that it is exclusively up to democratically elected parliaments to pass legislation that would close down coal-fired power plants, prevent binge drinking by providing a minimum price, protect animal welfare by providing detailed regulations, or impose on farmers obligations to protect the black-tailed godwit.

We disagree.[50] First, it is no less controversial to give exclusive recognition to economic interests in situations where non-economic interests are also at stake, than to acknowledge both sets of interests. In our view, therefore, it is the legal decisions by competition authorities that exclude non-economic interests which lack legitimacy. Once brought forward by one of the parties in the dispute, it is arbitrary to exclude non-economic interests to the advantage of the economic interests at stake. In political philosophy, it is widely recognized that only a democratic process which includes all interests at stake can gain legitimacy.[51] From this perspective, the political argument must be turned on its head. Moreover, if the weighing of an administrative agency dissatisfies groups of citizens and politicians, then nothing prevents law-making as a way of correcting those judgments and making regulations which express a different weighing of the interests for future cases. The explicit weighing of these interests by a competition authority will serve as a trigger for law-making authorities, who can still have the last word on the matter if they want to.

Second, we should not underestimate the potential for democratic elements to be added to the decision-making procedure at the administrative agency itself. For example, the public at large could participate through consultations. But more promising is to include elements of deliberative democracy, by involving a representative group of the public in the decision-making procedure where non-economic interests are raised. In this forum of debate, where all points of view are discussed and weighed on their merits, without the power base of the discussant being the defining factor of acceptance,[52] a balancing of interests would be at stake.[53] This means calling upon the public not as consumers, but also as citizens.[54] Judicial appeal of such a decision would ultimately place in the hands of the judiciary the question of the correct interpretation of the legal provision, its application to the facts of the case, and review of the procedures established to safeguard legitimacy of the decision-making process.

In conclusion there are legal, moral and political arguments for including non-economic interests in a competition law assessment. This brings us to the next and final step in our argument: applying the capability approach to the cases introduced above.

APPLYING THE CAPABILITY APPROACH

It is one thing to present general arguments – as we have done in the previous section – stating that noneconomic goals should be taken into account in competition law. It is quite another thing to show how this can be done. Therefore in this section we will show how the capability approach can be used in competition cases, using the three cases presented in Section 2: the Dutch Energy Agreement, the animal welfare case and the binge-drinking case. We will start by discussing these cases under the currently dominant consumer welfare approach, which as we saw does not incorporate non-economic goals (5.1). Then we will show how the capability approach can be applied, by making use of the framework introduced in Section 3 (5.2). Finally, we will show the differences between the capability approach and its economic cousin, i.e. the inclusive welfare approach (5.3).

Applying the consumer welfare approach

Above we distinguished two versions of the consumer welfare approach. Under the narrow consumer welfare standard, only direct effects on the consumers of the product in question can be considered, especially the price effect on consumer welfare. Under this standard all three agreements of our example cases would be prohibited. The

Dutch Energy Agreement concerns an agreement between energy companies and other stakeholders to move towards sustainable energy production in the Netherlands. A specific agreement to close down noxious coal-fired power plants was included in this overall agreement. Economic theory suggests that taking production out of the market will lead to a price increase (because of the decrease in supply).[55] Similarly, in the animal welfare cases higher production costs lead to an increase in the price of pork and an increase in the price of dairy products as a result of agreeing to protect the black-tailed godwit. Finally, in the binge-drinking case the agreement on prices of alcoholic beverages between supermarkets will also increase prices. All these agreements therefore lead to lower consumer welfare. Under the narrow standard, nothing counterbalances this effect, and therefore these agreements violate competition law.

In contrast, a broad consumer welfare approach allows for weighing these negative effects on consumer welfare against quantifiable benefits of these agreements for consumers. For example, the avoided healthcare costs of consumers of energy, pork (by ingesting less antibiotics), or alcohol (by drinking less) are calculated and taken into account. These benefits apply to the same group of consumers who suffer from price increases, albeit that the benefits occur on different markets. This approach was actually applied by the Dutch competition agency ACM in the Energy Agreement case. All consumers are affected by an increased price, but all also benefit from avoided healthcare costs of lower emissions of noxious gases. However, the ACM limited its acknowledgment of the benefits of avoided healthcare costs to the lowering of the emission of NO_x, SO_x and particulate matter, and – controversially – excluded the lowering of CO_2 emissions.[56] The compounds NOx and SO_x play a role in creating harmful particulate matter, smog and acid rain and have an effect on health (especially on the respiratory system), on visibility, on corrosion (of metals and statues), and on the environment and the ecosystem. A lowering of these emissions has both an immediate local effect on health and an immediate and long-term effect on the environment, locally and globally. As for particulate matter, these very small particles contain solids or liquids that can enter the lungs and thus result in serious health problems, as well as leading to environmental damage. Thus a lowering of particulate matter has a direct local effect on health, as well as a more non-local effect on the environment. The ACM calculated the healthcare benefits of these three types of emissions and weighed them against the welfare loss caused by the agreement (its conclusion was that the latter weighed heavier; thus the agreement was still declared to be in breach of competition law).

The energy case shows how the broad consumer welfare approach can take into account non-economic goals, such as health, but only in an indirect way: by calculating avoided healthcare costs. Similarly, it is possible to present the advantages of preventing binge drinking as a matter of avoided healthcare costs of the youths involved, just as it is possible – though the chain of causality is stretched – to include the notion that using less antibiotics to raise pigs leads to lower human healthcare costs. However, there is a difference in valuing health in itself, as a capability (as we will show below) and valuing the avoidance of (quantified) healthcare costs. The limits of the broad consumer welfare approach become even more apparent in the non-consideration by the ACM of the long-term ecological effects of the Energy Agreement. Greater resilience of the ecosystem, for example, cannot be accounted for in terms of avoided healthcare costs. Furthermore, a consumer welfare standard in competition law generally has difficulty with long-term effects and favours short-term consumer benefits.[57]

The consumer welfare standard also falls short when we consider the animal welfare case as there is no consumer welfare effect from increasing an animal's living space or protecting the black-tailed godwit. In the latter case one would need to stretch the notion of consumers to include a market for leisure, where consumers benefit from being able to hear and see different birds when hiking or biking, as these benefits do not necessarily accrue to the same consumers as those paying the higher price (on the dairy consumption market). All of this requires heavy conceptual gymnastics from the consumer welfare approach. Where benefits do not accrue in any straightforward manner to consumers, this standard therefore fails to integrate non-economic goals into a competition law framework.

Applying the Capability Approach

A capability approach would start by taking into account the three groups of capabilities mentioned in Section 3. First, consider the market-constituting capabilities for property and to contract. The capability for property of the energy production companies relates to their ownership of coal-fired power plants and other production assets.[58] This capability is in itself not limited by competition law. By contrast, the capability to contract is directly limited by competition law: concluding agreements restricting competition is prohibited. Prohibiting an agreement to diminish production capacity means limiting the energy producers' capability to contract. Interestingly, the market structure of this case means that this has a negative impact on the capability for property as well. For in this case there is a 'first mover disadvantage': a change to sustainable production by an individual producer is not feasible, because such a production mode is more expensive, leading to higher prices, so that consumers will switch to the producer offering a lower price for a less sustainable product. It is therefore unfeasible for one individual producer to take the lead.[59] If the alternative route of collective agreements is prohibited by competition law, then the capability for property is limited as well. More precisely: no capability is left to use one's property to produce in a sustainable manner. In the same vein, the market-constituting capabilities of producers of pork and dairy products, and those of supermarkets fighting binge drinking are at stake in the other cases.

Both the consumer welfare approach and the inclusive welfare approach fail to take into account these capabilities of producers. The capability approach is broader in that it values the freedoms (opportunities) of market participants both instrumentally and intrinsically: both for the consumption capabilities that market agents provide to each other, and for their abilities to enjoy and exchange their property.[60] This intrinsic valuation of producers' market freedom may be treated with suspicion by many in the competition context, given its historically primary aim of countering producer power to enhance consumer welfare. This historically grown focus is understandable, but in cases where non-economic interests are involved, we see its problematic implications. Producer capabilities cannot be taken into account, even where undertakings aim to protect a widely-valued public interest. Of course, this does not mean that market-constituting capabilities will be the only valuable thing on the table (such as in libertarian approaches which exclusively rely on the value of market freedoms) when using a capability approach. But they do need to be recognized and included as valuable capabilities, and then balanced against the other two classes of capabilities

Second are consumptive capabilities. In the Energy Agreement case, these are all capabilities that need the supply of electricity: cooking, warming, cooling, washing, lighting etc.[61] As a result of the Energy Agreement these capabilities are negatively impacted, as the goods necessary to realize them become more expensive. Less total consumption is possible, leading either to less consumption of energy or of other goods. Similarly, in the animal welfare and binge-drinking cases, there are clear consumer capabilities at stake, which are negatively affected by any price increases as a consequence of producer agreements. These consumer interests are also included in the assessments of the consumer welfare and the inclusive welfare approach. The difference with the capability approach is that the inclusive welfare approach evaluates consumptive capabilities differently once a threshold is reached (see Section 4). As long as basic/core capabilities can still be met (are still on a level above this threshold), individuals have sufficient capabilities. An increase of the price of energy, which does not result in a situation where basic capabilities cannot be met above the threshold, is therefore less problematic. If there are weighty (third-party) capabilities on the other side of the balance, this might lead one to accept a decrease in consumer capabilities due to price increases. The consumer welfare approaches obviously would not agree with this: they do not take the remaining budget of consumers into account when thinking about the value of price increases. But the capability approach can discriminate between situations above and below a threshold, and take into account that a given price increase for a generally affluent population is not the same thing as the same price increase for a poorer population.

Finally, third-party capabilities. As mentioned earlier, in this category we find a wide variety of capabilities. In the cases under discussion in this article we find four examples of third-party capabilities: capabilities for health, capabilities of future generations, animal capabilities and citizen capabilities

First, in most of the cases discussed the capabilities for health of consumers are at stake. In the Energy Agreement case health is negatively affected through emissions, in the animal welfare case through the use of antibiotics, and in the binge-drinking case by drinking too much. In these cases, a broad consumer welfare approach could take health into account by looking at avoided healthcare costs (as explained above). However, valuing such a capability is very different from valuing the avoidance of (quantified) healthcare costs. Being of good health is a basic capability to function, which has to be taken into account when applying a capability approach. This capability is affected by lower emissions immediately leading to greater health. Furthermore, as indicated in Section 3, although the set of basic (minimum) capabilities necessary for individuals to flourish may be the same for everyone, the 'amount' of resources needed to reach a threshold level of the capability for health may differ between persons (interpersonal variability in converting resources into functioning's). A reduction of emissions would immediately lead, for individuals with respiratory problems, to a higher level of functioning, even if for others the resulting improvements in health are negligible in this sense. The capability approach can take these differences into account.

Second, the capability approach may acknowledge capabilities of future generations. [62] In the Energy Agreement case, this would do justice to the fact that lowering emissions has important effects which go beyond any currently existing base of consumers. A reduction of emissions results in a (better chance of) flourishing of future generations, because of the expected long-term environmental effects. The ETS, of course, restricts the effect of lowering CO_2 emissions, which have a clearly long-term effect on the environment, unless the resulting allowances of CO_2 emissions are not traded back in the system: a capability approach would not change the fact that the case of the producers would be much stronger if this were the case.[63]

Third, in the animal welfare cases, the capability approach might introduce the notion of animal capabilities. Then the capabilities to flourish of the animals involved will have to be balanced against the capabilities of humans, in their roles as producers, consumers and third parties affected through health impacts. There is great debate regarding the extent to which a capability approach should take animal capabilities into account. Nussbaum has argued that we should, [64] but others have criticized her.[65] Some have argued that we should look at ecosystem capabilities instead.[66] We cannot conclude this argument here, but argue that the framework of the capability approach is at least open to the possibility for including animal capabilities.

Fourth, in the binge-drinking case there are some citizen capabilities at issue: capabilities of those living in the areas of consumption who are negatively affected by binge-drinking scenes. These might have to be specified as 'capabilities to live in a peaceful neighborhood'. This is a rather individualist interpretation of the problem, which focuses on citizens being able to live their own lives without being disturbed by noise in the middle of the night, or by excessive pollution in the street. But the case may also be given a more collectivist twist by framing citizens' worries about binge drinking as a concern over social cohesion, or as paternalist concerns with respect to the value of the leisure activities of youngsters. Again, we will not take a stance on these issues here, but argue that the capability approach gives reason to coherently discuss these elements in a competition law case.

Comparison to an Inclusive Welfare Approach

The discussion thus far has aimed at showing how a capability approach is superior to a (narrow or broad) consumer welfare approach in dealing with non-economic interests. This leaves us with another alternative to consumer welfare approaches, however: the inclusive welfare approach

With respect to all of the types of cases discussed in this paper, an inclusive welfare approach could also take these non-economic interests into account: it generally uses a willingness-to-pay method. For example, current consumers may be asked how much they are willing to pay (for their electricity today) for a better environment for future generations. Thus, in the Energy Agreement case, consumers would be asked whether they would be willing to pay the higher costs of energy – amounting to 3-4 euros per year per household over 5 years – for a (switch to a) sustainable energy production (knowing that these costs are higher than the avoided costs of healthcare).[67] A willingness-to-pay survey could also ask consumers how much they are willing to pay for using less antibiotics on pig farms and greater animal welfare through providing more living space. It is even possible to use such a method for 'non-use' (for example keeping the rain forest healthy, knowing one will never travel there), in the case of protecting the black-tailed godwit. If such an inclusive welfare approach can take these interests into account in a satisfactory manner, then it might be judged a better alternative to consumer welfare approaches than the capability approach.

We do not want to overemphasize our disagreement with the inclusive welfare approach as it does also take non-economic interests into account. Nonetheless, there remain important differences with the capability approach to competition law. A general point is the one which has been important in developing the capability approach as an alternative to preference-based utilitarianism: that preferences may be distorted by problematic processes of adaptation and socialization. As a consequence, the answers in willingness-to-pay surveys have a problematic normative status. If in these surveys no one attaches value to future generations, animals or the health of parts of the population, then these interests do not count. Thus, the protection of these groups is dependent on the contingent value attached to them in these surveys. This does not do justice to the interests involved. These are two other important theoretical differences: the inclusive welfare approach will not take into account the (non-welfarist) value of market-constituting capabilities (liberties) and the threshold structure of consumptive capabilities, at least as long as individuals do not include them in their preferences.

To all of this an advocate of the inclusive welfare approach might retort that there is no other basis for making social choices. This is what an advocate of the capability approach would deny.[68] Social choices are legitimately made, in the end, in a democratic process. In that process, of course, citizen preferences play a crucial role. But the context of a democratic process is different from the context of a willingness-to-pay survey. The most important difference is that the democratic process is a means to form preferences on the basis of reasons, not to aggregate pre-existing preferences. All the substantive conclusions that we have argued for here, then, should be seen as reasons that may or may not convince citizens in a democratic process. Willingness-to-pay surveys do not allow such a process of reasoning to take place, and thus do not allow the subjects that are asked to report their preferences to change them on the basis of new information.[69] To the extent that an inclusive welfare approach is used by competition authorities to shortcut such a process, this is deeply problematic from a democratic point of view.

CONCLUSION

In this article we have argued that there are good reasons to include non-economic interests in a competition law assessment, and we have shown the shortcomings of the dominant consumer welfare approach in this respect. We have proposed the capability approach as an alternative and have explored what an application of this approach to competition cases might entail. In all of the cases discussed above, when applying a capability approach a balancing act is still necessary to come to a conclusion on whether or not to allow the agreement at issue under a competition law assessment. Our aim has been to show how the capability approach leads to a different result, by introducing three types of relevant capabilities. This shows that the capability approach (i) values market freedom, i.e. the capabilities to own property and to contract directly; (ii) recognizes consumers' capabilities but limits their value when consumer budgets are above specified thresholds; (iii) can incorporate a wide range of third-party capabilities. As a result, where consumer capabilities are already securely above a certain threshold, they may be outweighed by the value of the capabilities of future generations, the capability to health of current generations, or even by animal capabilities. Whether this is the case, is for producers to argue in the public sphere when they defend their agreements; for competition authorities to assess; and for parliaments to legislate upon when they are unsatisfied with the conclusions reached by competition authorities.

NOTES

1. As is well known, the main provisions of European competition law are Art. 101 TFEU (prohibition on anti-competitive agreements (cartels)), and Art. 102 TFEU (prohibition on abuse of a dominant position). Mergers are subject to an ex ante regime of control as laid down in the merger regulation. Although we focus on agreements that fall within the scope of Art. 101 TFEU the general line of reasoning may equally apply to Art. 102 TFEU or to the scrutiny of mergers.
2. Other standards, e.g. concerned with market structure or processes may also play a role (see e.g. Case C-8/08, 4 June 2009, T-Mobile Netherlands and Others, [2009] ECR I-4529) and the Court of Justice has not embraced consumer welfare as a single standard for European competition law. The enforcement focus of the European Commission in Art. 101 TFEU cases however, is on consumer welfare. This is not to deny that the Commission has, especially in the past, also deviated from a narrow consumer welfare approach, especially in the seminal case on greening washing machines (CECED, Commission Decision of 24 January 1999, OJ L 187, 26.7.2000, p. 47). This case, however, predates the more economic approach and its focus on consumer welfare
3. K.J. Cseres, 'The Controversies of the Consumer Welfare Standard', (2007) 3 The Competition Law Review, no. 2, pp. 121-173
4. Following from European Commission, Guidelines on the application of Article 81(3) of the Treaty, OJ C 101, 27.4.2004, p. 97; European Commission, Guidelines on Vertical Restraints, OJ C 130, 19.5.2010, p. 1; see also B. Baarsma, 'Rewriting European Competition Law from an Economic Perspective', (2011) 7 European Competition Journal, no. 3, pp. 559-585. This is not to deny that the Commission has, especially in the past, also deviated from a narrow consumer welfare approach, especially in the seminal case on greening washing machines (CECED, Commission Decision of 24 January 1999, OJ L 187, 26.7.2000, p. 47).
5. A legal barrier to apply this 'weighing' to some agreements, however, lies in the text of Art. 101(1) TFEU: for 'object restrictions', connoting classic cartel arrangements such as price fixing or restrictions of production, negative effects

are assumed and weighing of possible benefits is generally impossible.

6. T. Prosser, The Limits of Competition Law. Markets and Public Services (2005); D. Zimmer (ed.), The Goals of Competition Law (2012); O. Budzinski, 'Monoculture versus Diversity in Competition Economics', (2008) 32 Cambridge Journal of Economics, no. 2, pp. 295324; C. Townley, 'Is Anything More Important than Consumer Welfare (in Article 81 ERC)? Reflections of a Community Lawyer', (2008) 10 Cambridge Yearbook of European Legal Studies, pp. 345-381; C. Townley, Article 81 EC and Competition Law (2009); A. Gerbrandy, 'Competition Law for a Sustainable Society: Government Action or Private Initiatives in Reaction to Science's Call for Sustainability', in A. Colombi Ciachhi et al. (eds.), Law and Governance. Beyond the Public-Private Law Divide? (2013).

7. Due to the wording of Art. 101(3) TFEU, where a 'benefit to consumers' is explicitly mentioned as a necessary condition for balancing, a total welfare standard is not imaginable in European competition law.

8. C. Rose, 'Environmental Faust Succumbs to Temptations of Economic Mephistopheles, Or, Value by Any Other Name Is Preference', (1989) 87 Michigan Law Review, pp. 1631-1711.

9. 9 M. Adler, 'Welfare Polls: A Synthesis', (2006) 86 New York University Law Review, no. 6, pp. 1875-1970.

10. D. Lewinsohn-Zamir, 'Consumer Preferences, Citizen Preferences, and the Provision of Public Goods', (1998) 108 The Yale Law Journal, pp. 377-406.

11. <https://www.acm.nl/nl/publicaties/publicatie/12033/Notitie-ACM-over-Sluiting-5-Kolencentrales-in-SER-Energieakkoord>, available in English at <http://www.energieakkoordser.nl/doen/engels.aspx> (last visited 2 November 2015).

12. The Verbond van Den Bosch is part of an ongoing process of restructuring the farming industry in the Province of Noord-Brabant and was signed 1 September 2011 (see: https://www.brabant.nl/dossiers/dossiers-op-thema/platteland/agrofood-in-brabant/zorgvuldigeveehouderij/transitie-veehouderij.aspx?document=ondertekenaars-verbond-van-den-bosch (last visited 14 December 2015).

13. See: 'Boerengilde kansrijker dan biologisch', Leeuwarder Courant, 15 February 2014.

14. See Townley 2008, supra note 6, p. 348.

15. See: <http://www.theguardian.com/society/2012/mar/23/coalition-minimum-alcohol-price-40p> (last visited 21 October 2015) and <www.parliament.uk/briefing-papers/sn05021.pdf> (last visited 21 October 2015).

16. A. Sen, Commodities and Capabilities (1985); A. Sen, The Standard of Living (1987).

17. M. Nussbaum, 'Nature, Function, and Capability: Aristotle on Political Distribution', (1988) 1 Oxford Studies in Ancient Philosophy, pp. 145–184; M. Nussbaum, 'Aristotelian Social Democracy', in R. Bruce Douglas et al. (eds.),

Liberalism and the Good (1990), pp. 203–252. The approach has also been used in development studies and quality of life studies (see: I. Robeyns, 'The Capability Approach: A Theoretical Survey', (2005) 6 Journal of Human Development, no. 1, pp. 93-117; I. Robeyns, 'The Capability Approach in Practice', (2006) 14 Journal of Political Philosophy, no. 3, pp. 351-376. The United Nations Development Programme (UNDP) has also used the capability approach to rank countries in a Human Development Index, which is an alternative to standard GDP rankings.

18. H. Brighouse & I. Robeyns (eds.), Measuring Justice: Primary Goods and Capabilities (2010).

19. M. Nussbaum, 'Capabilities and Human Rights', (1997) 66 Fordham Law Review, pp. 273-300; A. Sen, 'Elements of a Theory of Human Rights', (2004) 32 Philosophy & Public Affairs, no. 4, pp. 315-356.

20. M. Nussbaum, Women and Human Development. The Capabilities Approach (2000).

21. A. Sen, The Idea of Justice (2009).

22. There have not been many applications of the capability approach to law. Exceptions include work on property law (see: G. Alexander, 'The Social-Obligation Norm in American Property Law', (2009) 94 Cornell Law Review, no. 4, pp. 745-819; G. Alexander, 'The Complex Core of Property', (2009) 94 Cornell Law Review, no. 4, pp. 1063-1071; G. Alexander & E. Penalver, An Introduction to Property Theory (2012)), on contract law (see: S. Deakin, 'Capacitas: Contract Law and the Institutional Preconditions of a Market Economy', (2006) 2 European Review of Contract Law, no. 3, pp. 317-341; M. Hesselink, 'Capacity and Capability in European Contract Law', (2005) 13 European Review of Contract Law, no. 4, pp. 497-507) and social rights (see: S. Deakin & J. Browne, 'Social Rights and Market Order: Adapting the Capability Approach', in T. Hervey & J. Kenner (eds.), Economic and Social Rights under the EU Charter of Fundamental Rights – A Legal Perspective (2003), pp. 27-43).

23. Deakin & Browne, supra note 22.

24. R.J.G. Claassen, 'The Capability to Hold Property', (2015) 16 Journal of Human Development and Capabilities, no. 2, pp. 220-236.

25. Nussbaum does not mention this capability explicitly, but she does include a capability of 'being able to hold property' on her list of basic capabilities (Nussbaum 2000, supra note 20, p. 80).

26. R.J.G. Claassen, 'Institutional Pluralism and the Limits of the Market', (2009) 8 Politics, Philosophy, and Economics, no. 4, pp. 420-447.

27. Note that the efficiency arguments in favour of markets which are familiar in a standard economic framework are translated into the capability framework here. See also Claassen 2015, supra note 24.

28. S. Caney, 'Climate Change, Human Rights and Moral Thresholds', in S. Humphreys, Human Rights and Climate Change (2009), pp. 69–90. Sen has argued that we do indeed need to take into account future generations. See S. Anand & A. Sen, 'Human Development and Economic Sustainability', (2000) 28

World Development, no. 12, pp. 2029-2049.

29. Nussbaum has argued that animals have rights to capabilities to a minimally flourishing life as well. M. Nussbaum, Frontiers of Justice (2006).

30. This may be the case for citizens in rich and sufficiently egalitarian countries. Any criticism that a price increase makes some groups unable to satisfy their basic capabilities can also be resolved by general redistribution – it does not necessitate prohibiting the price increase.

31. P. Anand & M. van Hees, 'Capabilities and Achievements: An Empirical Study', (2006) 35 Journal of Socio-Economics, pp. 268-284; P. Anand et al., 'The Development of Capability Indicators', (2009) 10 Journal of Human Development and Capabilities, no. 1, pp. 125-152.

32. Nussbaum 2006, supra note 29, p. 85.

33. R. Alexy, 'On Balancing and Subsumption. A Structural Comparison', (2003) 16 Ratio Juris, no. 4, pp. 433-449.

34. See for an overview of reasons for companies to engage in social responsibility practices: J. Graafland et al., 'Motives of Socially Responsible Business Conduct' (July 1, 2010). CentER Discussion Paper Series No. 2010-74. Available at SSRN: <http://ssrn.com/abstract=1649987> or <http://dx.doi.org/10.2139/ssrn.1649987> (last visited 9 December 2015).

35. We provide a paper-length treatment of the moral and political arguments in R. Claassen & A. Gerbrandy, 'Doing Good Together. The Ethics and Politics in Competition Law' (manuscript under review, 2016)

36. M. Motta, Competition Policy: Theory and Practice (2004); O. Odudu, The Boundaries of EC Competition Law: The Scope of Article 101 (2006).

37. European Commission, Guidelines on the application of Article 81(3) of the Treaty, OJ C 101, 27.4.2004, p. 97; European Commission, Guidelines on Vertical Restraints, OJ C 130, 19.5.1010, p. 1.

38. For a discussion also: Townley 2008, supra note 6; I. Lianos, 'Some Reflections on the Question of the Goals of EU Competition Law', CLES Working Paper Series 3/2013, p. 15.

39. Art. 3 of the Treaty on European Union includes references to 'sustainable development', 'balanced economic growth' and a 'social market economy'.

40. Integration clauses are included in the Treaty and link general policy aims, such as the protection of culture or the environment, with all other policy domains, including competition policy. See specifically in relation to competition law and environmental protection: S. Kingston 'Integration Environmental Protection and EU Competition Law: Why Competition Isn't Special', (2010) 16 European Law Journal, no. 6, pp. 780-805.

41. Lianos supra note 38; Townley 2008, supra note 6.

42. We believe this position also fits the stance of the capability approach, although it is not dictated by it. Nussbaum has argued that the capability approach represents a distinct method of judicial interpretation, which pays attention to the social

and historical context of cases, and is in contrast to more formalist methods of interpretation (see M. Nussbaum, 'Constitutions and Capabilities: 'Perception' against Lofty Formalism', (2007) 121 Harvard Law Review, no. 4, pp. 4-97.

43. Baarsma for example, states that 'Competition law is only intended to solve problems concerning market power (…). The government must resolve different market failures using different policies', Baarsma, supra note 4, p. 585.

44. This is not to deny the possibility of companies 'greenwashing' an anticompetitive agreement. The argument here relates to the point that companies have a moral responsibility to take into account the effects of their actions with a wider scope than mere shareholder value, giving rise to the notion of a stakeholder model of corporate responsibility. The fact that companies may decide not to fulfil their moral responsibilities does not deny the existence of these responsibilities.

45. E. Garriga & D. Mele, 'Corporate Social Responsibility Theories: Mapping the Territory', (2004) 52 Journal of Business Ethics, pp. 51-71.

46. A. Bertland, 'Virtue Ethics in Business and the Capability Approach', (2009) 84 Journal of Business Ethics, pp. 25-32; B. Giavanola, 'Re-Thinking the Anthropological and Ethical Foundation of Economic and Business: Human Richness and Capability Enhancement', (2009) 88 Journal of Business Ethics, pp. 431-444.

47. Although the binge-drinking case shows that it is possible, the other cases are illustrations of the government being involved in (brokering) the agreements instead of choosing a legislative route.

48. 48 Giving rise to transnational private regulation, see on this e.g. C. Scott et al., 'The Conceptual and Constitutional Challenge of Transnational Private Regulation', (2011) 38 Journal of Law and Society, pp. 1-19.

49. At least not without a clear legal mandate, see e.g. T. van Dijk & P de Bijl, 'Mededingingsbeleid en Publieke Belangen: Een Economisch Perspectief', (2012) Markt & Mededinging, no. 4, pp. 149-156.

50. We have excluded here the role of judges in private competition law disputes and focus on the executive (including the judicial review of agency decisions).

51. A. Gutman & D. Thompson, Democracy and Disagreement (1996); J. Habermas, Between Facts and Norms. Contributions to a Discourse Theory of Law and Democracy (1996).

52. S. Chambers, 'Deliberative Democratic Theory', (2003) 6 Annual Review of Political Science, pp. 307-326.

53. As brought forward by A. Gerbrandy, 'Addressing the Legitimacy Problem for Competition Authorities Taking into Account Non-Economic Values: The Position of the Dutch Competition Authority', (2015) 40 European Law Review, no. 5, pp. 769-781.

54. On the impact of this difference also Lewinsohn-Zamir, supra note 10.

55. Although the parties to the Agreement argue that an increase in sustainable energy production and supply – also resulting from the. Agreement (but not a

direct result of the closing of the coal-fired power plants) – will balance this effect on supply. This was not taken into account by the competition authority in its preliminary opinion.

56. Lowering CO_2 emissions would normally result in lower healthcare costs (locally), and abate the greenhouse effect (globally and in the longer term). But because CO_2 emissions are regulated by the ETS, the ACM argued that any reduction of CO_2 emissions from the closed plants would not necessarily lead to reduction of total CO_2 emissions: the ETS is a system of trade in CO_2 emissions, which caps total EU emissions. Plants emitting CO_2 have an 'allowance' to do so, which, if not used (or not up to its maximum), can be traded. From the (publicly available) text of the Agreement it is unclear whether the parties intended, or are able to take their resulting allowance off the market completely or to trade this under the ETS. Thus, there may be no effect at all. Of course, if the parties to the Agreement were to state that the CO_2 emissions were to be removed from the ETS altogether, as has been suggested as a possibility, the resulting avoided healthcare costs would also have to be taken into account.

57. See e.g. Cseres, supra note 3, p. 167

58. The capability for property also concerns the allowances of emissions, but this seems to us a derived capability that is limited by competition law: it is not competition law itself that prohibits individual companies to remove their allowances from the ETS. Jointly deciding not to trade the resulting allowances back into the ETS would make a stronger case for the Energy Agreement from all perspectives, however.

59. On the issue of this collective action problem as a basis for cooperation in responsible business conduct see D. Vogel, 'The Private Regulation of Global Corporate Conduct', (2010) 49 Business & Society, no. 1, pp. 68-87.

60. A. Sen, 'The Moral Standing of the Market', (1985) 2 Social Philosophy and Policy, no. 2, pp. 1-19.

61. Indirectly, also the use of energy by other producers of goods and services, which consumers need for their capabilities are affected: clothing, street lighting, schooling, transport (trains, trams, and electric cars), etc.

62. R. Claassen, 'Ecological rights of Future Generations: A Capability Approach', in G. Bos & M. Düwell (eds.), Human Rights and Sustainability (London: Routledge, forthcoming 2016).

63. A signalling statement might have such an effect however (see note 58, supra).

64. Nussbaum 2006, supra note 29.

65. R. Ilea, 'Nussbaum's Capabilities Approach and Nonhuman Animals: Theory and Public Policy', (2008) 39 Journal of Social Philosophy, no. 4, pp. 547-563; E. Cripps, 'Saving the Polar Bear, Saving the World: Can the Capabilities Approach Do Justice to Humans, Animals and Ecosystems?' (2010) 16 Res Publica, pp. 1-22.

66. D. Schlosberg, Defining Environmental Justice: Theories, Movements, and Nature (2007). However, there might be important tension here: the survival

of ecosystems depends on predator relations which violate individual animals' capabilities for life.

67. It might also make a difference to the consumers whether or not the allowance resulting from the CO_2 emission reduction would be removed from ETS completely. Even if this were not the case, the consumers might still be willing to pay the higher price, either as a political signal against the ETS and as a minor price to pay for uncertain, but possible, longer-term environmental benefits.

68. R. Claassen, 'Making Capability Lists: Philosophy versus Democracy', (2011) 59 Political Studies, no. 3, pp. 491-508.

69. H.S. Richardson, 'The Stupidity of the Cost-Benefit Standard', (2000) 29 Journal of Legal Studies, no. 2, pp. 971-1003.

10
CHAPTER

COMPLIANCE PROGRAMMES IN COMPETITION LAW: IMPROVING THE APPROACH OF COMPETITION AUTHORITIES

Eva Lachnit

Keywords: Competition law, enforcement, compliance programmes, public/private domain

INTRODUCTION

'There are few branches of trade in this or any country which are not represented by associations which seek to prevent unprofitable competition.'[1]

This might look like a grim way of introducing an article about the role of compliance programmes in competition law, and to be fair, it is. However, this quote – dating from 1887 – was as true then as it is today. Competition authorities discover multiple cartels on a yearly basis, throughout various markets or 'branches of trade'. And even though we educate our future lawyers on the basics of competition law, many businessmen/women seem to be unaware of the prohibitions it contains, and might feel that preventing unprofitable competition is merely part of the game.[2]

How competition authorities should change such an attitude towards competition law is strongly debated in literature, and the suggested approaches vary as much as the fields of academia that have contributed to this discussion.[3] In this article, the focus will be on one suggestion in particular: the use of compliance programmes, which is

Citation: Lachnit, E., (2014). Compliance Programmes in Competition Law: Improving the Approach of Competition Authorities. Utrecht Law Review. 10(5), pp.31–50. DOI: http://doi.org/10.18352/ulr.299.

presented as an addition to (and not a replacement for) another important approach to enforcement: deterrence. This article explores the way in which competition authorities deal with compliance programmes, specifically in the light of the question whether this approach would, at least in theory, be capable of changing companies' attitudes towards competition law. The aim of the article is to explore whether competition authorities could do more to unlock the potential of compliance programmes.

Compliance programmes: FAQ

However, in presenting the aim of this paper this prematurely distracts from the questions at hand: what are compliance programmes, and how could they serve as an enforcement tool in competition law? Even though this article focuses on the domain of competition law, compliance programmes are in no way specific to this field. In fact, businesses usually have to comply with a wide range of rules and prohibitions, for which the use of compliance programmes is not unusual (think, for instance, of environmental law, safety regulations or food and health regulations). In its most basic form, a compliance programme is a way for a company to publically announce that it intends to follow all of these rules, and they have to be taken into account in day-to-day business. Often, but not always, compliance programmes are coupled with the company's corporate governance code or another code of conduct. Compliance programmes are examples of 'voluntary governance', whereby companies or organizations express their commitment to certain rules and to the values or objectives on which they are based. Such programmes generally also include a set of actions intended to assist companies in building a genuine culture of compliance with those rules, but also in detecting likely acts of misconduct, in remedying them and in preventing any repetition.[4]

Because compliance programmes are often publicly available, they serve an important external signalling function by stating that a company is aware of the law, and intends to comply with it. However, compliance programmes also create an educational responsibility in the internal structure of the company. By having a compliance programme in place, companies basically state that their employees are aware of the applicable rules and regulations, and that they take care to abide by them. This creates an obligation for companies, at least in theory, to educate all personnel about the laws to which they have committed themselves. For that reason, compliance programmes often contain an approach to the training and education of current employees, and they are usually provided to new employees at the outset.

Presumably, most corporate compliance programmes contain a reference to competition law, and to its two basic rules in particular: not to engage in anti-competitive agreements and not to resort to abusive conduct when a firm is dominant in the market.[5] These are rather broad prohibitions, and go hand-in-hand with an impressive body of case law, making it complicated to determine when an agreement could be regarded as anti-competitive, or when market behaviour could qualify as abusive. Committing oneself to complying with these rules is one thing, transferring their full meaning is another. Competition law compliance programmes therefore need some special attention, and it is easy to see that competition authorities could play a role within these programmes. From the foregoing it follows that this role should, at least partly, consist of explaining competition rules to businesses. However, as this is part of a competition authority's more general task of giving guidance on competition rules, this role is mostly disregarded in this article.[6] The other possible roles – promoting the adoption of compliance programmes and monitoring their application – are featured in this article, as they ensure that competition rules receive the special attention that they need.

Outline and delineation

This article aims to explore whether competition authorities could do more to unlock the potential of competition law compliance programmes with a view to increasing the company's commitment to the rules. However, the point can be raised whether competition authorities should even focus on increasing commitment, and why a focus on deterrence as an enforcement strategy is not sufficient. These preliminary points are discussed, though briefly, in Section 2. In this section, the potential role of compliance programmes is explained as well. Section 3 discusses the current approach to compliance programmes in practice by looking at the approach of competition authorities (the procedure) and the elements prescribed in a programme (the substance). These issues are relevant in Section 4 as well, in which some of the leading opinions in literature are depicted on these points. The most striking features of this discussion are bundled in Section 5, which explores whether the current approach of competition authorities, as seen in the light of the advantages that compliance programmes may have to serve enforcement purposes, could be improved or altered in any way.

The national practice as discussed in this article focuses on the approaches of the Dutch Authority for Consumers and Markets (*Autoriteit Consument en Markt*) and the French *Autorité de la Concurrence*. The differences between these authorities in their procedural approach is striking, though their views on what constitutes a good compliance programme are rather similar. The research is limited to their approach in the last decade (2004-2014), also with a view to the entry into force of Regulation 1/2003.[7] Lastly, it must be mentioned that this article is based on the research for the author's forthcoming thesis, in which the use of compliance programmes in competition law will play a role as well.[8]

DETERRENCE, COMMITMENT AND COMPLIANCE

Competition authorities enforce the law in order to secure compliance with competition rules, or in a broader context, in order to secure the goals which competition law pursues. People, and therefore also companies, can be led by various motivations to comply with the law. Generally, compliance can flow from a fear of detection and subsequent punishment or from a sense of normative obligation. These two kinds of motivations have been labelled the negative or affirmative basis for compliance.[9] In order to realize compliance, enforcement agencies must appeal to these bases by increasing the fear of detection and punishment, by focusing on stirring a sense of obligation, or by a combination of the two.

Enforcement & deterrence

The enforcement of competition law takes place through a structure of detection, investigation and sanctioning. In more detail, a competition authority detects a potential infringement – generally as a result of complaints or leniency, or by means of other indicators that a market is not working well – and investigates its scope. If an infringement is indeed established, a fine can be imposed. These fines can run up to fairly large amounts. Illustrative in this respect is the European Commission's Cathode Ray Tubes cartel, in which the cartelists incurred a fine of no less than €1.47 billion combined, or the Yen Derivatives cartel in which an aggregate fine of €1.71 billion was imposed.[10]

The concept of imposing high fines for competition law wrongdoings is based on the theory of deterrence. This entails that companies are dissuaded from committing and infringement based on the credible threat of detection and incurring a sanction. The underlying rationale of deterrence is that the decision to violate the law is based on a cost-benefit analysis.[11] Assuming that companies are rational actors,[12] their decision to comply with the law will depend on whether the benefits of compliance exceed the costs of non-compliance. To put it the other way around, a violation will occur if the benefits of violating the law exceed the costs. The factors determining these costs and benefits are the probability of detection and the severity of the sanction. Generally speaking, in order to increase the deterrent effect of enforcement, either the detection rate must improve, or the fines should increase.

In past years, competition authorities have attempted to increase the deterrent effect of their actions by increasing the maximum amount of the fine.[13] Apart from that, criminal and civil liability increase the perceived cost of infringement, as it leads to the conviction – and possibly incarceration – of cartelists and civil follow-on or stand-alone claims respectively. On the other part of the equation, the detection rate has surged since the introduction of national and European leniency programmes, which are intended to destabilize cartels through self-reporting. Other possibilities to increase the amount of cartels detected, such as *qui tam* provisions, informant rewards and structural market screens, have been debated in the literature, but have yet to be implemented in many jurisdictions.[14]

Enforcement & commitment

Despite the focus on increasing deterrence, competition law infringements still take place: durable cartels are found and fined every year, as well as long-standing abusive behaviour. Moreover, in many industries certain behaviour amounting to a competition law infringement is not perceived as 'breaking the law', but as business culture.[15] Another problem might be that studies have shown that those who have been caught and sanctioned seem to be more likely to violate the law again.[16] Somehow, despite its undeniable possible effects on companies and individuals who do make a deliberate cost-benefit analysis, increasing the deterrent effect of enforcement alone is not enough to induce compliance.[17] Instead of increasing deterrence by sanctioning illicit behaviour after it has taken place, competition authorities might attempt to increase the understanding of and the commitment to the rules beforehand. This approach, which is sometimes referred to as the increase of normative commitment,[18] is based on the assumption that compliance may stem at least as much from a personal commitment to law-abiding behaviour as from a fear of punishment.[19] However, it is difficult to imagine how competition authorities could increase normative commitment or change companies' objectives on their own. 'Imposed commitment' is almost a *contradictio in terminis*, and immediately indicates the necessity of involving companies in the process. In other words, if competition authorities do wish to appeal to the normative commitment of companies, these companies will have to participate in this actively. Therefore, appealing to a positive basis for compliance requires crossing the public-private domain and involving businesses in promoting compliance with competition rules.

The potential of compliance programmes

One of the ways in which companies can contribute to the level of compliance in their organizations is by designing and implementing compliance programmes. This is not a new or ground-breaking realization, certainly not in the field of competition law.[20] Competition authorities are aware of the possibilities of compliance programmes, and the authorities' most desirable role therein has been debated extensively in the literature. And for good reason, because compliance programmes are potentially a way in which market parties and competition authorities could work together in order to secure compliance across the board.[21]

For businesses, the benefits of compliance lie in the mitigation of the risks and costs of non-compliance. If a compliance programme functions well, infringements can be detected and halted at an early stage, thus preventing further damage to the company and to the market. From a more positive viewpoint, compliance programmes aid companies in being seen as 'ethical businesses', which can increase positive branding.[22] For competition authorities, compliance programmews can be seen as a method of disseminating a compliance culture, to keep tabs on the market, and to somewhat share the burden of detecting infringements.[23]

NATIONAL ENFORCEMENT PERSPECTIVE ON COMPLIANCE

Whether the way in which compliance programmes are treated in practice is capable of increasing a normative commitment to competition rules within companies is a difficult – if not impossible – question to answer. Therefore, the following sections focus on a number of circumstances that are believed to either facilitate or stand in the way of a successful compliance programme. Again, whether the approaches taken by the different authorities actually lead to more commitment to the rules is difficult to measure. However, it must be possible to determine obstacles in the authorities' current approaches, as well as suggestions that might promote the commitment to competition rules.[24]

General approach to compliance programmes

Considering that the use of compliance programmes has been heavily debated over the years, the Dutch Authority for Consumers and Markets (ACM) and the French *Autorité de la Concurrence* (*Autorité*) have not avoided the opportunity to make known their views on compliance programmes. However, the level of guidance given on compliance programmes differs between both authorities, as does the subsequent appraisal. In this last respect, attention is paid to the question of rewarding compliance efforts by granting fine reductions in formal procedures. The relation between compliance and other instruments – besides fines – is discussed briefly as well.

The Netherlands

The ACM has no legal obligation to engage in or actively promote businesses' compliance programmes. There is no model of what compliance programmes should look like, and no regulation on what the ACM is supposed to do with them. Still, the ACM views it as part of its task to promote the use of compliance programmes in general, and sometimes even in specific cases.[25] It derives this competence from its vision on enforcement ('using all instruments and approaches necessary to solve a problem') and its mission statement ('creating opportunities and choices for businesses and consumers').[26] In general, ACM views compliance programmes as potentially beneficial, even though it views its role in these programmes quite narrowly.

This is illustrated by the fact that the ACM does not often mention whether compliance has played a role in its decisions, and that it used to be quite hesitant about giving guidance on the contents of what it believes to be a good compliance programme. Naturally, a competition authority should be aware of not handing out 'stamps of approval' in advance, possibly exonerating companies which have 'trusted the authority's guidance on the matter'. Therefore the ACM's predecessor, the Netherlands Competition Authority (*Nederlandse Mededingingsautoriteit, NMa*), did underline the importance of compliance in some of its publications and annual reports, but not extensively. However, ever since the ACM started focusing on its full array of instruments under its new strategy, the Dutch authority seems to have become somewhat more forward on the subject. In an interesting speech, the Dutch chairman Chris Fonteijn has shed more light upon the matter, referring to international toolkits to illustrate the idea of a *bona fide* compliance programme.[27] This is further discussed below.

When compliance does seem to play a part in the ACM's decisions, it is mentioned most often in commitment decisions. In these decisions (in which no infringement is found, but companies offer commitments to remedy harmful behaviour[28]) compliance programmes could be offered as commitments, possibly increasing the future preventive effect of the decision. In the Netherlands, where ten commitment decisions have been taken since the introduction of the instrument in 2008, only three decisions contain specific compliance requirements.[29] In the other commitment decisions, mostly behavioural remedies were offered. In the cases containing a compliance programme the minimum requirements were already mentioned in the decisions. Also, in these cases the existing compliance programmes are still in place.[30] None of the companies involved in the other seven cases have given public attention to the question whether they have established a compliance programme.

Compliance programmes are not just of importance in the course of a commitment procedure; their existence can be a factor in determining a fine in a regular procedure as well. A widespread discussion in this respect concerns the question whether they should constitute a mitigating or an aggravating factor in the imposition of a sanction.[31] The ACM is neutral in this decision: a company should neither be rewarded nor punished for having a compliance programme in place. To support this view, the ACM holds that there are other mechanisms in the fining procedure which are more suitable for dealing with the benefits of a well-functioning compliance programme. For the early reporters (those who find an infringement and report it to the ACM voluntarily) there is leniency. For others, who have detected an infringement and have ended it quickly, there are benefits to be reaped from reporting a short-lived infringement instead of a long-lasting one. Nevertheless, the ACM's Fining Guidelines do not completely exclude a compliance programme from the realm of fine mitigation or aggravation. When a company uses a compliance programme for window-dressing purposes only, an increased fine is possible – at least in theory.[32] However, when a compliance programme is a basis for proactive participation with the procedure, fine mitigation must be possible as well.[33]

France

Also in France, there is no explicit legal basis for the promotion or evaluation of compliance programmes or for making them binding, but this is seen as a competence that the *Autorité* derives from its mission statement.[34] Especially because of the policy goals of preventing and educating, the *Autorité* feels that it has an implicit competence to promote compliance and to disseminate a compliance culture. The introduction of compliance programmes is seen as a particularly suitable way of doing so.

In 2012, the *Autorité* published a framework document on compliance programmes in order to help companies to set up a credible and verifiable compliance programme, which the *Autorité* can take into account when handling infringements. The framework document offers an overview of the *Autorité's* decisional practice and provides specific guidance for companies. In principle, this document is binding upon the *Autorité*, but it can deviate from it when this is justified. [35] The content of this framework document is outlined more extensively below, when the indicators of a successful compliance programme are discussed. It is however striking, especially in the light of the initial reluctance of the Dutch ACM to do so, that the *Autorité* has chosen to give extensive guidance on the content of compliance programmes. This might be because compliance programmes play an important role in a formal procedure: if companies can receive a reduced fine for a thorough compliance programme, good governance might require the authority to make known its views on what constitutes such a programme. To explain the role of fine reductions in formal procedures, the *Autorité* started accepting compliance programmes as commitments in the course of a settlement procedure. The French settlement procedure (or non-contestation procedure) differs from the European

Commission's settlement procedure in various ways, but the most striking difference in this respect is that the *Autorité* can make binding commitments offered by the companies in the course of a settlement, in return for a fine discount that might be up to 10%.[36] However, it has to be remarked that the *Autorité* has become somewhat more sceptical in reviewing compliance programmes that concentrate on educational aspects only. Already in 2005, it stated that such a compliance programme was not very substantial, but this was not reflected in the fine discount.[37] In 2007 the *Autorité* was more straightforward and held that 'such commitments, even if they are not devoid of importance, are nevertheless not likely to make improvements, substantial and verifiable, to the operation of competitive markets affected by the practices.'[38] Similar arguments have been repeated in other cases as well, resulting the *Autorité* disregarding the compliance programme and applying a 10% discount for just the non-contestation.[39] It appears from decisional practice that all published compliance programmes have been introduced in the course of such a settlement, for which reason it could be said that the development of the approach to compliance programmes in France has occurred along the lines of the development of the non-contestation procedure. However, with regard to the role of compliance programmes in regular fining procedures the *Autorité* takes a neutral stance towards the weighing of compliance programmes: it is neither seen as a mitigating nor an aggravating factor, as the existence of a compliance programme does not alter the reality of the infringement itself.[40] Having a compliance programme in place, however, does yield a special responsibility after the discovery of an infringement of competition law. The infringement must be immediately brought to an end, and in the case of a cartel the company must apply for leniency.[41]

Indicators of a successful compliance programme

As described above, the French *Autorité* is more forward in pronouncing elements of a (perceived) successful compliance programme. In a recent speech, however, the chairman of the Dutch ACM has referred to the International Chamber of Commerce's Compliance Toolkit and the United Kingdom's 'Wheel of Compliance' as an example of what a robust compliance programme should look like. It will become clear from the following that the ACM's and the *Autorité's* respective views on the content of compliance programmes are not far apart.

The Netherlands

The formal stance taken by the ACM is that compliance programmes have to be tailored to each company individually. First and foremost, a company wishing to ensure compliance must make sure that there is a decent risk management within its internal structure. According to the Wheel of Compliance, this comprises comprehensive risk identification, a thorough risk assessment, measures to ensure risk mitigation and a continuous review of this process.[42] Apart from that, it is mentioned that compliance programmes require the full commitment of management in order to be effective. However, it is not just management that needs to be involved, all employees who could come into contact with competition law have to participate actively in the compliance programme and they must receive permanent education. For that reason, the company must provide a clear explanation of what constitutes illegal behaviour, along with practical examples that illustrate this behaviour in the various branches of the company. The employees receiving this training must declare their compliance on a regular basis, not just when signing a declaration of integrity at the beginning of the introduction of the programme. Finally, the compliance programme must contain a protocol for the handling of infringements, and must be updated on a regular basis.

Indicators of Compliance	1. Commitment of management	
	2. Explaining the rules	
	3. Participation & education	
	4. Declaration of compliance	
	5. Risk management	Identification Assessment Mitigation Review
	6. Protocol for infringements	
	7. Updating	

Figure 1: Seven indicators of a successful compliance programme

Even though this was one of the first occasions that the ACM had made a public, general statement about what it deems important in compliance programmes, the ACM has published its views on compliance programmes in a number of specific cases. Two of the most fully-fledged compliance programmes are those of the Dutch trade association for pharmacy (KNMP) and the Memorandum of Compliance between the Dutch telecom operator KPN and the ACM's predecessor in telecom regulation, OPTA.[43] These compliance programmes contain provisions similar to the elements mentioned above, and are considered to be examples of what a compliance programme should look like. It seems that of these two examples the Memorandum of Compliance between KPN and ACM is the most detailed and far- reaching. This Memorandum contains a number of additional elements, such as the introduction of a whistleblowing system, efforts to achieve a change of culture within KPN and the obligation to perform an internal or external audit annually.[44]

France

According to the *Autorité*, compliance programmes have a double objective: to diminish the risks of infringements on the one hand, and to form mechanisms to detect infringements that could not be prevented on the other. It is only with a combination of these two objectives that compliance programmes are believed to be effective.[45] In order to attain this effectiveness, the *Autorité* is quite specific in describing the contents of a compliance programme. First of all, it must create a culture of real and determined respect for competition rules amongst all levels of the hierarchy; it must consist of measures to provide information and training and to increase awareness, combined with supervisory, control and punishment systems; and lastly, it must fit the size of the company and the nature of its activities, along with its organizational structure, mode of governance and business culture.[46]

Obviously it is quite difficult to determine, based on these broad requirements, whether a compliance programme will be effective for a specific company, in a specific situation. For that reason, the *Autorité* has developed and communicated a number of indicators (both ex ante and ex post) to review a compliance programme's effectiveness. The more detailed of the two are the ex-ante indicators, designed to represent a number of features that compliance programmes would ideally contain in order to be effective. First of all, the introduction of a compliance programme must go hand in hand with a clear, firm and public position adopted by the company's management bodies and, more broadly, by all managers and corporate officers. Secondly, a compliance officer must be appointed and, thirdly, effective information, training and awareness measures must be put in place. The compliance programme must furthermore include the design of effective control, audit and whistleblowing systems, along with an effective oversight and monitoring system, in which the treatment of information gained and the sanctions to be imposed have to be determined beforehand.[47] These features, also dubbed the 'five-step programme', are not just extensively elaborated upon in the *Autorité's* framework document on compliance, but also have an exemplary function in the OECD report on competition law compliance.[48]

Ex-post indicators are used after an infringement has taken place, despite the existence of a compliance programme. They are therefore sub-optimal as indicators of the effectiveness of compliance programmes, which have by then proven to be faulty. However, if a compliance programme, in case of an infringement, contributes to the fact that the company is able to detect this at an early stage within its own organization, and the company is able to apply the right consequences to the infringement because of it, the programme is nevertheless considered to be effective.[49]

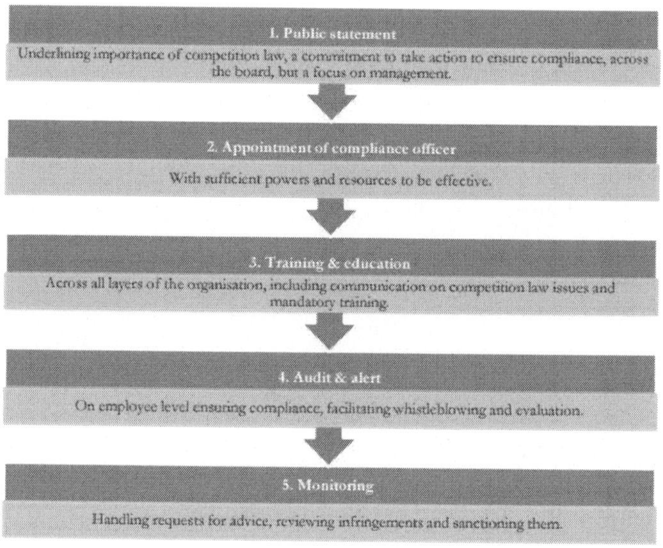

Figure 2: Five-step approach to compliance

As a final note it has to be remarked that the use of whistleblowing systems in French compliance programmes is a feature that first made its appearance in 2007, and which was considered an innovation in France.[50] It seems that compliance programmes including the implementation of a whistleblowing system can count on a 5% additional discount if offered in a settlement procedure.[51]

Public attention to compliance programmes

Because the starting points of the two authorities differ somewhat, the attention given to compliance programmes in publications varies as well. Because the Dutch ACM has not, in the past, issued formal guidance on compliance, publications about compliance programmes in which the ACM was involved have been scarce. The French *Autorité*, on the other hand, has been quite forward in publishing the compliance programmes which it has accepted as commitments. However, this is not so much based on compliance policy, but on the duty to be transparent about its reasoning in formal decisions. As discussed above, compliance programmes in France have been developed along the lines of the formal non-contestation procedure in antitrust cases.

The ACM is not as active in communicating about its role in compliance as the *Autorité* is (see below). Nevertheless, it is safe to say that compliance programmes are usually mentioned as an element in the use of other instruments, such as a fine or a commitment decision. The ACM seldom presses the use of compliance programmes in another, stand-alone context. [52] As already mentioned above, compliance has played a role in 3 out of 10 commitment decisions. Apart from that, the ACM has mentioned discussing compliance efforts with companies on 9 other occasions, usually in the course of a regular fining procedure.[53]

In France, the *Autorité* has published 37 non-contestation decisions since 2004. In 26 of these decisions the *Autorité* has accepted compliance programmes from one or more companies as a commitment. Apart from that, the *Autorité* has a separate section of its website dedicated to compliance, and offers guidance by means of a framework document, available in French and in English.[54]

COMPLIANCE PROGRAMMES IN THE LITERATURE

The analysis of national practice shows that there are different approaches to compliance, and that the approaches of the Netherlands and France differ slightly on a number of specific issues. First of all, in France compliance programmes have developed along the lines of the non-contestation procedure. For that reason, and from a transparency perspective, the French *Autorité* published guidelines on the contents and treatment of compliance programmes in 2012. The Dutch ACM has not provided such guidance until quite recently. Secondly, competition authorities could disagree on the question whether compliance programmes should be rewarded in fining procedures. The ACM and the *Autorité*, however, both take a neutral stance, stating that compliance should neither be a mitigating nor an aggravating factor in the amount of the fines imposed. Still, in the non-contestation procedure, a commitment to establish or improve a compliance programme might lead to an additional 10% fine discount in France, and the Dutch fining guidelines theoretically allow for compliance programmes to be taken into account in determining fines. Lastly, the opinion on what constitutes a 'good compliance programme' differs slightly between the two authorities. Even though the *Autorité* is more outspoken in its guidance, it seems that the ACM advocates more elements within the compliance programme, mainly in the domain of risk management.

Naturally, all of these previous topics are discussed extensively in the literature as well. In order to determine to what extent the approaches of the national competition authorities might be improved, this discussion is depicted below in a concise manner. This overview is in no way complete, but is intended to give an impression of the opinions that are out there, in order to see on which points the promotion of compliance programmes – if any are needed – could be enhanced.

Compliance programmes – do we need them?

It would be unfitting, however, to embark on a further analysis of compliance programmes without devoting attention to the more sceptical viewpoints in the literature, which state that compliance programmes in competition law might not be as useful as this article suggests. Even though one could probably think of more points of critique, this article focuses on the inherent differences between competition law infringements and other infringements and on the negative side-effects of compliance programmes.

In competition law, individuals commit infringements, but the companies pay the fines. Even though this might seem like a good reason for companies to monitor their employees' behaviour – something competition agencies benefit from as well –, there is no alignment of interests between the companies and the enforcement agencies on this point: the companies benefit from the infringements. Different from, for instance, embezzlement or corruption, the companies do not initially suffer from their employees' bad behaviour.[55] This could be a reason why company-based compliance programmes might not work as effectively as suggested.

Other reasons why compliance programmes might be ineffective is that cartelists – usually senior managers or those who enjoy more discretion and authority in the company – typically know what they are doing and go to great lengths to prevent discovery.[56] A compliance programme based on the education of employees and the self-discovery of infringements might therefore be ineffective.[57] In fact, many infringements have been committed in spite of the existence of a compliance programme.[58]

Finally, but very importantly, compliance programmes might have two unintended side-effects: the learning effect and the monitoring effect. The learning effect stems from the educational focus of compliance programmes. Employees unaware of competition problems might become aware of the opportunities that cartel behaviour has to offer. Instead of focusing on the prevention of infringements, they might be tempted to infringe the law themselves.[59] The monitoring effect is more serious – and probably more likely.[60] It entails that those responsible for monitoring compliance within the company are also particularly well placed to hide non-compliance. In other words, if one would know where to look for signs that things are going wrong, one would also know how to hide them or to erase them.[61]

These critical remarks on the effectiveness of compliance programmes cannot be swept under the carpet. However, some of the solutions advocated below might address these concerns, or at least outweigh them. Where possible, a reference will be made to these criticisms.

Substantive issues: content & culture

If compliance programmes are to address the concerns mentioned above, they must be of a substantial nature and cannot be mere checklists or a safety document meant for window-dressing. Even though the competition authorities have already provided extensive lists of what they consider to be important elements of compliance programmes, the lists in the literature are even longer. These elements are discussed below, though quite concisely. Next, three elements that are – to some extent at least – underexposed in the competition authorities' guidance are discussed: full commitment, culture and incentives, and the role of the compliance officer.

Elements of compliance programmes

Compliance programmes differ vastly from one another. Theoretically, it would be possible to call it a compliance programme if a CEO would list the competition rules on a sheet of paper, would declare the company's commitment to these rules and would present them to his employees during a one-hour PowerPoint presentation. This kind of compliance programme would, to nobody's surprise, be ineffective, and would constitute that dreaded window-dressing. However, these are not the kinds of compliance programmes advocated by many experts in the field. Compliance is not determined by declaring a commitment to a piece of paper alone, it is 'the multiple and complexly interacting factors of structure, culture and agency that determine real compliance.'[62] For that reason, a compliance programme has to be tailored to the specific company, and must include the full range of management techniques to prevent and detect misconduct.[63]

One of the most sophisticated examples of a compliance programme is found in the work of Murphy and Kolasky.[64] They advocate a list of no less than twenty elements that should be included in a compliance programme, which go beyond the more standard elements of a training manual, audits and the involvement of management.[65] Strikingly, there is a special focus on the organizational structure of a company and its capability of disseminating a real compliance culture. For instance, the role of the compliance officer is very articulated, and a system is advocated in which firms are aware of how much authority and discretion is given to people in key positions, and in what way this authority is delegated. It seems that the more complex the organization, the more prone it is to illegal behaviour, because it is easy to hide behind structures. Internal governance does matter, and this should be underlined in a compliance programme.[66] Naturally, a real compliance culture requires a commitment from employees, most particularly from those in management positions. Lastly, the list pays attention to incentives set by companies that might cause cartelistic behaviour. These elements of compliance programmes (the role of the compliance officer, commitment, culture and incentives) are discussed separately below. It is clear that compliance programmes that include the majority of these elements are far more extensive, aggressive and probably more successful than the Powerpoint-based compliance programmes mentioned earlier. However, extensive compliance programmes do require a great deal of investment on the part of the company. Organizational structures must be changed in order to promote compliance (think, for instance, of the questions of discretion and delegation, or the pivotal role of the compliance officer), and more attention must be paid to processes that must have played a smaller role in this context before (the protection of whistleblowers, the bonus structure). It is safe to say that these extensive compliance programmes are more suitable for larger firms, because of the financial burdens involved. Nevertheless, through guidance on more extensive programmes, smaller companies can become aware of the dangers of non-compliance and some of the business structures and incentives that provoke it.

Role of the compliance officer

One of the elements of a successful compliance programme is the creation of a pivotal role for the compliance officer: the person – or persons – responsible for overseeing and managing compliance with competition rules. First of all, a compliance officer must have a central role within the organization. It has to be someone – or a group of people – who is visible to all employees, and who has knowledge not just of the law, but also of the technical aspects of the work, of the market and of the functioning of the organization. A compliance officer does not operate in a vacuum, but must keep track of economic, social and political trends that might influence behaviour within the company.[67] Briefly stated: a compliance officer must be visible and informed. To meet this requirement, a compliance officer must have sufficient resources and independence to move around the company.

Apart from overseeing compliance, a compliance officer is also responsible for handling complaints and tip-offs. For that reason, it is important that the compliance officer is a person who can be trusted by the employees. Studies show that the main reason why misconduct or grey-area behaviour is not reported is mistrust in the person in charge of handling this report and subsequent retaliation, even more so than a lack of financial reward or company loyalty.[68] Companies must be aware of this, and be very careful concerning the impartiality and reputation of the compliance officer.

Commitment & culture

In many companies, the compliance office seems to be a different world, apart from day-to-day business. It is not uncommon for a compliance officer to draft some sort of statement for the CEO to sign.[69] It cannot be surprising that such an approach to compliance is not very effective, because it gives no sign of a strong compliance culture. If compliance culture is weak, there is no incentive for employees to comply themselves, let alone to report suspect behaviour.[70] Compliance culture must be spread across the board and, accordingly, the commitment of senior management is of the utmost importance.

Of course, true commitment cannot be coerced. Therefore it is important to pay attention to the circumstances in which senior management are more likely to abandon their commitment to the rules. It seems that this could be the case when financial reports are often revised, when the board of directors do not closely monitor management, and when the board of directors and the external auditor are not regularly replaced. [71] Consequently, merely saying that management are committed to the compliance programme is not enough; processes monitoring this commitment must be in place as well and these processes must take account of the circumstances mentioned above.

With antitrust violations it is an additional difficulty that cartel behaviour is accepted as normal business practice in many industries.[72] Compliance programmes should pay attention to this problem, and if they do, they can have an important external learning effect as well. Some authors have raised the 'part of normal business' argument in order to illustrate that compliance programmes will not be effective,[73] but the argument can also be made that an aggressive compliance programme can be used to attack this kind of business culture. In that case, a real commitment on the part of the entire firm is indispensable.

Incentives

Antitrust violations are typically committed by people with substantial authority, who are primarily motivated by company interest or by incentives set by companies.[74] Mechanisms such as profit-linked bonus schemes fuel the temptation for collusion,[75] because employees tend to focus on the threats and rewards within the organization, instead of focusing on external threats.[76] It seems that the incentives set by companies might be one of the main reasons why infringements of the law occur, and why compliance programmes – despite best efforts – might remain ineffective. This is understandable. If a company explains the importance of compliance, but sets impossible sales targets or promises bonuses for extreme results, the company sends mixed messages to its employees. Given that companies are mostly insular, and the responsibility for infringements is dispersed, it is to be expected that the benefits of reaching a target or receiving a bonus will outweigh the negative consequences of a competition law infringement.[77] When setting up a compliance programme, companies must be aware of this, and downscale their targets and bonuses accordingly. This does not mean that financial incentives for better performance are all bad, but they should be handed out with care and not be too high.[78]

Procedural issues: guidance and fining

The foregoing shows that compliance programmes should focus more on commitment and culture, and that businesses should be aware of the incentives within their organization. Also, a compliance officer should be appointed with care in order to implement a compliance programme successfully. This illustrates how companies could deal with compliance, but does not give an insight into how competition authorities should deal with compliance programmes. In this respect, two questions are highlighted in this section: whether competition authorities should do more to promote compliance programmes or to give guidance about their content and implementation, and whether competition authorities should grant a fine reduction for a compliance programme that contains the elements listed above.

Guidance & promotion

One of the points of discussion is whether competition authorities should do more to promote compliance programmes or to give guidance thereon. The two authorities under review here already give guidance about the content of compliance programmes and what is considered to be an effective compliance programme. The need for such guidance has been underlined in a recent survey. [79] On the other hand, competition authorities need to avoid creating a 'checklist for compliance', because this might discourage companies from looking beyond the elements mentioned in the competition authority's guidance. The message should always be that compliance programmes have to be tailored to the company, and that not two of them are the same. This makes sense, as real compliance is dependent on a multitude of factors within a complex organization.[80] However, from the point of view of transparency, but also with a view to promoting a compliance culture across the board, it can be important for a competition authority to underline a number of important elements that could constitute a real compliance programme.

Still, the best form of promotion is the successful compliance programme of others, as a good example tends to be followed. It has been argued that corporate compliance is a form of advocacy as well, which might even be more effective than the competition authority's advocacy.[81] In order to bring about such effects, public attention to the value of compliance is needed, which means that the importance of competition law should be underlined more often. Despite this, it seems that there is too little attention for competition law and competition law compliance in the traditional media.[82] There could be a task for competition authorities here, as competition culture could be used as an enforcement tool by increasing moral outrage about infringements and by publicly shaming non-compliance. Perhaps competition authorities could be more attentive to 'branding' by publishing more cartel stories.[83]

However, it is easy to see why this could be difficult for competition authorities. Cartel cases typically take many years to conclude, which means that the news is 'old' as soon as the case is ready for publication. Of course, the imposition of a fine is a novelty, but the real cartel story is often not told. This could be due to another factor: antitrust violations are often complex subject matter and it might be difficult to explain the elaborate legal reasoning to the general public.[84] Lastly, it has to be taken into account that companies have a stake in press outings. Reputational damage matters to them, and could even affect share prices.[85] This could be a reason to use the media as a leverage – which is a discussion in itself – but also a reason to avoid publishing cases too early in order to prevent naming and shaming.

Fine reductions

Probably the most discussed issue in the handling of compliance programmes by competition authorities is the matter of fine reductions and the question whether these should be granted to companies which have a compliance programme in place. Fine reductions come into play when an infringement has been detected in spite of a compliance programme and a fine is about to be imposed. Most European competition authorities do not grant fine reductions for compliance programmes, but a number of authorities outside of Europe do.[86] Within the European Union, the United Kingdom still grants fine reductions, and as shown above, compliance efforts are rewarded within the scheme of a non-contestation procedure in France.[87] The European Commission used to grant fine reductions, but has not done so since the 1990s.[88]

The proponents of fine reductions argue that not taking compliance efforts into account is weakening the incentive for companies to adopt these programmes, because the infringements detected through these programmes are usually heavily fined. Also, real compliance programmes take up a great deal of investments, resources and time by companies.[89] Granting a fine reduction for a genuine compliance programme might give companies that last push in deciding whether or not they should implement a compliance programme. Some argue that the fine reduction granted for compliance programmes should only be as high as is needed to stimulate companies to establish such a programme.[90]

The leading argument by those opposed to granting fine reductions for compliance programmes is that compliance with the law is the standard, and should not be rewarded separately. The benefit of a compliance programme should lie in the prevention of infringements, and not in a reward from a competition authority. [91] Compliance must rest on internal motivation, and not on external bonuses. By extension, heavy fines should provide a sufficient incentive for firms to take compliance seriously, and infringing firms should not be rewarded for failed compliance.[92] Besides, if a compliance programme leads to the detection of an infringement, there is always a possibility to apply for leniency. In that way companies might receive immunity, which is preferential to a fine reduction for compliance programmes.

Even though the leniency argument renders a large part of this discussion irrelevant – in many cases leniency may indeed be requested and granted – this article favours a fine reduction for compliance efforts, though it must be approached with care. First of all, there might be circumstances in which immunity from fines under the leniency guidelines is not possible or desirable.[93] In these cases, a fine discount might nevertheless encourage companies to report infringements or grey-area behaviour. On another level, a fine discount for a compliance programme might give businesses a sense of 'doing the right thing'. Naturally, it cannot be contradicted that compliance with the law should be the standard, but far-reaching efforts to secure this compliance across the board surely exceed this standard. Some sort of appreciation for these efforts might have a reinforcing effect. Moreover, compliance programmes are beneficial for competition authorities as well. If executed properly, they can be a source of information, and allow authorities to keep tabs on the market. The main conditions under which any reduction should be granted are that compliance programmes are genuine and that companies that do find an infringement have done as much as they could to prevent it. Even though there is some scepticism about whether competition authorities are able to ascertain this, it is also believed that the extensive investigations in competition law cases give competition authorities a pretty good idea of whether a compliance programme is genuine and a company has done everything it could to prevent an infringement.[94] Naturally, the culture indicators and contradictory incentives mentioned above should be taken into account as well. Instead of refuting compliance discounts altogether, competition authorities might need to optimize their systems to distinguish window-dressing from genuine compliance.[95]

UNLOCKING THE POTENTIAL OF COMPLIANCE PROGRAMMES

Discussing this vast number of elements that can be included in a compliance programme, along with their preferential treatment by competition authorities, has distracted slightly from the main issue at hand: whether competition authorities could do more to unlock the potential of competition law compliance programmes with a view to increasing the company's commitment to the rules. In that respect the literature clearly shows that there is a serious debate on whether guidance and promotion and granting fine discounts are possible ways of increasing the use of compliance programmes. However, with regard to the content of compliance programmes, the most important conclusion to be drawn from the literature is that compliance programmes should always be tailored to a specific company, taking into account a company's organizational structure and capability of disseminating a real compliance culture.

This final section discusses the ways in which the ACM and the *Autorité* could improve their approach to compliance programmes, by looking at the three important substantive conditions derived from the literature (the role of the compliance officer, business culture and targets), as well as the two procedural issues discussed above (guidance and fine reductions). The question of to what extent the competition authorities are already focused on these points is answered and suggestions are made for future practice.

Role of the compliance officer

If a compliance officer is appointed, he should be central to the organization, and knowledgeable about its functioning. He must have sufficient resources, powers and independence to oversee compliance. Additionally, employees must trust their compliance officer, and have faith in the mechanisms for dealing with complaints and tip-offs.

Out of the two competition authorities, the *Autorité* is the only one that stresses this aspect of compliance in particular. The appointment of the compliance officer receives attention in its guidance on compliance, including his need for resources, powers and independence.[96] It is underlined that this person must have unquestionable skills and authority within the company, suggesting that the issue of trustworthiness is something that should be seriously considered. Even though the Dutch ACM is less explicit about the role of the compliance officer, it is stressed – by reference to the OFT's Wheel of Compliance – that having a protocol for infringements is important. [97] However, this protocol seems to be less focused on the privacy and protection of whistleblowers, but more on the process for handling detected infringements. This is illustrated in quite a detailed fashion in the Memorandum of Compliance between KPN and ACM, in which a scheme for decision-making is elaborated.[98]

From the foregoing, it seems that the *Autorité* has progressed further in recognizing the potentially important role of the compliance officer, and the need for his impartial positioning within the company. The ACM could stress this point more, in order to make businesses understand that appointing a compliance officer is not just a matter of shifting the burden of compliance to the legal department. Furthermore, both competition authorities could pay more attention to a fundamental underlying issue in the good functioning of a compliance programme: trust. Mistrust in the compliance officer or the procedures for handling complaints could be an indicator that a compliance programme is not working well, and probably will not work well in the future. This could serve as an important signalling function, and should be addressed more in the design, but also in the review of compliance programmes.

Business culture and targets

A business culture geared towards compliance is indispensable for the success of a compliance programme. Unfortunately, a number of organizational defects can play into the hands of cartelisation, such as restatements of financial reports, a meagre oversight of managers and few changes to the board and auditors. Along with that, targets and incentives play an important role in business culture, as they can encourage employees to behave in a certain way.

Except for emphasizing that management should be fully committed to a compliance programme,[99] neither of the competition authorities express concerns regarding business culture or incentives. Naturally, it is not the task of competition authorities to impose all of these elements upon companies – since it is very unlikely that such an approach will genuinely change anything as far as commitment or culture is concerned. However, a competition authority is probably the designated institution to make companies aware of any red flags in the organizational structure, and to encourage companies to review their targets and bonuses in order to ensure that these do not inspire cartelistic behaviour. If there is no pressure upon a company to think about these issues or to review its business structure, infringements are bound to occur and compliance programmes are bound to fall short. It would be advisable for competition authorities to point out these dangers and to explain them, instead of only focussing on more tangible and controllable elements of compliance.

Guidance and promotion

First of all, with respect to guidance, it has been repeatedly stressed that there is a need for guidance on compliance. Not every company is as well educated about the content of competition rules and the value of compliance, and as a result the risks of infringements are often underestimated. Secondly, in the course of discussing guidance on compliance programmes, it became clear that competition policy in general suffers from a lack of attention by the general public. This makes compliance with competition law a less pressing issue on business agendas.

With regard to the first point, the ACM gives no specific guidance on the content of compliance programmes, although it has made a reference to the guidance documents of others. This provides some insight into what the ACM considers to be important. Additional information on compliance programmes can be gained from published cases and the recent Memorandum of Compliance, although this is fragmented at best. However, with regard to bringing competition law to the attention of the general public, the ACM gives the impression that it pursues a modernized publication strategy, by using less legal terminology in press releases, by using a digital, interactive annual report with short clips, and by actively involving consumers in the setting of priorities through a digital survey. The *Autorité,* on the other hand, is more active concerning the first point, having published an explicit guidance document on compliance programmes. Additionally, all non-contestation cases have been published, including the compliance efforts promised by companies and the *Autorité's* evaluation of these commitments. On the second point, no noticeable change in publication strategy has been noticed.

For the reasons mentioned above it would be advisable for the ACM to publish more extensive guidance on compliance programmes, so that companies are aware of what it considers to be 'good' or 'thorough'. The *Autorité's* guidance can be considered adequate in that respect. Regarding general promotion and publications, competition authorities should be more outspoken about their efforts, and not just limit themselves to the publication of fines which have been imposed. Despite the difficulties with press coverage in competition cases, the overall importance of competition law should be emphasized in the media, as this could increase the urgency of competition law compliance on the corporate agenda.

Fine reductions

The last issue discussed is that of granting fine reductions for companies that have adopted compliance programmes. In the Netherlands, the chairman of the ACM has pointed out that there is no fine reduction for improving or implementing compliance programmes. However, because of the Dutch Fining Guidelines, this remains possible in theory, leaving the opportunity open to change this in the future.[100] In practice, the opposite (a fine increase) has occurred in telecommunication regulation.[101] In France, there is no fine reduction for the existence of a compliance programme, but the commitment to improve such a progamme, or to implement one can yield a 10% discount in a non-contestation procedure. With that, the *Autorité* has found a middle ground in rewarding compliance efforts without possibly setting wrong incentives.[102] This article favours a fine reduction for compliance efforts, although this should be approached with care, because it rewards companies that go beyond what is necessary to secure compliance, and compliance programmes as such can be beneficial to competition authorities as well. The main condition for granting such a discount is that the competition authority makes sure that it is a genuine, well thought out and aggressive compliance programme that is in place. As a consequence, competition authorities might need to optimize their system to distinguish window-dressing from genuine compliance. From the foregoing it appears that both competition authorities are rather clear in their approach to compliance programmes and their decision not to reward them financially in a normal fining procedure. Even though this article argues an opposite solution, there as just as many voices in the literature stating that the approach of the ACM and the *Autorité* is the right one, and that companies should receive no additional reward. Whether it is absolutely necessary to adjust this approach in order to 'unlock the potential of compliance programmes' remains unclear. Both competition authorities have given guidance on the necessary elements of compliance programmes. However, both might also benefit from a more active publication strategy. Continuously praising compliance and condemning infringements could be a powerful signal to the general public that competition law compliance is important, thus creating a firmer moral basis for companies to establish a compliance programme.

CONCLUDING REMARKS

This article aimed to explore whether competition authorities could do more to unlock the potential of competition law compliance programmes with a view to increasing the company's commitment to abide by the rules. Even though the review of practice was limited to two competition authorities, and the debate in the literature has focused on a number of specific topics, some interesting recommendations can be made. First of all, competition authorities should pay more attention to the organizational aspects which play a part in generating compliance, not only with regard to the role of the compliance officer and the employees' trust in procedures, but also regarding structural indicators and performance targets. Naturally, changes to these aspects cannot be imposed – the imposition of these changes would not even be effective – but it can be seen as the task of competition authorities to make companies aware of these aspects. It cannot hurt to think beyond the firm as a whole, and to allow firms to think about themselves and their organization in a different way. Secondly, a fine reduction for a genuine, well-functioning compliance programme has been advocated in order to reward companies for their efforts, but also because of the external effect of these programmes on business culture and the fact that the programmes could be beneficial to competition authorities as well. Finally, there is a need for more attention to be given to competition law issues and the value of compliance. Even though this is, admittedly, not entirely in the hands of competition authorities, but is dependent on the media and the receptivity of the public, competition authorities should be aware of the effects that their publications potentially have, and the way this is perceived in business. Notwithstanding these improvements, both the ACM and the *Autorité* are already engaged in stimulating compliance in businesses in a distinct way. It is exciting to see if – and if so, in what way – their approach will alter in the future. In any case it is clear that the commitment of companies is a necessary ingredient for a successful compliance programme, and that in this respect the public authorities and the private parties must work cooperatively in order to achieve the necessary results.

REFERENCES

1. Montreal Journal of Commerce, 1887.
2. Researched by D.D. Sokol, 'Cartels, Corporate Compliance, and What

Practitioners Really Think About Enforcement', 2012 Antitrust Law Journal 78, no. 1, pp. 201-240, available at <http://scholarship.law.ufl.edu/facultypub/298> (last visited 7 November 2014).

3. The best way to enforce the law (not necessarily competition law) has been debated in, for instance, economics, behavioural sciences and social sciences.

4. Autorité de la Concurrence, 'Document-cadre du 10 fevrier 2012 sur les programmes de conformité aux règles de concurrence' (hereinafter: Framework Document Compliance), Para. 8. Translation is the official translation by the Autorité, available at <http://www.autoritedelaconcurrence.fr/doc/framework_document_compliance_10february2012.pdf> (last visited 7 November 2014).

5. Arts. 101 and 102 of the Treaty on the Functioning of the European Union (TFEU).

6. Apart from the concluding paragraphs mentioning the importance of press coverage for competition law actions. Competition authorities give guidance about competition rules in general. See for instance the brochures on competition law by the European Commission, accessible at <http://ec.europa.eu/competition/antitrust/publications_en.html> (last visited 7 November 2014). It is less common to give guidance in individual cases, since the competition rules are based on a system of self-assessment, rather than pre-approval by the competition authorities. In exceptional cases, competition authorities might give an opinion on a specific case. However, these opinions are not intended as a 'licence' for a certain behaviour.

7. Which significantly altered the enforcement of European competition law from a central to a decentralized system with competence for the national authorities. Council Regulation (EC) No. 1/2003 of 16 December 2002 on the implementation of the rules on competition laid down in Articles 81 and 82 of the Treaty, OJ L 1, 4.1.2003, p. 1.

8. Forthcoming in the spring of 2016. This comment is made due to the nature of some of the research (semi-structured interviews, see below) for which a more extensive methodological explanation will be provided in the thesis.

9. P.J. May, 'Compliance Motivations: Affirmative and Negative Bases', 2004 Law & Society Review 38, no. 1.

10. European Commission, press release Cathode Ray Tubes: <http://europa.eu/rapid/press-release_IP-12-1317_en.htm>, and European Commission, press release Yen Derivatives: <http://europa.eu/rapid/press-release_IP-13-1208_en.htm> (last visited 7 November 2014), although this decision concerned the Commission's settlement procedure.

11. There is extensive literature on this subject, see for instance A.M. Polinsky & S. Shavell, 'The economic theory of public enforcement law', NBER Working Paper, No. 6993, 1999. However, it is also argued that such a cost-benefit analysis is not always made, see for instance B.A. Jacobs, 'Deterrence and deterrability', 2010 Criminology 48, no. 2, pp. 417-442.

12. Which is an assumption often made in economic literature describing deterrence theory. However, see differently the work of R.H. Thaler & C.R. Sunstein, Nudge:

Improving Decisions about Health, Wealth and Happiness, 2009 or D. Ariely, Predictably Irrational: the Hidden Forces that Shape Our Decisions, 2008, though there are many more influential authors on behavioural sciences and its effect on economic assumptions.

13. See for another signalling of this trend van E. van Hasselt & H. Urius, 'The Deterrent Effect of EU Competition Law: Higher Fines and Extended Targets', National Law Review, blogpost 14 June 2014, available at <http://www.natlawreview.com/article/deterrent-effect-eucompetition-law-higher-fines-and-extended-targets> (last visited 7 November 2014). They refer to the intention of the Dutch Minister to raise the ceiling for fines. Minister H.G.J. Kamp, 'Kamerbrief over Boetebeleid Autoriteit Consument en Markt', 27 August 2013, available at <http://www.rijksoverheid.nl/documenten-en-publicaties/kamerstukken/2013/08/27/kamerbrief-over-boetebeleid-autoriteitconsument-en-markt.html> (last visited 7 November 2014).

14. See for a discussion of qui tam provisions W.E. Kovacic, 'Whistleblower Bounty Lawsuits as Monitoring Devices in Government Contracting', 1996 Loy. L.A. L. Rev. 29, pp. 1799-1858, p. 1804. An analysis of the possibilities of informant rewards and market screens is done by J. Polanski, 'Informant Reward Schemes in Competition Enforcement', available at <http://papers.ssrn.com/sol3/papers.cfm?abstract_ id=2457450> (last visited 7 November 2014).

15. Sokol 2012, supra note 2.

16. This is the 'positive punishment effect' as is mentioned in Jacobs 2010, supra note 11, p. 419.

17. However, it has also been argued that it might have affirmative effects as well, because a deterrent enforcement policy could reaffirm the commitment to compliance. W.P.J. Wils, 'Optimal Antitrust Fines: Theory and Practice', 2006 World Competition 29, no. 2, pp. 183-208 referring to J. Adanaes, 'The moral or educative influence of criminal law', 1971 Journal of Social Issues 27, no. 2, pp. 17-31.

18. J.G. Van Erp, 'Motieven voor naleving van regelgeving', in T. Barkhuysen et al. (eds.), Recht realiseren. Bijdragen rond het thema adequate naleving van rechtsregels, 2005, p. 16.

19. J. Jackson, 'Why do people comply with the law? Legitimacy and the influence of legal institutions', to be published in British Journal of Criminology, but more importantly: T.R. Tyler, Why people obey the law: Procedural justice, legitimacy, and compliance, 2006.

20. Actually, some of the debate on compliance programmes in competition law took place in the late 1950s, early 1960s, and is still relevant even today. See for instance C.V. Anderson, 'Effective Antitrust Compliance Programs and Procedures', 1962-1963 Bus. Law. 18, p. 739, or G. Geis, 'White Collar Crime: The Heavy Electrical Equipment Antitrust Cases of 1961', in M.B. Clinard & R. Quinney (eds.), Criminal Behavior Systems: A Typology, 1967, pp. 139-151.

21. However, as Section 4.1 below describes, a more sceptical approach towards

compliance programmes is equally possible

22. These drivers of compliance are mentioned by the European Commission, and by the Office of Fair Trading (OFT). European Commission, D-G Comp, 'Compliance Matters: What Companies Can Do to Better Respect EU Competition Rules', KD-32-11-985-EN-C, 2012. Office of Fair Trading, S. Preece (Deputy Director Competition Policy), 'OFT Competition Law Compliance Initiatives and Resources', 6 March 2012.
23. Assuming that infringements are indeed detected. Whether this is an appropriate stance for competition authorities is debatable.
24. In addition to national documents, previous cases and speeches by key people within the authorities, the following sections (on the national perspective and the incentives) have been based on a series of semi-structured interviews held at the competition authorities under review (ACM and *Autorité de la Concurrence*). These interviews took place between February and June 2014.
25. Speech by Chris Fonteijn on 24 January 2014 at the International Chamber of Commerce, available in Dutch at <https://www.acm. nl/nl/publicaties/publicatie/12571/Toespraak-Chris-Fonteijn-bij-International-Chamber-of-Commerce-over-compliance/> (last visited 7 November 2014). This speech is commented upon by R. Elkerbout, 'Robuuste Compliance Programma's Verdienen Meer Dan Een Lippendienst van de ACM', 2014 *Tijdschrift Mededingingsrecht in de praktijk*, no. 3.
26. The ACM advocates a problem-solving strategy, based on the work of Malcolm Sparrow. ACM, 'Strategie Autoriteit Consument en Markt', 20 September 2013, available in Dutch at <https://www.acm.nl/nl/publicaties/publicatie/11991/Strategie-Autoriteit-Consument-en-Markt/> (last visited 7 November 2014).
27. Speech by Fonteijn 2014, supra note 25.
28. Art. 49a Dutch Competition Act (*Mededingingswet*) and Art. 9 Regulation 1/2003.
29. ACM Case 7191, *Landelijke Huisartsenvereniging* 2012; ACM Case 7138,*Thuiszorg Midden-Brabant* 2011; ACM Case 13.0612.53, *Mobiele Operators*, 2014.
30. However, the companies involved in the *Thuiszorg Midden-Brabant* case opted to refer to the compliance programme of their joint association: Actiz. This association decided to introduce a general compliance programme as a response to the ACM's (then NMa's) activities in the sector.
31. See for this discussion, and an elaboration of the two arguments mentioned in this same section, OECD, Directorate for Financial and Enterprise Affairs – Competition Committee, *Promoting compliance with competition law*, 30 August 2012, DAF/COMP(2011)20, p. 15.
32. This is not merely theory, as the predecessor of the ACM's telecom branch (OPTA) had on one occasion increased a fine imposed on KPN, which had a Memorandum of Compliance in place. In an interim procedure, this reasoning was untouched (District Court (*Rechtbank*) of Rotterdam 24 October 2013,

ECLI:NL:RBROT:2013:8216). In competition law, such a fine increase has not yet been imposed.

33. ACM Fining Guidelines, Arts. 3.13 and 3.15 (Beleidsregels voor Boete en Clementie, *Staatscourant* 24 April 2013, no. 11214).

34. This statement includes the objective of safeguarding the functioning of the French competitive economy, implying a policy of preventing, detecting, correcting and sanctioning, and in which educational activities are essential., See Framework Document Compliance, supra note 4, Para. 14, but also see its mission statement on <www.autoritedelaconcurrence.fr>.

35. Framework Document Compliance, supra note 4, Para. 6. This document emerged after a round of consultations (in terms of information, transparency and dialogue) and a round-table conference on 20 December 2011.

36. See more extensively E.S. Lachnit, 'Alternative enforcement of competition law – Balancing legal requirements in practice', available at <http://renforce.rebo.uu.nl/wp-content/uploads/2013/11/RENFORCE-Working-Paper-Settlements.pdf> (last visited 7 November 2014). The legal basis for this non-contestation procedure is Art. L.464-2 Paragraph III of the Code de Commerce. The discount is found in the Framework Document Compliance, supra note 4, Para. 31.

37. Autorité de la Concurrence, decision 05-D-07 of 19 December 2005 (*Disney Videotapes*).

38. Autorité de la Concurrence, decision 07-D-26 of 26 July 2007 (*High Voltage Cables*), Para. 149.

39. Autorité de la Concurrence, decision 07-D-48 of 18 December 2007 (*Internal Removal*), Autorité de la Concurrence, decision 08-D-12 of 21 May 2008 (*Okoumé Plywood*) and Autorité de la Concurrence, decision 09-D-19 of 10 June 2009 (*Relocation of Military Personnel*).

40. Court of Justice of the European Union, Case C-189/02, *Danske Rorindustrie e.a. v Commission*. Also: Framework Document Compliance, supra note 4, Paras. 23-26.

41. Framework Document Compliance, supra note 4, Paras. 27-28.

42. ICC Antitrust and Compliance Toolkit, available at <http://www.iccwbo.org/advocacy-codes-and-rules/areas-of-work/competition/icc-antitrust-compliance-toolkit/> (last visited 7 November 2014). OFT Wheel of Compliance, not available as such, but published at <http:// www.mcguirewoods.com/news-resources/publications/international/competition-law-mar2012.pdf> (last visited 7 November 2014).

43. Memorandum of Compliance between KPN and ACM, renewed version of June 2014, available in Dutch at: <https://www.acm. nl/nl/publicaties/publicatie/13072/Vernieuwd-Compliance-Handvest-KPN-en-ACM/> (last visited 7 November 2014) (hereinafter: Memorandum of Compliance KPN/ACM), and the Compliance Programme of KNMP (current version), available in Dutch at: <http:// www.knmp.nl/downloads/organisatie-regelgeving/organisatie-regelgeving-wet-en-regelgeving/knmp-compliance-programma.pdf> (last visited

7 November 2014) (hereinafter: KNMP Compliance Programme).

44. Memorandum of Compliance KPN/ACM, supra note 43, pillars of compliance on pp. 2-3.

45. Framework Document Compliance, supra note 4, Para. 11.

46. Framework Document Compliance, supra note 4, Paras. 11, 16 and 19.

47. Here in a very short form, but described very extensively in the Framework Document Compliance, supra note 4, Para. 22.

48. OECD, Directorate for Financial and Enterprise Affairs – Competition Committee, *Promoting compliance with competition law*, 30 August 2012, DAF/COMP(2011)20.

49. Framework Document Compliance, supra note 4, Para. 18.

50. Autorité de la Concurrence, decision 07-D-21 of 26 June 2007 (Professional Laundry), Paras. 62 and 132.

51. See, most clearly, Autorité de la Concurrence, decision 11-D-02 of 26 January 2011 (Restoration Historical Buildings), in which the companies received a 10%, 15% and 25% discount for their compliance programmes.

52. One of the reasons behind this might be that compliance is perceived by the ACM as the standard situation. It is what companies should do in the first place, and is therefore not typically something that a competition authority would press upon companies without any reason to believe that there is non-compliance. Secondly, the compliance programmes mentioned by the ACM in publications would be those programmes introduced in a high profile or long-lasting case. In these cases, competition concerns are usually not removed by only introducing a compliance programme. An exception is the Memorandum of Compliance KPN/ACM, supra note 43.

53. Memorandum of Compliance KPN/ACM, supra note 43, KNMP Compliance Programme, supra note 43, *Verbond voor Verzekeraars* (press release 30 December 2010, available in Dutch at <https://www.acm.nl/nl/publicaties/publicatie/5471/NMa-meer-ruimte-voor-concurrentie-tussen-verzekeraars/> (last visited 7 November 2014)), *Veras* (mentioned in the Annual Report 2012, available in Dutch at <http://nmajaarverslag2012.acm.nl/jaarverslag/mededinging/activiteiten-in-2012/nma-beboet-rotterdamse-sloopbedrijven-wegens-verboden-afspraken/> (last visited 7 November 2014)), *Greenchoice* (press release 8/1/2013, available in Dutch at <https://www. acm.nl/nl/publicaties/publicatie/11008/NMa-wijst-bijna-alle-bezwaren-Greenchoice-af/> (last visited 7 November 2014)), *Uitgevers* (mentioned in the Annual Report 2007, p. 30), *Nederlandse Vereniging van Makelaars* (mentioned in the Annual Report 2007, pp. 28-29), *Garnalenvissers* (mentioned in the Annual Report 2005, p. 70) and *Nederlandse Vereniging van Banken* (mentioned in the Annual Report 2005, p. 74).

54. See the Autorité's website at <http://www.autoritedelaconcurrence.fr/user/standard.php?id_rub=421> (last visited 7 November 2014).

55. See in more detail W.P.J. Wils, 'Antitrust Compliance Programs and Optimal

Antitrust Enforcement', 2013 *Journal of Antitrust Enforcement* 1, no. 1, p. 9. Geradin has rebutted this objection in his reply to Wils by stating that this characteristic is in no way particular to competition law. For instance in the field of corruption, the company benefits as well, but compliance programmes are created and upheld nevertheless. D. Geradin, 'Antitrust Compliance Programmes & Optimal Antitrust Enforcement: A Reply to Wouter Wils', 2013 *Journal of Antitrust Enforcement* 1, no. 1, pp. 4-5.

56. A. Stephan, 'Hear No Evil, See No Evil: Why Antitrust Compliance Programmes may be Ineffective at Preventing Cartels', CCP Working Paper 09-09, 2009, pp. 6-10. But see also C.R. Leslie, 'Cartels, Agency Costs, and Finding Virtue in Faithless Agents', 2008 *Maryland Law Review* 49, p. 1621.

57. This is rebutted by the survey carried out by Sokol, which has shown that in many businesses there is a lack of awareness of competition law. Even where employees were aware of the rules, they were sometimes disregarded, because the consequences were perceived to be minimal. Sokol 2012, supra note 2, p. 28.

58. Wils 2013, supra note 55, p. 14.

59. See in more detail M.P. Schinkel, 'Nalevingsprogramma's', 2011 *Markt & Mededinging*, no. 6, p. 2.

60. Geradin compares the learning effect argument with the argument that drugs education in schools incites young children to experiment with drugs, instead of being aware of the dangers of taking drugs. Geradin 2013, supra note 55, p. 7.

61. This particular effect is addressed by Martijn Han in an econometric experiment. C. Angelucci & M.A. Han, 'Monitoring Managers Through Corporate Compliance Programs', Amsterdam Center for Law & Economics Working Paper No. 2010-14.

62. Quote from Wils 2013, supra note 55, p. 19.

63. J.E. Murphy & D. Boehme, 'Fear No Evil: a Compliance and Ethics Professionals' Response to Dr. Stephan', 2009, available at <http://papers.ssrn.com/sol3/papers.cfm?abstract_id=1965733> (last visited 7 November 2014), pp. 4-5.

64. J. Murphy & W. Kolasky, 'The Role of Anti-Cartel Compliance Programs In Preventing Cartel Behavior', 2012 *Antitrust* 26, no. 2, pp. 1-2. The full list includes the following elements: risk assessment, integrated approach, standards, controls, empowered chief ethics and compliance officer, resources and infrastructure, board oversight, senior management support, personnel practices, training and communication, third parties, audit and monitor, measure effectiveness, reporting systems, protection from retaliation, discipline, incentives, response to violations, diligence and industry practice, documentation.

65. These are considered to be the pillars of a compliance programme by the American Bar Association. ABA Section of Antitrust Law, 'Antitrust Compliance: Perspectives and Resources for Corporate Counselors', 2005, pp. 64-69.

66. R.M. Abrantes-Metz & D.D. Sokol, 'Antitrust Corporate Governance & Compliance', University of Minnesota Law School, Legal Studies Research

Paper Series, Research Paper No. 13-18, 2013, p. 4.

67. Anderson 1963, supra note 20, p. 4.

68. Murphy & Boehme 2009, supra note 63, p. 8. Another reason why people could be reluctant to report to the compliance officer is the lack of legal professional privilege (LPP) in the European Union. The Court of Justice has decided that LPP is not applicable to in-house counsel (Case C-550/07 P, *Akzo v Commission*), which means that complainants can rightfully fear for their privacy. However, a study shows that many employees are unaware of this distinction, see Murphy & Kolasky 2012, supra note 64, p. 16.

69. Murphy & Kolasky 2012, supra note 64, p. 1.

70. Abrantes-Metz & Sokol 2013, supra note 66, p. 11.

71. Abrantes-Metz & Sokol 2013, supra note 66, pp. 7-8. Yet, it appears from this same article that middle management seem to take compliance programmes more seriously than senior management.

72. Stephan 2009, supra note 56, p. 11. It seems that in many industries the illegality of cartel behaviour is dismissed or is not perceived as something which is really serious. Abrantes-Metz & Sokol 2013, supra note 66, p. 8.

73. See Section 4.1 above.

74. Wils 2013, supra note 55, pp. 8-9.

75. Stephan 2009, supra note 56, p. 2.

76. Murphy & Boehme 2009, supra note 63, p. 10.

77. Murphy & Kolasky 2012, supra note 64, p. 3.

78. Abrantes-Metz & Sokol 2013, supra note 66, p. 5. There is a role for a compliance officer there. See, e.g., J. Murphy, 'Using Incentives in Your Compliance and Ethics Program', 2012, available at <http://www.corporatecompliance.org/Resources/View/smid/940/ArticleID/724. aspx> (last visited 7 November 2014).

79. Sokol 2012, supra note 2, p. 22.

80. This is mentioned by Wils 2013, supra note 55, p. 19. For him, this is a reason not to create more detailed guidance on compliance programmes, which he calls check lists.

81. Geradin 2013, supra note 55, p. 7.

82. Sokol 2012, supra note 2, pp. 17-20,

83. Sokol 2012, supra note 2, p. 17. It is argued by Abrantes-Metz & Sokol that cartel offences suffer from a lack of stigma, see Abrantes-Metz & Sokol 2013, supra note 66, p. 11.

84. However, the fact that it might be difficult does not mean that they should not try to explain this more effectively. See for instance the efforts of the Working Group on Advocacy of the International Competition Network, which has listed this as a challenge in its assessment of advocacy in 2009. ICN, 'Report on Assessment of ICN Members' Requirements and Recommendations on Further ICN Work on Competition Advocacy', 2009, pp. 16-17.

85. Which happened in the Dutch Construction Cartel, as explained by Abrantes-Metz & Sokol 2013, supra note 66, p. 10.

86. The United States, Canada, Australia and Brazil give fine reductions for compliance programmes (typically 10%). Schinkel 2011, supra note 59, p. 2.

87. Office of Fair Trading in OFT's 'Guidance as to the appropriate amount of a penalty' (OFT423, September 2012), at 2.15; see also 'How your business can achieve compliance with competition law' (OFT1341, June 2011), and Framework Document Compliance, supra note 4.

88. See, for instance, case 91/532/EEC: Commission Decision of 5 June 1991 relating to a proceeding under Article 85 of the EEC Treaty (Case No IV/32.879 – Viho/Toshiba), OJ L 287, 17.10.1991, p. 39 but now take into account European Commission, *Compliance matters – What companies can do better to respect EU competition rules*, 2011, available at <http://ec.europa.eu/competition/antitrust/compliance/> (last visited 7 November 2014), pp. 19-20, in which fine discounts are firmly refuted.

89. Stephan 2009, supra note 56, pp. 11-12. Abrantes-Metz & Sokol 2013, supra note 66, p. 6.

90. Geradin 2013, supra note 55, p. 3.

91. Wils calls them 'subsidies for infringements'. Wils 2013, supra note 55, p. 24.

92. W.P.J. Wils, *Efficiency and Justice in European Antitrust Enforcement*, 2008, pp. 3-6.

93. For instance, when a competition authority was already tipped-off, when a company would rather request for a commitment decision instead, or when a cartel has operated internationally, and the A-status for leniency has been conferred on another, quicker cartelist.

94. Geradin 2013, supra note 55, p. 15.

95. Distinguishing bad input from bad apples, see Sokol 2012, supra note 2, p. 35.

96. Framework Document Compliance, supra note 4, Para. 22, sub 2.

97. See Section 3.2.1 above.

98. Memorandum of Compliance KPN/ACM, supra note 43, p. 8.

99. Speech by Fonteijn 2014, supra note 25 and the Framework Document Compliance, supra note 4, Para. 22, sub 1.

100. See, for instance, Elkerbout 2014, supra note 25.

101. District Court (Rechtbank) of Rotterdam 24 October 2013, ECLI:NL:RBROT:2013:8216. In competition law, such a fine increase has not yet been imposed.

102. Non-contestation has been called the ultimate form of proving its commitment to compliance, see Wils 2013, supra note 55, p. 33. This, however, is questionable, because there might be external reasons for a company to contest the findings of a competition authority.

11
CHAPTER

CONTRACTUAL CONTROL AND LABOUR-RELATED CSR NORMS IN THE SUPPLY CHAIN

Louise Vytopil

INTRODUCTION

This article explores the choices that multinational companies make in order to regulate corporate social responsibility aspects of their supply chains. The first part will look at the context in which these companies operate and explain the relevance of the questions which are central to this article. Furthermore, the methodology will be set out. The second part provides a theoretical private law background with respect to contracts, general terms and conditions and codes of conduct in the Netherlands. The final part will answer the following research questions: what do the codes of conduct and CSR contracts currently used by best-practice players look like? What are the contractual consequences (both in terms of possibilities and limitations) of these instruments? The article will answer these questions by describing the initiatives that fourteen Dutch multinational companies currently use in order to regulate their supply chains. Furthermore, it will qualify these initiatives in terms of contract law and highlight some patterns found in these initiatives.

SETTING THE STAGE

Over the past couple of decades, the world in which companies operate has changed dramatically. Since the early 1990s, there has been a strong increase in the amount of companies that operate multination-ally. At the end of the 1960s, only 7,000 multinational companies (MNCs) had been registered, expanding to over 30,000 in the

Citation: Louise Vytopil, "Contractual Control and Labour-Related CSR Norms in the Supply Chain", http://www.utrechtlawreview.org Volume 8, Issue 1 (January) 2012 | URN:NBN:NL:UI:10-1-101426.

early 1990s and 60,000 at the start of the new millennium.[1] An important role in this respect has been played by globalisation.

The process of globalisation encompasses many different aspects, such as deterritorialisation, in-creased use of technology and heightened transparency. These factors combined create – what the Neth-erlands Socio-Economic Council (*Sociaal-Economische Raad, SER*) refers to as – increased intercon-nectedness.[2] Companies may export their products to countries around the world or relocate part of their production process to lower-wage countries.[3] Companies located in low-wage countries, such as India, China and Bangladesh, increasingly do business for firms based in Europe and the United States. Furthermore, many developing countries have set up export processing zones.[4]

By operating in multiple countries, MNCs can take advantage of the weak points that each specific legal system offers, while planning the legal structure of their daughter companies so that the corporate veil is best utilised to avoid liability for any violations of the law.[5] This can lead to undesirable consequences: through their daily operations, MNCs may damage the local environment or they may commit human rights abuses. So how is the behaviour of MNCs governed when they operate across borders?

While companies are traditionally governed by the law of their corporate seat, their home states, generally speaking, do not have any legislative power or control when their corporate citizens operate across the borders of nation states as the result of the territoriality principle. At the same time, host states may lack the expertise or resources to regulate adequately.[6] Globalisation has also eroded the power of the nation state. As a result, regulating the behaviour of companies operating across the borders of na-tion states is complex. Thus the behaviour of MNCs is often not (effectively) regulated. What remains is a regulatory gap in which multinationals operate.

Western multinationals thus make use of global supply chains in order to provide their goods and services to the public, but these global supply chains are often not regulated by public law. At the same time, information processes have changed as a result of globalisation. If things go wrong, the world be-comes aware of this within a matter of minutes.

And as has been shown by various examples, things do go wrong. Consider, for example, the suicides at a Foxconn factory in Shenzen, Southern China, producing electronics for – inter alia – Dell and Ap-ple.[7] Or Shell's massive oil-spills in the Ogoni delta in Nigeria, resulting in the devastation of many square kilometres of water and farmland, for which it recently accepted liability.[8] MNCs are held accountable (both by the media and – to a slightly lesser extent – in the legal arena) for these wrongdoings.

MNCs themselves now take action in order to prevent human rights violations from occurring. These private initiatives are often brought together under the umbrella term of corporate social responsi-bility (CSR); in the words of Freer Spreckley described as the 'triple P bottom line' of People, Planet and Profit.[9] In the words of the European Commission: initiatives that 'contribute to a better society and a cleaner environment'.[10]

This concept of CSR as encompassing the 'triple P' is currently widely accepted among academics and companies alike. This article will not elaborate on the question whether or not companies should undertake CSR measures.[11] After all, I believe that it is clear that companies do undertake CSR measures and, therefore, the focus should not be on whether they should do so, but rather, on gaining greater in-sight into their CSR initiatives. What do they look like and how can they be qualified?

While in the early days of CSR many companies did not concern themselves with written policies, over the past few decades the code of conduct (COC) has taken off.[12] Rule-setting in CSR is now mostly undertaken by private actors rather than public actors: MNCs increasingly rely on self-regulation, soft law and codes of conduct. And while CSR and these private law initiatives are largely voluntary[13] by nature, they are not entirely non-committal. The same holds true for CSR in the supply chain. It is generally held that MNCs are no longer simply responsible for preventing wrongdoings by their own company, but rather that they also have a (limited) responsibility with regard to their business partners, including supply partners.

This conclusion is supported by the business and human rights framework drafted by the United Na-tions Special Representative for Business & Human Rights, John Ruggie. The framework, entitled 'Protect, Respect and Remedy' (the 'UN Framework'), describes the obligations that businesses have with re-gard to human rights. This framework was endorsed by the UN Human Rights Council on 16 June 2011 and sets out the responsibilities that – inter alia – businesses have with regard to their operations and human rights. They are to respect human rights, acting with due diligence and dealing with any problems that may arise. This responsibility extends to the supply chain that companies use when producing their goods or services. According to Ruggie, companies are to take on responsibilities with regard to CSR in the supply chain.

These responsibilities are echoed in the 2011 update to the OECD Guidelines, [14] which incorporates and builds upon the UN Framework. For the first time, the 2011 update contains both the general notion that enterprises are to exercise due diligence and the view that companies are to avoid any negative impact as a result of their business, regardless of whether such a negative impact is caused by their own operations or by others in their supply chain.

Such a 'responsibility' in respect of CSR and responsible supply chain management is therefore widely accepted at this moment in time; however, it should be noted that it is only that: a 'responsibility', not a (legal) obligation.

Many companies feel the demand for responsible supply chain management from society and NGOs. This is reflected in their CSR policies: nowadays, these often include supply chain issues. In the Netherlands, 60% of the largest companies investigated in the 2010 Transparency Benchmark addressed supply chain issues in some way or another in their CSR policy.[15] There is currently no strict liability for MNCs who engage with suppliers in low-wage countries, although, from time to time, politicians have called for further responsibilities. In the Netherlands, such a call came from Parliament in 2007, when it requested the SER to advise on the necessity of legislation on supply chain responsibility. The Labour Party (PvdA) had proposed an Act on the Transparency of Product Chains (*Wet Openbaarheid Ketens*).[16] The European Parliament, as well, has called for legislation that would create a strict liability for any MNC that included child labour in its supply chain, regardless of where this child labour would take place.[17] Furthermore, calls have come for European legislation in respect of the use of conflict minerals throughout the supply chain; up until now, however, no such legislation exists.[18]

So while no legislation on CSR in the supply chain exists in the Netherlands, it is widely accepted that companies have a certain degree of responsibility with regard to their supply chain. The extent of this responsibility is not yet clear, however. The question whether and, if so, how these CSR issues in the supply chain are incorporated in contractual documents has not yet been answered. Moreover, it is not always clear what the contractual consequences of these choices are in terms of both tort and contract law.

This article attempts to answer these questions in terms of contract law and their binding nature. It investigates the content of the codes of conduct and the CSR contracts of best-practice players in the Netherlands. It examines how these documents are incorporated in contractual relationships between multinationals and their suppliers and what is required in order for these documents to be contractually binding. Finally, it proposes a categorisation of these measures and investigates their binding nature.

METHODOLOGY

The first part of this research attempts to answer the following question: what do the contractual measures taken by MNCs in respect of CSR in the supply chain consist of? The sample of approached companies consisted of 45 Dutch multinationals: the top 25 stock exchange (AEX) listed companies[19] and an additional 20 companies from industries that have traditionally developed CSR policies (the food and garment industries). It was expected that approximately 25% of these companies would be willing to participate. For this qualitative research, a sample of 10-15 companies would provide sufficient information upon which to build a model of possible choices. These multinationals were first approached by telephone, then sent a letter with more information on the research. This letter was – if necessary – again followed up with a phone call to further discuss the research.

A total of 16 companies participated, of which 14 were interviewed before this research was con-cluded (30%). Seven of these companies were AEX listed at the time of participation and six were also represented in the Dow Jones Sustainability World Index 2010 (out of a total of 13 Dutch companies in that Index). A variety of sectors were represented: finance (2), energy (2), clothing (3), food (2), electronics (2), services (1) and chemicals and construction (2). All companies requested that they remain anonymous.

Scripted interviews were held with each participating company, nearly all of which took place in person. Relevant documentation was gathered from the internet where possible; documents not publicly available were obtained from the company. Non-public documentation mostly consisted of model agreements (such as purchasing agreements) and general terms and conditions. All companies were requested to provide all relevant documentation regarding CSR in the supply chain (i.e. both in respect of 'people' and 'planet' aspects). However, in order to make the analysis manageable, not all possible aspects of CSR could be included in this research. After all, this would lead to comparing documents on corruption (common in, inter alia, the building industry) and CO_2 reduction with documents on health and safety (common in the food industry). It was therefore necessary to find some 'common ground' in the CSR measures adopted by these companies.

In respect of assessing the *content* of CSR measures (which aspects were included and how they were described), only labour rights embodied in the eight ILO Core Conventions were included.[20] The reason for focusing on these core labour rights is threefold. First of all, all companies included in the sample included most or all of those rights in their CSR documentation. Furthermore, the ILO Core Conventions are historically widely accepted and lie at the heart of core CSR documents such as the OECD Guidelines and Ruggie's framework.[21] Finally, the rights embedded in these core conventions are fairly unambiguous: one can include quantitative standards with regard to – for example – child labour and list the grounds of discrimination. This makes a comparison of the content of the CSR measures that companies take in respect of these aspects fairly easy.

The empirical research was conducted between February 2011 and August 2011. Any new policies or codes of conduct dated thereafter were not included in this research.

The second part of this research analyses the contractual instruments in terms of content. The con-tent of the codes was analysed based on an adaptation of the model by Kolk and Van Tulder.[22] That model analyses codes on the basis of their stringency, focusing on which human rights standards have been incorporated, to what degree codes will be implemented, what type of control is established and how stringent that code is. Codes were then classified as strong, moderate or weak.

In the third part of this research, the contractual aspects of these model choices studied were analysed on the basis of Dutch private law. The possibilities and limitations of these options in terms of private law are explored: are codes binding? Are there any issues in terms of contract law? In a later stage of the research, aspects of contractual and extracontractual liability will also be investigated for these options.

It should be noted that this research does not attempt to answer the question of *why* companies choose certain CSR measures and how effective the implementation of these measures is.[23] The subject is approached from a private law angle and is not looked at from a business ethics or law and economics perspective.

INSTRUMENTS FOR CONTRACTUAL CONTROL AND DUTCH LAW

Once a company decides to take control of corporate social responsibility in its supply chain by means of contractual control,[24] it has a wide range of private law instruments at its disposal. It may choose to connect with existing codes of conduct, for instance with those that exist in the sector in which the company operates, or it may find that a better fit can be obtained if the company drafts its own code of conduct or incorporates specific clauses in its contracts or general terms and conditions.

In order to assess these instruments correctly, some aspects of international private law must be dis-cussed. After all, the nature of these contracts is inherently international, and while MNCs would prefer to see their own law applied to the contract, this may not always happen. This section will therefore first explore some aspects of private international law. Next, the theory behind various instruments will be discussed. First, the option of a contract. What is required for a binding contract to come into existence under Dutch law? The second option is to shape a CSR instrument in the form of general terms or conditions. What consequences does this have for the validity of the instrument? How does a 'battle of the forms' play out under Dutch law? Finally, I will discuss codes of conduct. I will propose a model in order to analyse and compare them, based on the model proposed by Van Tulder and Kolk,[25] and will answer the question whether codes of conduct are binding upon the MNC under Dutch law.

Private international law

The nature of the contracts is international; supply contracts that concern CSR-sensitive products or services are generally concluded between a Western MNC and a low-cost country supplier. As a result, it is necessary to study which legal system is to apply to these contracts and codes of conduct.

In respect of the Netherlands, the Rome I Regulation on the Law Applicable to Contractual Obligations (Rome I) will govern which law is applicable to contracts in civil and commercial cases (Article 1 Rome I). Rome I has been in effect since 17 December 2009 and it is universally applicable. As a result, the law specified by Rome I will be applied, regardless of whether it is the law of an EU Member State. Article 3 Rome I states that if a choice of law has been made, the law chosen will be applicable to the contract. Parties are free to choose which legal system applies to the agreement, except in those cases where Rome I only provides for certain legal systems. This is not the case for the contracts at hand. If no choice of law has been made, Article 4 Rome I prescribes that the law governing the contract is the law of the state with which it is most closely connected. Article 4 Rome I provides a number of examples: in the case of a sales contract (Article 4(1)) this will be the law of the state in which the seller is located. If more than one specific element listed under Article 4 is present, the law of the state of the 'characteristic performance' will govern the contract, unless it is clear that the contract is more closely connected to another country; in that case, the law of the latter country will apply. If the contract does not include a choice of law, the law of the home state of the MNC will often therefore not be the law which governs the contract, but rather the law of the country in which the supplier is located.

Generally speaking, however, most MNCs will include a choice of law in their contract. In approximately 90% of all contracts investigated, the MNC will choose the law of its home state as the law applicable to the contract.[26] In most cases, the law that governs the contract will therefore be the law of the home state.[27]

If parties engage in a discussion as to whether a contract has been concluded at all or whether general terms and conditions apply, there may also be a discussion with regard to which law governs these pre-contractual questions. These issues are relevant in the case of CSR codes of conduct and contracts, since MNCs may argue that no legally binding contract has come into being since the parties did not intend to be legally bound. Article 10 Rome I indicates that the 'existence and validity of a contract shall be determined by the law which would govern it (...) if the contract were valid', in other words: the lex causae. This is only different (Article 10(2)) if one party states that it has not consented to the contract; in such a case, the law of its home state applies if, considering the circumstances, it would not be reasonable to base the consequences of that party's behavior on the law specified in Article 10(1). These questions will therefore be governed by the law that would have governed the contract if it were assumed that a contract had validly been concluded; this is usually the home state of the MNC, unless one party disputes that it has consented at all, in which case the law of its home state may apply.

Contracts

The most straightforward choice a company could make if it wanted to regulate CSR issues with its sup-ply partners would be to include one or more CSR clauses in its supply contracts. This section will briefly explore how and where contract law is regulated in the Netherlands. Furthermore, it will set out which requirements need to be met in order for a contract to come into place, and – to some extent – how third parties may be impacted by the content of the contract.

Contracts are regulated in the *Burgerlijk Wetboek* (Dutch Civil Code, DCC). A contract comes into being by an offer and a subsequent acceptance (Article 6:217 Paragraph 1 DCC). An offer is only qualified as such if a proposal to enter into an agreement is made, containing all essential elements of that agreement, so that a simple 'yes' by the contracting party can suffice. Acceptance of the offer flows from the 'yes' by the contracting party. If the acceptance differs from the offer, the 'acceptance' should in fact be qualified as a new offer (Article 6:225 DCC) and as a rejection of the original offer.[28]

In practice, there may be some discussion as to whether a statement qualifies as an offer or not. A company may state that it did not wish to express an offer, but rather that its statement was the expression of an aspiration, and that those statements were not intended to have any legal consequences. How does Dutch law deal with such a scenario? In order for a contract to come into existence, parties must declare their intention (*wilsverklaring*), this declaration of intent being a kind of legal act as described in Article 3:33 DCC. If the intention of a (legal) person diverges from its declaration, such as when an MNC does not wish to be legally bound by its statement, the question is what should prevail. Should that be the appearance of the party's declaration or its intention?

Article 3:35 DCC states that the outward appearance of the declaration prevails over the internal will of the person acting, as long as the other party has justifiably relied upon the intent of the person acting. This system is known as the will/reliance doctrine (*wilsvertrouwensleer*) and it not only applies to the question whether an offer has been made but also to the question whether an offer has been accepted (see also Section 4.3). Generally speaking, most companies will clarify whether a policy or document is intended to be legally binding by inserting wording to that effect. If this is not clear, however, it will depend on the circumstances of the case at hand whether or not a statement could have been interpreted as an offer.

The enforceability of a contract furthermore depends on whether the contract contains determinable terms (Article 6:227 DCC) and is sufficiently certain. This criterion is met if the content of the obligations is sufficiently clear or determinable.[29] Assuming this is the case, the obligations arising from the contract are legally enforceable.

Besides being held to the obligations that flow from the contract, contracting parties also have other legal obligations. Article 6:2 DCC states that contracting parties are required to act in conformity with the requirements of reasonableness and fairness. This requirement of reasonableness and fairness is elaborated upon in Article 6:248 Paragraph 1 DCC: the agreement has the consequences that the parties have agreed upon, although the nature of the agreement, law, custom and demands of reasonableness and fair-ness may colour the agreement.

Furthermore, if the content of a contract is unclear or incomplete, the '*Haviltex* criterion' will form the basis of its interpretation. In that case, the interpretation of such a written contract should not be based on a purely textual explanation of that contract, but rather on what the parties, in the given circumstances, could reasonably expect from one another, taking into account their social background and any legal knowledge they may have.[30]

A contract between two parties may, under certain circumstances, also have consequences for others that are not party to the contract. The following may be relevant within the context of CSR contracting.[31] The first option is that of a perpetual clause (*kettingbeding*) in a contract. This option provides for the possibility that contractual obligations between two parties are continued by their successors. Dutch law poses no specific requirements on the validity of a perpetual clause. An example of a perpetual clause in a CSR context (and one that is used in practice, as we will see) is that the MNC provides that the COC not only applies to their contractual relationship, but that the supplier must also include this COC in the contracts with its sub-tier suppliers. In this way, the COC of one MNC can possibly apply to the entire supply chain.

However, there are issues in the case of non-compliance with such perpetual clauses under Dutch law. The MNC only contracts with its supply partner, not with sub-tier suppliers. If, contrary to its con-tractual obligations, the supplier fails to include a certain clause in the contracts with its sub-suppliers, on the basis of contract law the MNC can only make claims vis-à-vis its own supplier. But the MNC cannot force the sub-tier supplier (which, after all, is not its contracting partner) to observe certain clauses from a contract to which it is not a party. At the same time, Dutch case law has deemed it impossible for the stipulator of a perpetual clause to claim damages from the third party on the basis of extra-contractual liability.[32]

A qualitative obligation is not the solution in these cases since qualitative obligations can only cover acts of tolerating facts or refraining from acts (Article 6:251 DCC). Despite their limited effectiveness– there is no possibility to restore the contractual clause, it is difficult to claim damages from sub-tier suppliers – perpetual clauses are the only contractual solution for such a situation.

It may also be possible for third parties to derive rights from a contract to which are not a party. If the MNC and the supplier include a clause in their contract that indicates that employees must be granted a certain minimum protection of employment rights or a minimum salary, one can question whether these employees can directly make claims under this contract, despite not being parties to it. The clause on behalf of a third party is regulated under Dutch law in Articles 6:253 and 6:254 DCC. If A and B agree upon a clause on behalf of C, B is contractually obliged to fulfil this obligation if C accepts the clause. Until C has accepted this clause, C cannot claim rights under the agreement. Such acceptance may be implicit, as with 'regular' two-party contracts. If a clause on behalf of a third party is not complied with, both the third party and the stipulator may request performance, unless the stipulator has no interest in performance or the third party resists the stipulators' claim for performance.[33]

If a contract has been validly concluded between parties through an offer and a subsequent acceptance of that offer, it has the consequences that the parties have agreed upon, as well as any other consequences stipulated by law. If the supplier does not comply with the contract, the MNC will have various legal options at its disposal to pressure the MNC into observing the contract.[34] Contracts will therefore be a legally effective option that is at the MNC's disposal in order to regulate its supply chain. It may nevertheless be more convenient for a MNC not to have to draft a new contract for each separate supplier. If the MNC wants to use a standard set of clauses, it may either use a standard contract form which can be adapted for each individual supplier, or it may use a set of general terms and conditions that is applied to all contracts of a certain type. Most legal systems provide some sort of separate regulation for these terms and conditions. They will be discussed in the next section.

General terms and conditions

Most companies use general terms and conditions in some shape or form within the course of their daily business. Some incorporate CSR terms in their general terms and conditions, or make a reference to a CSR policy or COC. But what are general terms and conditions and how are they regulated under Dutch law?

General terms and conditions are a set of standardised conditions, which are used repeatedly and do not encompass the core terms from the contract. Title 6.5.3 of the DCC regulates general terms and conditions.[35] Article 6:247 DCC of that title contains scope rules in respect of three situations. First of all, if both parties are professionals and located in the Netherlands, Title 6.5.3 applies, regardless of the law that governs the agreement (Paragraph 1). If both are professional parties but one or both are located *outside* of the Netherlands, Title 6.5.3 does *not* apply, regardless of the law that applies to the agreement (Paragraph 2). Lastly, if the contracting party is a consumer and is located in the Netherlands, Title 6.5.3 applies, regardless of the law that applies to the agreement (Paragraph 4). The reason for not applying Title 6.5.3 to professional contracting parties in international situations is to create greater legal certainty for parties which operate in such an international setting; foreign users of general terms and conditions do not have to take Title 6.5.3 into account when drafting their terms that may be used for Dutch contracting parties. Given the nature of the agreements studied in this research, it is very unlikely that either the situation mentioned in Paragraph 1 or in Paragraph 4 of Article 6:247 DCC would apply. In virtually all cases, the supplier will be a professional party located outside of the Netherlands (Paragraph 2). As a result, Title 6.5.3 will generally *not* apply to the agreements studied, even if Dutch law applies to the agreement.[36] If this title does not apply to the general terms and conditions at hand, those terms and conditions will only be governed by the applicable contract law.[37] As a result, in order to evaluate whether the terms and conditions used are valid and binding, one should refer to the general framework for contracting as set out above. Furthermore, the following should be noted.

General terms and conditions become part of the contract as a result of an offer and an acceptance; upon accepting the user's general terms and conditions, its contracting party is bound by them. In practice, it may occur that two parties each refer to their own general terms and conditions and want them to be applied to the agreement. This is referred to as a battle of the forms.

Different legal systems adhere to different systems in respect of the battle of the forms. The Netherlands adheres to the 'first shot' system of the battle of the forms. Article 6:225 Paragraph 3 DCC covers the battle of the forms. This clause is *not* part of Title 6.5.3 and therefore also applies if the parties are international professionals. This article stipulates that the first reference is valid; the second reference only has effect if the first set of general terms and conditions is explicitly rejected. A standardised announcement that one's own terms and conditions will apply is not sufficient to meet the criterion of an 'explicit rejection'. Mentioning that one's own set will apply, to the exclusion of all other terms and conditions, will however suffice, subject to the condition that it is presented in a manner that is to be taken seriously.[38]

Another issue which is specific to general terms and conditions is the following. At times, general terms and conditions refer to yet *other* terms and conditions, which may or may not be provided to the contracting party at the time of contracting. Under Dutch law, such a reference to a second set of general terms and conditions will not mean, generally speaking, that this second set also becomes part of the contract. Only if the contracting party has read the second set of terms and conditions, or creates the impression of knowing their content, is this not an issue, since – as Jongeneel points out – the contracting party has either intended to be bound by these terms (Article 3:33 DCC) or has created the impression that it has such an intention (Article 3:35 DCC).[39]

All in all, the nature of general terms and conditions (i.e. their repeated use) makes them a practi-cal instrument for CSR contracting. Under Dutch law, general terms and conditions that are used in an international setting are not specifically regulated and are only subject to general contracting laws, mak-ing them a fairly flexible and convenient option. But there is another option at the disposal of the MNC wishing to regulate its supply chain: the code of conduct.

Codes of conduct

What constitutes a code of conduct? There are a number of aspects that scholars generally agree upon. The first is the principle of voluntariness. This is not necessarily voluntariness in the sense that once a company uses a code, it does not need to abide by it, but rather that the target group creating or adopt-ing the code was under no (legal) obligation to do so. Another aspect often highlighted is that codes of conduct contain a set of norms and standards. Van Tulder and Van der Zwart [40] define codes of conduct as 'a set of agreements with which an organization indicates which behavior it expects from its members (and possibly business partners) in certain, defined situations.'

If a company decides to include a code of conduct as part of its broader CSR policy, it has a wide range of policies that it can choose from, varying from codes created by international organisations such as the OECD, sectoral initiatives such as the Electronic Industry Citizenship Coalition, or it may draft a code itself. Codes of conduct may contain a wide range of topics: societal responsibility, human rights, the environment, responsible investment, the integrity of employees, and so on.[41]

In order to make reasonable comparisons on the basis of a fairly small sample, this research only focuses on the labour norms and standards laid down in the eight core conventions of the International Labour Organization (ILO). The following four categories are covered by a total of eight ILO core conventions: (i) freedom of association and collective bargaining, (ii) prohibition of child labour, (iii) prohibition of forced labour, and (iv) non-discrimination. These principles are widely recognised and have been included in the ILO's Tripartite Declaration of Principles Concerning Multinational Enterprises and Social Policy as well as in the UN Global Compact principles.

In order to identify the legal status of (voluntary) codes of conduct, one must distinguish the question whether a MNC can be held accountable by a third party on the basis of such a code, from the question of the binding nature between the MNC and its supply partner. I will first answer the question whether a MNC is bound by its own COC in relation to third parties. This is also the question that most of the discussions concerning the binding nature of codes of conduct in the literature have revolved around. Although the first question is more relevant in respect of liability for CSR violations by MNCs, and this research relates to the use of private law instruments in the supply chain (rather than the use of COCs in general), I will briefly discuss these theories since they provide background information on how codes of conduct are classified in private law in general. I will then discuss the question of the binding nature of a COC on supply partners. This section will restrict itself to situations where the code of conduct is not embedded in another kind of private law initiative, such as a contract or general terms.

The answer to the question whether codes of conduct are legally binding upon the MNC that publicly adheres to them is not clear-cut. Generally speaking, there are two streams of thought in the international literature. The maximalist perspective argues that codes of conduct are legally binding and that the clauses of these codes should be enforceable in the courts. The minimalist view believes that the character of codes of conduct is not legally binding and that compliance with these codes should be voluntary. A third perspective is that of the 'zebra code', which contains both legally binding and non-binding clauses.[42]

From an international perspective, the minimalist view is dominant. [43] An example of this is the reference in the OECD Guidelines, which indicates that 'observance (...) is voluntary and not legally enforceable'.[44] Similarly, in the Netherlands the general notion is that voluntarily drafted or accepted codes are not legally binding for those that adhere to them.[45] It is often also claimed that the provisions contained in a code are not legally binding, at least that such a binding nature does not naturally flow from the instrument of a code of conduct. Koelemeijer asserts that if any binding nature of clauses in a code is to be induced, this does not flow from the code itself but rather from general or more specific (inter)national legislation, if a code contains legally binding clauses.[46]

The general view, therefore, is that a COC is not in and of itself binding for the MNC that adheres to it. What, if anything, does that mean for the status of the COC in supply relationships? I believe that a mere reference to a code of conduct ('Please take note of the Code of Conduct of Company X, enclosed as Annex A') in a contractual document is insufficient for a contract to be concluded. After all, it is not clear to the supplier that the MNC expects him to uphold the COC and does not constitute an offer in the private law sense.

In order for the COC to be binding upon the supplier, this code of conduct should therefore be contractually embedded. As has been set out supra, an offer and an acceptance is needed under Dutch law in order to conclude a contract. Therefore, it must be clear to the supplier that the reference to or provision of the COC is, in fact, an offer, which he may or may not accept. This may be done by requesting that the supplier signs for the receipt of and compliance with the COC. Another option is to refer to the COC in a contract and to declare that that COC is applicable to the contract, as a form of special terms and conditions.

Having set out the theory above, it is time to look at what CSR contracting in the supply chain looks like in practice. What are the contractual consequences of choices made by Dutch MNCs? Are the instruments used binding?

CONTRACTUAL CONTROL IN THE SUPPLY CHAIN IN PRACTICE

Introduction

In the Netherlands, 16 companies were willing to participate in this research. A total of 14 were inter-viewed before August 2011; those companies were included in this article. All of them provided their codes of conduct, and, if applicable, the general (purchase) terms and conditions that contained CSR clauses and/or CSR clauses from their contracts. A twofold analysis was carried out on the basis of these documents.

The first type of analysis related to content. As indicated, the analysis of the content was carried out on the basis of an adaptation of the model proposed by Van Tulder and Kolk.[47] The adapted model is included as *Figure 1* infra. Secondly, the structure of the contractual control mechanisms was analysed. Which instruments were most frequently used by companies? Could a pattern be discovered that would distinguish various types of initiatives? To what extent were instruments legally binding? Did they also include clauses in relation to third parties?

Content of CSR instruments

In order to compare and assess codes of conduct, one needs a set of indicators and variables. Kolk and Van Tulder have proposed such a model, binding together the content of the issues included, the nature of the wording, references to legal systems which they make and compliance aspects.[48] For the purpose of assessing the COCs of the participating companies, I have adapted this model, thereby only including issues in respect of the 8 ILO core conventions. This adjusted model is proposed in the final section of this article.

The content of all 14 contractual control initiatives was inserted into the model inserted as *Figure 1.*

			Classification
Binding	*Code signed separately?*		yes / no
Issues		– non-discrimination, equal remuneration	Ranging from: 0 out of 4 to 4 out of 4.
		– industrial relations (freedom of association, collective bargaining)	
		– child labour	
		– forced labour	
Nature	*Quantitative standards?*	100% (predominant), 75% (majority)	predominant, majority, medium or frail
		50% (medium)	
		0-25% (frail)	
Measures	*Reference?*	Reference to local legal system or international standards or other COC?	none defined; home country; host country; international or combinations
Compliance	*Monitoring systems and processes*	Good insight into systems (clear), reference to some parts but criteria or time frames lacking (clear to vague), only general reference to monitoring without details (vague).	clear / clear to vague / vague
	Position of monitoring actor	Firms themselves (1st), business associations (2nd), external professionals (3rd), combination (4th).	1st, 2nd, 3rd, 4th
	Sanctions	Warnings and exclusion of membership (mild), threat to business activities (severe).	none / mild / severe

Figure 1: The analysis led to three types of content: weak, moderate and strong content.

Weak codes

Content described as weak often did not include all four issues of the ILO core conventions; sometimes, issues such as freedom of association, collective bargaining or force were not included. The wording was general and left much room for interpretation; e.g., phrases such as ‘promoting respect for people and their work environment’, ‘supplier will not indulge in acts of discrimination’ and ‘supplier will recognise its employees’ rights to freedom of association’. Such phrasing does not make it clear what the MNC exactly expects from the supplier. There was no reference to legal standards (home state, host state or international). Codes did not generally include any compliance mechanisms, such as auditing or self-assessment questionnaires. The codes are not signed for by suppliers. Out of the 14 codes, 4 were classified as weak (29%).

Moderate codes

The contents of three codes (21%) were considered moderate. These codes used either general phrasing or predominantly general phrasing; they did, for instance, describe exactly what was expected from the suppliers in terms of non-discrimination and they mentioned all possible grounds for discrimination, but only referred to freedom of association in general terms. Limited quantitative standards were included (for instance, only relating to child labour). Codes mentioned legal standards but did not make it clear which legal standards those are; e.g., codes stated that 'all legal standards must be observed'.

Strong codes

The contents of seven codes (50%) were classified as strong. These codes included clear norms for all four issues. They usually included relevant references to ILO conventions and all included references to a mix of legal standards (home state, host state, international and international trade standards). The norms also usually set out what was expected in the case of conflict between the various norms. Quantitative standards were usually included with respect to child labour.[49] These codes frequently referred to or included external, third-party COCs as well.

All codes of conduct were signed for by supply partners. Furthermore, all strong codes included compliance mechanisms, either by means of auditing (usually by a third party; sometimes by the company itself) and/or self-assessment questionnaires.

With the exception of one COC, all strong codes included obligations in respect of sub-tier suppliers: any further sub-suppliers that the supplier engaged with would also need to agree to the content of the code of conduct.

Form of initiatives: COCs, general terms and conditions or contracts?

All three types of instruments – contracts, general terms and conditions, and codes of conduct – were seen in practice. Most companies chose a mix of these instruments and the instruments used often did not strictly fall into one category.

All companies investigated used some type of code of conduct. Almost all codes of conduct (with the exception of two) were signed for by supply partners. This has some consequences for the relevance of the concept of a 'code of conduct' in the original, voluntary sense. By requiring that all suppliers sign the code of conduct, these 'codes' would in fact qualify as general terms and conditions. They are a set of standardised terms, to be used repeatedly within the context of a certain type of contract. While this does not have major consequences in terms of Dutch private law – after all, title 6.5.3 of the DCC does not apply to international contracts – it does provide us with an excellent indication that the discussion concerning to what extent codes of conduct are binding is of limited importance in the supply chain. Furthermore, these codes of conduct become contractually binding. The MNC extends an offer to its supplier, which the supplier –

by signing for the code of conduct – accepts. It turns out that MNCs do not wait to see whether courts deem codes of conduct to be binding upon those who adhere to them; rather, they take matters into their own hands and ensure that COCs are binding on their supply partners through the means of contracting. Furthermore, the *content* of COCs does not bar them from becoming binding. In my opinion, even the content of weaker codes of conduct would meet the criterion of having sufficiently determinate terms.

Using a CSR clause in a contract was the least popular option among this sample. Apparently, CSR contracting is very much standardised (either through the use of COCs or general terms or conditions). Only 5 of the 14 companies also included some kind of ethical clause in their contracts. Usually, these were fairly general clauses that described the CSR obligations of the supply partner on an abstract level. For example, 'manufacturer is obliged to demonstrate that it is actively promoting good labour conditions for its workers'. The companies that *did* include CSR clauses in contracts indicated that they only did so in the case of contracts where the risk of CSR violations would be high. In such cases, a CSR clause would be inserted to draw extra attention to CSR issues. When asked why companies did not include such a clause, most answered that they felt such an ethical clause would not be necessary since the code of conduct had already been signed for and was therefore a contractual obligation in and of itself.

Patterns

Another important discovery was that a pattern could be deduced from the choices that companies made. Those companies that used CSR codes of conduct or general terms and conditions of which the content qualified as weak did not create contractual mechanisms to embed these codes of conduct. As a result, these codes would not be contractually binding for supply partners. Furthermore, the implementation of these instruments was lacking: the use of these codes was not widespread among employees dealing with supply partners and they were often overlooked in the contracting process.

Those companies that had moderate codes of conduct and general terms and conditions made some effort in respect of the content of the code, but often one or more issues concerning implementation did arise. A number of MNCs indicated that while elaborate codes were in place, employees neglected to include them in contracts in the heat of the commercial process. Another company explained that not all supply partners signed the code, but that the general terms and conditions contained a reference to the COC. The set of general terms and conditions provided on the company website did not include such a reference. Another example was a code consisting of both a company COC and a third-party, NGO COC (the second COC being much more specific and stronger), while the form that must be signed by the NGO only referred to the weak company COC. Yet other MNCs chose to include a reference to their code of conduct in their general terms and conditions. As set out above, this would be problematic if the code of conduct is then not provided to the supplier at the time of concluding the agreement. These companies would therefore need to make sure that the code of conduct is provided with the general terms and conditions (for instance, by attaching the code to the general terms and conditions). Those MNCs that used the strongest COCs from a content perspective also embedded their codes in the broadest manner from a contractual perspective. They not only requested that their suppliers sign their code of conduct, but they also frequently drafted specific general terms and conditions for suppliers that related to CSR and included CSR clauses in contracts. Finally, with the exception of one MNC, all strong codes included a perpetual clause in respect of sub-tier suppliers: any further sub-suppliers that the supplier engaged with would also need to agree to the content of the code of conduct.

Private international law, battle of the forms

All general terms and conditions included a choice of law. With the exception of two sets, all chose the law of the Netherlands as the law applicable to the agreement.[50] On the basis of Rome I, this will generally mean that Dutch law applies to the agreement.

Assuming that Dutch law applies, it is not likely that any battle of the forms would cause any problems. All general terms and conditions explicitly rejected any other set of general terms and conditions, thereby meeting the criterion of a sufficient rejection described supra. Furthermore, COCs are almost always signed for separately by suppliers. This means that these codes do not run a great risk of becoming 'victims' of a battle of the forms. If a set of general terms and conditions loses the battle of the forms, only that set of general terms and conditions will not apply; only CSR clauses laid down in those general terms and conditions would then not apply. Only one company investigated in this research had only anchored its CSR policy through general terms and conditions without requesting that suppliers sign for it. All other companies either also requested that suppliers sign for their COCs, or made the COC applicable through a reference in the standard contract.

Other aspects: third parties, implementation

As set out in Section 5.2, all strong COCs and most moderate COCs extended obligations to sub-tier suppliers by means of a perpetual clause. While such a perpetual clause is not perfect, it is the only contractual option that MNCs have available in such a case. The options that MNCs have available in case their suppliers do not include a perpetual clause are exceptionally limited – they may claim damages from their supply partner on the basis of non-performance, but there is no way to restore a CSR contract in a clause between supplier and sub-tier suppliers or to claim damages from the sub-tier supplier on the basis of tort.

All of the codes included references to the rights of workers, such as clauses on non-discrimination and freedom of association. Under certain conditions, such clauses may be considered clauses for the benefit of a third party, as set out in Section 4.2. In order for a third party to derive rights from a contract between a MNC and its supplier, this clause must be sufficiently determinate. In the case of strong codes of conduct, this is generally the case. Furthermore, the clause (the offer, as it were) should be accepted by such a third party.

Within the context of CSR contracting, the most likely category of 'third parties' to accept such a clause would be the employees of the supply partner. It is not clear whether the codes of conduct that contained clauses for the benefit of a third party are in practice always provided to the employees of suppliers, so that they can accept these clauses and derive rights under the supplier code of conduct. In the Netherlands, it has also been considered sufficient for third parties to accept clauses by means of instigating a procedure requesting that the promissor fulfils its obligations in respect of the third party.[51] It is therefore not unthinkable that employees would be able to derive rights from the supplier codes of conduct.

All three types of codes of conduct included the possibility to terminate the agreement. On the basis of the conducted interviews, however, it quickly became clear that all companies were reluctant to terminate relationships; they rather engaged with the supplier in order to draft a plan for improving the points that fell short from a CSR perspective.

CONCLUSION

In conclusion, codes of conduct are not used in the true sense of the term in the supply chain. Companies really attempt to obtain contractual control; not only by requiring that their supply partners sign their code of conduct, but also by anchoring the code of conduct in their general terms and conditions or in the contract. Furthermore, within the context of the supply chain and supplier codes of conduct, the discussion revolving around whether these codes are binding is virtually irrelevant; after all, nearly all companies with any kind of serious supply chain corporate social responsibility system in place ensure that these codes are contractually anchored.

Moreover, companies that have weaker codes of conduct from a content perspective less frequently anchor their code contractually by means of signing codes of conduct or references in contracts or general terms and conditions. This would support the idea that multinationals which have really thought their CSR policy through would also have thought better about how to implement that policy; not only from a practical point of view but also from a contractual point of view.

The findings so far provide material for further research. All companies interviewed have shown a great interest in the question of what the consequences of their policies and contracts are in terms of extracontractual liability. All of the general terms and conditions and contracts included some kind of limitation of liability. Could such a limitation of liability also be valid in respect of claims on the basis of CSR violations by third parties? Furthermore, many of the investigated MNCs use the same instruments in all companies they operate. But the same instruments may have different consequences (in terms of validity and their binding nature) in different legal systems. Do companies need to adapt their instruments for each state they operate in? The continuation of this research project will attempt to answer these questions.

The research to date nevertheless already provides MNCs with a frame of reference for evaluating their own codes of conduct. They can gain more insight into the extent to which their own instruments are binding on their supply partners, as well as exploring some of the best practices of other MNCs in the Netherlands.

REFERENCES

1. R. van Tulder & A. van der Zwart, Reputaties op het spel: maatschappelijk verantwoord ondernemen in een onderhandelingssamenleving, 2003, p. 43.
2. Sociaal-Economische Raad, Duurzame Globalisering: een Wereld te Winnen, 2008, p. 30.
3. Ibid., p. 42.
4. EIRIS Foundation, A Risky Business? Managing core labour standards in company supply chains, 2009, p. 17.
5. M.T. Kamminga in J.J.A. Hamers et al., Maatschappelijk Verantwoord Ondernemen: Corporate Social Responsibility in a Transnational Perspective, 2005, p. 64.
6. M.P. Vandenbergh, 'The New Wal-Mart Effect: The Role of Private Contracting in Global Governance', 2007 UCLA Law Review, p. 919.
7. See, inter alia, 'Apple and Dell investigate Foxconn plant', The Financial Times, 26 May 2010, (last visited 10 August 2011).
8. See, inter alia, 'Shell accepts liability for two oil spills in Nigeria', The Guardian, 3 August 2011, (last visited 10 August 2011).
9. F. Spreckley, Social Audit - A Management Tool for Co-Operative Working, 1981.
10. European Commission, 'Corporate Social Responsibility: Encouraging best behavior', 15 June 2006, at: (last visited 16 November 2011).
11. For further reading on the moral and legal foundations of CSR, see inter alia the report by the SER, supra note 2; D. McBarnet et al., (eds.), The New Corporate Accountability: Corporate Social Responsibility and the Law, 2007, and A. Crane, The Oxford Handbook of Corporate Social Responsibility, 2008.
12. A. Kolk, & R.J.M. van Tulder, 'Child labor and multinational conduct: a comparison of international business and stakeholder codes', 2002 Journal of Business Ethics 36, p. 293.
13. Examples of exceptions being CSR reporting obligations under the corporate governance code in the Netherlands, and an obligation to create tracking systems for conflict minerals in the United States under the Conflict Minerals Act
14. To be found at: <http://www.oecd.org/document/28/0,3746,en_2649_34889_2397532_1_1_1_1,00.html> (last visited 4 November 2011).
15. Transparantiebenchmark, The Hague, Ministerie van Economische Zaken, 2004, p. 30.
16. See: <http://www.ketens-netwerken.nl/resources/uploads/files/documenten/WetOpenbaarheidvan productieen Ketens.pdf> (last visited 10 August 2011).
17. See: European Parliament resolution 'Towards an EU strategy on the rights of the child' 2007/2093(INI), accessible through <http://www.europarl.europa.eu/oeil/file.jsp?id=5479632> (last visited 11 November 2011).
18. See inter alia, Report by MakeITFair, Roundtable on Conflict Minerals Legislation, 26 May 2011, http://somo.nl/news-en/long-but-hopeful-path-towards-legislation-

on-conflict-minerals/at_download/attachment (last visited 19 September 2011).

19. Date listed: 1 January 2011.

20. Convention C87, Freedom of Association and Protection of the Right to Organise Convention (1948), Convention C98, Right to Organize and Collective Bargaining Convention, (1949), Convention C138, the Minimum Age Convention (1973), Convention C182, Worst Forms of Child Labour (1999), Convention C29, Forced Labour Convention, (1930), Convention C105, Abolition of Forced Labour Convention, (1957), Convention C100 (Equal Remuneration, 1951) and C111 (Discrimination, 1958).

21. This in contrast to other, more 'progressive' human rights that can be brought within the umbrella of CSR, such as the right to a living wage and the right to a healthy environment (including measures to reduce CO2).

22. R. van Tulder, & A. Kolk, 'Multinationality and Corporate Ethics: Codes of Conduct in the Sporting Goods Industry', 2001 Journal of International Business Studies 32, pp. 267-283.

23. For further reading on these topics, see inter alia: I. Mamic, 'Managing Global Supply Chain: The Sports Footwear, Apparel and Retail Sectors', 2005 Journal of Business Ethics 59, pp. 81–100; A. Kolk & R.J.M. van Tulder, 'Multinationality and Corporate Ethics: Codes of Conduct in the Sporting Goods Industry', 2001 Journal of International Business Studies 32, no. 2.

24. The term contractual control was first coined by D. McBarnet & M. Kurkchiyan, 'Corporate social responsibility through contractual control? Global supply chains and "other-regulation"', in D. McBarnet et al. (eds.), The New Corporate Accountability, The new corporate accountability: corporate social responsibility and the law, 2007.

25. Van Tulder & Kolk, supra note 22.

26. Out of the 14 Dutch model agreements, 13 effectively included a choice for Dutch law.

27. Art. 9 of Rome I relates to the application of overriding mandatory provisions (respect for which is regarded as crucial by a country for safeguarding its public interests, such as its political, social or economic organization) of national law, which depends on the scope of the provision. Provisions of the law of the forum as well as of the country in which the contract is to be performed may be applied. It should be noted that there may be some overlap between these provisions and the subjects governed by the CSR contract or COC (e.g. labour standards). This article investigates matters of validity and the binding nature of these documents, as well as the consequences of these codes and contracts for liability, rather than the validity of the content of these documents under national law.

28. If parties each refer to a different set of general terms and conditions, the acceptance will be different from the offer. This is referred to as a 'battle of the forms' and this is elaborated upon in Section 4.3.

29. C. Asser et al., Mr. C. Asser's Handleiding tot de beoefening van het Nederlands burgerlijk recht: 3, 2010, no. 283. Case law e.g.: Hof Den Bosch 15 October

2002, NJ 2003, 477; Hof Leeuwarden 8 June 2010, Prg. 2010, 169.

30. HR 13 March 1981, NJ 1981, 635.
31. The next paragraphs relate only to the obligations on the basis of a contract. The content of a contract may also have consequences for the extracontractual liability of contracting parties in respect of third parties. Such liability is – unfortunately – outside the scope of this article but will be further explored in my PhD research.
32. HR 4 June 1965, NJ 1965, 381 and HR 28 June 1974, NJ 1974, 400.
33. Hof Arnhem 8 March 1985, NJ 1985, 678.
34. It should be noted that under Dutch law, performance – rather than damages – is the primary obligation in case of non-compliance with contractual obligations.
35. This title is partly based on EU Directive 93/13/EEC on Unfair Contract Terms for Consumers
36. Which, as we will see, is highly likely.
37. See, for example, Rechtbank Rotterdam 12 March 1998, S&S 1999, 45 and Hof Arnhem 2 December 2003, LJN AO 1612.
38. S. A. Kruisinga, 'Battle of Forms', in B. Wessels et al. (eds.), Algemene voorwaarden, 2010, p. 35.
39. R.H.C. Jongeneel, 'Gebondenheid', in B. Wessels et al. (eds.), Algemene voorwaarden, 2010, p. 113.
40. Van Tulder & Van der Zwart, supra note 1, p. 108.
41. R.C.J. Galle, Ondernemen en ethiek, 2000, p. 65.
42. S.C. Eyk, The Oecd Declaration and Decisions Concerning Multinational Enterprises: An Attempt to Tame the Shrew, 1995, p. 20; M. Koelemeijer, 'Gedragscode: effectief instrument voor maatschappelijk verantwoord ondernemen?', 2004 Ondernemingsbestuur, no. 1, p. 13.
43. R.J. Hoff, De Integere Onderneming, De Bedrijfscode En Het Recht, 2006, p. 130.
44. OECD Guidelines for Multinational Enterprises, 2011, Concepts and Principles I.1.
45. M. Koelemeijer, 'Naar een Nederlandse gedragscode maatschappelijk verantwoord ondernemen?', in J.J.A. Hamers et al. (eds.), Maatschappelijk Verantwoord Ondernemen: Corporate Social Responsibility in a Transnational Perspective, 2005, p. 108.
46. See note 45 supra.
47. Van Tulder & Kolk, supra note 22.
48. Ibid.
49. As well as in respect of working hours, which lies outside the scope of this research.

50. One company chose English law. Another chose the law of the country where the relevant contracting entity was located, which would often, but not always, be Dutch law.

51. HR 19 March 1976, NJ 1976, 407.

INDEX

N

S

T

U

W